88 $\dfrac{1200}{4-88}$ 1140

CCCP

The White Arctic

The White Arctic

Anthropological Essays on Tutelage and Ethnicity

Robert Paine, Editor

Newfoundland Social and Economic Papers No. 7

Institute of Social and Economic Research
Memorial University of Newfoundland

© Memorial University of Newfoundland 1977
Printed in Canada
by University of Toronto Press
ISBN 0-919666-14-0

Canadian Cataloguing in Publication Data

Main Entry Under Title:

The White Arctic

(Newfoundland social and economic papers; no. 7)

ISBN 0-919666-14-0

1. Eskimos – Northwest Territories – Addresses, essays, lectures.   2. Eskimos – Labrador – Addresses, essays, lectures.   3. Northwest Territories – Native races – Addresses, essays, lectures.   4. Labrador – Native races – Addresses, essays, lectures.
I. Paine, Robert, 1926–   II. Memorial University of Newfoundland.   Institute of Social and Economic Research.   III. Series.

E99.E7W45   970′.004′97   C77-001664-2

Contents

"The problems of the Canadian Arctic may be said to be as old as Canadian history, since the first attempt to colonize Canada was made not along the St. Lawrence, but in Baffin Island at Frobisher Bay. ... [T]here is cause for wondering if things have improved greatly in Canada's North since 1578."

Michael Marsden in *The Arctic Frontier*.

List of Abbreviations

A.C.N.D. – Advisory Committee on Northern Development
C.O.P.E. – Committee for the Original Peoples Entitlement
C.Y.C. – Company of Young Canadians
D.N.L.A. – Division of Northern Labrador Affairs
D.O. – Development Officer
D.P.W. – Department of Public Works
H.B.C. – Hudson's Bay Company
I.G.A. – International Grenfell Association
I.T.C. – Inuit Tapirisat of Canada
L.I.A. – Labrador Inuit Association
L.R.A.C. – Labrador Resources Advisory Council
L.S.D. – Labrador Services Division
N.L.T.O. – Northern Labrador Trading Operation
N.W.T. – Northwest Territories
P.A. – Periodical Accounts
P.C. – Privy Council
P.T.A. – Parent Teacher Association
R.C.M.P. – Royal Canadian Mounted Police
R.R.C.L. – Report of the Royal Commission on Labrador
S.F.G. – Society for the Furtherance of the Gospel
U.I.C. – Unemployment Insurance Commission

Acknowledgements

Most of the research in this volume was undertaken for the project *Identity and Modernity in the East Arctic*, which was sponsored by the Canada Council in 1968 as part of its Killam Awards Programme. Phased through five years, 1968–72, it was directed by the present writer. Members of the project and their publications in its connection are listed in the Bibliography (Chapter 20), and several other monographs can be expected.

The majority of the book's contributors participated in the Killam project as M.A. or Ph.D. Fellows. In addition, there are four guest contributors: Professor Shmuel Ben-Dor of the University of Negev, Israel, a one-time Fellow of ISER; Mr. Hugh Brody of the Scott Polar Institute, Cambridge; Professor Evelyn Kallen of York University, Ontario; and Ms. Ditte Koster, who took her M.A. in Anthropology at Memorial University at the time of the Killam project.

On behalf of all of us who were associated with the Killam project, I wish to thank the Canada Council for the gamble they took with us, and the Institute of Social and Economic Research (ISER), Memorial University, for logistic as well as financial support for our work. On behalf of all who have essays in this book, I wish to thank Sonia Kuryliw Paine without whose labours over our sentences, paragraphs and chapters, the book would have looked ragged indeed (Ben-Dor's essay is reprinted from his 1966 monograph); and Jeanette Gleeson whose typing and re-typing, and her patience with us all ensured that we eventually made it to the press.

In thanking the contributors, who put up with my editorial intrusions into their manuscripts, I add an apology for the delay in getting the job finished. For suggestions concerning the different chapters that I wrote, I wish to thank David Alexander, Fredrik Barth, Harald Eidheim, Milton Freeman, Robert Hill, Gordon Inglis, Anita Jacobsen, Ditte Koster, Roger Krohn, Ignatius La Rusic, Per Mathiesen, Axel Sommerfelt, Stephen Strong and Cato Wadel. Much of the argument of Chapters 2 and 3 could not have been documented without the co-operation of government departments and the work of a research assistant, especially engaged by the Northern Science Research Group of the Department of Indian Affairs and Northern Development. Chapter 5 is also a desk study, resulting from thoughts about the field reports of other anthropologists; I wish to record a special debt to Jean Briggs for her generosity and patience when faced with my questions and ideas.

The excerpt from *The Rise and Fall of the British Nanny* by J. Gathorne-Hardy is quoted with the permission of Hodder and Stoughton; the chapter by Brody appears in similar form in *The Peoples Land* published by Penguin Books (Brody, 1975).

Tromsö, Norway   Robert Paine
Easter, 1977

Preface

The title of our book, *The White Arctic*, is a response to the most insistent message coming from those who live today in the settlements of Canada's far north, whites and Inuit alike: "Don't waste your time with the Eskimos, it's the whites you should really be studying!" (Hugh Sampath, personal communication). If, then, this book should have a message, it is (besides concentrating upon 'native' behaviour) the needs that both whites and natives have of learning about white behaviour. Much of the book may be read as a discussion of the place that learning actually has, as opposed to the place it *should* have in Inuit-white relations. For government northern policy does, in fact, find its *raison d'être* in a learning process: the whites (it is said) are in the Arctic to teach the Inuit.

The first few chapters consider the government programmes of northern development and administration together with the geo-political constraints and ideological suppositions in which they were conceived after World War II and which are maintained today. We find a colonialism based on welfare, and a moral 'double bind' in the situation of those persons who make decisions on behalf of others. Chapters 5 to 12, based on anthropological field work in the Baffin Region of the Northwest Territories (N.W.T.), focus on the colonial encounter at the level of the individual settlement. Although their topics range from Inuit notions of social roles, through white notions of 'proper' behaviour, to gossip among whites, it is the praxis of white tutelage that is, at all times, under consideration. The field research in Labrador (Chapters 14 to 19) reveals a situation that is a good deal more complicated than the one in the N.W.T. Inuit and Settlers are two native populations in Labrador, and their relations with each other today cross-cut those between tutor and tutored. For this reason I delay the introductory discussion of the Labrador scene (Chapter 13) until the N.W.T. material and the 'prototypical' situation of tutelage that it represents have been examined.

The notion of tutelage itself is borrowed from *Eskimo Townsmen* (1965) by John and Irma Honigmann; or rather, it is their notion of tutelage that is placed under critical review. Briefly, their assumption, erroneous in our view, is that it is by being taught by whites that Inuit will gain the new identity they need in the modern world. Important to the argument in the present book is the deleterious effect this tutelage relationship has on the (white) tutors – as well as on the tutored – and thus on white-Inuit relations.

Although an increasing number of whites in the N.W.T. have become disillusioned and although the turn-over rate is high, it is unlikely that the whites are ever going to leave for good. Nor are the Inuit, though at one time there was talk of Inuit resettlement to the south. There is little hope, however, of the whites ever understanding the Inuit – a sad fact that this volume elucidates; on the other hand there is reason to suppose that Inuit will continue to improve their own understanding of white ways, thereby also improving their grasp of what it means to be an Inuit in the Canadian north today. This process of Inuit learning is markedly different from that of tutelage: Inuit are their own teachers, learning *about* whites, and not simply from them. This means that to a significant extent the learning is on their own terms; that the conclusions drawn are as much theirs as they are 'white.'

Yet, the betterment of ethnic relations and of the lot of the Inuit – even by this route – seems predicated on whites increasing their understanding of their own behaviour in the north. As was said years ago (in the columns of *Eskimo*), ''Before beginning to educate the Eskimo it would be wise to begin educating the whites who will do the job.'' For, so long as whites are uncertain about themselves and their mission, it is difficult for Inuit to put the 'white lore' they learn to socially constructive use. Nor should it be overlooked that whites, themselves, as they arrive in the north to assume the role of tutor, look to other whites to learn about the north, about the Inuit, and about proper white conduct. Or, what seems more common, the ''old-timers'' indoctrinate the newcomers whether they wish it or not, and whether or not what they say is accepted. Too often this learning process is larded with cynicism.

The White Arctic may be thought by some readers to be cynical. But the evaluatively negative aspect of our reporting of the place of whites in Inuit settlements – and of Canadian northern policy – does not derive from either malice or misplaced 'liberalism' or sensationalism; nor do we resort to any general set of psychological postulates about whites. Instead, our selection of facts, and our explanations, consistently refer to (1) structural considerations, such as the role in which a white person finds himself *vis-à-vis* Inuit and other whites in the settlement to which he is posted (for example, how he must work according to a system of rule and how the rules make less sense when transplanted to the north than they do in the south, their culture of origin); and (2) the emotive strains that many experience as a result of the position in which they find themselves.

Others may charge this book with taking an altogether too soft a view of colonialism, as though we have forgotten the hard economic facts of colonial exploitation. These are not forgotten (and they have been analysed by others), but we feel that the 'everyday' of colonial life – of the encounter between colonizer and colonized – needs sociological study. If anything, it is this which tends to be glossed over when taking apart a colonial situation. I see this book, then, as belonging to the responsibility of anthropological research in the Canadian North at this time. Following upon work begun in the '50s by colleagues such as R. W. Dunning and Frank Vallee, the aim is to provide an explanation of ethnic relations as we found them at the time of our research and as they may develop in the future. The ultimate objective, in which anthropological research should be able to play some part, is the improvement of those relations.

R. P.

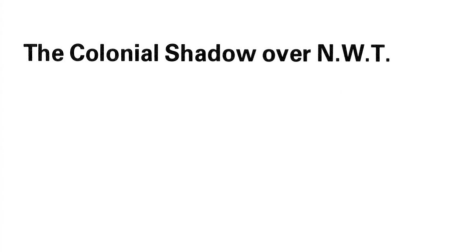

The Colonial Shadow over N.W.T.

Introduction

1

Robert Paine

> "Popular interest and concern in the North – stimulated by dramatic discoveries, technological achievements and up-to-date information on the media – have made northern development a national endeavour and the whole area a showpiece in which a distinct image of Canada can be identified and reflected for all Canadians and other nations to see."
> *Jean Chretien*, Minister of Indian Affairs and Northern Development, March 28, 1972.

To understand Canadian northern policy, one has to recognize that it was conceived in colonial circumstances: only then can it be appreciated how life today in the individual northern settlements is dominated by the colonial encounter. The colonialism is of a kind that is increasingly prevalent in the contemporary world and different in many important respects from that of the 'old' colonial empires. It might be called *welfare colonialism,* which should suggest, correctly, the connection it has with centre-periphery relations generally.

The social scientist faces a particular problem here: the context in which welfare colonialism is likely to take place makes its objective existence difficult to demonstrate. For example, white behaviour towards Inuit may be (and sometimes is) characterized as solicitous rather than exploitative, as liberal rather than repressive. Both descriptions hold true. In other words, we are apparently faced with the phenomenon of non-demonstrative colonialism. In general terms the problem is, then, to demonstrate non-demonstrative colonialism. The view that I take of this kind of colonialism is that it is based on two illegitimate positions: the colonizers are illegitimately privileged, whereas the colonized are illegitimately devalued. Specifically, the problem is to show how this state of affairs pertains, as I believe it does, even in present-day Canada where the Inuit are recipients of expensive educational and health programmes; to show how an administration that apparently wishes to increase Inuit control of their own affairs is, nevertheless, colonial; and to suggest how the Inuit respond.

The next two chapters follow in chronological sequence: Chapter 2 deals with the emergence of programmes for the administration and development of the north (insofar as they affect the Inuit) after World War II; Chapter 3 reviews the more recent programmes with regard to changes, apparent changes and failures to change. The primary data in the two chapters are (1) official statistics, (2) what can only be described as rhetoric – within and outside government – concerning policy, and (3) critically evaluative memoranda of senior government officials and others. Supplementary source material and a short discussion of problems in the use of official statistics are presented in Chapter 4.

The Canadian North is known to be large, but it is probably not appreciated, even among Canadians, how much of the area of Canada is inside its north: "Forty percent of Canada is not in its provinces – it is in the Yukon and Northwest Territories – and large areas of two provinces, in northern Quebec and northern Labrador, are land like the Territories" (Lantis, 1966:89). The Northwest Territories (N.W.T.) accounts for approximately one third of the total land area of Canada, but its population is no more than 41,000. Just under half live in six urban or urban-like communities (of which one, Frobisher Bay, is in the East Arctic), and the remainder are dispersed throughout the area in 54 small settlements, the largest of which has less than one thousand people (Hunter, 1976:77). The West Arctic, and the Mackenzie Delta in particular, is the ethnically heterogeneous area (Indian, Métis and whites, besides Inuit), as well as the more heavily populated.

The population of the part of the East Arctic with which we are concerned, the Baffin Region, is 80 percent Inuit (approaching 6,000 persons), and 20 percent white (over 1,000 persons). Aside from a concentration of residents in the administrative centre of Frobisher Bay (it has the largest number of Inuit anywhere in Canada), this population is widely dispersed throughout twelve settlements, each having no more than a few hundred Inuit and a handful of whites. In contrast to the West Arctic, the whites of the Baffin Region, composed mainly of government personnel (including teachers), Hudson's Bay traders, and missionaries, are almost all transients who have no intention of making a permanent home there (Davidson, 1973:110, 113). In short, the population dynamics of the Baffin Region features an Inuit population that maintains itself by natural fertility (which is dropping) and a white population (transient) based on immigration. There is also some out-migration among the Inuit population.

TABLE 1
Some Population Figures, 1941–75

A. N.W.T. and Arctic Quebec: Population by Ethnic Group

	1941	1951	1961	% increase	1968	1971	1973	1975	% increase
Inuit									
– N.W.T. only	5,500	7,000	8,000	45.5					
– with Arctic Quebec	7,000	9,000	10,500	50	11,000	13,000	13,500	14,500	32
Indians					6,000	7,000	7,500	7,500	25
Others					13,500	15,000	16,000	17,000	26
Total					30,500	35,000	37,000	39,000	28
Inuit as % of Total					36	37	36	37	

Note: Figures rounded off to nearest 500 (and percentages to nearest whole or half). "Others" includes Métis and whites.

B. Percentage Distribution of Inuit Population Throughout the Regions of N.W.T.

	1968	1975
Mackenzie	20	19
Inuvik	16	15
Keewatin	21	26
Baffin (including Arctic Quebec)	43	40

C. Baffin Region (including Arctic Quebec): Population by Ethnic Group

	1941	1951	1961	% increase	1968	1971	1973	1975	% increase
Inuit	2,100	2,600	3,000	30	4,600	5,500	5,500	5,700	24
Whites					800	900	1,100	1,100	37.5
Total					5,400	6,400	6,600	6,800	26
Whites as % of Total					15	14	16.5	16	1

Note: Figures rounded off to nearest 100 (and percentages to nearest whole or half).
Sources: 1941–61: Statistics Canada; 1968–75: Chief Medical and Health Officer, N.W.T. Government.

References

DAVIDSON, D. A.
1973 "The People in the North." In N. Ørvik (ed.), *Policies of Northern Development*. Kingston, Department of Political Studies, Queen's University.

HUNTER, RICHARD
1976 "Development of Local Government in the Northwest Territories." In N. Ørvik and K. Patterson (eds.), *The North in Transition*. Kingston, Centre for International Relations, Queen's University.

LANTIS, MARGARET
1966 "The Administration of Northern Peoples: Canada and Alaska." In R. St. J. MacDonald (ed.), *The Arctic Frontier*. Toronto, University of Toronto Press.

The Path to Welfare Colonialism

Robert Paine

2

> "The purpose now seems to be to protect the Eskimo from the missionary, but who will protect him from the Administration?"
> *Eskimo*, 1958 (Sept.):6

A specifically Canadian presence in the Northwest Territories dates realistically only from World War II. However, a 'white' presence there, non-governmental and for the most part non-Canadian, is much older. Our interest centres upon two questions: Why did Canada linger along the path to colonialism in the north? What form of colonialism emerged eventually? Even though the history has been told several times before (cf. Jenness, 1964, 1968; Hughes, 1965; Zaslow, 1971; Graburn and Strong, 1973), it is necessary to begin with a brief review of white contact prior to World War II, particularly for the reader unfamiliar with the north or its history.

Before World War II

> "So completely did we forget the north that as recently as ten years ago ... [it] was left to the missionaries, the fur traders, the Eskimos and the Indians."
> Deputy Minister of Northern Affairs and National Resources, 1957.

'White' incursions into the Canadian Arctic over the last hundred years have taken five principal forms: trade, mission, law, welfare, and capital investment. They arrived in the north approximately in that order, but none was wholly replaced by those that followed, so that today, all five are present; but the noteworthy triumvirate of the pre-war Arctic were the traders (with whom we include, for convenience, the whalers), missionaries and police.

The control that the traders wished to exercise over their Inuit clients should be distinguished from *latifundia* colonialism known in other parts of the world: the traders' *raison d'etre* was not land appropriation and they were interested that the Inuit retain (with certain important qualifications) a pattern of dispersed settlement. Unlike those who followed them to the Arctic, they and the missionaries had unequivocal reasons for being there, reasons which the Inuit understood better than they do many white activities in the north today. On this basis there developed a transactional relationship between whites and Inuit in which each side was able to derive benefit from the other, even though their respective bargaining powers were unequal.

Preeminent among the trading agencies has been the Hudson's Bay Company (H.B.C.), which came to the Arctic as a fur-trading enterprise, but did not open its operations there until relatively late. According to Usher (1971:207),

"The white fox trade had its beginnings in the last days of the whale fishery, in both the eastern and western Arctic. The establishment of the Cape Wolstenholme, Quebec, post in 1909 marked the real beginning of the Hudson's Bay Company Arctic trade, for although they had regularly sailed through Hudson Strait for 240 years they had never exploited its shores.[1] The expansion of the trade was extremely rapid; the network of posts and the induction of the Eskimos into the trapping and trading system being virtually completed within 15 years. The Company extended its operations to eastern and northern Baffin early in 1920s, and by 1925 ... had obtained an effective monopoly throughout the eastern Arctic."

This "initial heavy penetration was partly in response to competition, and partly a means of establishing trade relations with the Eskimos at a time when the fur prices were high and the incremental cost of operating additional posts low" (Usher, 1971:123). The competition came from smaller companies, of which the most active was the Paris firm of Revillon Frères, and from ex-whalers of the British and American whaling fleets that operated off the east coast of Baffin Island throughout the latter half of the 19th century (Usher, ibid.).

However, a failing world market a generation later caused the fur-trading posts to close down almost as quickly as they had been opened a generation earlier; in the East Arctic, for instance, "the Company had opened 23 posts ... prior to 1940, but by the end of that year maintained only nine of these" (Usher, ibid.). Woodcock (1970:174–75) gives this description of more recent changes in the role of the H.B.C. in the Arctic:

Until little more than a decade ago, the posts were simple log buildings where the Eskimos and northern Indians traded their furs for the Company's metal tokens, which they exchanged for goods. The traditional exchange of furs against manufactured goods was still the basis of the trade. But there has been an extraordinary change in the last few years. ... Today the Hudson's Bay posts, even those on the bleak shores of Baffin Island ..., have become miniature department stores, supplying a great variety of sophisticated commodities as well as traditional items like snow knives and ice chisels.

Only one-eighth of the Company's present trade in the northern stores is in furs; nowadays most of its furs are ranch-grown. But some of the old features of the trade remain. At the Arctic posts, merchandise still arrives only once a year, by the annual ship whose arrival is a major event. But the old isolation has given way to the bush plane and the short-wave radio, and the old self-contained life of the trader is a receding memory. Nevertheless, the Company remains one of the dominant elements in the life of the land that stretches beyond the edges of cultivation to the margins of the permanent ice.

As Usher notes, "in 1959 the Fur Trade Department of the Hudson's Bay Company changed its name, significantly, to the Northern Stores Development" (1976:207); yet, although the fur trade has been reduced as an enterprise on the international markets, it is still important to the Inuit household economy: "... even today, among the native population, more people receive income from furs than from any other resource-based activity" (Usher, 1971:15).

Significantly, Bishop Marsh opens his short history of the Anglican Diocese of the Arctic with the statement that "to appreciate the work of the Anglican Church in the far north and the Arctic, one must have some understanding of the fur trade" (n.d.:4). The point he is making is that without the help of the H.B.C., the logistics of setting up mission stations in the far north would have severely strained the resources of the mission, including arctic expertise. As it was, the Anglicans set up seven stations in the East and Central Arctic (including New Quebec) between 1852 and 1899, the missionaries often travelling to these stations with the help of H.B.C. transportation and pilotage (op. cit.: 4, 22). Nineteen more stations were opened in this same enormous region (and others in the West Arctic) in this century (op. cit.:23). By the early 1900s the Oblate (R.C.) missionaries had also arrived, and between 1912 and 1947 nine mission stations were opened, followed by a further six in the years after World War II (Oblate archivist, personal communication). Policy towards the Inuit varied according to denomination, but even missionaries of the same denomination sometimes pursued (and still do) different, even radically different, policies at their separate mission stations. In place of government agencies, the missionaries were able to assume far-reaching responsibilities for the Inuit congregations (cf. Briggs, 1971).

It is not my intention to consider in any detail the implications for Inuit of these early white contacts. However, I draw attention to the following intepretative comment by Williamson (1968:486) on the interrelation between the replacement of Inuit shamans by Christian missionaries and the change from aboriginal hunting to trapping for fur traders.

The shamans of the Eskimo have been the intellectual elite in a culture in which profound respect for intelligence was one of the most important values. ... [However] the Eskimo [also] respected people whose technology showed evidence of intellectual power, though they found the white men often childlike in their helplessness in arctic settings ...

[Now,] the arctic fox was little valued in traditional times and, therefore, of limited significance in the religiosity of the hunt. The need to hunt to serve the fur trade, then, brought about a steady diminution of religiosity, as fox trapping was clearly a secular pursuit.

Changed in their motives and impelled to question old beliefs now undervalued by the non-believing Kablunait (whites), who came provided with a store of goods for years ahead, without the practices and rituals the Eskimo had once thought vital to survival of man and perpetuation of his soul, the thinking people found a void of intellect and spirit which old resources could not fill.

This need was met, to some extent, by yet another force of change that came in from the south with establishment of trading posts. The Christian missionaries, who also spoke of souls and preached a moral code analogous to that which Eskimos had largely followed in their unconverted lives, were closely associated by the Eskimo with the traders whom they followed and whose culture they shared.

Regarding the H.B.C., it is important to realize that this merchant enterprise has always operated on the basis of the ability of each local station to maintain a balanced account; a deficit often meant the closure of a particular trading station. Perhaps it is this prerogative of *withdrawal* that was the most injurious feature of the trading relationship to the Inuit; it also underwrote the ultimate asymmetry in the power relationship between trader and client.[2]

It was in 1903 that Canada – with Dominion Status since 1867 – established the first two posts of the Royal North West Mounted Police in her far north, precursors of the posts of the Royal Canadian Mounted Police (R.C.M.P.) that "today ... stretch from one side of the Arctic to the other" (Jenness, 1968:24). These Canadian policemen made long sledge patrols, winning accolades from, among others, Stefansson, the explorer; later the patrols were also made by sea and by air (Kelly, 1973:167–71). It was the responsibility of the Commissioner of the North West Mounted Police to 'govern' the N.W.T., and his policemen brought Canadian law to both non-native and native (with or without the latter's comprehension of it). They also engaged actively, as did the missions, in unofficial 'welfare' activities, setting up temporary hospitals, soup kitchens and the like (*ibid.*). Later, when Family Allowances were instituted in Canada, it was the R.C.M.P. detachments who administered the programmes in the Arctic; but first they had to register the Inuit population and for that purpose issued ID discs (*op. cit.*:221). Today, the duties of most R.C.M.P. detachments in the Arctic are more routine and less diffuse, as many of their previous tasks are distributed among other government agents.

Jenness' summary comment on the lack of Canadian responsibility for the Inuit within her territory during the first four decades of this century is blunt (and supported by other authorities): "Canada's police faithfully imposed the reign of Canada's law on her Arctic ... [but] the education and training of Eskimos and care of their health, the government abandoned to the missionaries because it was easier and more economical" (1968:25). However, the missions did not have the resources to provide education beyond kindergarten and notably, "completely failed to check the ravages of European-introduced diseases" (*ibid.*). Jenness concludes: "the fault lay in Ottawa, where the government, though overly jealous of its sovereignty in the region, could not decide what it should do with it, or with the Eskimos who inhabited it" (*ibid.*). And as for the Inuit, their economy had become so entwined with the fur trade that the fall in fox prices again in the late 1940s resulted in an Arctic-wide depression. ... "by comparison the Eskimos had come through the Great Depression of the previous decade unscathed" (Usher, 1976:207). The situation was exacerbated by outbreaks of tuberculosis and the failure of seasonal caribou hunts, and wherever these happened in combination, the consequences were fatal for many Inuit.

Although Canada neglected her north during this period, it is from there that two 'Canadian' institutions came, in fact as well as legend: the H.B.C. and the R.C.M.P. Woodcock (1970:179) calls them "institutions that Canadians criticize but never dismiss." A third 'institution' also emerged during these years as peculiarly Canadian (at least in the eyes of the rest of the world): the "Eskimo."

Encapsulated descriptions of the communities of the Baffin Region, as published by the N.W.T. government, are set forth in Chapter 4. These tell us a little about how whites perceive the Arctic even today: some settlements are noted as "primitive," others brought to the attention of sports enthusiasts, yet others singled out for their industrial prospects. Particularly noteworthy is the pronounced tendency of settlements still to carry their 'historical' names that refer back to events and personages of European (British) exploration and patronage. The "Dorset" of Cape Dorset and the Dorset culture, for instance, is the name of a 17th-century earl; similar examples abound. In the case of Igloolik, the Inuit name is kept, and yet the government guide book, even while mentioning the Inuit prehistory associated with Igloolik, can still note (without any apparent sense of incongruity) "the first person to visit the island was Thomas Button in 1613" (N.W.T., 1974a).[3]

World War II and After: Geopolitics and Resettlement

> "[We] are fulfilling the vision and the dream of Canada's first prime minister – Sir John A. Macdonald. But Macdonald saw Canada from East to West. I see a new Canada. A Canada of the north!"
> *John F. Diefenbaker*, February 12, 1958.

With World War II and the Cold War after it, the Canadian Arctic became a strategic military area. For example, a U.S. Air Force base was built at Frobisher Bay in 1942–43 and between 1952–57, the U.S.-Canadian DEW-Line project, stretching from Alaska to the east coast of Baffin Island, was completed at a conservatively estimated cost of five hundred million dollars.[4] A direct consequence of these military activities was a radical change in Canadian involvement in its north. Decisions were taken for government-sponsored capital investment in mineral and oil exploration and (possibly) extraction (Rea, 1968:358 f.). With respect to the Inuit population, the change ushered in the epoch of colonialism infused with concepts of social welfare.

"Some form of rational justification" of its policy decisions in the north, especially its expenditures, was never much of a problem for the Canadian government:

"Insofar as Canada shared in the great military undertakings throughout the north, the justification for this diversion of resources from alternative uses was simply that it was 'in the national interest.' No one asked whether such projects would yield a profit. Similarly, in the field of welfare, despite the qualms of neo-Malthusians, the provision of relief to a population facing famine could be for political purposes adequately justified on humanitarian or moral grounds without recourse to more elaborate argumentation" (Rea, *ibid.*).

The alarm raised from time to time, by public media reports, about continued U.S. "occupation" of posts in the Canadian Arctic (cf. Rea, 1968:53 f.) must have assisted the Canadian government with its provision of "rational justification" for expenditure in the Arctic, however embarrassing such reports were to them at the time of their release.

It was principally as a result of its geopolitical interest in the north that the Canadian government found itself, at last, facing the question of what was to be done about the Inuit who lived there (in 1951, there were 7,000 in the N.W.T. and 2,000 in Arctic Quebec). Their resettlement to southern Canada was rejected as a solution, perhaps most of all for fear of the disastrous consequences such an operation could have for Canada's international image (though the possibility is still mentioned from time to time). But if the Inuit could be "rehabilitated" (the official expression) without moving them physically out of the north, then scandal might be avoided. Jenness (1968:31), for example, charges that Canadian neglect of its Inuit had been scandalous for some time "and the fear that it might damage Canada's international prestige, belatedly aroused the nation's leaders, who hastily improvised a program for Eskimo rehabilitation."

There are, however, two other factors to be taken into account. The first concerns the provision of relief to a population facing famine. Awareness of the Inuit in their north brought Canadians face-to-face with a system of population dynamics that was shocking to them; that the government would intervene in order to 'correct' that system was a moral inevitability from the first. For, Inuit society was markedly one with "a high death rate which tends to fluctuate in response to varying and uncertain economic productivity and periodic health crises" and with high birth rates that are matched only by the high mortality rates among children (Freeman, 1971:216). The government was determined to eliminate not only the periodic famine among the Inuit, but their high infant mortality rate as well.[5]

Secondly – and supportive of the above – one should recall that the dramatic commitment to its northern people began at the time when the Canadian government was embarking on new social programmes for its southern population as well (and was soon to find itself with a considerable annual welfare bill).[6] The Family Allowance Act was passed by Parliament in 1944 and the Old Age Pensions Act the following year; in 1945, the responsibility for the health of both Inuit and Indians was transferred to the Department of National Health and Welfare. Thus, "officialdom for the first time publicly recognized the Eskimos as citizens of the Dominion by distributing among them the family allowances to which a bill enacted a few months before entitled all Canadian citizens" (Jenness, 1964:77).

Whatever the combination of motives, by the early 1950s both money and personnel flowed into the Arctic to redress the 'Eskimo problem': a second 'DEW-Line' was constructed. This time it was a Canadian line of schools, nursing stations, supply depots, workshops, co-operatives and subsidized housing, including living quarters for the cohorts of white personnel. The two main 'planks' in the government's rehabilitation of the Inuit were its health and education programmes (see next section); it was felt, however, that the long-term success – or even implementation – of either was dependent on a rationalization of the traditionally dispersed and semi-nomadic Inuit pattern of camp living. Thus, early in the fifties there began the uneven match between "the pulls of the settlement (schools, health services, housing) and the pushes of the land (starvation, disease, uncertainty). ... Before the mid-1950s, most of the Inuit visited the settlements a few times a year to trade. ... By the mid-1960s, most of the Inuit were living in permanent settlements, and visited the land a few times a year. Some were using modern technology (motor toboggans and planes) to continue hunting and trapping with wage employment" (Lotz, 1976:26).

A concomitant government concern at this time was with the efficiency of Inuit resource management and the limits of the natural resources; a number of Area Economic Surveys were commissioned.[7] In his review of these Surveys, Lotz (*ibid.*) finds it paradoxical that "though [the research] was intended to help the Inuit to make better use of the land resources ... the area surveys chronicled the increasing dependency of these people on the government and the resources of the settlements." But this development should also be considered in the light of Usher's (1976:207) conclusion, in the context of the earlier dependence of Inuit upon fur-trading, that "increased opportunities for wage employment after 1955 proved both the immediate salvation and the subsequent (although still inadequate) basis of the Arctic economy." Lotz notes, on the basis of several reports, how it is "obvious that in some areas the limits of resource use were being reached" (*ibid.*). Nor was it found that a movement from camp to settlement necessarily meant a reduced harvest of the natural resources. From southern Baffin Island Higgins (1968:188) reported that "exploitation has in many ways improved with the abandonment of camps and may, in fact, be approaching a state of near over-exploitation." In any case, it was already recognized that the problem of Inuit employment would transcend any camp-versus-settlement argument: "Hanging over all the reports is the shadow of a basic problem: the resources of the land will support only so many people. There are jobs for only so many people in the settlement (and the best paid and most permanent of these are held by white outsiders). And a generation has grown up that knows neither the life on the land nor the world of steady wage employment" (Lotz, *op. cit.*:28).

Remembering that besides Inuit resettlement and the health and school programmes, there was also considerable activity in connection with quite different white-related enterprises, one wonders how these events were perceived by the Inuit at the time? Here, at least, is how one first-hand observer (an Oblate) wrote about them:

"The Eskimo of today is confronted by revolutionary changes. During the past few years, radio and meteorological stations have been established around him in increasing number and now a gigantic air lift accompanied by an extensive unloading operation has dumped hundreds of men and thousands of tons of material all over his native land for the construction of radar stations" (*Eskimo*, Sept.: 1958).

"Each year he sees a number of his compatriots take off towards the hospitals in the south, while many of his children live for months in boarding schools situated hundreds of miles away. Others of his fellowmen have left their country to work as labourers elsewhere" (*ibid.*).

The only vocal criticism, at that time, of the government "rehabilitation" programmes (aside from Jenness' protestations) came, indeed, from missionaries. But it was not until senior government officials, in the officially-blessed spirit of self-criticism of government northern policy (see Ch. 3), took up several of the same points some twenty years later that the criticism was 'heard.' The government, of course, believed that part of its job was to 'free' the Inuit from the missions: an explicit objective of the educational programme, for instance, was the replacement of the church schools (Davidson, 1973:12). Recognizing the cultural as well as religious secularity of the government programmes, the Anglicans claimed that "at the time the Government took over the Church schools and set up their own...more than 80% of the Eskimos were literate in their own language" (Marsh, n.d.:10). On resettlement and the abandonment of camp life, the Anglicans declared "this decision forced the Eskimos on to relief...and increased their dependency" (Marsh, p. 15). The Oblates protested at what they perceived to be the erosion of Inuit rights: "[the right] to live where they wish in their own country...the right to send their children to the school of their choice," and so on (*Eskimo*, Sept., 1958).

A sombre warning, spared of sentimentality, came somewhat later from an anthropologist concerning the likely relationship between poor health, large families and poverty. It was widely and uncritically accepted that these problems would be solved when Inuit were moved into permanent settlements. However, Freeman found that "it is the consequences of sickness (particularly the lack of economic security for dependents) rather than sickness itself that is minimized by settlement living, for in many localities the incidence of sickness rises dramatically with movement to permanent settlements and concomitant destruction of a viable ecologic adaptation" (1971:226–7). He urged the government to heed seriously the fact that "decreasing fertility [is] a pre-condition for, or concomitant of rational [rehabilitation] programs" (*op. cit*.:228); furthermore, the Northwest Territories is "heading for serious social, economic and political problems unless effective measures are taken, without delay, to slow down the rate of population increase" (p. 231).

Government Programmes: Expenditure and Ideology

> "The development drive has taken on an energy of its own, based on the false assumption that what is good for the rest of Canada is good for the native northerners."
> *M. K. Petrie* (1974b:9).

At the close of 1953, the prime minister observed that "apparently we have administered these vast territories of the north in an almost continuing state of absence of mind" (Canada, 1953:698); he could have added with 'almost an absence of money.' Yet, only two years later government expenditure in the N.W.T. was $12 million; by 1959 it was $61 million, with a revenue of under $7 million (Lantis, 1966:89–90). Since the early '70's, the government has been investing about $300 million a year, receiving in return about $200 million, thus creating an annual deficit of $100 million (Ørvik, 1973b:6).

In citing figures for government expenditure in the north, my intention is not to suggest that the spending has been big or generous – for how does one judge? Rather, it is to point out how the government of a modern nation can use its money to try to redress a perceived social problem; to demonstrate how the way in which money is allocated influences the definition (and, of course, the 'progress') of the social problem; and to consider some of the social and demographic consequences of this governmental campaign. Among unwanted consequences which were apparently unforeseen – an incredible matter, itself, were it not a depressingly familiar feature of government programmes anywhere – have been those arising from the effects of government action in one sector of its programme on other sectors.

By 1961–62, three million dollars were being spent annually by the Northern Health Service (Jenness, 1964:143),[8] and according to Statistics Canada, the Inuit population of the N.W.T. increased from 6,800 in 1951 to

8,000 in 1961; by 1971 it totalled 11,400 – a 68 percent increase over twenty years. Probably more than any other single factor, it is this demographic growth that has ensured the continuation of a welfare colonialism among the present-day Inuit of Canada. Exactly which socio-economic and cultural pattern a welfare colonialism takes is not of course predictable from the demographic factor alone; yet this factor did make predictable the "low per capita income ... with concomitant dependenc[ies] on outside sources of influence and control" (Freeman, 1971:218) such as the Inuit are now experiencing.

In the event, government expenditures on the implementation of a school programme exceeded even those of the health programme. In the Commissioner's Annual Report from 1968–69, the N.W.T. Director of Education begins thus:

Prior to 1955 the education program of the Northwest Territories was a loosely organized service of partly public and partly private sponsorship, involving churches, local governments, company operations and the federal government. Less than 15% of the school age children of the Territories had received any appreciable amount of formal instruction. The remainder, largely children of the indigenous population, were almost completely illiterate in either their own language or in English. The introduction of a school system which was free, and universally accessible was a primary requisite to meet the desires and needs of northern people.[9] Consequently in 1955 a program of formal schooling was developed by federal authorities to provide the requirements under the direction of a single authority.

During the course of the past fifteen years in which this education program has been developed in the north, significant and in some cases even spectacular changes have occurred in the "education scene" north of the 60th parallel.

Approximately 90% of the school age children of the N.W.T. are now in regular school attendance. Staff, facilities and educational resources equal to those found in the provincial systems are now available.

The same report also mentions progress at the pre-school and vocational school levels: 148 Inuit from the East Arctic, for instance, were enrolled at the Churchill Vocational Centre; adult training centres and "southern exposure courses" had been instituted; and "approximately twenty Eskimos were relocated in southern Canada for employment." The mood of the educational bureaucracy appears to have been one of confidence, even self-congratulation. The message at the time was that the figures speak for themselves. But when looking at them one should remember that the pace-setter – a hard one – for the educational programme was the health programme[10] and its 'successes.' The Inuit population, traditionally among "the most fertile population[s] known" in the world (Freeman, *op. cit.*:220), was now also an exaggeratedly young one: in 1969–70 about 60 percent of the Baffin Inuit, for instance, were under 20 years of age, and 90 percent under 45 years (see Ch. 4). Secondly, it is assumed that school enrollment figures would correlate with employment possibilities; but there has never been an employment programme comparable to those in health and education, nor even comparable claims of success by officials.

The principal tasks of government are the supply, distribution and administration of social services ("hard" and "soft," to follow the official language). The population receiving these services is small but disproportionately 'expensive.' It is so because of its scattered spatial distribution, its cultural heterogeneity and yet overall cultural marginality to the rest of Canada, and its negligible capacity to generate tax dollars. Notice should also be taken here of the minimal autonomy afforded to local communities, as the N.W.T. government sponsors and controls (still today) a variety of projects that elsewhere in Canada are usually left to local councils (see Ch. 4 for a description of local government) and even private individuals (N.W.T., 1974b:11). Whereas in Ontario there is a civil servant for every 114 people, in the N.W.T. there is one for every 29 people (N.W.T., 1974b: Appendix I); and whereas the combined per capita expenditure of all levels of government for Canada (and for Ontario) for 1970/71 was about $1,500, in the N.W.T. it was $4,200 (Table 3, below).

Government is, of course, the largest single employer (by far) in the N.W.T. Most government jobs and almost all those requiring formal educational skills have been and still are in the possession of whites. Whites inherit from whites, and this pattern maintains itself even while the civil service expands. In the early post-war years, the job of administrating the N.W.T. was "hardly as important ... as the administration of the National Museum"; indeed both tasks belonged to the same federal department (Rea, 1968:47). But by 1969 there were almost 3,000 persons on the Federal Government northern payroll which was in excess of $16 million and accounted for 25 percent of the "total personal income of the north" (Palmer, 1971:ii and Table 1).[11]

A clue to the place of Inuit in this system – or the place that they did not have – at about this time is contained in Lantis' comment (1966:118): "... probably the largest single category of steady wage employment for Canadian Eskimos is 'janitorial-maintenance.'"

On the other hand, the government makes important and widely distributed contributions to Inuit (and others') personal income through social transfer payments. Table 1 shows that expenditure listed officially under the inclusive heading of "Welfare"[12] in 1973–74 accounted for 11.2 percent of all government expenditure in the Canadian North (including the Yukon); the projection for 1976–77 is 13.9 percent. The corresponding figures for "Health" are 7.8 and 9.3 percent; and for "Education," 12 percent in 1973–74 (above that of Welfare), dropping in 1976–77 to a projected 9.4 percent, which is significantly below that allocated to welfare. Combining now the three budgetary items of health, education and welfare, we find (Table 2) they account for a little over 30 percent of the total government (federal and territorial) budget for the Canadian North

TABLE 1

Itemized Government Expenditures in the Canadian North
Including the Yukon (1973/74–1976/77)

Rank Order of Expenditures	1973/74 % of Total	1974/75 % of Total	1975/76 % of Total	1976/77 % of Total	New Rank Order
(1) Transportation	22.3	20.0	19.0	19.7	(2)
(2) General Govt. Services	22.2	23.5	22.1	20.7	(1)
(3) Education	12.0	10.8	10.5	9.4	(4)
(4) Welfare	11.2	11.8	13.0	13.9	(3)
(5) Health	7.8	8.6	8.3	9.3	(5)
(6) Econ. Dev't. (Other)	6.6	5.6	7.6	6.7	(7)
(7) Short Range Research	5.1	4.4	3.7	3.2	(8)
(8) Local Govt.	4.5	5.8	6.6	6.9	(6)
(9) Defence	2.6	2.6	2.5	2.4	(12)
(10) Communications	2.1	2.4	2.6	2.6	(10)
(11) Econ. Dev't. (Human)	2.0	2.3	3.2	2.8	(9)
(12) Culture and Recreation	1.6	2.2	2.4	2.4	(11)
Totals	100	100	100	100	
(millions of dollars)	(345.5)	(407.5)	(513.0)	(583.5)	

Source: Canada, 1976: Tables VII, VIII, IX, X and XI.
Note: The figures are the combined expenditure of the Governments of Canada,
N.W.T. and the Yukon Territory. For separate expenditures of the Federal and
Territorial Governments, see Chapter 4. Figures for 1975/76 are "forecast" and those
for 1976/77 are "planned."

over the same time period. Although their combined value, as a percentage
of the gross budget, remains constant, the welfare budget alone shows the
greatest growth of all expenditures. Expressed as per capita costs, the
figure for all social assistance programmes in the N.W.T. during 1970–71
was $124, of which nearly $29 were absorbed by the administration of the
programmes; the Candian per capita figure outside the north was $59
(Table 3). It has been suggested that the health programme acted as a
pace-setter for the educational programme; it is now becoming clear that
these two programmes have functioned as a pace-setter for the welfare
programme.

To grasp the meaning of these payments to Inuit households, it is
important to realize that they are used by the Inuit as a fourth source of
income in a scheme of limited occupational pluralism. The other three
sources are wages and salaries, hunting/trapping/fishing, and handicrafts.
Officially, transfer payments are regarded as unearned income in contrast
to earned income, which is derived from the other three sources, and it is

TABLE 2

Health, Education and Welfare: Government Expenditures in the
Canadian North, Including the Yukon (1973/74–1976/77)

A. Dollars

	1973/74	1974/75	1975/76	1976/77
Health	26,840,000	35,072,000	42,674,000	54,354,000
Education	41,443,000	43,863,000	53,920,000	54,693,000
Welfare	38,576,000	47,856,000	66,596,000	81,236,000
Sub-total	106,859,000	126,791,000	163,190,000	190,283,000
All government expenditures in the north (Table I)	345,500,000	407,500,000	513,000,000	583,000,000

B. Percentage increases over the 1973–74 expenditures

	1973/74	1974/75	1975/76	1976/77
Health	—	30.6	59.0	102.5
Education	—	5.8	30.1	32.0
Welfare	—	24.0	72.6	110.6
Sub-total	—	18.6	52.7	78.0
All government expenditures in the north (Table I)	—	17.9	48.5	68.7

C. As percentage of all government expenditures in the Canadian north

	1973/74	1974/75	1975/76	1976/77
Health and education and welfare	31.0	31.2	31.8	32.6

Source: Canada, 1976: Tables VII, VIII, IX, X and XI.
Note: See note to Table I.

convenient to accept this usage in the following cursory survey of work and income among the Inuit of the Baffin Region during the sixties.

In the east-coast settlements of Baffin Island, *unearned* income accounted for about a quarter of the total personal income (Haller, 1967: Table 51). Along the south coast the percentage was lower, ranging between eleven and twenty (Higgins, 1968: Tables 25 and 38). These data are from the early and middle '60s and exclude Frobisher Bay.[13] The Manpower Survey data at the end of the '60s (see Ch. 4) show that the greater part of the *earned* income of men (Frobisher Bay included) is from wages – although in six of the settlements the imputed value of fresh meat, as income in kind (that is, hunters' earned income), exceeds income earned from wages (Palmer, 1973: Appendix IV); and the source of over half of the wages is government. Totalled, earned income is *less than* one thousand dollars in the case of nearly 40 percent of the men and over 80 percent of the

TABLE 3

Representative Costs of Social Services in N.W.T.
(1967/68 and 1970/71)

A. Per capita expenditures (all levels of government)

	1967/68	1970/71	% increase
N.W.T.	$2,936	4,256	45
All Canada	1,142	1,555	36

B. Per capita costs of Social Assistance Programmes[1]

	1970/71
N.W.T.	$124.15
Outside the North	59.08

Source: Ørvik, 1973a; Appendix IV.
[1]Costs of administering the programmes are included.

women.[14] As one would expect, it is in Frobisher Bay, the administrative centre itself, that wage employment has the greatest place in Inuit economy, and there the percentage of unearned income is appreciably lower than in most of the other settlements of the region (cf. MacBain Meldrum, 1975: Tables 4 and 5). Yet even in Frobisher Bay, few Inuit have advanced in the occupational structure much beyond the "janitorial-maintenance" level of which Lantis spoke; in 1969, the figure was perhaps ten persons and most of them were in clerical jobs (MacBain Meldrum, 1975:129). Meanwhile, an Inuit employment crisis has become imminent in Frobisher Bay (op. cit.: 137–38).

In closing, I want to take a preliminary look at the ideological side of the government programmes; to consider the relation between dollar inputs and the "quality of life" (a common phrase in government circles from 1972 on) of Inuit. Any conclusion to the effect that Inuit are now better off than ever before must take into account how government ideology has been directed to giving the Inuit a white lifestyle (Davidson, 1973). The principal result has been to impress upon those who live in the Arctic, Inuit and whites alike, how the circumstances of the Inuit are, in fact, not as good as the whites'. For instance the Inuit now live in houses and their rents are subsidized (see Ch. 4); yet the subsidized housing of their white neighbours is of a different quality. The Territorial Government recently admitted to "two often conflicting objectives" in this connection: "On the one hand, it is necessary for Government to provide adequate accommodations at a reasonable cost if it is to be able to attract and keep competent employees; on the other hand it must always be conscious of keeping within the range and quality of accommodation available to the public as a whole" (N.W.T., 1974b:20). The Inuit are aware of these "conflicting objectives" (re: the film The People's Land). Then again, whites move in and out of permanent government jobs (there is no effective government stipulation regarding minimum length of tenure in these jobs) at the higher levels of responsibility and remuneration, the Inuit at the lower levels; and a large proportion of the Inuit jobs are part-time only.[15]

The educational programme for the native peoples of the north was, in the late '60s, held by one observer to be "undeniably socially destructive" (Freeman, 1969:75). Guemple (1969:45–6) elaborates:

"The most pointed educational goal to date has been learning English together with a set of tastes and social skills appropriate to the average school child of metropolitan Canada. What the precise advantages of obtaining these skills are I am unable to ascertain after some investigation. Eskimos are all quite anxious to acquire them; and the young work quite diligently to become accomplished in them. When I enquired what they thought they might be useful for, the results were disappointing. No one could find any very useful purpose in obtaining them, and no one interviewed – man, woman, or child – could suggest more than five ways in which they could be used. They were certain that the skills would enable them to get along better with whites, read and listen to radio broadcasts in English, work as a handyman in the Hudson Bay Company Store, work for the government in some capacity, or simply "get a job." But this hardly approaches an "orderly plan" for developing the Eskimo world.

I interviewed government people as well, and they too found it difficult to suggest precisely how these skills could be put to good use. There seems to be general agreement that the "plan" is to have the Eskimo remain in the Arctic permanently. Yet there does not appear to be any substantive "work" for them to do there. ..."

In local government and even in the co-operative movement, southern models have been brought north and imposed on local communities – or what are held by government to be southern models; for when "what is good for the rest of Canada" (Petrie, 1974b) is taken north, it in fact usually changes. Thus, local government institutions that, in the south, provide communities with significant autonomy, in the north become tightly controlled from outside the community: this will be considered more precisely in our evaluation of the situation of the '70s.

With respect to other services and industry, instead of southern 'models' being taken north, the north is held in direct economic bondage to the south:

A needlessly large proportion of total earnings of the north at present leaves [the north] to pay for the basic services and goods required in the north. For example in the eastern and central arctic there is no northern-based transportation service, no construction industry, no manufacturing of domestic, school or office furniture, no light engineering for repairs or modification of marine, aircraft or construction equipment, no printing facilities (outside of school and office typing and duplicating equipment), no manufacturing or assembly of hunting equipment, no clothing or shoe manufacturing or repair facilities, and virtually no boat-building or repair facilities. Even efforts to establish a tannery in the Eastern Arctic are delayed by endless procrastination (Freeman, 1969:70).

Others have noted, and regretted, the same phenomenon over a wide range of context. Guemple (1969:53) thought that more effort should be made "to find and promote economic activities and industry which make 'sense' to the native in his own world. The value of carving, for example, completely escapes the native with the result that he thinks the white man rather mad for desiring it and for paying money to possess it. A good knife, on the other hand, is something that does make a good deal of sense to him.'' In the field of mental health (see Ch. 4), Atcheson (1972:16) observed:

> Practitioners, nurses, native public health personnel are constantly seeking advice from the consultant as to the management of disturbed people. Usually the first request has been for means of expediting their removal from the community. However, if they knew that a consultant would be available, even on a radio-telephone communicating basis, they demonstrated a willingness to cope with the problem in their local community.
>
> It [is] my opinion that the majority of the mentally ill people in the Arctic could be successfully maintained and cared for through the existing facilities within the community.

All the evidence, then, appears to support the conclusion that the government—whether willfully or unwittingly – has 'shut out' the local community and the native people from the processes directed towards their own modernity. That being so, it is important to know about native reaction and to include that, as well, in our account of the situation. As a first step in this direction, we begin by asking some questions. Why, for instance, should Inuit want responsibility if it is to be on whites' terms? Perhaps Inuits' 'inferior' standing to whites can be explained, in part, by their reluctance to help whites incorporate them? This view is plausible with respect to Inuit employment. Why should they *want* wages rather than an income from hunting? Why a permanent and full-time job if they can still manage to make their own seasonal arrangements? Yet, as Brody and Riches (this volume) each demonstrate, this line of thinking is not adequate as an explanation for Inuit response to local government and even some local co-operatives: though they may not wish or be able to play an active role in these institutions, they may have wanted them there in the first place.

That a factor is still missing in the general explanation we are seeking concerning low native involvement in white-sponsored plans and institutions becomes particularly evident when one asks why there were only seven "native" (including Indian and Métis, as well as Inuit) elementary school teachers in the N.W.T. as late as 1971 (Girard & Gourdeau, 1973:115–17)? What this other factor may well be is that in 'helping' Inuit, whites allow their own thinking about the white 'system' – or more precisely, their predispositions towards 'southern rules' of that system – to keep the Inuit 'down.' As Inuit see this happening when they become involved with the white system, they proceed to withdraw from it. We can safely say, already here, that the degree of Inuit involvement in the conduct of their own affairs has been – as a matter of fact and not only Inuit perception of the facts – very small; this it seems, is one of the principal results of government programmes and dollar inputs from the '60s. We must now take a closer account of the '70s.

NOTES

1 See, however, Cooke, 1969.
2 At the level of on-going exchanges between trapper and trader, it is the "grubstake" system of credit that should be examined; cf. Salisbury, 1976.
3 Although I think this is a subject that needs closer study, one must be careful about the conclusions that might be drawn from such data in isolation. Dr. Gordon Inglis (personal communication), for example, suggests that what we have here is rather an all-Canada pattern and not one peculiar to the Canadian Arctic: "In Canada, for most of the time, the frontier was an administrative one (unlike the opening of the U.S. west) of which the leading edge was more often surveyors, cartographers, policemen, judges, or crown-chartered companies. In this respect Canada's expansion into the Arctic is quite consistent with the development of the rest of the country, and my general impression is that Canadian Arctic place-names are probably much like place-names in most of the rest of the country."
4 "... the DEW line was conceived as an instrument for continental defence ... it entailed the performance of prodigious engineering feats; the expenditure of enormous amounts of public money (perhaps more than $500,000,000); and the establishment of facilities in the far north possessing little direct economic value for the area itself. ... The basic elements of the programme were the 50-odd radar stations to be strung out along the arctic coast of North America from Alaska to the east coast of Baffin Island – a distance of some 3,000 miles. ... The actual construction was undertaken by a large United States firm which built the stations in the western arctic, and two Canadian firms, which built the eastern two-thirds of the system" (Rea, 1968:308–91).
5 Note should be taken of the strong probability that the extreme "precariousness" (Lee, 1968:40) of the Inuit ecologic-economic-demographic adaptation was aggravated by contact with whites throughout the previous century.
6 This point is taken up by Professor David Alexander (personal communication) who warns against the tendency to discuss the situation in the Canadian north in "something of a national and historical vacuum: the lack of government involvement in the north in the early decades of this century, and then the rush to supplant church services with secular services and administration, does not strike a historian as a uniquely northern course of events: it was a general trend that moved through Canadian society in this century." Moreover, the standards implicit in the judgements of such northern critics as Diamond Jenness need to be evaluated: perhaps they were based on "what they found and expected as middle-class persons in the south? For the working class in the south, the neglect of the north might not have looked very extreme, and the absence of a government presence would not have been at all surprising." (Cf. Notes 9, 10 and 11.)
7 The Area Surveys were concerned almost exclusively with natural renewable resources – as though mineral and fossil resources could not possibly have any connection with the Inuit; given this restricted focus, it was all the more regrettable that "the Inuit perspective" concerning land usage was "almost entirely missing" (Lotz, 1976:26). More seriously, though predictably, the Surveys contained "almost no information on the economic and social structures – and the attendant costs – of the non-Inuit residents of the Arctic" (ibid.). For a superlative documentation of Inuit land use (hunting, trapping, and fishing), area by area, see Freeman, 1976, vol. 1.
8 Regarding Jenness' (ibid.) claim that this sum was one hundred times the amount spent in 1939, Professor Alexander (personal communication) responds as follows:
  "If you deflate the expenditures with the general wholesale price index (1935–39 = 100) then the real increase in expenditure between 1939 and 1961 was 43 times rather than 100 times. Over the same period, all government expenditures rose by 20 times in money terms and 8 times in real terms. Federal Government expenditures rose by 270 times in money terms and 116 times in real terms (reflecting entry into shared-cost hospital programmes with the provinces).
  If northern health service expenditures rose from $30,000 in 1939 to $3 million in 1961, then expenditures per head of NWT and Yukon population rose from $1.77 to $79.73.
  For Canada as a whole, Federal Government expenditures per capita grew from

$0.11 to $18.11, and *all government* expenditures from $4.18 to $52.04.

Thus, without considering the differential real costs of health delivery in the north and south, populations serviced by provincial governments in 1939 did better than the north serviced by the Federal Government; but by 1961 the situation was substantially reversed. (All calculations from Urquhart and Buckley, 1965).''

9   This state of affairs bears direct comparison with that in the south a quarter of a century or so earlier. For Canada as a whole in 1921, 54% of population aged 5–19 were at school for 7–9 months, 39% were not in school, and 8% attended for less than 6 months (Canada, 1929). In 1930, of all children in school, 40.4% were attending grades I-III and 30% grades IV-VI (Canada, 1932). These data were provided by Professor Alexander who comments: ''school attendance was supposed to be compulsory up to age 14; but many children that were registered never attended because there was no space for them. In these years in Canada, schooling was an entirely local affair, and compared with most countries in the western world the Canadian population was very badly educated, or at least schooled'' (personal communication).

10   Health care in Canada before World War II ''varied incredibly because it was in the private sector and the different provinces provided public health facilities with varying commitments. While in Ontario and generally in the west of Canada, the statistics compared favourably with the developed world, in Quebec and the Maritimes infant mortality rates were dreadful'' (Alexander, personal communication). In fact, the infant mortality rates (per 1000 livebirths) in eastern Canadian cities in 1929 (Canada, 1932) exceeded those for N.W.T. Inuit in 1966 (cf., ch. 4).

11   ''By comparison, in Canada, the payment of wages and salaries by the Federal Government amounted to only 3.4% of personal income. These figures excluded payments by Crown Corporations, the Territorial Governments and military pay and allowances'' (*ibid.*).

12   Figures cited are for the '70s as those for earlier years are officially deemed ''unreliable'' (personal communication). Re: my introductory remarks to Chapter 4.

13   In Newfoundland in 1965, government transfer payments were 16% of personal income (Newfoundland and Labrador, 1970); and for Canada as a whole in 1969 they were 10% (Canada, 1973).

14   The gross incomes of these Inuit of the Baffin Region were (following Meldrum and Helman, 1975, Table 26) as much as 75% lower than those among the Inuit of the West Arctic whose percentage of earned to unearned income was also about 5% higher.

15   It is significant to note this communication from 'industry' to D.I.N.A.: ''Industry has recently warned us of the negative effect of casual labour, from major projects (highways, oil industry, gas pipeline construction) on native communities. These are: (1) Increase in school drop-outs when teenagers see their parents, without schooling, earning large pay cheques. (2) Stable labour force in the communities attracted to higher paying jobs with resultant loss of a full-time position and families unsettled. (3) The temporary masking of deep-rooted change problems which if continually avoided only make their ultimate solution more difficult'' (Petrie, 1974a: 18).

References

ATCHESON, J. D.
    1972 "Problems of Mental Health in the Canadian Arctic." *Canada's Mental Health*, XX(1).
BRIGGS, JEAN
    1971 "Strategies of Perception: The Management of Ethnic Identity." In Robert Paine (ed.), *Patrons and Brokers in the East Arctic*. St. John's, Institute of Social and Economic Research, Memorial University of Newfoundland.

Canada
1929 *Canada Yearbook 1929*. Ottawa, F. A. Acland.
Canada
1932 *Canada Yearbook 1932*. Ottawa, F. A. Acland.
Canada
1953 Debates of House of Commons, Official Reports. 22nd Parliament, First Session, Vol. 1. Ottawa, Queen's Printer.
Canada
1973 *Canada Yearbook 1973*. Ottawa, Information Canada.
Canada
1976 *Annual Northern Expenditure Plan, 1976–77*. (Advisory Committee Northern Development) Ottawa, Department of Indian and Northern Affairs.
COOKE, A.
1969 *The Ungava Venture of Hudson's Bay Company, 1830–1843*. Unpublished Ph.D. thesis, University of Cambridge.
DAVIDSON, D. A.
1973 "The People in the North." In N. Ørvik (ed.), *Policies of Northern Development*. Kingston, Department of Political Studies, Queen's University.
Eskimo
1958 Quarterly Magazine. Churchill, Oblate Fathers of the Hudson Bay Vicariate.
FREEMAN, MILTON, M. R.
1969 "Development Strategies and Indigenous People in the Canadian Arctic." In M. M. R. Freeman (ed.), *Intermediate Adaptation in Newfoundland and the Arctic*. St. John's, Institute of Social and Economic Research, Memorial University of Newfoundland.
FREEMAN, MILTON M. R.
1971 "The Significance of Demographic Changes Occurring in the Canadian East Arctic." *Anthropologica*, XIII(1–2).
FREEMAN, MILTON M. R.
1976 *Inuit Land Use and Occupancy Project* (3 vols.). Ottawa, Department of Indian and Northern Affairs.
GIRARD, G. and E. GOURDEAU
1973 "Southern Teachers for the North." In *Man in the North; Technical Reports: Education in the Canadian North*. Montreal, Arctic Institute of North America.
GRABURN, N. H. H. and B. S. STRONG
1973 *Circumpolar Peoples: An Anthropological Perspective*. Pacific Palisades, Goodyear Publishing Co., Inc.
GUEMPLE, D. L.
1969 "The Eskimo and Intermediate Adaptation in the Canadian Arc-

tic." In M. M. R. Freeman (ed.), *Intermediate Adaptation in New-foundland and the Arctic*. St. John's, Institute of Social and Economic Research, Memorial University of Newfoundland.

HALLER, A. A.
1967 *Baffin Island – East Coast: An Area Economic Survey*. Ottawa, Department of Indian Affairs and Northern Development.

HIGGINS, G. M.
1968 *The South Coast of Baffin Island: An Area Economic Survey*. Ottawa, Department of Indian Affairs and Northern Development.

HUGHES, C. C.
1965 "Under Four Flags: Recent Culture Changes among the Eskimos." *Current Anthropology*, 6(1).

JENNESS, DIAMOND
1964 *Eskimo Administration: II. Canada*. Montreal, Arctic Institute of North America: Technical Paper No. 14.

JENNESS, DIAMOND
1968 *Eskimo Administration: V. Analysis and Reflections*. Montreal, Arctic Institute of North America; Technical Paper No. 21.

KELLY, WILLIAM and NORA
1973 *The Royal Canadian Mounted Police: A Century of History 1873–1973*. Edmonton, Hurtig.

LANTIS, MARGARET
1966 "The Administration of Northern Peoples: Canada and Alaska." In R. St. J. MacDonald (ed.), *The Arctic Frontier*. Toronto, University of Toronto Press.

LEE, R. B.
1968 "What Hunters do for a Living, or How to Make Out on Scarce Resources." In R. B. Lee and I. DeVore (eds.), *Man the Hunter*. Chicago, Aldine Publishing Co.

LOTZ, JIM
1976 "Area Economic Surveys: Critique and Assessment." In M. M. R. Freeman (ed.), *Inuit Land Use and Occupancy Project* (vol. 2). Ottawa, Department of Indian and Northern Affairs.

MACBAIN MELDRUM, SHEILA
1975 *Frobisher Bay: An Area Economic Survey*. Ottawa, Department of Indian Affairs and Northern Development.

MACBAIN MELDRUM, SHEILA and MARIAN HELMAN
1975 *Northern Manpower Survey Program in the Yukon and Northwest Territories*. Ottawa, Department of Indian Affairs and Northern Development.

MARSH, D. B.
n.d. "A History of the Work of the Anglican Church in the Area now known as the Diocese of the Arctic." (Publisher unknown)

Newfoundland and Labrador
1970 *Historical Statistics of Newfoundland and Labrador*. St. John's,
Northwest Territories
1968–69 *Annual Report of the Commissioner of the N.W.T.* Yellowknife, N.W.T. Government.
Northwest Territories
1974a *Community Data 1974*. Yellowknife, N.W.T. Government.
Northwest Territories
1974b *Report of the Task Force on Personnel Policy and Management*. Yellowknife, N.W.T. Government.
ØRVIK, NILS
1973a *Policies of Northern Development*. Kingston, Department of Political Studies, Queen's University.
ØRVIK, NILS
1973b "The North as Politics." In N. Ørvik (ed.), *Policies of Northern Development*. Kingston, Department of Political Studies, Queen's University.
PALMER, JOHN R.
1971 *Social Accounts for the North: Interim Paper No. 1; The Federal Government Sector: Employment and Payrolls*. Ottawa, Department of Indian Affairs and Northern Development.
PALMER, JOHN R.
1973 *Social Accounts for the North: Interim Paper No. 3; The Measurement of Income in the Yukon and N.W.T.* Ottawa, Department of Indian Affairs and Northern Development.
PETRIE, M. K.
1974a "Factors Affecting Northern Program Employment Policies." Ottawa, Department of Indian Affairs and Northern Development. (Stencil)
PETRIE, M. K.
1974b "Factors Affecting Native Employment North of '60.'" Ottawa, Department of Indian Affairs and Northern Development. (Stencil)
REA, KENNETH J.
1968 *The Political Economy of the Canadian North; an Interpretation of the Course of Development in the Northern Territories of Canada to the early 1960s*. Toronto, University of Toronto Press.
SALISBURY, RICHARD F.
1976 "Transactions or Transactors? An Economic Anthropologist's View." In Bruce Kapferer (ed.), *Transaction and Meaning*. Philadelphia, Institute for the Study of Human Issues.
URQUHART, M. C. and K. A. M. BUCKLEY
1965 *Historical Statistics of Canada*. Toronto, Macmillan.
USHER, PETER J.

1971 *Fur Trade Posts of the Northwest Territories 1870–1970*. Ottawa, N.S.R.G. 71-4.

USHER, PETER J.
   1976 "The Inuk as Trapper: A Case Study." In Milton M. R. Freeman (ed.), *Inuit Land Use and Occupancy Project, vol. 2*. Ottawa, Department of Indian and Northern Affairs.

WILLIAMSON, ROBERT G.
   1968 "The Canadian Arctic, Sociocultural Changes." *Archives of Environmental Health*, 17(4).

WOODCOCK, G.
   1970 *The Hudson's Bay Company*. Cromwell, Collier Press.

ZASLOW, M.
   1971 *The Opening of the Canadian North 1870–1914*. Toronto/Montreal, McClelland and Stewart, Ltd.

An Appraisal of the Last Decade

Robert Paine

3

> "Canadians can no longer afford to romanticize about their North as an 'Arctic Wilderness' with quaint people living exclusively off the land. Canadians as well as people in other countries must be given an up-to-date picture of our developing North – the direction it is moving and the dramatic changes taking place."
>
> *Commissioner of the Northwest Territories*, 1971 Annual Report.

In the '60s, Diamond Jenness indicted Canadian northern policy in these words: "We have set up a complex government ... but offered them [the native people] no real place in it; and, what is worse, we have not inspired any hope that there will be a real place for them" (Jenness, 1964:161). If true at the time, is it still true? Alternatively, what is one to make of the government claim, early in the '70s, that "northern development [is] a national endeavour and the whole area a showpiece"? This passage occurs in the policy statement of March 1972 by Jean Chretien, Minister of Indian Affairs and Northern Development (Canada, 1972a), and the question in the forefront of the discussion that now follows is, did Chretien's statement really mark a watershed in government thinking, and praxis, or was it just window-dressing?

For many, this may be an absurdly academic question: for them the answer is as plain as the window-dressing is elaborate. In this view, the real concern since 1968 has been with oil and gas, and northern policies and programmes in the social field have taken their cues from that basic national purpose. Accordingly, "at no time did Ottawa's inner circle consider the interests of the native people as a central component of northern development" (Dosman, 1975:213). Apparently the "national interest" itself has fared no better. Dosman's verdict is, "Ottawa's true religion is *drift*" (*ibid.*). However, policy options are left open so that "Ottawa [can] bend more easily with the prevailing winds from the South" – that is, the U.S. Thus, "what appears as drift was in fact a method" (p. 215). Even so, "crisis succeeded crisis in the period 1968–75. ... senior officials found themselves outflanked again and again in a rapidly changing northern policy environment" (p. 213).

Such analysis is at the macro-level but the research in this book is concentrated at the micro-level; and whereas Dosman assesses "government and business relations in the North from 1968 to 1975'' (p. ix), the appraisal in this chapter limits itself to the possible relationships between government policies and the everyday circumstances of two of the populations of the North, Inuit and white. As research foci, these are complementary. Regrettably, Dosman's and my conclusions are broadly similar, and in order to show why this is so, we must answer the questions asked above.

Government: New Structure; New Praxis?

> "In 1966, Canada began an exciting new phase in
> northern political development, with possibilities
> emerging for the evolution of a process unlike any
> that had previously taken place."
> *Marquand and McNeill* (1975:i).

The last decennium has repeatedly been noted as one of significant periods in the history of Canadian northern administration. The events making it so include the Carrothers Commission on the development of government in the N.W.T. (1965–66), the establishment of the federal Advisory Committee on Northern Development (A.C.N.D.) (1966), the transfer from Ottawa to Yellowknife of the seat of the Territorial Government and the creation of its own civil service branch (in 1966–68), the transfer of administrative responsibility for the East Arctic from the Federal to the Territorial Government (1970), and the achievement of a fully-elected N.W.T. Council (1974). (Representation in the House of Commons was extended throughout the Arctic in 1962; Fingland, 1966:156.) All this activity is in marked contrast to the inertia of previous decennia. Though when Rea (1968:36) describes the government of the N.W.T. between 1921 and 1951 as "entrusted in effect to a group of senior civil servants," one must ask whether things are much different today (behind the new structural façade)?

Comment on the recent inclusion of the East Arctic in the N.W.T. political and administrative structure is necessary here. For a long time the more 'isolated' and 'backward,' and still the distinctly Inuit area of the Canadian Arctic, it had been administered directly (without representation) by the Federal Government throughout the '60s. Indeed, serious consideration was given in the early '60s to proposals for withholding the East Arctic from the planned political development of the remainder of the N.W.T. (centred on the Mackenzie District) (N.W.T., 1961:12–13). It was argued that in the East Arctic "... the level of education and sophistication among the Eskimo population had not reached the point where more than a small minority understood what was meant by an election and representation. ... If an Eskimo were appointed to give special representation to

Eskimos in the Eastern Arctic, there was the danger he would be looked upon as someone selected to put forth the view of the Administration" (*ibid.*). In fact, the division of the N.W.T. into two separate territories, with the East Arctic (as one Territory) remaining under the direct administrative care of Ottawa, came to naught. Finally, in 1970, "just two-and-a-half years after the first plane-load of Territorial public servants put down on Yellowknife airstrip to establish the new Capital" (N.W.T., 1970:6), the administrative responsibility for the East Arctic was assumed by the Territorial Government. Today the area makes its contribution to the N.W.T. council debates in Yellowknife, and it is from the East that the (vestigial) concept of an Inuit Territory – *Nunavut* (Sanders, 1973) – has come.

The Territorial Government consists of a council (now officially called the Legislative Assembly) and an executive over which the commissioner of the Territories presides. The progress of the council in becoming an elective assembly must not obscure the fact of its continuing subordinancy to the commissioner and his executive. (In 1951, three out of eight members were elected; in 1954, four out of nine; in 1970, six out of ten; and in 1974, all of its fifteen members.) Although the council may pass resolutions with "instructions" to the commissioner, and although three councillors now have places on the executive, the power of the council is constitutionally curtailed so that it has not attained a position comparable to a provincial legislative assembly. This position of the council is to be seen, not as much as a consequence of a strong executive, but of the control exercised by the Federal Government over the Territorial. The operation of the N.W.T. government depends on a budget most of which is provided by the Federal Government. It is not surprising, then, that the commissioner and other members of the executive are federal appointees; ... "the statutory channel of responsibility lies exclusively between the commissioner, a federal civil servant, and his superiors in Ottawa" (Fingland, 1966:130–45).[1] Fingland's conclusion, from the mid '60s, that the existence of territorial councils "give an impression of equality which is deceptive" (p. 131), still stands today despite a number of formal changes. Put bluntly, the Territorial Government is in many respects – the financial the most important among them – but "a puppet government" of the Federal (N.W.T., 1975a:26; cf. Patterson, 1976:140).

Although overstated with regard to the administrative responsibilities of some sectors of government (for example, education is now in the hands of the Territorial Government), this view is a usefully pointed summary of the situation. In one important *political* respect, however, it is a conservative view, taking too little account of the growing influence of the council – notwithstanding its constitutional limitations – as a vocal arena in deliberating and publicizing the affairs of the N.W.T.

Government: New rhetoric; New Thinking?

> "The heaviest emphasis in current thinking is on the
> needs and aspirations of the native peoples ... Pov-
> erty is their most pressing problem with all its
> psychological as well as physical characteristics."
>   *Jean Chretien*, Minister of Indian Affairs and
> Northern Development, March 28, 1972.

Leaving aside now the structure of government in the north, it is important to enquire about possible changes in government ideology and – what may only amount to pretences in changes of ideology – in the image that government holds of itself or the image it wishes to impart to the public. The ministerial statement of March, 1972 is important in respect to both ideology and image; it is remembered principally for the priorities it lay down for northern development, first among which was the betterment of the quality of life. Since then a number of statements of reappraisals, of varying degrees of candour and penetration, from government sources have followed (cf. Canada, 1972b; Davidson, 1973; N.W.T., 1974, 1975b; Petrie, 1974a and b).

In 1973, Queen's University invited "representatives of government institutions that are responsible for developing Canada's North to present their views" (Ørvik, 1973, ii). Although justifiably criticized, at the time, for not including Inuit contributors to the debate, in which government representatives faced a "group of scholars and policy practitioners, mostly from Canadian universities and research institutions" (*ibid.*), the conference produced, nevertheless, a number of quite valuable background papers.

In particular, I want to consider the one by Davidson who, at that time, was Acting Director of the Territorial Affairs Branch of the Federal Government. First, let us consider his remarks on the northern education programme. He makes it clear that government no longer found virtue exclusively located in "staff, facilities and educational resources equal to those found in the provincial systems"[2] (N.W.T., 1968–69; cf. Table 1). On the contrary, "... the process of assimilation of native youngsters into a southern white Canadian culture, upon which was based most of the thinking not only in education but in everything else, simply does not work" (Davidson, 1973:126). The new curricula in N.W.T. schools is described by Davidson in broad and uncritical terms: "Over recent years new curricula have been developed that recognize the way of life, the language, history, heritage and culture of the native peoples. It is [now] the policy of the government of the Northwest Territories to teach native people in their mother tongue in the primary grades. This program is just beginning"[3] (*ibid.*).

That was in 1973; there is, however, still much apprehension among northerners and other observers concerning the kind of educational pro-

TABLE 1

Growth Figures in Education in N.W.T., Baffin Region,
and Frobisher Bay

A. N.W.T.

	1960	1974
Pupils		
Total	5,029	12,803
Inuit Only	1,710	4,951
Schools	45	65
Teachers	197	660

B. Baffin Region, excluding Frobisher Bay; elementary schools only

	1966	1973
Pupils (virtually		
all Inuit)	630	1,425
Schools	11	12
Teachers	32	68
Pupil-Teacher		
Ratio	20	21

C. Frobisher Bay; pupil enrollments

	1972			1976		
	Inuit	White	Total	Inuit	White	Total
Elementary	n.d.	n.d.	n.d.	309	133	442
Pre-vocational	73	0	73	54	0	54
Secondary	92	56	148	160	86	246

Sources: Canada, 1975: Tables 18 to 21. Superintendent of Education, Baffin
Region (1976), personal communication.

cess the young are exposed to (personal communications). From the
N.W.T. Council debates, we hear that "... the kids who have been through
the system either for any length of time or even a short period are the people
who are unhappy, who are disillusioned, who are in the correction camp,
who are the layabouts, the people whom you are trying to encourage to take
on these jobs. These are the people who have a smattering of your so-called
education" (N.W.T., 1975a:99). Anxiety was also expressed recently in
Council over what Welsman (1976:37) calls "the invasion of informal
education," via the Canadian Broadcasting Corporation, since the launching of Anik, the telecommunications satellite, early in 1973.

I have a theory that the C.B.C. has an ill motive in the North and that is to Anglicize. Anik
sends programmes coming up from the South, you cannot imagine the effects of this tremend-
ous influence. When I think of the possibility that the C.B.C. has, what they can possibly do, it
just astonishes me and I cannot help but be very pessimistic about the future because in ten
years we will have everybody acculturated with the southern programmes with the result that
northern cultures will be seriously hindered (N.W.T., 1975a: 15).[4]

Returning now to Davidson, we are left wondering if government has understood its part in the relative failure of local government in the north. For, recognizing that "government is, in many ways, an over-exposed and over-used part of the social structure in the North," Davidson believes "this has come about, in part, because of the low capacity of the local people to provide themselves with acceptable social services and the resulting pressures on senior government to fill the void" (p. 130). Such a statement from a senior civil servant but affirms how political tutelage has smothered local expression (cf. Ch. 2, this vol.), assuring the continuance of government 'from the top down.' As much is recognized by another Federal Government source:

"In most N.W.T. communities there is an over-abundance of associations and committees, each dealing directly with some Department of the N.W.T. Government. The net effect here is to so water down the areas of responsibility of the local councils as to leave them simply with the responsibility of spending a limited budget supplied by the Territorial Government. The areas in which this budget may be spent are pre-determined except for a small per-capita community development grant which tends to get spent in the same way each year" (Petrie, 1974a:16).

The same source concludes that "in the N.W.T. one has, in effect, representation without taxation, local government without responsibility" (*ibid.*). Another source adds that a local council cannot do anything with its budget "except spend it on things we are told we can spend it on" (N.W.T., 1975b:26; cf. Hunter, 1976:71–5).

There is a tendency in government circles to point to the establishment and operation of co-operatives in the Arctic[5] as a successful development programme; and as Table 2 indicates for the Baffin Region, co-operatives certainly play an important – though somewhat skewed[6] – part in the economic and occupational structure of many settlements. Their community role, however, falls far short of that of co-operatives in southern Canada. As Riches (this volume) shows in a detailed case study, the affairs of a co-operative in the Arctic are likely to be closely monitored by (white) government administrators who can wield powerful sanctions to obtain the acquiescence of a local board of directors in official policy (which is not necessarily in accordance with the principles of the co-operative movement). Thus the role of a co-operative as an institution that fosters and generates local autonomy and local work groups can be undone, and the question of government aid to co-operatives becomes one of paramount sociological importance. "[The] co-operatives will never be completely institutionalized until they are independent of Government aid" is the verdict of one contemporary commentator (Paterson, 1976:63); for, as long as the financing of the co-operatives is from governmental sources, government "will continue to have a say in how the money is spent" (*ibid.*).

It is in the area of the (white-controlled) occupational and wage structure and the places that Inuit can expect to have in it – an area in which one

TABLE 2

Co-Operatives of the Baffin Region (1974–75)

Location (Population)	Members	Employees	Activity of Co-operative
Arctic Bay (311)	57*	3*	Carvings, crafts, sewn products, artifact replicas, contract fuel and gasoline sales, contract freight haul to and from airstrip.
Cape Dorset (690)	133	33	Consumer and producer operation, general store, prints, soapstone carvings, Shell Oil Distributors, Bell Tel. and weather station operator (34 employees).
Frobisher Bay (2365)	75	4	(Information not available)
Grise Fiord (100)	42	9	General store, fur and handicrafts, municipal service.
Hall Beach (315)	25*	1*	Handicrafts and carvings.
Igloolik (611)	88	75	Consumer Co-op; arts and crafts, municipal contracting, equipment rental.
Lake Harbour (260)	71	5	Mainly buying and selling carvings and sealskins. Holds contracts for municipal services.
Pangnirtung (906)	150	10	(Information not available)
Pond Inlet (550)	110	6	Sale of arts and crafts, carry out water contract, sewage and garbage contract and fuel oil contract.
Port Burwell (121)	25*	5*	Domestic foods, carvings, eiderdown, handicrafts, sealskin parkas, char fishing and cod fishing, raw fur sales.
Totals	776	151	

Sources: Paterson, 1976: Appendix 1; Buchanan, 1977: Table 2.
Note: Where possible membership and employment figures based on returns for 1974 or 1975; asterisked entries, however, are "estimation only, no recent data available." Employment includes part-time.

might reasonably expect *effective* government action – that there has been least change of all. Table 3 shows that in the early '70s, the number of federal employees in permanent jobs, actually located in the N.W.T., approached 1,500; but no more than 8 percent of these were filled by Inuit. A number of key departments (for example, Indian Affairs and Northern Development) were, according to the returns filed, without any Inuit on their permanent staff in the N.W.T., although there were vacancies. Indeed, the total number of vacancies (in 1972) was only slightly less than the total number of Inuit in permanent jobs. The situation with the Territorial Government appears to have been worse, particularly when one considers that the gross figures for 1972 (Table 3) are *not* restricted to permanent positions. (On the other hand, it is unlikely that the figures provide an inclusive coverage of seasonal, casual, or part-time employment.)[7]

Government officials have expressed concern over this. At times, what they say has that hollow ring of departmental rhetoric: "We must ensure

TABLE 3

Public Sector Employment Located in the N.W.T.

A. Federal and Territorial Governments, 1972–75

Year Govt.	Positions		Vacancies (Permanent Positions)	Native Employees (Inuit, Indian, Métis)		Inuit Employees		Native Employees as % of Permanent Positions	
	Permanent	Other		Permanent	Other	Permanent	Other	All Natives	Inuit Only
1972 Fed.	1,465	n.d.	109	228	n.d.	121[1]	n.d.	16	8
1972 Terr.[2]	2,110	265	423	291		148		12(?)	6(?)
1973 Fed.	1,693	262	n.d.	224	29	n.d.	n.d.	13	n.d.
1973 Terr.	2,344	735	n.d.	n.d.	n.d.	n.d.	n.d.		n.d.
1974 Fed.	2,085	456	n.d.	295	62	n.d.	n.d.	14	n.d.
1974 Terr.	2,144	n.d.	n.d.	436	n.d.	n.d.	n.d.	20	n.d.
1975 Fed	1,420	n.d.	n.d.	246	n.d.	115[1]	n.d.	17	8

Notes: [1]See B of this Table.
[2]Distribution of native employees between permanent and non-permanent positions not clear.

See Chapter 4 for the (much larger) figures of permanent northern service employment – including southern Canadian locations as well as N.W.T. and Yukon.

B. Departmental Distribution of Inuit in Permanent Positions with Federal Government in the N.W.T.

	1972	1975		1972	1975
Indian Affairs and Northern Development	14	11	Defence (civilian)	0	4
Environment	0	0	Energy, Mines & Resources	7	0
Health and Welfare	0	0	Communications	46	55
Transport	0	0	Justice	16	27
Public Works	19	n.d.	Power Commission	n.d.	3
Post Office	0	n.d.	R.C.M.P. (regular)	n.d.	14
Manpower	19	n.d.	Special Constables	0	1

Note: Under "Comments" attached to the return for 1972, 78 casual employees are mentioned: these are for the Yukon as well as the N.W.T. (not differentiated) and only 13 are identified as Inuit (one in Environment and 12 in Energy, Mines and Resources).

Sources: Northern Services Division, November 14, 1972; A.C.N.D. Secretariat, April 10, 1974 (at December 31, 1974, May sources).

that for all government work at least, jobs offered to native people are real as opposed to make-work projects ... [and that] there should be opportunities for advancement" (Hunt, 1973:15–16; writing about "positive employment practices"). But among themselves officials sometimes admit the bleak situation in which native employment programmes operate; a memorandum, at the end of 1972, to the A.C.N.D. (Advisory Committee on Northern Development) sub-committee on the employment of native northerners states:

"On the basis of these figures, it is clear that a great deal of work remains to be done to ensure that native northerners gain their rightful representation on the Federal labour force in the North. ... It may be recalled that in 1970 the A.C.N.D. ... adopted the target of 75% northern residents to be employed in Federal positions by 1977. ... the term "Northern Residents" was intended to refer chiefly to Indians, Eskimos and Metis; it would appear that no progress has been made in trying to reach the target set" (Canada, 1972b).

Yet, when Davidson (p. 134) says "the better jobs are usually filled by white workers and many of the native people are not capable of holding down responsible jobs even if they were available in their part of the North," we most likely come closer to government thinking or closer to the predispositions of government. (One notes, too, the self-validating and non-verifiable way in which the government position is defended: ... 'the jobs are not there, but even if they were ...') To 'complete' Davidson's statement, we have only to refer to the policy statement of Chretien's the year before: "[the North] will depend heavily for quite some time on attracting Canadians from the South, whether as individuals or corporations of high calibre and capability" (Canada, 1972a). In short, the present situation may be due less to government's lagging behind its intentions than to shortcomings of the intentions: they are less than what they are proclaimed to be.

The situation in Frobisher Bay (see Honigmann, 1965; Koster, 1972; MacBain Meldrum, 1975) is particularly critical because of its large Inuit population. The recently published Area Economic Survey Report recognizes "an obvious need" to find more jobs for this population, but observes that: "Unlike the indigenous labour force of many underdeveloped countries, the Eskimos of Frobisher Bay are not low cost labour, but neither are they particularly skilled labour. As they have become accustomed to high wages, it may be necessary to subsidize any private enterprise in order to attract it to the settlement and utilize Eskimo labour" (MacBain Meldrum, 1975:138). This view endorses the government's own concerning the need to attract Canadians of "ability" from the South; it also appears to be based on the same kind of argument used by Davidson (above) in connection with local government. Regarding the place of Inuit in the occupational structure, MacBain Meldrum comes close to saying, 'the (better) jobs are not there, but even were they ...'

Here, it is important to consider this view of Frobisher Bay's labour situation against the background of the community's short history. Invariably it is characterized as an "artificial community."

"It is an artificial community which has continued to exist simply because the Federal Government needed to maintain officials in the region to implement programs for northern development. In a sense, it remained in existence because for most of the time no final decision about its future was reached by government planners. They could decide neither to develop it nor to close it down" (MacBain Meldrum, *op. cit.*:133).

"... the more successful communities [in the Canadian Arctic], like Frobisher Bay and Inuvik, appear to me to be little more than empirical tests of Parkinson's Law, that is, they tend to prove that, given enough money, an artificial community can be set up whose bureaucratic functions can be expanded and elaborated enough to provide everyone with a make-work job" (Guemple, 1969:46).

While Frobisher Bay was still only an air force base and radar station, it attracted Inuit from the dispersed settlements of the Baffin Region, many of whom literally had to scrounge their living in the precincts of the base. With the decision, in 1966, to make it the administrative centre for the East Arctic, the future of the town was assured, and the problem became what future it could offer the Inuit. The community was provided with a façade of modern urban living: high rise buildings (apartments and offices), shopping plaza, clinics and schools – including an ultra-modern, multi-million dollar regional high school with academic and vocational streams. The community also assumed a reputation throughout the East Arctic for sexual, alcohol and drug abuse. Inuit parents across the East Arctic became concerned over the prospect of sending their children to school (for the higher grades) in Frobisher Bay; and instead of an expected enrollment of about 400, the high school opened in 1971 with only 275 students – 211 of them Inuit, of whom but 82 came from the settlements of Baffin Region and 10 from those of Keewatin (Koster, 1972).

Now, the reason MacBain Meldrum gives for the need to introduce non-Inuit private enterprise from the south (to ensure the employment of Inuit labour) is "the inadequate education and lack of financial and management experience" of the Inuit themselves (*op. cit.*:141; cf. p. 145). If that is the case, then it seems clear that it is white programmes (community planning and educational) that have failed. Yet it is the Inuit who are to pay for these failures. Because Inuit lack management experience after thirty years of white tutelage, white management will be brought in, and the inexperience of the Inuit extended, indefinitely.

Such thinking concerning the occupational structure in the north has also to be considered in relation to the new approach to native education (see Davidson, above). If the Inuit duly took their places at the bottom of the occupational structure through the years in which the educational programme was devoted to a replication of Euro-Canadian skills and attitudes, then what chances will be left to them when, on the one hand, their education is not directed solely to their assimilation (if one can believe the government on this point) and, on the other, the managerial and entrepreneurial positions continue to be offered to Southerners? Put another way, why does the government's wish to stimulate the private sector of the economy in the north have to mean that that sector has to become white-dominated and south-controlled (what the public sector already is)? The viewpoint expressed in earlier years (see p. 21, this vol.) by Freeman, Guemple, and Atcheson still seems to have no place in government thinking. The more one considers the 1972 statement of Jean Chretien, the harder it is to put aside the conclusion that what helps to maintain what he called the "poverty ... with all its psychological ... characteristics," which the native people suffer and which the government wishes to eliminate, is government insistence (in the same statement) on the need to offer "powerful incentives [to] non-native residents" (Canada, 1972a).

Government: Public Image

> "To our knowledge this is the first time anywhere that an Annual Report has been produced as a high quality bound book."
> *Commissioner of the Northwest Territories,*
> 1970 Annual Report

We have had little to say about the way government manages its public image, and the Annual Reports of the N.W.T. government, for instance, deserve closer attention than we can give them. As an important shop-window of a young and earnest bureaucracy, each report tends to call the 'successes' of the year; on the occasion of the N.W.T. centenary, the report was decked out in glossy pages and colour photographs, and that fact itself was recorded by the Commissioner. However, the public image imparted by these reports undergoes subtle changes in accordance with the changing times. For example, the section entitled "The Year in Review," for 1960–61, stresses industrial development; announcements such as a "grant of exploration permits, leases, or reservations for 95,000,000 acres" and a paragraph on the building of a railway in connection with a mining project are given precedence over such items as "the increase in the educational level," "the Territorial Hospital Insurance Services Plan," and "a dramatic improvement in the incidence of TB among the Eskimo citizens." Today, the emphasis is reversed. Generally speaking, the magic of numbers as evidence of progress is also worn thin today: perhaps the escalation of figures over the years has produced its own inflationary effect, and it is surely recognized that there is, by now, widespread scepticism about dollar inputs' ever achieving what it is said they will achieve. The accent is likely to be placed, if still rhetorically, on quality rather than numbers, and at times even upon problems rather than solutions.

Reaction to Government: Inuit

> "Despite increasing numbers of native people graduating from the school system, and from vocational training programs, the percentage of native people within the public service has not increased significantly."
> *N.W.T. Government Task Force Report* (N.W.T., 1974b:44).

Along with a crisis of unfulfilled expectations among younger Inuit as an increasing likelihood, there persists today, as we have seen, a situation of gross underemployment in the public sector among Inuit and the other native peoples of the N.W.T. The size of the problem has been recognized officially for some time. The nature of the problem, however, is more equivocal than often supposed. It is not enough to say, for example, that the problem is simply one of white refusal to employ native persons; there is also a strong element of native non-involvement.[8] With impressive candour, the recent N.W.T. government Task Force Report on employment makes it clear that "education alone is not the major barrier to increasing the numbers of native people in the public service."

[T]he public service, Federal and Territorial, remains the largest and most visible employer within the Northwest Territories, and the employer with which native people will most frequently come into contact. It would be natural to assume that it would be to this employer that native people would most often look for employment opportunities or careers. We must ask ourselves why they do not.

One of the reasons they do not is, ironically, the pervasiveness of the public service within Northern society, and the large degree of contact native people have had with it. As a native person grows up, his contacts with the public service, either directly or through family or friends, are extensive, and are inevitably, given the composition of the public service, with non-native people who come from a different back-ground and culture. It would be natural to assume, therefore, that many native people who might otherwise be qualified and interested, might not regard employment in the public service as a realistic avenue for the development and growth of their natural and acquired experience and skills, and where their inborn experience and skills will be valued (N.W.T. 1974b:44)

This affirms the hypothesis put forward in the previous chapter; namely, that even while wishing to diversify Inuit participation in the occupational structure and to increase Inuit representation in Inuit affairs, the whites allow their own thinking about the white 'system' to keep the Inuit 'down.' It was further suggested that as Inuit observe this to be a consequence of their involvement with the white system, they proceed to withdraw from it.

In other words, the marginal places that Inuit occupy in institutional life in the N.W.T. reflect not only a white refusal (of Inuit) but also Inuit refusals of white terms.

The N.W.T. Task Force suggested a number of ways in which they believed the situation could be rectified. These included:

"a major expansion in the number of training positions available to native peoples. ... Emphasis should be placed upon junior and intermediate level positions, in particular 'assistant' positions, in the future expansion of departmental personnel positions" (p. 45);

"existing recruitment practices must be altered significantly. ... much greater use should be made of local and community radio stations where they are available, and ... greater efforts should be made to contact native people directly" (p. 45);

"regular competitions [should be] carried out for each category, rather than when individual positions fall vacant" (p. 46);

"compulsory quotas [for] the number of native people in the Territorial public service was considered, and rejected" (p. 46).

Although the Task Force recognized the need to "change the perception that native people have of the public service as being an institution foreign to them" (p. 44), one wonders whether their proposals, which call for reforming bureaucratic procedure for recruitment into a bureaucracy, reach the root problem. If the problem can be reduced to a matter of "[differential] access to different opportunities" (Smith, 1974:6), then proposals of that kind are probably adequate; but not if the problem is also rooted in differences of "culture" (*ibid.*). In the latter case, account also has to be taken of the differing expectations of whites and Inuit; and we find this argued even from within D.I.N.A.:

"In his own community no native may claim openly a superior position to others; in the larger community surrounding him he is faced by a bewildering array of open and covert strata. ... The native person interacts with the larger (natural) community around him by living in it and as part of it; the non-native attempts to dominate by stressing his superior nature. The native community is self-regulatory; the non-native [is regulated] by enforcing written law. The native community's need is to survive, while the non-native [community] has added acquisition of goods to its needs. The native community expects no more than survival without growth while the non-native [community] must grow to survive" (Petrie, 1974b:3).

If true, even in part, this cuts like a swathe through the kind of proposals forwarded by the Task Force.

Before moving on to a consideration of the whites in government service, I want to draw attention to an 'event' among Inuit families which I interpret as an adjustment of their lives to the modernization of their own world: something which should be distinguished from Inuit action motivated by ideas of 'non-involvement' in the white world.

The White Arctic

Reaction to Modernization: Inuit

> "It is important to understand about contraception.
> It is also ... important to want to have children."
> *An Inuk woman*, cited in Freeman (1971b: 18).

The statistics issued by the Chief Medical and Health Officer of the Northwest Territories show that the "natural increase" rate among Inuit, calculated as livebirths per 1,000 population, less total deaths per 1,000 population, dropped from 41.9 and 43.1 in 1966 and 1967, respectively, to 21.7 and 26.3 in 1974 and 1975. (Fuller coverage of the statistics is given in chapter 4). Although the current rate is still high,[9] this is, nevertheless, a remarkable drop and wholly unpredicted.

The crude death rate (total deaths) for these same years dropped from 12.6 and 10.3 to 6.7 and 6.1, with a significant drop in the infant (under 1 year) death rate: in 1968 (*sic*), infant deaths accounted for nearly half of the total deaths, but for only a quarter of them in 1975. We find that the infant death rate dropped from 108.8 and 83.8 (in 1966 and 1967) to 70.7 and 48.0 (in 1974 and 1975). While impressive, these drops were to be expected as a direct consequence of the government health programme.

Yet, without a concomitant lowering of the livebirth rate, all improvements in the infant death rate will simply exacerbate the socio-economic problems (alluded to earlier: Ch.2) arising from a 'young' population with a high fertility rate. The need to lower the livebirth rate was not effectively addressed by the government health programme (Freeman, 1971a), almost certainly for fear of raising the spectre of white-inspired Inuit genocide; it is, therefore, all the more remarkable that it does show a marked decline over the decennium: from 54.5 and 53.4 (for 1966 and 1967) to 28.4 and 32.4 (for 1974 and 1975). It is this that needs explaining.

In an unpublished paper, Freeman (1971b) characterizes the few steps taken by government prior to 1971 as "a lamentable public non-program of birth control" (p. 22). Yet he has to admit surprise over the relatively high degree of local birth control practice. Among the sociological factors that may help to account for it, Freeman points to the reduced involvement of Inuit women with familial roles (p. 23) and, relatedly, the "considerable inter-generational gulf" that has arisen at the same time as children (now at school) no longer make important work and economic contributions to their households (p. 24). One may also have in mind here other changes in the parent-child relationship reported by Brody (1975:206; cited on p. 234, this vol.). In general terms, Inuit are now in their second generation of 'modernization' (with attendant degrees of immiseration), and it is to be expected that young married couples have different domestic (and socio-economic) strategies from their parents'; but what they are is not exactly known.

Elsewhere in the world, birthrates have generally dropped immediately following a reduction in the infant mortality rate – fewer children are born but more of those survive. The important question is whether this will prove to be but a passing demographic phase or one that becomes normative in Inuit culture. If the latter, will Inuit families limit themselves to a few children? Or will the realization of the traditional value of having large families simply be 'deferred' during the early years of marriage? The evidence from other parts of the world is distributed between these two outcomes. The broader correlation between modernization and falling birthrate is, however, well supported within the Arctic itself by the lower birthrate of the Inuit of the Mackenzie Delta (55.6 in 1968, 29.4 in 1975) compared to the more isolated Inuit of the Baffin Region (56.4 in 1968, 37.2 in 1975).

Reaction to Government: White

> "Problems arise as well for non-native residents in the two Territories very few of whom will settle there for any length of time without powerful incentives."
> *Jean Chretien*, Minister of Indian Affairs and Northern Development, March 28, 1972.

It was, of course, the Inuit that Diamond Jenness had in mind when he said "we have set up a complex government ... but offered them no real place in it" (1964:161). Yet today, it is ironically a relevant comment on the situation of many whites as well. In fact, the Task Force on employment (N.W.T., 1974b) was concerned primarily with the "unduly high rate of [white] turnover of staff within the Territorial public service" (p. 2) and only secondarily with native underemployment.

In the years 1972 and 1973, over one thousand employees, or 27 percent of the total, left the Territorial public service; at this rate "the entire public service turns over once in each four year period." The Task Force calculated that "the average cost of replacing a Territorial Government employee is $7,000, which when applied against the number of employees terminating each year results in an expenditure of approximately $3.5 million." The Task Force was especially concerned and puzzled at the high rate of turnover "within the senior and middle management levels ... because it is in this management group, comprising the minority of positions within the public service, that organizations would normally expect to find a minimal rate of turnover" (p. 2).

The Task Force noted that the N.W.T. bureaucracy had an "abnormally high ratio of officer level positions to support staff" (p. 10). At the same time as this tends to reduce the number of jobs within reach of the native population, the Task Force also found it to be a factor in the white turnover rate. On the one hand, in order to provide the high salaries which, it is believed, are necessary "to attract the right type of person," there is a "tendency to expand [and inflate] the duties of positions beyond those that actually exist" (*ibid.*). On the other hand, "the chief reason for employees leaving the Territorial public service, as indicated in the personal interviews conducted with terminating employees, was the fact that the work they had been assigned was less responsible than that which was stated in the advertisement they responded to, or that their experience qualified them for" (*ibid.*).

Among other factors identified by the Task Force as contributing to the problem, there are several that relate directly to points raised in the previous section. There is, for example, the fact of "our present dependence upon recruitment rather than training" when staffing the territorial service (p. 16). A consequence "is the necessity of competing in outside job markets for employees whose technical and professional skills have already placed them in high demand. ... Often this results in employees with a limited personal commitment to the Northwest Territories, and whose skills ensure that they will be in constant demand as opportunities within their field develop in more settled parts of the country" (*ibid.*).

A pervasive effect of this situation is "that problems of the Territorial Government are inevitably administered by individuals of limited experience with the organization, the peculiar problems of northern administration, and the experience and needs of northern communities" (p. 2). "Often too, ... positions vital to the effectiveness of the Territorial administration [remain] vacant for long periods because of our inability to attract suitable candidates" (p. 16).

Little wonder, then, that "also missing is a system which would ensure that employees throughout the organization are informed of the underlying philosophy beneath Government programs and policies, the priorities that have been set, and the problems that are being experienced" (p. 12). Indeed, the Task Force found general dissatisfaction among territorial employees, with a situation in which "levels of authority and responsibility are not clearly defined, frequently unrelated, and not delegated to the lowest practical level of the organization" (*ibid.*). Instead, "control often appears to exist through the withholding of authority ... this frequently results in only the illusion of control, while contributing to poor morale and organizational inefficiency" (*ibid.*).

It is much to the credit of the N.W.T. civil service that they undertook this self-examination, and this, rather than some of the shortcomings that were revealed, distinguishes it from other civil services. However, our concern here is with the circumstances of the special problems that face the public service sector in the N.W.T. The Task Force paid particular attention to the turnover in the higher echelons; other data show, however, that

TABLE 4

Turnover Rates: N.W.T. and Baffin Region

A. Territorial Government Employees (excluding the educational
sector)—Percentage Turnover by Region and Year. Permanent
positions Only.

(percentages)	1971	1972	1973	1974	1975
Yellowknife	24	20	33	23	31
Fort Smith	26	22	38	48	45
Inuvik	27	23	34	46	38
Keewatin	36	39	29	52	57
Baffin	27	39	39	37	37

B. Teachers in the N.W.T.
"Only 23% of elementary school teachers in the North stay there
for more than three years" (Girard and Gourdeau, 1973:119).

C. Baffin Region—Turnover in Medical Service Branches. Permanent Positions Only.

| | 1974/75 | | 1975/76 | |
(Actual numbers)	Positions	Terminations	Positions	Terminations
Medical Officers	3	2	4	1
Nurses	18	28	24	22
Dentists	2	1	3	0
Pharmacists	1	0	1	1
Stenographers	2	0	2	2
Clerks	10	8	14	4
Administrative	1	0	1	1
Technical	7	2	8	1
General Labour and Trades	3	1	3	1
Certified Nursing Assts.	6	4	4	6
Environmental Health	1	0	1	1
Totals	54	46	65	40

Note: Where terminations exceed positions, there were several persons in the one position
in the course of a year.
Sources: N.W.T. Government, Personnel Department (personal communication). Federal
Government, Department of Health and Welfare (personal communication).

the rates for whites located in the settlements are higher still; nor is there
any abatement in the rates (Girard and Gourdeau, 1973:119; Brody,
1975:42 f.; and Table 4). Now, it is particularly at the level of the individual
settlement – rather than at Yellowknife, the Territorial capital where senior
managerial staff are concentrated – that the pressures of the 'colonial'
situation are felt by whites. I return to this problem in Chapter 5; meanwhile, the fact that whites do not stay very long in the 'white'-invented jobs
may be noted as a powerful index of non-involvement.[10] These turnover
rates also negate the possible assumption that because the bureaucracy in
the N.W.T. is 'white,' the individual white finds his corporate identity
through it; what is rather surprising is that he is apparently even less likely
to find this bureaucracy supportive of his own long-term interests. What-

ever it may have been in the past, the N.W.T. for the whites there today –
again especially in the east – is little more than a letter-head; it is without
gemeinschaft.

It is often asked of the 'people problems' in the north whether they are
rooted in the kind(s) of person who ventures north in the first place, or
whether they are generated by the circumstances of living there. It would
be naive to suppose that these really are either/or alternatives (or that the
problem is one for mental health research only; cf. Atcheson, 1972; Sampath, 1972). If we wish to improve our understanding of how the two
possibilities act upon each other, then a follow-up of Dunning's (1959)
seminal report, concentrating on the backgrounds of the whites who go to
the Arctic and, for that matter, on what happens to them when they leave,
should be given high research priority.

To conclude, not only Inuit, but also whites demonstrate a strong element of non-involvement in public and professional life, though the form it
takes is likely to diverge along lines of ethnic membership. This broad
conclusion is probably tacitly accepted today in Ottawa and Yellowknife,
although by the nature of the case, one cannot expect 'government' to be
able to do much about it. It seems as though this is the price of, what
Davison termed, the "over-exposed and over-used" place of government
in "the social structure of the north." The effect has been to sap rather than
strengthen institutional commitment. The only exception is the sense of
corporateness among Inuit of being a 'people,' and this flows from a
cultural reservoir beyond the reach of government, notwithstanding government support from time to time.

The Dilemma of Welfare Colonialism

> "Two general solutions have been tried in the matter
> of Eskimo living standards.[11] ... neither solution ...
> results from consideration of the aspirations of the
> Eskimo themselves but reflect the values of exter-
> nal agencies."
> *Damas* (1969:60–61).

In conclusion, I want to consider an inherent dilemma of the welfare
colonial encounter. Any decision taken by the colonizers has a basic flaw: a
decision made for the material benefit of the colonized at the same time can
be construed as disadvantaging them; a 'generous' or 'sensible' decision
can be at the same time, morally 'wrong.' This is so because it is the
colonizers who make the decisions that control the future of the colonized;
because the decisions are made (ambiguously) on behalf of the colonized,
and yet in the name of the colonizers' culture (and of their political,
administrative and economic priorities).

Freeman (1969:78) states boldly, "I go so far as to say that the omnipresence of some effective stabilizing influence must be considered a pre-requisite for sound long-term planning in the north, and enlightened government may provide the necessary, indeed the only conceivable element of regional stability." But what will the criteria be for "enlightened government"? At what point along the culturally-ideological axis is "stabilization" to take place? In bringing forward these questions, I am not overlooking the fact that they are important and difficult wherever one turns in the world, but am urging that we do not overlook that, in the Canadian north, they are being decided *for* the local native majority and not *by* them.

Itself so obvious (and so inevitable), there is still a reason for emphasizing this last point. While one may wish to query whether pure 'made by' decisions ever occur anywhere, one must also acknowledge that it is common to find societies providing mythological support for the belief that some decisions – even important ones – are 'made by' the people they affect. It is this support that the Inuit have been conspicuously without (for signs of change, see Ch. 12). An outcome of welfare colonialism has been to make Inuit aware how decisions are 'made for' them by the whites and this cognitive aspect of the colonialism can prove to be its most alarming dimension.

Decisions of the 'made for,' rather than the 'made by,' kind are probably (for reasons of power) the least easy to revoke or revise. On the other hand, they are especially open to criticism: perhaps on the charge that they are, indeed, 'made for' decisions, but also because among planners (that is, the practitioners of 'made for' decisions) other 'made for' decisions nearly always come to mind. Jenness' stand against the Canadian government's post-war Inuit policy is an important example. He characterized (Jenness, 1968:45) the government's decision to "rehabilitate" the Inuit in the north as establishing "a New World Bantustan in which European immigrants are discreetly confining the aboriginal Eskimos and segregating them from the rest of the continent." That was not only a 'made for' decision by the Canadian government but, in Jenness' view, also the wrong one. His was among the strongest voices in favour of Inuit relocation in the south (*ibid.*). But surely – other observers of the Inuit scene will argue – this would have placed Inuit in a still more hapless situation of assimilation?

As it happened, because they were in faulty health and 'illiterate,' the Inuit justified the government's own decision. The Inuit were even 'useful' to the Canadians, so long as they themselves did not possess the health and educational services which Canadian society is geared to provide its citizens. That is cynically put; yet it may help us to understand what has been happening on the colonizers' side ever since the original decision of "rehabilitation." It also prompts the question, what is going to happen (how can the Inuit be kept 'useful'?) should the Arctic be TB-free and should all Inuit complete grade school?

Clearly, arguments over 'made for' decisions can continue endlessly among whites (each argument or thesis freely generating its own antithesis). The principal reason for this is that answers are not being provided to the basic question of Inuit aspirations: still wanting after 30 years of welfare colonialism is a true insight into what the aspirations of the Inuit are (cf. Petrie, 1974a:2) – though recently, the Inuit have begun voicing their wishes (see Ch. 12). By the same token, these have been years of misunderstandings and ambiguities, rather than outright Inuit-white conflict – the subject of Chapter 5.

NOTES

1   Only in 1963 was the position of resident commissioner "detached from that of deputy minister of Northern Affairs and National Resources" (Fingland, *ibid*.).
2   In 1974, 21% of the N.W.T. government personnel in permanent positions were teachers; the highest figure for the same category of all the provinces was 10.6% for Alberta, whereas the lowest, in British Columbia, was 0.9% (N.W.T., 1974:Appendix II).
3   Recent innovations in N.W.T. education are discussed by Brown, Tizya and Gourdeau (1973a and b), and Girard (1972); Girard and Gourdeau (1973) review the place of the southern teacher (non-Inuit, non-Indian and non-Métis) in the northern school.
4   On the other hand, *Anik* has made inter-settlement telephone communication more reliable. What this can mean for Inuit is suggested by Kallen (personal communication): "When opposition of various Inuit settlements to the establishment of the secondary school in Frobisher Bay was being expressed, each community was being unaware of the [same] stand being taken by the others. Lack of effective communication between settlements at this time severely hampered the ability of the Inuit to coordinate their efforts in order to take concerted action."
5   In the late 1950s "the co-operative movement was initiated in small communities in the N.W.T. and Quebec as a completely subsidized Federal Government project. However, it was hoped that the enterprises would eventually be independent of government support. To speed the development of fiscal autonomy Co-operative Development Officers were sent to the communities to train the Eskimos in bookkeeping, purchasing and almost all aspects of business life. In some communities the local R.C.M.P. assisted in the initial education process" (Paterson, 1976:50).
6   Towards arts and crafts production for the 'white' market and local sales of southern consumer goods. In this connection note should be taken of the relation between local H.B.C. stores and the co-operatives: "[The] seeming contradiction of the H.B.C.'s roles as both a supporter and competitor of Arctic co-operatives can be readily explained. Because the original co-operatives were primarily production-oriented, notably in arts and crafts, it was to the Company's advantage to encourage the establishment and expansion of co-operatives and to thereby increase the spending powers of the native peoples. However, many (although not all) co-operatives gradually became more consumer-oriented. By 1970 the Port Burwell co-operative was 70% consumer-oriented and the George River co-operative was 90% consumer-oriented. As a result of this economic diversification there now exists direct competition between the co-operative and the Company in many communities" (Paterson, 1976:53).
7   See note at the beginning of chapter 4 regarding the reliability of data. The 1976 figures for native employment in the Federal public service in the north are: permanent jobs, 14.8% (Federal Depts.) and 12.1% (agencies); permanent and casual jobs, 18.2% (Federal Depts.) and 21.4% (agencies). Figures include Indian, Métis and Indian populations. The percentages are lower for the Yukon (A.C.N.D. Secretariat, Feb. 16, 1977).
8   This does not necessarily imply, and usually does not, withdrawal from Inuit-white relations of the client-patron type described in Chapter 5.
9   For instance, the Canadian rates for 1966 and 1973 are, respectively, 7.5 and 7.4. On the other hand, the Inuit rate since 1972 has been slightly *below* that of N.W.T. whites (whereas it was significantly above the white rate in the '60s). However, a word of caution is necessary

concerning all demographic statistics for the whites in N.W.T.: in terms of age structure, it is not a 'natural' population because of the near absence of old people and the very young; it is basically a middle-aged population. As the statistics confirm (see Ch. 4) such a population may be expected to exhibit little demographic change through the years.

10   See Paine (1965:169–86) for a detailed treatment of the employment of 'non-involvement' strategies in village relations.

11   "The first of these has been to arbitrarily tie the local living standards to the actual productivity of the community. A low standard of living and confort is thus maintained with the minimum of outside subsidization. This philosophy was for years the basis of the trader-dominated community and its satellite camps. ... The second solution has been the attempt to establish a standard of living among the Eskimo which approximates parity with southern rural villages or hamlets as to diet, housing, possessions and medical services. This model is at least implicit in government policy for the Eskimo" (Damas, *ibid.*).

References

ATCHESON, J. D.
1972 "Problems of Mental Health in the Canadian Arctic." *Canada's Mental Health*, XX(1).

BRODY, HUGH
1975 *The People's Land: Eskimos and Whites in the Eastern Arctic.* Aylesbury, Penguin Books.

BROWN, D., R. TIZYA and E. GOURDEAU
1973a "Apprentice Teachers." In *Man in the North; Technical Reports: Education in the Canadian North.* Montreal, Arctic Institute of North America.

BROWN, D., R. TIZYA and E. GOURDEAU
1973b "Community-guided Education." In *Man in the North; Technical Reports: Education in the Canadian North.* Montreal, Arctic Institute of North America.

BUCHANAN, M. A.
1977 *Statistical Analysis of the Northwest Territories Co-operatives and Credit Unions.* Yellowknife, Government of the N.W.T., Dept. of Economic Development and Tourism.

Canada
1972a *A Report by the Honourable Jean Chretien, Minister of Indian Affairs and Northern Development, to the Standing Committee on Indian Affairs and Northern Development.* Ottawa, Department of Indian Affairs and Northern Development.

Canada
1972b "Memorandum to Members of the A.C.N.D. Sub-committee on the Employment of Native Northerners." Ottawa, Department of Indian Affairs and Northern Development.

Canada
1975 *Northwest Territories, Statistical Abstract.* Ottawa, Department of Indian Affairs and Northern Development.

DAMAS, D.
    1969 "Problems of 'Rural' Canadian Eskimo Adaptation." In M. M. R.
    Freeman (ed.), *Intermediate Adaptation in Newfoundland and the
    Arctic*. St. John's, Institute of Social and Economic Research, Memo-
    rial University of Newfoundland.
DAVIDSON, D. A.
    1973 "The People in the North." In N. Ørvik (ed.), *Policies of Northern
    Development*. Kingston, Department of Political Studies, Queen's
    University.
DOSMAN, EDGAR J.
    1975 *The National Interest. The Politics of Northern Development,
    1968–75*. Toronto, McClelland & Stewart Ltd.
DUNNING, R. W.
    1959 "Ethnic Relations and the Marginal Man in Canada." *Human
    Organization*, 18(3).
FINGLAND, F. B.
    1966 "Administrative and Constitutional Changes in Arctic Territories:
    Canada." In R. St. J. MacDonald (ed.), *The Arctic Frontier*. Toronto,
    University Press.
FREEMAN, MILTON M. R.
    1969 "Development Strategies and Indigenous People in the Canadian
    Arctic." In M. M. R. Freeman (ed.), *Intermediate Adaptation in New-
    foundland and the Arctic*. St. John's, Institute of Social and Economic
    Research, Memorial University of Newfoundland.
FREEMAN, MILTON M. R.
    1971a "The Significance of Demographic Changes Occurring in the
    Canadian East Arctic." *Anthropologica*, XIII(1-2).
FREEMAN, MILTON M. R.
    1971b "The Utterly Dismal Theorem." Presented to the Canadian
    Sociology and Anthropology Association Annual Meeting, St. John's,
    Newfoundland.
GIRARD, G.
    1972 "Training of Native Teachers in Quebec." In Frank Darnell (ed.),
    Education in the North. University of Alaska and Arctic Institute of
    North America.
GIRARD, G. and E. GOURDEAU
    1973 "Southern Teachers for the North." In *Man in the North; Techni-
    cal Reports: Education in the Canadian North*. Montreal, Arctic Insti-
    tute of North America.
GUEMPLE, D. L.
    1969 "The Eskimo and Intermediate Adaptation in the Canadian Arc-
    tic." In M. M. R. Freeman (ed.), *Intermediate Adaptation in New-
    foundland and the Arctic*. St. John's, Institute of Social and Economic
    Research, Memorial University of Newfoundland.

HONIGMANN, J. J. and IRMA HONIGMANN
1965 *Eskimo Townsmen*. Ottawa, Canadian Research Centre for Anthropology, Saint Paul University.

HUNTER, RICHARD
1976 "Development of Local Government in the Northwest Territories." In N. Ørvik and K. Patterson (eds.), *The North in Transition*. Kingston, Centre for International Relations, Queen's University.

HUNT, A. D.
1973 "The North in Canada's National Policy: Problems and Approaches." In N. Ørvik (ed.), *Policies of Northern Development*. Kingston, Queen's University.

JENNESS, DIAMOND
1964 *Eskimo Administration: II. Canada*. Montreal, Arctic Institute of North America, Technical Paper No. 14.

JENNESS, DIAMOND
1968 *Eskimo Administration: V. Analysis and Reflections*. Montreal, Arctic Institute of North America, Technical Paper No. 21.

KOSTER, D.
1972 "Ambiguity and Gossip in a Colonial Situation." Unpublished M.A. Thesis, Memorial University of Newfoundland.

MACBAIN MELDRUM, SHEILA
1975 *Frobisher Bay: An Area Economic Survey*. Ottawa, Department of Indian Affairs and Northern Development.

MARQUAND, JOHN and DON MCNEILL
1975 "Evolution of Political Process in the Northwest Territories." Ottawa, Department of Indian and Northern Affairs (stencil).

Northwest Territories
1960–61 *Annual Report of the Commissioner of the N.W.T.* Yellowknife, N.W.T. Government.

Northwest Territories
1961 *Votes and Proceedings*. Yellowknife, N.W.T. Government.

Northwest Territories
1968 *Council Debates*. Yellowknife, N.W.T. Government.

Northwest Territories
1968–69 *Annual Report of the Commissioner of the N.W.T.* Yellowknife, N.W.T. Government.

Northwest Territories
1970 *Annual Report of the Commissioner of the N.W.T.* Yellowknife, N.W.T. Government.

Northwest Territories
1974 *Report of the Task Force on Personnel Policy and Management*. Yellowknife, N.W.T. Government.

Northwest Territories
1975a *Council Debates*. Yellowknife, N.W.T. Government.

Northwest Territories
1975b *A Paper on the Philosophy of the Department of Local Government.* Yellowknife, N.W.T. Government.

ØRVIK, NILS (ed.)
1973 *Policies of Northern Development.* Kingston, Department of Political Studies, Queen's University.

PAINE, ROBERT
1965 *Coast Lapp Society II. A Study of Economic Development and Social Values.* Tromso, Oslo, Bergen, Universitetsforlaget.

PATERSON, LESLEY
1976 "The Co-operative Movement in the Canadian Arctic." In N. Ørvik and K. Patterson (eds.), *The North in Transition*, Kingston, Queen's University.

PATTERSON, Kirk R.
1976 "The Theory and Practice of Home Rule in the International North." In N. Ørvik and K. Patterson (eds.), *The North in Transition.* Kingston, Queen's University.

PETRIE, M. K.
1974a "Factors Affecting Northern Program Employment Policies." Ottawa, Department of Indian Affairs and Northern Development (stencil).

PETRIE, M. K.
1974b "Factors Affecting Native Employment North of '60.'" Ottawa, Department of Indian Affairs and Northern Development (stencil).

REA, KENNETH J.
1968 *The Political Economy of the Canadian North; an Interpretation of the Course of Development in the Northern Territories of Canada to the Early 1960s.* Toronto, University of Toronto Press.

SAMPATH, H. M.
1972 "Migration and Mental Health of the Non-Eskimos in the East Arctic." Paper presented to the Third International Conference on Social Science and Medicine.

SANDERS, D. E.
1973 *Native People in Areas of Internal National Expansion; Indians and Inuit in Canada.* Copenhagen, International Work Group for Indigenous Affairs.

SMITH, DEREK G.
1974 "Occupational Preferences of Northern Students." *Social Science Notes −5.* Ottawa, Department of Indian and Northern Affairs.

WELSMAN, PAUL
1976 "Education of Native Peoples in the Northwest Territories: A Northern Model." In N. Ørvik and K. Patterson (eds.), *The North in Transition.* Kingston, Queen's University.

Further Source Material and Some Questions

Robert Paine

4

> "This publication is designed to provide an interested public with a comprehensive view of the nature and purpose of these resource allocations."
> *Warren Allmand*, Minister of Indian Affairs and Northern Development (Introduction: Canada, 1976).
> "What are the measures by which to judge the performance of the police, education, social services, justice, and so forth?"
> *Shubik* (1971:362).

Beginning on page 57, data are assembled from official sources on the following:

A. the distribution of government personnel and expenditures in the northern programmes;

B. summary descriptions of the communities of the Baffin Region;

C. local government ordinances;

D. the Inuit of the Baffin Region in the 1969–70 manpower survey;

E. vital statistics for N.W.T. Inuit and whites, Baffin and Mackenzie Delta Inuit;

F. health in the N.W.T.

Other official data have been presented in the preceding chapters, and a short critical discussion of these data sources is warranted. Although our concern is with the problems arising over the collection, codification and possible use of official data in the N.W.T., I draw upon Shubik's (1971) general discussion as an aid in identifying the problems and placing them in a wider perspective.

The Collection and Coding of Information in the N.W.T.
What Shubik (1971) has to say about information as a resource of modern government should be of particular relevance to the 'young' government of the N.W.T. (with its recent computerized data facilities) and the polyethnic population it serves. As a changing world places people in larger units, so there is a pressing need for social statistics which, Shubik insists, *can* (and must) "treat individuals as individuals rather than as parts of a large aggregate" (p. 363). But the achievement of this goal is beset with prob-

lems, and the first among them seems to be the preservation of our traditional values in a world of increasing economic and social scale.

What Shubik observes globally may be applied to the N.W.T. Because the nature of government for the N.W.T. is neither quantitatively nor qualitatively the same as that required for an isolated Inuit settlement, we face the question: "What freedoms do we intend to preserve?" – or, "what new concepts of freedom do we intend to attach the old names to?" (*ibid.*). Here Shubik is particularly concerned with the protection of privacy;[1] this is already a deeply embedded problem in the N.W.T. because of the tutelage practices there: for the Inuit, white tutelage is so intrusive that it is difficult for them to maintain a perception of self independent of situations of white help, and the whites themselves are placed in situations that engender anxieties and dilemmas concerning their privacy (Chs. 5 and 12). Then again, the pronounced 'made for' character of many decisions in this colonial situation (Ch. 3) leaves the native population with few rights *vis-à-vis* the inquisitive intruder whose officially sanctioned task is the collection of information.[2]

Priority of values is at the same time entwined with the problem of measurement, and here Shubik's message is directed not only to the administrator but also to the social scientist who "may claim that we can scarcely define values, can hardly measure them, and cannot compare them" (p. 363). Shubik reminds us that at the same time as the social scientist may wish to eschew the whole question of value-measurement as unanswerable, answers *are* given to it, politically and administratively. The problem here is exacerbated by the global historical fact that refinements in the coding of information have been directed towards economic values rather than social. Accordingly, the administrator who is faced with the task of coding social information is still inclined to make use of such instruments as "national income accounting, input-output tables, [and] gross national income figures" (p. 362). The social scientist is often able to do little more than point out the error in such a procedure. Shubik's plea is that "the next thirty years must be characterized by the development of social statistics and measures for the control of the services and joint processes of society" (*ibid.*).

Shubik also urges the view – somewhat unexpected, though in accord with his sense of a need for pragmatism – that "even the crudest approximation provides a guide for behavior where a decision *has* to be made" (p. 363; his emphasis). Certainly much of the data from the N.W.T. is but an approximation; moreover, different official sources may make different approximations of the same data. As much is evident even regarding basic demographic figures, and it is particularly noticeable in the native employment figures. One wonders why.

One also wonders about possible political consequences of the fact that there exists the category "official data." Governments are likely to claim that they make many of their decisions on the basis of these data and where this is true, it can mean that the data substitute for the 'real world': the planner and politician are able to apply their skills to a restricted universe encompassing a limited number of *selected* variables. Such procedures can lead to self-validatory conclusions; indeed, that may be the political intention. Such conclusions may even reflect bureaucratic (departmental) interests; in other words, the discrepancies between the figures of different departments may themselves not be random. To permit approximation in this situation may simply have the effect of licensing such a procedure. Perhaps the most serious aspect of this problem is not that decisions (on the basis of data supplied) are taken at a high organizational level, but that the selection of the data is itself determined at that level.

Turning now to a brief examination of the situation in the N.W.T., there are two matters to be considered: the accuracy of the data and their scope – or viewpoint.

The Advisory Committee on Northern Development (A.C.N.D.) is responsible for drawing up an "annual northern expenditure plan" (Federal and Territorial); this is now published (since 1975)[3] and contains precise allocations of dollars and personnel (see Tables 1 and 2, Ch. 2 and section A, below). Now, *if* these allocations are made on the basis of figures supplied by the 25 (or more) departments and agencies involved in "northern-related activities," then this is a matter of some concern. For government officials, while adding that the situation will soon be brought under control, candidly admit to serious problems of "coordination" in the task of data-collecting (personal communications).

An important example is the collection of primary demographic data. A relatively simple task, one might suppose, and yet the figures from Statistics Canada and those from several government departments disagree (sometimes by as much as 20 percent in a population of under 1,000). Part of the explanation is that whereas Statistics Canada has a standardized methodology that is strictly adhered to, the procedures of different departments can be altogether more 'inspirational.' Statistics Canada makes a strict count of persons *in situ* on census day, and although there will always be a percentage of persons who are missing (or wrongly placed) in such a procedure, a longtitudinal population profile providing dependable comparisons over a span of census years is achieved. Other departments and agencies, by contrast, attempt to aggregate returns from local communities, not all on the same day but over a period of time. The intention here is to provide an inclusive count of the population of each community in a certain year (itself open to various interpretations); however, standardization of procedure is more difficult to maintain or to control, and the operation is likely to be undertaken with differing degrees of resourcefulness.

The problem is a general one in the N.W.T. Whereas we mention varying resourcefulness as one contributing factor, officials themselves may draw attention to a lack of resources. The Supervisor of Co-operatives, for example, writes, "we face internal problems with respect to qualified management, extended credit requirements, lack of adequate working capital to do the job, and lack of the support services which are normally taken for granted in the south." He concludes that until this situation is rectified, "objective statistics ... will be difficult to attain without considerable, but reasonable, interpretation being placed on them" (Buchanan, 1977:ii).

The N.W.T. Task Force (1974) on personnel policy and management points to the lack of an "effective information process" (N.W.T., 1974:12): "At the present time the Territorial administration lacks any effective means of providing information to managers at all levels, upon which programs can be evaluated, decisions reached, and adjustments made. There are no mechanisms which ensure the integration of up to date information."

Other sources, particularly non-governmental, show equal concern over the restricted significance of the information that *is* collected. We may instance demographic work again. At the first Northern Population Workshop, organized by the Arctic Institute of North America in 1976, it was insisted that "demographic implications have not been a factor in planning northern activities and, as recently as 1971, a review of federally-sponsored or -supported scientific activities in the North revealed that no demographic work related to northern development had been sponsored by the government" (Arctic Institute, 1976:4). The Workshop discounted "routine periodic census-taking."

Efforts made to collect data on income have (not unexpectedly) run into special problems. The 'white' population of N.W.T. is likely to be deliberately evasive in their answers, and the native population (it is said) are unaccustomed to answering such questions (Macbain Meldrum, personal communication). One of the most ambitious data-collecting undertakings in the N.W.T. was the 1969–70 Manpower Survey (see section D, below), and it is appropriate to conclude with relevant excerpts from the principal researchers' comments on the methodology of the Survey and its problems (Meldrum and Helman, 1975):

"The method used in the Baffin and Arctic Coast surveys was to send one or two officers from Ottawa to the field to each settlement where enumerators were hired and given instruction. Where suitable Eskimo enumerators could be found they were used. In each settlement the job of supervision of enumerators was handled by a local non-Eskimo resident such as a school teacher's wife or R.C.M.P. constable's wife. In some instances it was necessary to hire persons such as these to carry out the survey, using Eskimo interpreters. Payment was made to the enumerators on a per questionnaire basis, with supervisors receiving set amounts according to the time involved and size of the population to be covered. Control of the progress of the survey in each of the regions was maintained from Ottawa. The Ottawa-based supervisor tried where possible to return to each settlement to collect the completed questionnaires, taking the opportunity to go over them while in any given community, calling for corrections or further interviews in those cases for which the questionnaires did not appear to be complete or consistent (pp. 10–11)."

"[The question] on income, suffered through not being sufficiently detailed to allow for provision of information on income obtained from each job, for those respondents who held more than one job in the previous 12 months. It was also found impossible to handle these questions as originally designed, i.e., to call for income after expenses or before deductions for taxes were made, as the question then became entirely too complicated for the majority of the respondents.

[The question] on kinds of work done in the past 12 months was by and large too complicated in design and wording for many enumerators to fully understand. The concept of full-time and part-time work was not sufficiently clear, nor was the concept of describing different kinds of work done in the same year. Confusion also arose from the fact that many people did the same kinds of work for different employers in any given year. While it was possible to recover a great deal of important information from this question, considerable work was required at the questionnaire editing stage (p. 20)."

The situation, outlined in these brief notes, posed something of a dilemma regarding the inclusion of official statistics in this book. In the end, a great deal more was rejected than included; absolute figures, in a number of cases, were converted into percentages; and – without being very satisfied by it – justification was sought in Shubik's statement that "even the crudest approximation provides a guide."

A. DISTRIBUTION OF GOVERNMENT PERSONNEL AND EXPENDITURES IN NORTHERN PROGRAMMES

Source: Annual Northern Expenditure Plan, 1976–77. (Advisory Committee Northern Development) Ottawa, Department of Indian and Northern Affairs. 1976

A:1 *Public Sector Employment: by Government (1973/74 – 1976/77)*

Government	1973/74 No.	%	1974/75 No.	%	1975/76 No.	%	1976/77 No.	%
Federal	4,233	50.5	4,312	49.2	4,632	50.2	4,754	49.9
Northwest Territories	2,911	34.7	3,117	35.6	3,227	34.9	3,353	35.2
Yukon Territory	1,238	14.8	1,334	15.2	1,377	14.9	1,421	14.9
Total	8,382	100.0	8,763	100.0	9,236	100.0	9,528	100.0
% increase	(base year)		4.5		10.2		13.7	

A:2 *Location of Federal Employees in Northern Programmes (1976/77)*

	No.	%
NWT	2,592	54.5
Yukon	1,063	22.4
Southern Canada	1,099	23.1
Total	4,754	100.0

A:3 Federal Government Employment in Northern Programmes in Earlier Years (1965-69)

	1965	1966	1967	1968	1969
Total personnel	2,803	3,087	3,177	n.d.	2,703
Payroll ($)	14 million	16 million	16.7 million	n.d.	16.5 million

Note: "Public service employment includes all regular, seasonal, casual and part-time employees, but not persons engaged under professional and special service contracts. ..." Supplementary source: John R. Palmer, *Social Accounts for the North: Interim Paper No. 1; The Federal Government Sector: Employment and Payrolls.* Ottawa, Department of Indian Affairs and Northern Development. 1971.

A:4 Health, Education and Welfare in NWT: Distribution of Expenditures Between Governments (1973/74 and 1976/77)

Items	1973/74		1976/77 (planned)	
		Expenditures by Federal Govt.		Expenditures by Federal Govt.
	NWT Govt.	(for NWT & Yukon)	NWT Govt.	(for NWT & Yukon)
Health	$ 7,057,000	16,484,000[1]	19,354,000	28,123,000[1]
Education	30,670,000	1,386,000[2]	40,837,000	1,502,000[2]
Welfare	17,457,000	17,417,000[3]	39,072,000	35,090,000[3]

Notes: Federal expenditures include sums spent in the Yukon.
[1] Expenditure by Department of National Health and Welfare.
[2] Expenditure by Department of Indian and Northern Affairs.
[3] Expenditures by Central Mortgage and Housing, Department of Indian and Northern Affairs, Department of National Health and Welfare, and Unemployment Insurance Commission.

A:5 Total Government Expenditure on NWT: by Government and as Percentage for Canadian North (1976/77 - planned)

Distribution between governments

	Total	NWT Govt.	Govt. of Canada
$	386,200,000	216,100,000	170,100,000
%	100	56	44

As part of total government expenditures on the Canadian North

	Total	NWT	Yukon	"North Generally"[1]	"Outside the North"[1]
$	583,400,000	386,200,000	145,600,000	33,500,000	18,100,000
%	100	66.2	25.0	5.7	3.1

Note: [1] Expenditures by federal agencies only.

B. THE COMMUNITIES OF BAFFIN REGION

Source: *Community Data, 1974.* Department of Information, Government of the Northwest Territories.

The Baffin Region extends from Port Burwell in the south-east to Grise Fiord in the north, and includes the islands of the High Arctic – a land and water mass exceeding 1,500 miles in longitude and of some 900 miles in latitude (cf. Ch. 1, this vol.).

Arctic Bay

"Arctic Bay was named after the whaling vessel "ARCTIC" under the command of Captain William Adams who first visited the bay in 1872. Seal, polar bear and white fox are still the basis of the Settlement's economy. In recent years mineral exploration has been carried out. Plans are to open a lead-zinc mine at Strathcona Sound some 17 miles east of Arctic Bay. A local soapstone quarry containing a unique stone called Kooneak has been a factor in the arts produced by carvers in this community. Wage employment was increased considerably in 1971 when workers began travelling to Panarctic Oil sites. Population 311."

Broughton Island

"Broughton has a very short history in comparison with other settlements on Baffin Island. The Eskimo population, although there was a few families in the area before the 1950's, have since the establishment of the DEW Line Base, moved into the area from the camps that existed on Cumberland Sound. The population again increased during the mid 60's when D.I.A.N.D. closed down the nearby settlement of Padloping Island. The Hudson's Bay Company established a post there in 1960 which burned to the ground in 1965 but has since been rebuilt. This settlement, for the adventurous traveller is a 'must.' Sea mammals are very plentiful in the area and char fishing is excellent. Population 390."

Cape Dorset

"Cape Dorset was named after the Earl of Dorset by Captain Foxe on September 24, 1631. Because the first ruins of an ancient Eskimo culture were found at this place, this ancient culture became known as the Dorset Culture. The first trading post was established by the Hudson's Bay Company in 1913. The West Baffin Eskimo Co-operative is the largest employer. Soapstone sculpture, prints, hunting and trapping are the mainstays of the economy. Fish, water fowl and walrus also contribute to the economy of Cape Dorset. Population 690."

Clyde River

"The history of Clyde River dates back to 1923 when the Hudson's Bay Company established a post there. The Bay relocated a number of Eskimo families to the area and for the next 20 years the population remained fairly steady. In 1942, Clyde River started to expand again as defense-related facilities were constructed. In 1954 a U.S. Coast Guard Station was established at Cape Christian, 10 miles from Clyde. The Base expanded in 1957 with the construction of a 2,500 foot airstrip and in 1960 the strip was extended to 5,000 feet. This strip is gravel as was the new strip which was built at Clyde River in 1970. Clyde River is considered to be one of the more primitive settlements on Baffin. There still exists in this area outlying camps. Hunting is good. Population 357.''

Grise Fiord

''Grise Fiord was established in the early 1960's by the R.C.M.P.; thence Eskimos from Pond Inlet, Port Harrison, Arctic Bay and Pangnirtung were relocated to Craig Harbour, thence to Grise Fiord. The economy is traditional with hunting, trapping and fishing with fur marketed through the local Co-op store. Population 100.''

Hall Beach

''Hall Beach is named after Captain C. F. Hall who spent a number of years on Melville Peninsula in the mid 1800's. Most of the economy is based on fur trapping and wage employment with the Government and DEW Line station. The present settlement is comparatively new, most inhabitants coming from the surrounding communities – Igloolik, Repulse Bay, and other places in the Keewatin district. The people moved here to take on wage employment during the construction phase of the DEW Line in the mid 1950's, and then remained to continue working as equipment operators, mechanic's assistants, etc. Population 315.''

Igloolik

''The first person to visit the island was Thomas Burton in 1613. The island was also the wintering site of Parry's expedition in 1822/23 and subsequently visited by the fifth Thule expedition in 1921/24. Evidence exists that the island has been populated since the last glaciation about 2000 B.C. Although the area is rich in fur and sea resources including walrus and seal, the increase in population exceeds the availability of the area to support them. An ever increasing proportion of the economy is therefore of a wage type through employment with government, etc. Population 611.''

Lake Harbour

''Lake Harbour was visited regularly before the 1900's by whaling ships who employed local people in their operations and to mine mica in the settlement. In 1900 an Anglican Mission was established and a Hudson's Bay Post in 1911. The main economy is based on sea mammals and fishing. This is a good seal hunting area. Carving – the light green serpentine stone is found near the settlement and is very popular. The Department of Economic Development is exploring the possibilities of mining and processing a small deposit of Lapis Lazuli. Population 260.''

Pangnirtung

"Situated on the southeastern shore of Pangnirtung Fiord, which leads to the sea on the northeastern shore of Cumberland Sound, Pangnirtung is surrounded by steeply rising mounts. The Penny Ice Cap to the north rises to 7,000 feet. Pangnirtung Fiord is the terminus of one of the two main passes and sledge routes through the Baffin Mountains. The present economy is based on excellent sealing, whaling and fishing resources as well as caribou and walrus. Pangnirtung is the access point to the newly created Baffin National Park. Population 906."

Pond Inlet

"The first recorded visit to Pond Inlet was W. W. Parry in 1820. The Inlet, however, was named in 1888 by John Ross after John Pond, Astronomer Royal. The economy is based mainly on seal, whale, fishing, trapping and carvings. Wage employment with Panarctic Oil Company is gaining in importance and the majority of the working force is employed by them. Population 550."

Port Burwell

"Between the years 1884 and 1940, Port Burwell has seen a number of enterprises come and go. The Federal Government Meterological Station, the Moravian Mission and Trading Post and later the Hudson's Bay Company, who with the decline of game, departed with most of the residents in 1940. With the return of game, the residents also returned and in 1960 started a producer-consumer co-op which still flourishes. Seal hunting is very good both by hunting and in the fall netting. In the summer month there is a fish plant operating with the main fish [being] char and cod, the cod is filleted and sold in Frobisher Bay and also there is a growing demand for Port Burwell cod in Fort Chimo. Population 121."

Resolute Bay

"Cornwallis Island was discovered in 1819 by Parry in search of the Northwest Passage. Resolute Bay was named after the ship Resolute that wintered there in 1850. The island was inhabited by Eskimos of both the Thule and Dorset cultures. The first recent occupation was the establishment of a joint U.S. /Canadian weather station in 1947. In 1953 Eskimos were re-introduced to Resolute Bay from Port Harrison in Quebec and Pond Inlet on Baffin Island, to harvest the game resources there. The economic base is wage employment at the airfield, fishing, hunting, trapping and polar bear sports hunting. Population 209."

Frobisher Bay – the administrative centre

"The Settlement is named after Sir Martin Frobisher who discovered the

Bay in 1576. In 1942 a military base and gravel runway was established at the head of Koojasse Inlet. A new 9000' asphalt strip was built by the U.S. Airforce in 1955 during the build-up of the Strategic Air Command Base. The main increase in civilian population took place during the 50's when the Canadian Government established an Elementary School at Apex Hill, some three miles from the Air Base site. A new multi-million dollar town-centre complex was constructed in 1970 and the settlement became incorporated as a Hamlet on April 1, 1974. Population 2360.''

C. LOCAL GOVERNMENT ORDINANCES

Source: Marquand, John and Don McNeill, ''Evolution of Political Process in the Northwest Territories.'' Ottawa, Department of Indian and Northern Affairs. 1975. (stencil).

C:1 *Local government ordinances*

Communities of the N.W.T. are allocated status either as 'unorganized communities,'' ''settlements,'' ''hamlets,'' or ''villages.'' In Baffin Region, in 1975, eleven communities were of settlement status; two, Pond Inlet and Pangnirtung, had hamlet status; and Frobisher Bay was a village.

Unorganized Communities

''[T]hose communities which have no local tax base and where the administrative services of the community are performed or overseen by a Territorial Government representative. These communities with two exceptions have populations of less than 150 people and are all located in the District of MacKenzie, in the Northwest Territories.''

Settlements

''There are 23 communities in the Northwest Territories classed by the Government of the Northwest Territories as *settlements*.''

''The settlements are looked upon as the training grounds for the practical and orderly development of local government, and ultimate incorporation as municipalities. Each settlement has a fully elected Council which acts as the advisory body to the local government Territorial officer. This officer in turn acts as the Secretary to the Council and is required to maintain a local person in training at all times. While the Territorial officer in fact does have the power of veto over Council proposals, in practice this is mostly exercised in the form of advice. He is required to consult the Council on all matters that affect the community. The Council receives from the Territorial Government a per capita grant of $20 per head of population per year for use in providing community facilities over and above the provision of an approved level of municipal services.''

Hamlets

"Section 3 of the Hamlet Ordinance allowed for the establishment of Hamlets in the Northwest Territories when '... it appears desirable to the Commissioner that a settlement in the Territories that (a) is not incorporated as a municipality established under an Ordinance of the Territories; and (b) has developed sufficiently so as to warrant participation of its residents in the governing of its local affairs.'"

"Hamlet Councils consist of either six or eight members, and Council members hold two year terms. Elections are held annually for one-half of the council."

"The Hamlet Ordinance defines their powers under the following headings: Highways, Public Health and Nuisances, Fire Prevention, Domestic Animals, General By-laws relating to the protection of Persons and Property, and Zoning."

"Hamlet Councils may also make by-laws regulating and controlling all businesses within the hamlet that are not regulated or licensed under an Ordinance, and set and collect fines and fees subject to those regulations. Hamlets also raise revenue by the levy by Council of a 'Community service charge,' amounting to $15 for each person, making in excess of $500 per year and having resided in the hamlet for more than 3 months. Revenue from fines, licences and the community service charge are the only monies that a hamlet may *collect* and control directly for the administration of the Hamlet."

"Hamlets are given an approved level of municipal services from the Government of the N.W.T., and submit operating budgets to the Territorial Government."

C:2 *Housing Associations*

"Provision was made for the Eskimo people to assume the responsibility of local management. The tenants, that is those who sign the rental agreement, automatically become members of a Housing Association. The members elected, from their membership, one director for every ten houses to a maximum of nine and a minimum of three. The directors formed the Council of the Housing Association. Each local housing association would then apply to have the association incorporated under the Societies Ordinance of the Northwest Territories. This gave them the right to enter into contracts on behalf of the Association. It also provided for annual reports and audited statements of accounts. Directors may receive remuneration."

"The development of local Housing Associations continued, pursuant to the N.W.T. Housing Corporation Ordinance. Section 48 of the N.W.T. Housing Corporation Ordinance established the authority of Housing Associations in that 'the Commissioner may rest in a Housing association such power, functions and duties as he deems necessary to operate, manage and maintain any housing unit or housing project under an agreement entered into pursuant to this ordinance.' Housing Associations now receive funding through the N.W.T. Housing Corporation in the form of accountable grants administered quarterly. These grants are used by the Associations to pay for utilities, services, housing maintenance, materials, labour and administration of government low-cost housing units."

D. THE INUIT OF THE BAFFIN REGION IN THE 1969–70 MANPOWER
    SURVEY

Source: MacBain Meldrum, Sheila and Marian Helman, *Northern Manpower Survey Program in the Yukon and Northwest Territories*. Ottawa, Department of Indian Affairs and Northern Development. 1975.

D:1 *Age-group as Percentage of Baffin Inuit Population (1969–70)*

| Age-group | % of Population | | Accumulative % | |
	Male	Female	Male	Female
0–14 years	48.6	52.2	—	—
15–19	10.6	10.4	59.2	62.6
20–44	30.2	28.6	89.4	91.2
45–64	9.0	7.5	98.4	98.7
65 and over	1.6	1.3	100.0	100.0

Source: Table 2.

D:2 *Percentage Distribution of Highest School Grade Completed among Baffin Inuit Population over 14 Years of Age (1969–70)*

School Grade	Males	Females	Total
Never attended	57.4	55.1	56.4
Kindergarten (grade 5)	28.7	29.4	29.1
Grades 6–9	8.2	9.6	8.8
10–11	0.5	0.2	0.3
12–13	—	—	—
Unknown	5.2	5.7	5.4
Totals	100.0	100.0	100.0

Source: Table 8.
Note: Figures for Baffin similar to those for Arctic Coast and Keewatin Inuit; notably higher figures among the Mackenzie Inuit. No notable differences between sexes.

D:3 *Age-groups as Percentage of Two Languages' Ability among Baffin Inuit Population over 14 Years of Age (1969–70)*

Age-groups	Speak Inuttitut and English (%) Male	Female	Proficiency of Males over Females (%)
14–24 years	73.1	69.8	3.4
25–44	30.9	11.7	19.2
45 and over	12.5	2.5	10.0

Source: Table 9.
Note: Proficiency among Arctic Coast and Keewatin Inuit runs at about 10% higher and among the Mackenzie Inuit considerably higher still (in the 14–24 years age-group, none of the Mackenzie Inuit are without proficiency in English and 39.3% have proficiency in English only).
    The authors (p. 35) provide this definition: "A person was listed as able to speak a language if he or she could speak it easily for long periods, e.g. to answer the questionnaire."

D:4 *Age-groups as Percentage of Baffin Inuit Labour Force; Percentage Participation of Age-groups in Labour Force (1969–70)*

Age-group	Age-group as % of Labour Force Male	Female	% Participation in Labour Force Male	Female
15–19 years	11.3	25.2	40.2	13.3
20–44	70.3	67.7	87.8	13.0
45–64	17.9	7.1	74.8	5.2
65 and over	0.5	—	13.2	—

Source: Tables 17 and 18.

D:5 *Percentage Distribution of Labour Force by Activity and Week's Work (1969–70)*

Weeks	Wage & Salary Male	Female	Hunting, Trapping, Fishing Male	Female	Self-employment Male	Female	Without Work Male	Female
1–3	5.7	3.1	2.4	—	6.7	5.4	0.4	—
4–17	22.5	14.0	14.3	0.8	21.0	11.6	5.7	4.6
18–31	15.4	8.5	15.0	—	7.6	3.1	10.3	7.0
32–45	10.3	8.5	10.7	—	2.9	2.3	5.7	8.5
45–52	28.1	34.1	8.0	1.5	1.6	14.0	6.5	17.1
No weeks	18.0	31.8	49.6	97.7	60.2	63.6	71.4	62.8
% Totals	100.0	100.0	100.0	100.0	100.0	100.0	100.0	100.0

Source: Table 20.
Note: Work as "housewife" not included as self-employment (no income); but home handicrafts, house-cleaning and baby-sitting are (MacBain Meldrum: personal communication).

D:6 *Percentage Distribution of Earned and Unearned Incomes (by Activity and Income Group) among Baffin Inuit Population over 14 yrs. (1969–70)*

Income Group	Wage & salary Male	Female	Hunting, Trapping, Fishing, Male	Female	Self-employment Male	Female
$1,000–4,999	41.6	22.9	5.8	—	10.3	2.1
$5,000–9,999	16.3	1.6	—	—	0.2	—
Over $10,000	0.4	—	—	—	—	—
Sub-total	58.3	24.5	5.8	—	10.5	2.1
Under $1,000	40.2	72.5	71.8	60.0	86.4	93.3
Unspecified	1.5	3.0	22.4	40.0	3.0	4.6
% Totals	100.0	100.0	100.0	100.0	100.0	100.0

Income Group	Total Earned Income Male	Female	Total Unearned Income Male	Female	Total Income all Sources Male	Female
$1,000–4,999	45.3	13.2	7.4	23.3	51.3	19.2
$5,000–9,999	14.1	0.8	—	—	15.2	0.9
Over $10,000	0.6	—	—	—	0.5	—
Sub-total	60.0	14.0	7.4	23.3	67.0	20.1
Under $1,000	37.4	82.4	89.4	67.3	30.4	75.4
Unspecified	2.6	3.6	3.2	9.4	2.6	4.5
% Totals	100.0	100.0	100.0	100.0	100.0	100.0

Source: Table 13.
Note: See note to D:5.

D:7 *Distribution of Average Earned and Unearned Incomes (Inuit only) among Baffin Settlements (1969–70)*

MALES

Settlement Average Incomes	Wage & Salary	Hunting, Trapping, Fishing	Self-employment	Unearned Income
Two lowest	$1,403	$ 234	$162	$280
(excl. Frobisher)	1,448	265	171	309
Two highest	2,715	735	759	619
(excl. Frobisher)	3,233	1,230	828	629
Frobisher Bay	4,061	506	302	366
All Baffin	2,411	387	372	431

FEMALES

Settlement Average Incomes	Wage & Salary	Hunting, Trapping, Fishing	Self-employment	Unearned Income
Two lowest (excl. Frobisher)	$ 182 231	$— —	$ 27 82	$330 389
Two highest (excl. Frobisher)	972 1,467	— —	247 617	792 978
Frobisher Bay All Baffin	1,433 810	— 180	229 179	429 600

Source: Tables 26 and 52.
Note: See note to D:5.

D:8 *Distribution of Per Capita Income (Inuit only) among Baffin Settlements (1969–70)*

Settlement Per Capita Income	Male	Female
Two lowest (excl. Frobisher)	$ 544 780	$ 61 70
Two highest (excl. Frobisher)	1,192 1,720	194 376
Frobisher Bay All Baffin	1,768 1,147	276 170

Source: Tables 25, 51 and 52.
Note: "Per capita" includes children under 14, and unearned as well as earned income sources.

E. VITAL STATISTICS: N.W.T. INUIT AND WHITES; BAFFIN AND MACKENZIE DELTA INUIT

Source: Annual Reports of the Chief Medical and Health Officer of the Northwest Territories.

E:1 *N.W.T. Inuit and Whites*

Livebirths per 1000 population

Year	1966	1967	1968	1969	1970	1971	1972	1973	1974	1975
Inuit	54.5	53.4	53.3	49.4	40.8	38.3	35.1	32.8	28.4	32.4
Whites	28.2	25.5	32.1	28.0	32.1	34.1	31.9	34.2	29.3	32.4
All Canada	19.4		17.6				15.9	15.5		

Stillbirths per 1000 livebirths

Year	1966	1967	1968	1969	1970	1971	1972	1973	1974	1975
Inuit	43.1	23.6	22.7	12.6	17.4	17.9	21.4	15.6	20.2	8.7
Whites	3.2	11.9	9.1	15.3	10.2	7.8	8.1	7.3	12.4	12.9
All Canada	11.4		10.8				11.4			10.6

Infant deaths (under 1 yr.) per 1000 livebirths

Year	1966	1967	1968	1969	1970	1971	1972	1973	1974	1975
Inuit	108.8	83.8	89.1	90.5	105.0	97.8	72.9	44.7	70.7	48.0
Whites	52.4	29.6	27.4	20.5	21.7	19.7	26.2	12.7	18.7	12.9
All Canada	23.1				18.8		17.1	15.5		

Total deaths (crude death rate) per 1000 population

Year	1966	1967	1968	1969	1970	1971	1972	1973	1974	1975
Inuit	12.6	10.3	10.6	10.1	11.1	11.2	8.9	6.1	6.7	6.1
Whites	7.7	6.8	6.6	4.1	4.6	5.9	5.2	5.8	5.7	5.1
All Canada	7.5		7.4				7.4	7.4		

Natural increase per 1000 population

Year	1966	1967	1968	1969	1970	1971	1972	1973	1974	1975
Inuit	41.9	43.1	42.7	39.3	29.7	27.1	26.2	26.7	21.7	26.3
Whites	24.3	21.6	28.9	23.8	27.5	28.1	26.7	28.4	24.7	29.0
All Canada	11.9		10.2				8.5	8.1		

Livebirths in hospitals – as percentage of total livebirths

Year	1966	1967	1968	1969	1970	1971	1972	1973	1974	1975
Inuit	63.8	74.4	80.2	85.9	92.4	95.8	98.0	97.3	98.9	97.8
Whites	71.7	86.9	90.6	100.0	99.6	99.8	99.1	98.3	98.0	98.5
All Canada	99.2	99.5					99.6	99.8		

Deaths in hospitals – as percentage of total deaths

Year	1966	1967	1968	1969	1970	1971	1972	1973	1974	1975
Inuit	47.2	40.6	47.4	54.8	62.3	64.1	56.8	57.1	48.9	52.8
Whites	51.5	47.0	50.7	57.0	59.1	60.9	60.1	55.7	56.0	53.2
All Canada	65.2		67.7							

E:2 *Baffin Inuit and Mackenzie Delta Inuit*

Livebirths per 1000 population

Year	1968	1971	1973	1975
Baffin Inuit	56.4	37.6	37.3	37.2
Mackenzie Inuit	55.6	43.9	31.8	29.4

Stillbirths per 1000 livebirths

Year	1968	1971	1973	1975
Baffin Inuit	23.2	24.3	19.3	0
Mackenzie Inuit	17.1	27.5	12.2	25.6

Infant deaths (under 1 yr.) per 1000 livebirths

Year	1968	1971	1973	1975
Baffin Inuit	85.2	86.5	48.3	75.1
Mackenzie Inuit	99.1	100.9	36.6	12.8

Total deaths (crude death rate) per 1000 population

Year	1968	1971	1973	1975
Baffin Inuit	10.9	7.9	6.5	7.5
Mackenzie Inuit	13.7	11.3	9.3	6.4

Natural increase per 1000 population

Year	1968	1971	1973	1975
Baffin Inuit	45.5	29.7	30.8	29.7
Mackenzie Inuit	41.9	32.6	22.5	23.0

Livebirths in hospitals – as percentage of total livebirths

Year	1968	1971	1973	1975
Baffin Inuit	70.9	96.5	96.6	95.3
Mackenzie Inuit	83.5	92.6	97.5	100.0

Deaths in hospitals – as percentage of total deaths

Year	1968	1971	1973	1975
Baffin Inuit	34.0	77.3	66.6	58.1
Mackenzie Inuit	33.3	64.3	45.8	29.4

Note: The rates (except those for "All Canada") are computed on statistically small populations. The actual numbers for 1968, for instance, are as follows:

	Total pop.	live-births	still-births	infant deaths	total deaths	natural increase
Inuit	10736	572	13	51	114	458
Whites	13596	437	4	12	43	394
Baffin Inuit	4571	258	6	22	50	208
Mackenzie Inuit	2177	121	1	12	30	91

F. N.W.T. HEALTH
Source: *Annual Report on Health Conditions (1973)*. Department of Health, Government of the Northwest Territories.

F:1 *Major Notifiable Diseases: Inclusive Population (1967–73)*

Year	1967	1968	1969	1970	1971	1972	1973
Inclusive Population	29,243	30,304	31,283	32,340	35,000	n.d.	37,010
Influenza	464	999	1,154	1,109	3,478	1,591	1,140
Measles (German and Red)	505	15	44	509	29	22	480
Chicken Pox	81	76	47	—	—	—	—
Mumps	—	100	—	—	—	—	—
German Measles	—	42	—	—	—	—	—
Scarlet Fever	—	—	58	—	—	—	—
Whooping Cough	—	—	—	31	8	1	7
Dysentry (unspec.)	53	—	95	—	—	—	—
Dysentry (bacillary)	18	19	27	25	109	93	49
Infectious Hepatitis	37	12	26	31	268	122	435
Meningitis (unspec.)	36	22	20	8	—	—	—
Meningitis (meningococcal)	2	3	13	5	3	4	9
Pertussis	8	—	—	—	—	—	—
Rubella	35	—	178	449	36	30	36
Trichinosis	3	2	—	—	—	—	—
Food Poisoning	10	—	—	—	—	—	—
Tapeworm	7	—	—	—	—	—	—
Typhoid	1	1	—	—	1	6	1
Botulism	1	—	10	—	—	—	—
Diptheria	1	—	—	—	—	1	6
Gastroenteritis	—	18	—	—	—	—	—
Brucellosis	—	3	—	—	—	—	—

F:2 *Infectious Hepatitis (1973)*
"The increase in Infectious Hepatitis was largely to be accounted for by the occurrence of two major outbreaks in Baffin Zone, at Igloolik and at Pond Inlet."

"The spread of this disease is to be connected directly with conditions of insanitation. Although epidemics may be associated with contamination of water supplies by sewage, there is no indication that such a route was involved anywhere in the Northwest Territories in 1973. Rather, the absence of adequate water supplies for hand washing, or the failure to take advantage of what is available must be cited. The outbreak, which was very thoroughly analysed in retrospect by our nursing staff, appeared among young children of elementary school age, being spread by them to other family members at home. This is a common pattern for this disease."

"The original introduction of the disease to the communities has not been traced though many possibilities exist. The transfer occurred most probably towards the end of the shipping season, at the time when there is much traffic in and out of the communities."

F:3 *Red Measles (1973)*
"The increase in red measles during 1973 was alarming in view of the heavy emphasis on measles vaccination."

"Review of the figures indicated that a substantial proportion (more than half) of the cases of Red measles occurred before the recommended time for measles vaccination (12–18 months according to the American Paediatric Association). Accordingly, our programme has been amended to include early measles vaccination (at six–nine months) and a repeat vaccination at eighteen months to catch those who missed the first does along with those who failed to react by virtue of left-over maternal immunity."

"This one little exercise is an example of the problems that can result from trying to apply the principle of southern medicine to the Northern situation. They do not always fit."

"In short, the communicable disease picture is labile and convincing evidence, if any is needed, of our overcrowded and insanitary environment."

F:4 *Tuberculosis (1965–73)*

New Cases	1965	1966	1967	1968	1969	1970
Inuit						
Nos.	50	83	114	119	103	52
Rates	0.53	0.84	1.1	1.1	0.92	0.44
White						
Nos.	17	10	17	18	14	13
Rates	0.16	0.09	0.13	0.13	0.1	0.09

"There were 49 new and reactivated cases of tuberculosis reported in the calendar year 1973, a decrease of 28% from the previous year. This decrease provides a low rate of 132 per 100,000 which is the lowest in the recorded history of the Northwest Territories."

"It is of interest to note that of the 49 new and reactivated cases only 30 were adult pulmonary tuberculosis, again indicating a downward trend in the spread of tuberculosis."

F:5 *Syphilis (1973)*

"Comparatively speaking, Syphilis is a minor problem in the Northwest Territories. Only four cases were discovered and of these, only one was potentially infectious, the remaining three being old infections only recently identified by blood tests."

"The probable reason for our favorable syphilis experience in the face of such a high incidence of Venereal Disease in general, is the extremely active programme of case finding and treatment aimed at Gonorrhoea. The drugs used and the dosage employed for gonorrhoea treatment are calculated to be effective for the abortion of all incubating syphilis cases as well. This, however, cannot be the whole story and if syphilis did become introduced at all regularly, the evident promiscuity would undoubtedly lead to a rapid spread within the community. Constant vigilance is essential."

F:6 *Gonorrhoea (1971–73)*
Inclusive population, 1971–3

	1971	1972	1973
Confirmed and unconfirmed cases	1,804	2,147	3,269 (44% of cases were Inuit)
% increase on 1971	—	19	81

F:6 cont'd on p. 72

"The year 1973 saw an increase of 38% of confirmed gonorrhoea over the comparable figures for 1972."

"In addition to this, there was a 110% increase in unconfirmed gonorrhoea which may in part reflect the actual increase in disease but also an increased awareness of the likelihood of this disease being recognized by medical and nursing personnel."

"Because of this disproportionate incidence, a heavy emphasis is being given to our V.D. educational programme in 1974 with input from this department into the schools as a primary point of attack."

F:6 cont'd
Gonorrhoea: Confirmed and clinical cases (unconfirmed cases not included) for 1973

Ethnic Group	Total by Sex M	Total by Sex F	Age Groups 0-9	10-14	15-19	20-24	25-39	40-59	60+	Age not stated
Indians	404	236	1	6	145	215	218	50	5	
%			.02	0.9	23.09	34.08	34.78	7.86	.08	
Eskimos	589	464	3	24	257	331	343	87	3	5
%			.02	2.28	24.71	31.73	32.95	8.36	.02	.03
Others	576	115			98	234	292	63	2	2
%					14.18	33.88	42.51	9.37	.03	.03
Total Cases 2384	1569	815	4	30	500	780	853	200	10	7
%	65.82	34.18	.16	1.25	20.9	32.7	35.7	8.3	.4	.29

F:7 *Mental Health (1973)*

"The main stay of the psychiatric program to the Northwest Territories in 1973 continued to be the provision of visiting psychiatrists from southern centres. Consulting psychiatric services to Mackenzie Zone were provided by the Zone Psychologist (resident in Yellowknife), a psychiatrist from the University of Alberta, and the Regional Psychiatrist from Edmonton. Inuvik Zone which had previously been serviced by the University of Alberta will, in future, be serviced by the Regional Psychiatrist and it is planned that in 1974 there will be extension of these visiting services to both Mackenzie and Inuvik Zones."

"The University of Manitoba continues to provide the psychiatric consultation visits to the Keewatin district."

"A new agreement has been signed between Northern Health Services and the Clarke Institute of Psychiatry in Toronto whereby the Clarke Institute will be sending a team composed of a psychiatrist, a child psychiatrist and a psychiatric resident three to four times per year to Frobisher Bay and Cape Dorset. Two such visits were made during 1973 and on one visit, the team included a specialist in speech problems and learning disabilities. The costs for this specialist were met by the Department of Education, Northwest Territories. This co-operative venture between the Department of Health and Welfare, Canada and the Department of Education, Northwest Territories was found to be extremely useful and, hopefully, such joint teams will be a feature in future services."

"Very much has been achieved by our visiting specialists but there is still a need for further service from locally based people. To date, the only member of our Department working strictly in the area of mental health is the Zone Psychologist for Mackenzie Zone in Yellowknife. Budgetary restraints did not allow us to increase the numbers of personnel working in mental health in the North during 1973 but plans are afoot to begin programs involving psychiatric nurses in selective settlements in 1974."

"The total admissions to mental hospitals in 1973 was 41 patients. This figure is down from 1972 when 50 patients were evacuated. As in previous years, the number of male patients vastly outnumbered females in a ratio of 3 to 1. Similarly, non-native people outnumbered native patients in the ratio of 3 to 1. This high number of male non-native patients can probably be attributed to the fact that many of these are transient individuals not residents of the Northwest Territories, at least only resident for a brief period of time."

"As in previous years, the vast majority of suicides occurred in the non-native population. ... The total for 1973 was 10 suicides. ... One particularly disturbing feature of the suicides in 1973 was the fact that 7 of 10 occurred in persons under the age of 30 (3 occurring in persons under the age of 20)."

NOTES

1   It is, paradoxically, the intention to treat individuals as individuals that can especially threaten individuals' privacy.
2   The role of the social anthropological (sociological) field worker used to present the same problem; however, the native population has recently acquired and begun to exercise the right to sanction this information-gathering activity.
3   A.C.N.D. was constituted in 1948; its first meetings were in secret.

References

Arctic Institute
   1976 *Northern Population Workshop I. Summary Report*. Montreal, Arctic Institute of North America.
BUCHANAN, M. A.
   1977 *Statistical Analysis of the Northwest Territories Co-operatives and Credit Unions*. Yellowknife, Government of the NWT., Dept. of Economic Development and Tourism.
Canada
   1976 *Annual Northern Expenditure Plan, 1976–77*. (Advisory Committee Northern Development) Ottawa, Department of Indian and Northern Affairs.
MacBAIN MELDRUM, SHEILA and MARIAN HELMAN
   1975 *Northern Manpower Survey Program in the Yukon and Northwest Territories*. Ottawa, Department of Indian and Northern Affairs (stencil).
Northwest Territories
   1974 *Report of the Task Force on Personnel Policy and Management*. Yellowknife, N.W.T. Government.
SHUBIK, M.
   1971 "Information, Rationality, and Free Choice in a Future Democratic Society." In D. M. Lamberton (ed.), *Economics of Information and Knowledge*. Harmondsworth, Penguin Books.

Case Studies from N.W.T.

The Nursery Game: Colonizers and the Colonized

Robert Paine

5

> "The [Eskimo] has been invested with the needs, the reactions, the mentality of the white – in other words, under pretext of the evident technical superiority of the white, a superiority which is rarely of a moral nature, the white's mode of life, culture and even defects, have been set up as an ideal for the Eskimo to follow."
> *Eskimo*, 1958:4 (Sept.).

This chapter introduces the field studies from the N.W.T. A shared focal concern about white tutelage (see Preface) and its implications for local Inuit and white populations relate these studies to the preceding chapters on government policy and praxis in the north.

Still pursuing the theme of welfare colonialism, I now attempt to portray likely *subjective* experiences that Inuit and whites have of each other and of themselves as an outcome of the colonial encounter. To do this I draw upon social anthropological work, particularly that of Vallee (1962), Brody (1975) and the Killam Project (see Preface and Ch. 20).

It is a relatively simple matter to document (Chs. 2–4) the establishment and 'progress' of welfare colonialism; the demonstration of its invidious consequences – embedded, as they are, in ambiguities and ambivalences – for interpersonal relations is, however, an altogether more subtle task. In Chapter 1, I spoke of the problem as being that of having to demonstrate non-demonstrative colonialism (p. 3); here, I would call attention to the way in which the form or structural context of this colonialism may obscure its impact, particularly on the individual's relationships. The situation aggravates a confusion of motives and of images of self among both colonizers and colonized, though particularly (as far as I can discern) among the former. Indeed, an important part of our task is to show how whites – finding themselves in the colonizers' role – increasingly sense a moral predicament, even though they are unwilling, or find it too difficult (for theirs looks like a double-bind situation) to admit as much. One other point before beginning: although we may recognize that whites going north carry with them, if only as Westerners and (in some cases) metropolitans, dispositions that can easily lend themselves to colonialism, the more noteworthy feature about the Canadian north is the degree to which colonialism was unintended – even accidental. "Reluctant imperialists" is how one observer (Wilkinson, 1959) described the Canadians who went north after the war, armed with programmes.

Tutelage – and Nannies

> "Tutelage is socialization. Eskimos learn either
> through being confronted with opportunities that
> challenge them to master new behavior or through
> teachers' personal direction and encouragement.
> Doubtlessly, personal attention proves more effec-
> tive than unsponsored, trial-and-error learning."
> *Honigmann* (1965:225).

At a relatively early date, Canadian Inuit policy received legitimacy from the distinguished anthropological field team of John and Irma Honigmann, whose work in Frobisher Bay in 1963 was published in 1965 as *Eskimo Townsmen*. The key evaluative term in their analysis is tutelage, which is described above. An inevitable sub-structure of tutelage is "sponsorship" whereby "individuals who conform to Euro-Canadian cultural standards and values" are rewarded; and when there is deviation from what "tutors ... deem appropriate," support is withdrawn (p. 227).

One might be excused were one to confuse tutelage with what is analysed as patronage elsewhere in the anthropological literature. The Honigmanns, however, wish that the relations encompassed by tutelage be thought of as existing on a higher moral plane than those of patronage. Nor is tutelage seen as demeaning for the tutored: "We don't suggest that they [Eskimos] conform only in order to attract special favors. Once a sponsor confers his support, pressure to continue to conform and develop in the direction set by the new culture becomes even greater. A new incentive for learning has been added to the Eskimo's life" (p. 227).

Nevertheless, tutelage is appropriate not simply because there is "a setting of change, where guidance is needed," but also on account of the specific needs of "a people with a personality and culture like that of the Eskimo" (p. 241). A persistent conclusion of the Honigmanns is, then, that "the white man can be described as filling a social vacuum" (*ibid.*).

 There is also the claim that through tutelage, Inuit will experience "autonomy"; that, indeed, they were already experiencing it in 1963.

Here, for example, is a passage from the Honigmanns' report of a meeting of the Housing Co-operative Society at Frobisher Bay:

"As the meeting concluded, the officer gave the men another inspiring message. The Eskimos, he said, for the first time are their own bosses. Too often in the North the white man is the boss and pushes the Eskimo around. But in a co-op like this, the Eskimo is the boss and he can tell the white man what to do. You (speaking to the interpreter) know this. You (speaking to the group as a whole) are now in a co-op. These words assured Eskimos of their autonomy, just as the co-operative conference did" (p. 223).

Not written tongue-in-cheek, this amounts to a rhetorical legitimation of tutelage. "These words assured Eskimos of their autonomy": yet tutelage is, as the Honigmanns themselves explained it, based upon conformity whose inducement includes subtle coercions, and, as Vallee (1962:128) noticed, implies a relationship in which manifest "superiority" is attributed to the tutor.

I shall try to show how this assumption of superiority has become a vexing factor in white-Inuit relations; and how the "officers" themselves no longer always believe that the messages they give are inspiring. I will also consider the cognition and thought processes that are seen and believed by the Honigmanns to explain Inuit acceptance and need of white tutelage. But first, the political use to which the metaphor, tutelage, has been put should be challenged. Supposing we tamper with the metaphor by replacing tutor with nanny? I suggest that the following imaginary mealtime conversation in Gathorne-Hardy's *The Rise and Fall of the British Nanny* (p. 121), between a nanny and her charge should be taken seriously as an allegory of the white-Inuit relationship of tutelage:

"May I get down, Nanny?"
"Not until you have finished your bread and butter, dear."
"But Nanny – "
"Eat up your bread and butter, dear."
The bread and butter is eaten.
"Not too fast, dear, and don't cram your mouth like that. It is bad manners."
"Can I leave the crust, Nanny?"
"No, dear. Waste not, want not."
"But I don't like crusts, Nanny."
"Never mind. Eat it up. You may be glad of it someday."
"It's all gone now, so may I get down, Nanny?"
"If you say please, dear."
"Please, Nanny."
"Wait till I take your bib off and then say Grace."
"For wehavereceivedmaythelordmakeustrulythankfulamen. May I get down now, Nanny? Please."
"Yes dear, you may."

Do the Inuit ever "get down"? Could whites stop playing nanny, even if they wanted to?

White Nannies, Inuit Dilemmas

> "We are but little toddlekins,
> And can't do much, we know,
> But still we think we must be nice,
> For people love us so."
> Gathorne-Hardy (1972:177).

> "One does not wish to be loved too much
> ... because of the connotations of
> pitiableness and of personal inadequacy
> that are attached to a need for nurturance."
> Briggs (1968:51) on the Utkuhikhalingmuit[1]

It has been suggested that nannies in their heyday were "socio-cultural 'tricksters' who ... behaviourally and effectively separated child from mother" (Boon, 1974:138). In context, this notion of the trickster is useful in understanding the concept of tutelage prevailing between whites and Inuit: the Inuit 'mother,' however, has already been displaced (a casualty of culture contact), but not forgotten (both whites and Inuit have memories of her and, on occasion, these are invoked). In her place is a 'step-mother,' the Canadian government, and it is in her employment that the local whites find themselves. A sense of these allegoric relationships is sometimes apparent in statements by the Inuit themselves: "Those administrators have been pretty good to the people here, but they are all carrying orders from bosses far away, and these bosses have decided how the Eskimos should live, what they should do. So the administrators here are not free to do what they need to do (Brody, 1975:169).

Vallee (1962:129) was among the first to observe and to describe how relations with whites place the Inuit in a child-like role. Parsons (1970:38), in one of the very few studies devoted to whites in the north, finds, among the government employees living at Inuvik in the Mackenzie Delta, "the widespread conviction that natives tend to behave in a manner which is essentially child-like, and thus, like children, they must be taught to exercise initiative, develop self-reliance, practise self-restraint, and generally cope with a complex, changing world." Vallee (op. cit.:195) also suggested that Inuit have evolved behaviour appropriate to this role when dealing with whites: let the white person initiate action, never displease a white by open resistance to his suggestions or commands, and conceal from him behaviour that would be displeasing. Williamson (1968:489) mentions Inuit "ingratiation" as a deliberate measure of cultural defence. Reciprocal parental role behaviour is, Vallee suggested, equally in evidence among the

TABLE 1

Public Employees in Three Selected Baffin Settlements, 1973

Grise Fiord Pop.100 (1974)	Inuit			White		
	Permanent and Full-time	Casual and Seasonal	Part- time	Permanent and Full-time	Casual and Seasonal	Part- time
Settlement Manager				1		
Co-operative Manager	1					
& assistant	1					
& municipal services[1]	5					
Teachers				2		
& assistants	2					
& custodial	1					
Nurse				1		
& assistants	1		1			
RCMP Corporal				1		
& special const.	1					
Mechanics	3			1		
Totals (22)	15	—	1	6[2]	—	—

[1]Grise Fiord Co-operative listed as the employer of those in municipal services.
[2]Of the six whites, four entered as "Northerner" and two (the nurse and RCMP corporal) as "Other."

Broughton Island Pop. 390 (1974)	Inuit			White		
	Permanent and Full-time	Casual and Seasonal	Part- time	Permanent and Full-time	Casual and Seasonal	Part- time
Settlement secretary		1				
HBC Manager				1		
& clerks		1	1	1		
Municipal Services	4					
Welfare Officer		1				
Teachers				5		
& janitors	1					
Nurse				1		
& assistants	1	2		1		
Mechanic				1		
& labourers		2				
Cooks	2					
Housing Assoc. secretary			1			
Totals (27)	8	7	2	10	—	—

Note: No settlement manager listed, only a settlement secretary on casual employment by the government of NWT. The two cooks employed by the settlement council. All of the ten whites listed as "Northerner."

TABLE 1 cont'd.

Pond Inlet Pop. 550 (1974)	Inuit			White		
	Permanent and Full-time	Casual and Seasonal	Part-time	Permanent and Full-time	Casual and Seasonal	Part-time
Settlement Manager				1		
& secretary (trainee)	1					
& clerk	1					
Co-operative manager	1					
& asst. manager		1				
& water delivery	2					
& garbage pick-up	2					
& fuel delivery	2					
H.B.C. manager				1		
& clerks	4			2		
Welfare officer				1		
& assistant	1					
Teachers				8		
& assistants	2					
& maintenance supervisor	1					
& custodial		1				
Adult educ. officer	1					
adult educators				2		
Nurses				1		1
& janitor/interpreter			1			
& asst. janitor	2					
RCMP 1/c				1		
& constable				1		
& special const.	1					
Postmaster			1			
Telephone operator			1			
Radio announcers			3			
Game management				1		
& assistant		1				
& manual worker			1			
Housing Association secretary	1					
& assistant			1			
& stove cleaner		1				
& maintenance		3				
Mechanic	1					
& apprentice	1					
& assistant	1					
& helper	1					
& janitor	1					
& asst. electricians		2				
Dog officer			1			
Other janitors			2			
Totals (67)	27	9	11	19	—	1

Note: Thirty-five Inuit also listed as part-time employees of Pan Arctic.
Source: Individual settlement returns (N.W.T. government forms) "Employment in the Northwest Territories." (My selection of settlements was guided by relative completeness of returns and contrast in size of settlements.)

whites: they conceal strains in their own relations, they are careful about their conversation, and so on. In sum, concealment (in various possible forms) plays a major tactical part in these paired roles of parent (tutor-nanny)/child.

Of course, there are some circumstances under which this relationship may develop without giving rise to a sense of inferiority (or of ambiguity) among the Inuit. The adoption of Anglicanism and tea-drinking are two examples: these traits have become accepted by Inuit as part of their culture. Yet Inuit self-esteem is continually threatened in a way that the self-esteem of a real child would not be by the process of tutelage. One can begin to understand why this is so from the following generalized description by Vallee (1962:210):

"Although the Kabloona [whites] make a favorable, if romantic, judgment on the Eskimo past, this does not prevent them from showing contempt for the living Eskimos they meet, either openly or by implication. Consider what is implied where one learns that untidiness is sinful, and one's parents are untidy; that receiving handouts is a mark of inferior status while one's parents are forced to accept handouts to keep the household going; that self-respecting men are capable of protecting their womenfolk from human predators while one's sisters and mother have to be protected behind a social wall of non-fraternization, erected by the guardian of the predators. Under such conditions it is not unlikely that children will devalue their parents."

Vallee wrote the above on the basis of fieldwork (in the central Arctic) done some fifteen years ago, and if it has become dated, then this happened in a singular way. Consider what Brody (1975:205, 206) has to say about the relationship between Inuit parents and children today: "... the word *ilira* ... may be used to suggest the sort of awe or fear young children are supposed to feel towards a strong father, and it has an extended usage that captures Eskimo feeling about Whites in general. Today it is the young who have become relatively powerful and unpredictable, and inspire the feelings of awe, respect and apprehension. ... This respect for the young is in part an extension of respect for Whites."

A different aspect of the generational problem (but one that is reconcilable with Brody's reporting) is revealed by Atcheson (1972:14), a psychiatrist with consultancy experience in the Canadian Arctic since 1965: the majority of his Inuit cases have always been children and adolescents (referred to him by teachers?). Regarding children, he believes their psychiatric disorders relate principally to experiences at school (particularly where children have had to be sent to hostels – a practice that is no longer general) and to parental neglect associated with "excessive use of alcohol." Regarding adolescents, Atcheson writes: "I have examined many cases of serious depression in adolescents reactive to the hopelessness of having found themselves adequately trained to service or run heavy machinery, but being returned to a settlement where there was no possibility of employment."

In the context of tutelage, the assumption of political office by Inuit is likely to be a problematic matter. Here, Brody's observations (*op. cit*.:196) contrast sharply with the Honigmanns' interpretation but confirm the findings from other sources (cf. Ch. 3): ''White officials expect the [Inuit] men to take prominent positions in local government institutions. But since those positions all too often are seen to be devoid of power, the men who occupy them are criticized as ineffective. ... Some men refuse to accept positions of 'authority' for precisely that reason: to accept is to become a target for criticism and ridicule.''

But the criticism and ridicule of fellow Inuit are not all that a protégé of the whites has to worry about. The whites themselves generally judge Inuit according to two standards; one refers to a 'civilized Eskimo' who will emerge from white tutelage: ''Generally speaking, the image of the ideal Eskimo of the future which emerges ... is that of a steady, predictable bourgeois adult who has a sentimental attachment to the Eskimo past, who is proud of the way in which the Eskimos have manipulated nature and kept alive, but ...'' (Vallee, 1967:130 f.). The other refers to a 'real Eskimo' of the 'noble savage' kind (Brody, 1975; Atcheson, 1972) – a fictive and romanticized historical portrait. Both are unreal and between the two there runs a harsh contradiction between progress (white-defined) and tradition (white-defined). The Inuit who are most likely to be hurt by it are those who respond to pressures from their white tutors – pressures to 'conform' and to assume positions in their community. For, as soon as they are judged to be inadequate in some way – something that is likely to happen sooner or later – they run the risk of being characterized by their white sponsors as ''lazy, untrustworthy, useless and stupid''; Atcheson (1972:11) notes, ''these opinions are often offered openly, with native people present, and with a complete lack of sensitivity as to the effect on the Eskimo.''

It is important to consider the distribution of government welfare in the context of tutelage relations. Many Inuit, as we have seen, draw upon government welfare. Are we to conclude, then, that along with Anglican-ism and tea-drinking, this is a case of successful incorporation of a white item into Inuit culture? Before welfare was introduced, a man who pos-sessed more foodstuffs than his neighbours had the responsibility of sharing it with them; welfare payments from whites is probably perceived in much the same way. Yet there is this important caveat: in the Inuit system of sharing a person did not want to be in the role of receiver for too long or too often, and Inuit were diffident about *asking* for help (cf. Briggs, 1968:52). Certainly the government welfare programmes are used by many Inuit families as one economic resource among several, but whether it is a successful Inuit adaptation depends upon the whites' response to it – given the control whites exercise over Inuit. Generally speaking, whites deplore what they take to be Inuit 'dependence' on welfare. They have this attitude at the same time as they are the dispensers of welfare – and at the same time as it is the impermanence of much wage labour that itself contributes to the dependence on social assistance.

Behind this difference between Inuit and white responses to welfare lie a number of ambiguities and misunderstandings that tend to prejudice Inuit-white relations in other spheres. First, it is, of course, the whites themselves who are responsible for the inception of the programmes, and the programmes themselves are largely responsible for the stimulation of the dependency needs of Inuit which the whites deplore. Secondly, many Inuit may have insufficient knowledge of the actual welfare system; a particular complaint of white welfare officers has been that Inuit do not understand the limits attached to welfare payments: "We always try to get across to these people that the government isn't made of money, that there's a limit to what we can spend, but I guess they don't believe us or they don't understand" (Vallee, 1962:193). In addition, the system is not one of uniform practice: "the provision of welfare differs from settlement to settlement, from official to official, and from time to time" (Brody, 1975:178). A third difficulty is the likelihood that when whites and Inuit meet over a welfare decision, their relationship becomes symbolically-charged: the applicant's knowledge (or lack of it) becomes secondary to his interpretation of the welfare system and rights by it. Noteworthy, too, is the likelihood of Inuit interpreting the discrepancies they observe between welfare officers' procedures as evidence, not of the officers' knowing best but of their thinking they know best (Briggs, personal communication).

Significantly, another important matter over which Inuit-white relations are symbolically-charged is that of work. From the welfare applicant's point of view, an officer judges his work competence and settles (or tries to) what his work priorities should be. This, probably a feature of welfare systems wherever they occur, is particularly stressful when the perception of work and of the contingencies attached to particular tasks or pursuits is itself an expression of ethnicity. The scene in the Arctic is once again well-depicted by Brody (1975:178):

"Eskimo hunters everywhere are vulnerable to accusations of indolence, for the [welfare] officer may think that here is a fellow claiming that he cannot feed his family. This feature of the system is exacerbated by availability of wage-labour as an alternative to hunting, for this alternative puts pressure on hunters and trappers to supplement their land-based activity with wage-labour in the settlement, whereas hunters and trappers, if they are serious, must wait on weather and game, not on the chance of work around the settlement. A man who determinedly pursues land-based activity is likely to be faced periodically with poverty and then to have to seek welfare; an administrator faced with such a man in such a situation is likely to see other ways he could earn a living in the settlement."

To conclude, Inuit-white relations concerning welfare[2] place in relief this important aspect of white tutelage: whites perform for Inuit extremely personal services (in the course of which Inuit are open to personal cross-examination) in the absence of personal relations.

White Nannies, White Dilemmas

> "Many [whites] believe that each degree northwards
> is a degree closer to the margins – or beyond them."
> *Brody* (1975:80).

> "Oh, my!
> Other people's babies."
> *A. P. Herbert* (in Gathorne-Hardy, 1972:170).

Turning now to those whites who actually live in the settlements, let me begin with a generalization which, for all its likely exaggeration, should focus attention where attention is needed: it is that most of them are as much exposed to misunderstandings and ambiguities – and hence to cognitive and emotive distress – as are the Inuit, but they are less adroit in coping with their situation. This lack of adroitness occurs not despite their nanny role, but because of it.

It is possibly helpful to relate here the nanny aspect of tutelage to Gans' (1962:143–44) discussion of the caretaker role of government and private agencies in a low-income neighbourhood in Boston. The crux of the role is that "caretaking is not an altruistic act, but a reciprocal relationship in which the caretaker gives his services in exchange for a material or non-material return." The whites in the north are to 'take care of' the Inuit, and what they expect of the Inuit in return is that they accept the "middle-class" (Vallee, Parsons, Brody, and others) package. In such a relationship, Gans continues, "the caretaker also asks his clients to defer to his superior expertise – and status – thus placing them in a subordinate position during the care process." However, "clients are not always, or entirely, bound by these demands. Rather they can select from them, responding to those which satisfy their own goals, and rejecting those which they do not."[3] The conclusion is that (for various reasons) "most caretakers ... must ... take on some clients who do not entirely accept their requirements"; as much is borne out in the complaints of whites about their Inuit charges. Inuit accept some of the 'gifts' but not others; and 'why aren't they grateful?' the whites ask, or (showing their own frustration) 'why don't they help themselves?' It must sometimes seem to the whites that the Inuit attitude is one of, 'when it's jam (that's offered) it's mine, when it's crust it ain't!' (George Park, personal communication). Indeed, a persistent suggestion from Gans is that it is the client, and not the caretaker (who is constricted by his ideological mandate), who is the "freer" party.

The burden whites have assumed by always defining for the Inuit what they should do and be makes it difficult for whites to remember that Inuit still do make decisions for themselves. Indeed, at the root of the difficulties is the official insistence that social problems in the north are reducible to 'the Eskimo problem'; this carries the corollary that their mission and their own lives in the north are publicly presented as unproblematic. Perhaps this white view of the situation was more true of the first two decades after World War II than it is today, although Koster (1972) reports it as persisting among Frobisher Bay whites in 1971. Perhaps, too, the resentment whites express about their Inuit charges (though rarely to Inuit directly) is a symptom of their current bewilderment and anguish over their mission and their own lives: an increasing number of them have difficulty in accepting unequivocally that they, the whites, are only givers; they may also see themselves as takers (of the natural resources, for instance); as deprivers, depriving a people of their prerogative to make decisions; and even as "destroyers" (Brody, 1975:54).

But one thing has not changed since World War II; namely, how whites live in the north (among other sources, compare Wilkinson, 1959; Vallee, 1962; Fried, 1963). Their houses – to begin there – are the better ones in a settlement, and it is exceptional for them not to be grouped together. In other words, whites still insulate themselves not only from the cold but also from the Inuit in their settlement. Individuals venture out-of-doors remarkably little; "very few whites have winter clothing that is adequate for any journey longer than a walk through the settlement" (Brody, 1975:36). On the other hand, they remain in contact with the south by radio, telephone and plane. But the sociologically salient fact is, I think, the stark disjunction maintained by whites between their public and private lives or roles. Whites are either on-duty (public) or off-duty (private). When on-duty they face Inuit with problems and in these performances they are characteristically competent and confident-appearing: nannies (are meant to) know best! Off-duty, however, is a white social world in which Inuit have no assigned place except at its edges.

Yet, it is particularly the private off-duty world of the whites that is affected by long shadows of ambiguity and self-doubt: nanny no longer knows what is best either for 'them' or for herself. When a white does meet an Inuk in an off-duty context, "such an encounter is atypical ... [and] there is no formula for handling it" (Brody, op. cit.:77). The generalized and polarized notions of 'Eskimos' that whites carry leave them with little to say to individual Inuit.[4] Nevertheless, Inuit still intrude upon the whites' off-duty life. "Whites [arrange] each other in an invisible hierarchy with positions determined by whether or not Eskimos like them. ... They frequently denigrate colleagues by saying, 'The Eskimos don't like him, you know'" (Brody, op. cit.:73, 76).[5]

The evident paradox in this situation draws attention to the way whites tend to isolate themselves from *each other* as well as from the Inuit. It is common for whites not to get along with each other. Underlying this are the sharp lines whites draw between culture and nature, between the settlement and the "bush," and between themselves and the Inuit, distinctions that effectively constrict them to a kind of spaceship living in which physical, psychological, and social components are closely entwined.[6]

For example, there will always be accommodation for a white coming to the north but, as Sampath (1972:5–9) notes, "he has very little choice in deciding where he will live or the type of housing assigned to him … [and] it is virtually impossible for him to own his own house and furniture, all of which are highly subsidized by the government." Remembering that the white-in-the-arctic is likely to spend much more time indoors than he would in the south, one sees the force of the conclusion that "while his emotional investment in his house is great, his economic investment is totally lacking, and this produces a marked ambivalent feeling towards his house as home" (*ibid.*).

Sampath (*ibid.*) also suggests that the closed-society features which pertain in arctic settlements "provide for the dependency needs of those [white] individuals who conform to the rules of the society … [but] these people are extremely vulnerable if the protective trappings prove at times to be somewhat fragile." With this, some of the balance that is totally lost in local whites' reporting of 'problems' (particularly of the perceived Inuit dependency syndrome) is restored: the whites too have dependency needs; and it is surely significant that this is so even though "there is no valid statistical evidence to indicate that any specific personality type is attracted to the North, nor that such personalities as are attracted are vulnerable to mental breakdown" (Atcheson, 1972:13).

What Sampath (*ibid.*) found was that when whites "receive what they consider to be indifferent treatment from the benevolent authoritarian figures, e.g. medical staff, police and especially the administrator, they quickly become angry, demoralized and depressed." Atcheson's report throws some light on the still sketchy picture of the mental health of whites in the Arctic (see Ch. 4). Atcheson had very few white referrals, since those suffering from a mental breakdown were "almost universally evacuated to a southern city, for treatment" (*op. cit.*:11). The principal exception to this practice were persons suffering from "cabin fever," who "were usually cases of married women with their husbands in the north" (*ibid.*). Abbott and Kehoe (1972:7–8) describe cabin fever in the Yukon as prevalent in late winter among housewives with small children. It is characterized by "depression, irritability, easily provoked anger and a breakdown of relationships with those persons with whom the sufferer is living." It seems that the commonsense explanation for this malaise would not be wrong: it is a reaction to being cooped-up. Its high frequency and intensity is probably peculiar only to the Arctic – a reaction to the 'spaceship' conditions in which the whites live.

But it is the widespread tendency towards clique formation, rather than the (not unrelated) occurrence of cabin fever, that marks sociologically the small white communities in the north. By this reduction (socially) of the already small number of white persons who are available to each other, the spaceship conditions become still more accentuated, and white relations across a settlement become injected with the animus of hostility and secrecy. Riches (this volume) traces clique formation to the disjunction we have mentioned between public and private domains.[7] On the one hand, all whites in the Arctic must overtly support and subscribe to the public norm of intra-white solidarity; explicit in this code of conduct is that whites help one another in their role as tutors to the Inuit. This ideal code is maintained in public – when Inuit, or white superiors are present. However, out of the contradictions associated with their mission, a private norm of behaviour develops, antagonistic to the public one. Earlier writers (for example, Dunning, 1959) pointed to status ambiguities between whites of the same settlement as the principal source of these contradictions, but an elaborate white division of labour and command have developed so that the present situation is one of jealous concern over the prerogatives of each particular status. When a white is suspected of a status transgression (invariably it involves an Inuk client), he will be charged with "meddling."

If charges of meddling promote clique-formation, it is also true that cliques, upon establishment, direct the laying of such charges. There are naturally other factors at play: one clique is likely to group around the administrator (the senior white with special authority); one clique is likely to be known as "drinkers" and another as "dry";[8] each clique is likely to claim that (only) it understands 'Eskimos.' Competition for the favour of local Inuit is also likely to follow clique lines, and in this way differences can emerge, otherwise rare at the settlement level, in professed attitudes to 'Eskimos.' The drinkers may fraternize with Inuit and, if necessary, defend their doing so by asking 'how else is one to get to know them?' Though a drinking clique behaves in a way unbecoming to nannies, its members are unlikely to lose their jobs, for it is difficult to sanction a clique; a lone drinker or fraternizer, however, is entirely another proposition, as we shall show below.

Koster's analysis (this vol.) of white gossip is congruent with Riches' of cliques on several points, even though her material is from the town of Frobisher Bay whereas Riches' is from a much smaller settlement.[9] Cliques and gossip are both associated with the need experienced by individual whites to belong to a group of intimates: but a symptom of the situation in which they find themselves is that both cliques and gossip are themselves tainted by illegitimacy.[10] Gossip functions also as a means of learning how one should conduct oneself with reference to the public and private norm structures. Thus, the new arrival to Frobisher Bay is involved in gossip mostly as a listener (in the process of joining), but later his involvement is broadened and differentiated when he begins to use gossip, himself, as an instrument for allocating distance between himself and the various groups and categories of people in town.

Koster is convinced of a close association between gossip and a strong sense of ambiguity among the whites concerning their presence there. But instead of each person asking himself "why am *I* here?," the question (virtually an accusation) is directed to others: "why is *he* here?" By thus drawing attention to the motivation of others, an individual seeks to divert his misgivings about his own motivations and his own self-image. This is an important part of the explanation, I think, for inter-clique denigration.

It should be noted that this burden of white discomfiture is distributed by the whites *among themselves*; on the available evidence there is little displacement onto the Inuit (cf. note 5, above). The reason appears to be that it is the validation of his behaviour as white by other whites that is the preying concern of a white-in-the-Arctic. Competition for Inuit affection, even though it is turned into a means by which whites award relative status to each other, cannot, by definition, satisfy this concern. But clique membership and the supporting gossip do so, if only in a limited arena and in a somewhat indirect manner. This is why the occasional parties to which all whites of a settlement are invited are so important to the participants: the parties have been described as "the clearest and most forceful affirmation of southern ways. At parties the Whites are on show to one another" (Brody, 1975:65). Although the parties may be anomalous events in the small world of the settlement where sociability is usually restricted to cliques, the important point is that, for all the difference in outward form, they serve the same motivational end as do cliques and gossip – not intimacy but validation.

Antipathetic Systems

> "These patterns serve as lenses through which [Eskimos] perceive the kabloona world. And kabloonas [whites] in turn view these Eskimo patterns through the lenses of their own habitual behavior and attitudes."
> *Briggs* (1968:53–4).

Thus far the whites have been considered in their role of colonizer and the Inuit in theirs of the colonized, but only incidentally as members of their respective cultures. It is this cultural variable of the colonial encounter that I now wish to consider. When I introduced the Honigmanns' (1965) notion of tutelage, I did not discuss the view of Inuit cognition and thought processes on which they appear to base their belief of the Inuit need and acceptance of white tutelage. Let us begin there:

Inuit show "slight interest in motivation ... [and] are as unconscious of the regularities of their actions as of grammatical regularities" (p. 5; cf. pp. 238, 239).

"[I]deals to which behavior should conform little concern Eskimos" (p. 242).

Inuit "compete to maximize their satisfaction, to enter positions that will better gratify their impulses" (p. 237; cf. p. 240).

The only reason for taking these observations seriously is that they approximate those held among whites generally. We want to know how the Honigmanns reached them. It seems that an important factor was their frustration (to which they candidly admit) with their Inuit informants, and behind that was the Inuit informants' own unease with the Honigmanns' questions: a typical scenario of white-initiated, white-Inuit encounters. The Honigmanns demanded (a) interpretative answers to questions about (b) life-style and other Inuit; but (p. 5) "to many of our questions they responded with an impotent *atchiw* (I don't know; I can't say)." Now, *atchiw* in this context is, of course, a defence, and Williamson (1968:489) notes how it can be used "until the contact agent wearies or until silent withdrawal becomes possible." This seems to have happened with the Honigmanns who "hired and lost four young men – though we paid them up to $2.00 an hour – in spite of the fact that they had no other steady work" (p. 5).

At one level, the Honigmanns recognize that Inuit "don't customarily pressure one another"; "are reluctant to hazard interpretations beyond what is concretely known"; and "value deference in interpersonal relations" (pp. 5, 244). Yet when seeking to explain why Inuit were reluctant to answer their questions, the Honigmanns posit lack of interest in motivation; and in trying to explain that trait, they emphasize "thinking concretely" as being distinctly Inuit (237 f.). On both these points, Briggs (1968:53) makes an important comment:

"Three kinds of questions are particularly unwelcome [among Inuit]: those concerning motivation (one's own and other people's); the nature of other people's activities; and the future. Inquiry into these areas is likely to be met with evasive ... professions of ignorance ... [*White*] *observers tend to explain these traits in terms of the Eskimos' action-orientation and preoccupation with concrete reality.* ... this may indeed be a factor in some cases [but] there are also other reasons for evasiveness on these subjects. *In the case of questions about motivation, respect for personal privacy and autonomy, one's own and other people's, is an important factor*" (emphases added).

There can be no doubt that Inuit are concerned with motivation and ideal behaviour and hence with the will to control impulse gratification (cf. Briggs, 1976).[11] Given that whites are also concerned about these things, one cannot assume that Inuit and whites think and act in the same way regarding them. The relevant difference between Inuit and white modes of thought rests upon, firstly, Inuit reluctance to subordinate their thinking about individuals to thinking about groups: Inuit make conclusions about white individuals rather than about the white man. Secondly, Inuit try to avoid subordinating their thinking about individuals to a trait type of analysis whereby once a trait is attributed to a person, it is his forever; rather behaviour is regarded as situational and hence subject to changes within the same individual (Briggs, personal communication; Lange, this vol.).

Generally speaking, white agencies in the north have probably over-emphasized Inuit expectations of problems with 'the white man' and ignored Inuit expectations of problems with individual whites. If anthropological analysis has not addressed itself explicitly to this point, it has stressed the primacy of three related values in Inuit society which, taken together, underwrite the importance of *context* in Inuit thinking and behaviour. The first is *deference*, whose place in Inuit culture has been identified by the Honigmanns as behaviour "which includes people being patient with one another, not pressing one another to conform, not trying to change or reform each other, and withdrawing from strong, threatening interpersonal relations" (p. 244). Secondly, value is placed on the *personal autonomy* of others as well as of oneself; Briggs (1968) sees the extension of autonomy to a person as acknowledgement "that one is a person of sense and reason" (p. 49) and, hence, responsible for one's own actions. For example, "No one, even a child, ought to have to explain his actions to anyone unless he chooses to do so, and to inquire is to interfere. 'Why?' is the rudest of questions; it has, not surprisingly, a critical, even hostile, connotation which may be translated as 'What on earth do you mean by doing (or thinking) a thing like that!'" (p. 53). The third value, *flexibility*, is the one which anthropologists have written most about (cf. Honigmann, 1959; Willmott, 1960; Adams, 1971; Burch, 1975; Guemple, 1976). This is perceived as referring not only, or even primarily, to the flexibility of individuals – which is taken care of by the other two values – but to flexibility in social structure and institutions.

These Inuit concepts are the building blocks for Lange's essay (this vol.) on the inapplicability of the textbook notion of role, as being status-derived, to Inuit social relations. For the Inuit base much of their social relations on a consensual role system whereby persons select each other for particular relationships or tasks on the basis of what they know or believe about each other, and not on an *a priori* ascriptive basis.[12] Lange would not deny that consensual role relations, even among Inuit, operate within restrictions set by status. But the interesting point is the broad margins which are allowed in Inuit society for individual and (what Lange calls) "creative" solutions. For example, women usually confide in other women and not in men (status-derived restriction), although not necessarily in women of their own age or from among close kin. A woman seeking a confidante among older women does not necessarily go to her mother; more startling for us, older women may confide in teen-agers who are not their daughters. This relative freedom from ascription has important implications for Inuit leadership – a subject on which almost every anthropologist who has lived with Inuit has something to say. Here I would include another caveat on Lange's behalf: certain Inuit roles are status-derived and, as such, may be expected to carry constant (but still situationally limited) expectations of leadership; the roles of husband and wife are the outstanding examples. But obedience (of the wife) is conceived as voluntary, and leadership (of the husband) as not threatening to personal autonomy (cf. Briggs, 1974).[13]

Returning to the Honigmanns and their notion of tutelage, they see the values that we have described as supporting their claims that Inuit respond well to tutelage. Yet white tutelage is not flexible – either in precept or practice – and repeatedly disregards the values Inuit place on deference and personal autonomy. Rather, white tutelage is a white confrontation to which Inuit respond well only in the sense that their own culture teaches them to avoid confrontations whenever possible. Affronted, they withdraw. It is also important to remember that whites (whose system of learning and expectations we shall describe), if not affronted (in the same way) by Inuit behaviour, are certainly frustrated by it. They regret the attention Inuit give to individual, even idiosyncratic, considerations at the expense of (bureaucratic) rules; for if not the source of autonomy in the white world, the rules both govern and protect the extent to which autonomy is afforded to an individual. Mutual offence, therefore, is the result: Inuk and white each offends the context and meaning which the other gives to the notion of autonomy. There is reason to believe that tutelage relations also lead to a mutual loss of self-esteem. I have dwelt on the metaphoric parent-child relationship of tutelage which catches the asymmetry in white-Inuit relations; Inuit and whites, however, also place another metaphor on their interaction: each is inclined to view the behaviour of the other as childish (Vallee, Briggs, Brody, Lange, and others). The symmetry is one of frustration and non-communication.

In theory, whites 'meet' the Inuit as administrators – the role into which they were trained; and since their administration is designed to work as a bureaucracy, it is more precise to refer to their ideal role as that of the bureaucrat. But in the reality of everyday, whites find themselves in the role of patron as much as of the bureaucrat. The formal sociological separation of these two roles[14] collapses in the circumstances of life in smaller settlements, though in Frobisher Bay, the bureaucratic office (protected and controlled by assistants, secretaries and protocol) is maintained with more success. This disjunction between theory and practice, out of which occurs a hybrid, what we may call the *bureau-patron* role, is a constant source of uneasiness and ambiguity among whites especially, and of misunderstandings between them and the Inuit. Are the Inuit wards of the white bureaucrats or clients of white patrons? When are they the one and when the other? What happens when Inuit select the patron-client, and whites the bureaucrat-ward relationship on the same occasion (each with its own system of deference and reward)?

One reason for the intrusion of the patron role is that Inuit look for patrons in their relations with whites. But from the white point of view, it is often the wrong person who is approached; for in the white role system, status, and not trust (or simply familiarity), is the criterion of selection. One of two things can then happen, and in both cases there are stressful implications: the white may refuse to help, and his explanations as to why he cannot help are likely to be resented. Or he does help, assuming a patron role, in which case he is likely to be accused by another white of ''meddling'' (see Lange and Riches, this vol.). It is important to notice how the notion of meddling is, itself, differently perceived in the two cultures. Among whites it refers to action taken *without* status legitimation, whereas among Inuit it is when a person acts only on the assumption of a status-derived role that he is liable to be rebuked for meddling in the personal autonomy of another. However, there is also the obligation in the Inuit code to respond to requests for help regardless of who makes them, and a refusal to help can bring as much scorn on a person as meddling (Lange, this vol.).

An empirical consequence of these opposing points of view about meddling is that whites and Inuit frequently find themselves in situations where minimization of strain for one of them occurs at the cost of heightened strain for the other. It is also likely (though empirically, one is on less firm ground here) that whites are more troubled by the ambiguities they experience in this way than are Inuit. Operating with a bureaucratic learning system, which is a 'rule' system, whites expect Inuit to learn it also and to abide by it: when this does not happen, the whites are left relatively helpless. By contrast, the important place that context has in the learning system (and hence the system of expectations) of the Inuit helps to take (for them) much of the sting out of ambiguity (cf. Briggs, 1976).

Why, then, do whites get involved in patron roles with Inuit when to do so today can have high social costs? We have already suggested that Inuit look for (white) patrons, and that the whites' positive responses are probably conditioned by the desire to be liked by Inuit and by the ambivalence many of them experience as tutors – destroyers at the same time as they are helpers. Other reasons are the competition for power between whites, and the fact that some roles involve the distribution of material resources to Inuit. Whites also expect to be able to conduct bureau-patron roles on their own terms. They are sensitive to Inuit "ingratiation" (Williamson, 1968), and should they feel that they are being 'used' by a client, they may peremptorily break off the relationship. In short, besides getting involved in patron roles, they also move out of them with notable frequency.

Note may well be taken here of Memmi's (1965) delineation of a likely psychodynamic feature of colonial life that faces even Canadians in the far north of 'their' country. He speaks of the "tormented dance" of the colonialist who rejects colonialism, but continues to live in a colony, "resign[ing] himself to a position of ambiguity" (p. 44). This is true of many in the north. Then, Memmi says, there are those who reject colonialism and leave. The north knows them too. Some leave, however, more out of frustration over a system they wish to support than out of ideological protest against it. Even if they are not colonialists in the full sense of the word as used by Memmi, these persons come to the north committed to the idea of tutelage and, once there, fall naturally into a patron role. Realization of being trapped in this role causes them to leave eventually: such was the case with Travis, the Settlement Manager (Administrator) who is the subject of Brody's essay (this vol.). The trap was set by two interlocking pairs of contradictions. The first pair focussed upon Inuit expectations: they expected Travis to behave like a (benevolent) patron, but they also expected (on the basis of government statements) decision-making to be increasingly handed over to them. The second pair of contradictions centres around Travis' own expectations of and performances in a patron role, and the restrictions placed upon him by government regulations – regulations that were also seen by the Inuit as obstacles to the promised government programme of local development. In sum, Travis faced his Inuit public in the hybrid bureau-patron role which left him caught between local (Inuit) demands, his own sense of what was best, and government regulations.

From the Inuit point of view, the present situation is a deteriorating one on at least two accounts: on the one hand, the turn-over of white personnel (see Ch. 3) makes it harder, if not impossible, to build up a relationship with a white on the basis of what one has observed of his behaviour; on the other hand, the degree of specialization or compartmentalization of white administration today, even at settlement level, forces upon Inuit, as they perceive it, the need for several patrons. In sum: the situation forces upon them contradictions of their own (Inuit) role system. At the same time, contradictions in the application of the bureaucratic system are becoming more evident to Inuit as their opportunities (through travel and the media) to compare conditions in different settlements increase. Both Brody and Riches cite examples of this; Riches' essay on the co-operative at Port

Burwell suggests how Inuit knowledge of (what amounts to) idiosyncratic rulings by whites, or what is meant to be 'the rule,' can buttress belief in the necessity of following a patron-client ideology in their dealings with whites. Variations in the welfare officer role are more likely to be thought of as variations in the good will of the individual welfare officers than in Ottawa-made rules (Briggs, personal communication): this leaves one to speculate whether such observations and deductions of the Inuit lead them to conclude, privately, that whites are Inuit 'under the skin' after all?

What now remains is to single out from this rather discursive discussion of differences between Inuit and white systems of behaviour the one from which most of the others are derived; it is, I think, that the Inuit social system is characterized by corrective learning and the white as much by the opposite process of self-validation (Bateson, 1968; cf. Paine, 1976). Ecologic studies of Inuit culture have always stressed the adaptive process that I call here corrective learning. For example, Gubser (1965:22) observed that "as a Nunamiut accumulates experience, he gradually modifies his conceptions about the nature of the environment." The same process has been observed in Inuit camp and settlement life (Willmott, 1960; Lange, 1972). My suggestion is that it may also characterize the way Inuit attempt to handle their 'white environment'; that is, the way Inuit stalk their prey, all the while taking account of precise contextual information (Laughlin, 1968), may be considered as a metaphor for the Inuit model of conducting relations with individual whites and white culture. Inuit 'stalk' whites.

The limitations that we are able to recognize in this metaphor should also be of help to us. Gubser, Laughlin and others demonstrate that the way Inuit handle information about the natural environment is functionally adaptive: the hunters' information-gathering provides a basis for predictions, and in this sense the hunters exercise control. But the first limitation in the usefulness of our metaphor is that in their relations with whites, Inuit, even though they attempt to apply principles of corrective learning, find many of the factors determining white behaviour hidden from view. Thus, Inuit are denied the 'control' (in the sense of ability to make predictions about others' behaviour) they seek. Similarly, the learning processes in the hunt bring the Inuit 'closer' (metaphysically as well as physically) to the animal on which they depend; but can the same be said of Inuit learning about whites? Indeed, when that does happen, one can again question whether Inuit corrective learning, in this context, *is* functionally adaptive.

Turning to the white system of behaviour, I start with the general assumptions that (a) white roles in the north are bureaucratically conceived, and (b) this bureaucratic system of relations leaves little place for corrective learning. All the evidence at hand supports both assumptions. A status-derived role system governs the lives of the whites in so many ways that there is little or no *legitimacy* for social action on an inductive basis, or in response to personal experience in local conditions. There is, of course, particularistic behaviour among whites – in their patron role, for instance – but it occurs *despite* the system; this being so, the possibility of its transformation into new but institutionally-acceptable behaviour is always minimal. On the other hand, the kind of sanction that may be brought down locally upon a non-conformist (without it being commanded by superiors outside the settlement) is fully supportive of the system and has manifest self-validating implications. The non-conformist is likely to be declared "bushed" (see Koster and Riches, this vol.). "A White is bushed when he lives in the settlement but not actively within the White community" (Brody, 1975:57). A bushed person is said to be tired when he withdraws from company (Briggs, personal communication). Another symptom is one's (alleged) neglect of personal or household hygiene. In fact, a white may be judged bushed because he caused confrontations among his fellow whites; or (here the language of the social logic behind witchcraft accusations seems appropriate) accusations of meddling may precede a verdict of bushed. But the most serious misdemeanour associated with a bushed person is his seeking the social company of Inuit; far from changing the diagnosis that this person is tired, it is taken as the decisive confirming symptom.[15]

This last point also offers the strongest clue regarding the forces behind the system of sanctions in which the charge of bushed, while dramatic, is, after all, a predictable feature. The whites live in a "total institution" situation (Goffman, 1961), in which they draw a tight circle around themselves and exclude non-whites: self-validation as opposed to learning. In these circumstances, exclusion by a fellow-white, or even worse, inclusion of Inuit within the circle is gravely disturbing. Such an offence can be met only by the exclusion of the offender. Moreover, by passing its verdict of 'bushed' on non-conformists, the white community confirms (tautologically) that there is only one possible mode of behaviour. What one might call the failure rate of the system is thereby disguised. For it is the ejected individuals (bushed persons are usually sent south) who fail, and not the system.

Tradition and Ambiguity

> "The colonizer who accepts his role tries in vain to adjust his life to his ideology. The colonizer who refuses, tries in vain to adjust his ideology to his life. ... The most serious blow suffered by the colonized is being removed from history and from the community."
> *Memmi* (1965:45, 91).

"Tradition" and "ambiguity" recur in much of what I have had to say about the subjective meanings of Inuit-white relations, and in conclusion I want to gather together such insights as may have come from these two notions.

Tradition. Ortega y Gasset once wrote of culture as not what is given but what is sought; similarly, Inuit use tradition not so much to explain what was, but as a means of coming to terms with the present and the future, over which they otherwise have little control. The Inuit are a people under a state of siege, culturally and socially. Much of what was once theirs by history and custom is nowadays irrelevant; yet they do not simply abandon their past: they 're-write' it. For example, the Inuit capacity for flexibility, which has caught the attention of anthropologists, can be seen as assisting them along their path to modernity. It also says something important about how they handle tradition. In the customary historical sense, there is not one traditional Inuit community in all of the Arctic today, and yet tradition is a potent force among Inuit in their management of their affairs. Put differently, Inuit, as a group, cannot afford to act as though custom were king. Yet they still manage to keep alive a sense of behaving towards each other as Inuit (cf. Lange, this volume). What they seek is a basis for predictable behaviour among themselves, and secondarily with the whites. It is this – the maintenance of predictable behaviour – that is surely one of the important sociological functions of tradition. The case of the Inuit, then, shows that it is not least in 'non-traditional' times, when so much is changing, that tradition becomes important. In short, Inuit use tradition as an instrument in their subjective presentation of their culture (cf. Arima, 1976).

Among Inuit, one senses cultural forces at work expressing tradition-in-change (as well as changes in tradition). This is absent among the whites; instead, the dominant impression is of cognitive disjunction, amounting even to contradictions, between tradition (of the north – whether white or Inuit) as one separate matter and progress as another. Tradition is relevant only for what it tells of the past as something that has been left behind. For example, whites make a crude distinction between Eskimos now and Eskimos before; whites themselves become "old-timers" just three or four years after arrival, and there is no feeling of kinship with their white predecessors. By handling tradition in this way, discontinuities are forced between the past and present that can exacerbate tensions and ambiguities in the present (whereas the Inuit handling of tradition reduces their likelihood). Here, then, it is individuals who come to find themselves under a state of siege, and not their culture itself – that is 'secure' in the south. Yet, many whites feel that their southern culture is inadequate for the situation in which they find themselves. Many have begun to ask themselves why they are there – even while knowing that the answer is likely to involve them in a kind of betrayal. Though members of a culture that prevails over the Inuit in so many ways, whites find themselves without legitimate recourse to a re-interpretation of the public role of their culture in the north: but a re-interpretation is necessary for many of them, if they are to reconcile their lives in the north.

Ambiguity. I turn now to the place that ambiguity has had in the analysis.[16] Many of the problems encountered in arctic settlements surely stem from the paradox that the whites there are not living in 'white' communities, but that the Inuit are. While this statement exaggerates, distorts and simplifies, I believe it points to one of two major sources of ambiguity among whites and Inuit; the other is the colonial roles of whites and Inuit, which I have tried to express figuratively through the nanny metaphor. The nanny and child roles are put upon grown-up men and women – not merely by the caprice of the present writer, but also by the demands of the colonial encounter. The disjunctions noticed between whites' private and public lives and the artificiality of their public norms – around which ambiguity grows – are themselves traceable to the assumption of a nanny role. Their casting in a child role would have similar consequences for the Inuit, were it not for their cultural defences in this regard.

We should clarify our use of the term ambiguity by distinguishing between misunderstanding and ambiguity, proper (Briggs, personal communication). Misunderstandings arise in situations where two or more individuals, or groups, each interpret differently the 'same' (by external criteria) message or event (cf. Shibutani, 1966). Those concerned may, therefore, come to be at cross-purposes. This situation, however, is different from one in which the *same* individual or group suffers from the ambiguity – in the strict sense – resulting from two or more equally strong, different interpretations of one message or event.

Misunderstandings may occur in the normal course of events among either Inuit or whites, but it is their repeated occurrence in Inuit-white interaction that catches our attention. There is no better example than the one provided by the Honigmanns (1965:244) in their insightful description of Inuit withdrawal from white employees:

"Withdrawal may strike a Euro-Canadian as more abrupt than it is ... Exaggerating the Eskimos' degree of commitment, Euro-Canadians fail to see disenchantment and resistance build up. Instead of politely protesting or declining with a conventional excuse when he seeks to withdraw, the Eskimo evinces little show of protest at all. As a result, an employer doesn't know how deeply an Eskimo employee is offended, or how far he has transgressed on the Eskimo's feelings."

A misunderstanding such as this seems to imply an incapacity in one party (or both) to understand the metacommunication of the other; the misunderstanding also appears to be genuine, rather than intended. Even so, there will be instances when 'misunderstanding' is put to tactical service, and the suspension of communication at the meta-level is contrived. This has been noted in the cross-cultural literature almost exclusively as a tactic of the politically weaker group in confrontation situations. In the Arctic, it is true of the Inuit sometimes, but the device is also used by whites. Confronted by a role system different from their own, both whites and Inuit can fall back on a position of apparent lack of comprehension of the others' behaviour. In this way, misunderstanding is used as an alternative to direct confrontation in difficult situations.

Alternatively, misunderstandings may be suppressed. Thus, a discredited group may put to tactical service the discrediting image in which it is held by a politically stronger group: the weaker group affirms by its behaviour that the stronger group is right, and the 'misunderstanding' between them is suppressed by the weaker group. We find this in the following interpretation of a fairly common pattern of behaviour among Canada's native peoples: "Native people have had imposed on them the lazy-drunk image. This image has its practical uses in that it allows a native person to opt out of the tensions of the cultural shock he is experiencing, without having to explain to himself or his employer the tension he feels" (Petrie, 1974:2). The delicateness of the difference between this situation and that of withdrawal (by the Inuit) as depicted by the Honigmanns, begins to emerge: "Cultural differences in attitudes towards work and in social interaction with non-native workers creates tensions which the native worker is unable to relieve. Being unable to cope he engineers his own dismissal, thus conforming to a self-image created for him" (Petrie, *ibid.*). Among the costs to a native person of choosing to reject the image (lazy/drunk) imposed upon him is that he is then least able to hide from himself his disadvantaged status: for here the weaker is raising a misunderstanding with the stronger.

Although ambiguity, in the strict meaning we speak of, appears within an individual or group, its occurrence can be directly related to misunderstandings. A good example is white-Inuit interaction through the bureau-patron role (misunderstandings), and the problems which it presents separately to whites and Inuit (ambiguities).

For reasons that were raised in our discussion of white and Inuit systems of learning and expectations, it is likely that ambiguity *per se* is a greater problem among whites than among Inuit. The whites' situation, furthermore, is made more problematic, more ambiguous, because of their living on the margin of their own (southern) culture and in a colonial role; that is, in the capacity of both givers and takers. It was noticed (following Brody, 1975) how the all-white parties, which are sometimes held in northern settlements, serve to validate white culture for the whites. At the same time, however, the parties can sow a seed of ambiguity among whites.

"Only rarely did I see local Eskimos at these events," reports Brody (p. 64). Now, for whites, the unwritten but blatant assumption of social 'apartheid' between themselves and Inuit is a symbol of the natural order of tutelage; but at the same time, it can confront them with their own moral double-standard. There is no ready solution: the ambiguity cannot be pushed to the perimeter of the group (as Inuit are, and as bushed whites are) and made a boundary-marker (cf. Douglas, 1966; Leach, 1964), for here it is the group itself that is ambiguous. In this kind of situation, the "self-validating" defences of the white enclave society, by which non-conformity is regarded as deviance, are penetrable.

This suggests that ambiguity in a colonial situation is especially likely to occur when one or both sides are aware of their involvement in the maintenance of the other's illegitimate position (see discussion of colonialism; p. 1, above). Our data have shown this to be true of the whites (and I suppose this to be a likely development in any welfare-colonial situation): as colonizers they have become increasingly aware of how they devaluate the colonized, the Inuit. This tends to produce among the whites themselves a sense of self-devaluation, ushering in one of the paradoxes of welfare colonialism in the north. As they become more aware that 'colonial' behaviour conflicts with white (Euro-Canadian) egalitarian philosophy, so they realize that their position is one in which the more they succeed, the more they fail. Regarding the Inuit, it may be a case of the weak finding some measure of protection through the confusion of the strong, and we ask: what else, besides Inuit-white misunderstandings and the ambiguities that whites suffer among themselves, stands between the Inuit and their ethnocide?

NOTES

1　Briggs (personal communication) stresses how the lover, as a 'controller', can use his/her 'concern' as an excuse for interfering in the beloved's life.

2　Because of the difficulties, white administrators have begun to delegate to selected Inuit some of the work in distributing welfare cheques, in particular, the first screening of applicants.

3　"For example, the settlement-house-user may come to use the athletic equipment, but he will simultaneously resist efforts [that] make him act in middle-class ways" (Gans, 1962:144).

4　White avoidance behaviour regarding Inuit is not necessarily deliberate, but just a fact of life: Koster (1972:149) reports how the wife of a government department head in Frobisher Bay took the trouble to attend an Eskimo language course; when the instructor told the class to practise speaking with Inuit, she exclaimed, "but I don't know any Eskimos!"

5　It is possible that this behaviour is symptomatic of welfare colonialism. In Tunisia where the colonizers had no welfare mission, this behaviour seemed to be out of the question. Instead, efforts were made to increase "the distance which colonization places between [the colonizer] and the colonized," whose position was "degraded" and made "despicable," (Memmi, 1965:54–55).

6　Lantis (1968:578) believes that "today the important environmental stresses come from the social rather than the physical environment, since technology ameliorates the effects of climate and other physical factors.'' Although basically in agreement, I am uneasy with this formulation lest it draw attention away from the fact that the 'removal' of climate and the physical environment by technology produces its own set of problems (social and mental). In other words, effects from the physical environment are still evident, though they may be different from what they were in earlier times.

7   The stressful features of white-white relations in a colonial situation have been investigated in this book (by Koster, and Riches). The assumption is that characteristics of spaceship living are generated by the colonial situation of which the disjunction between public and private norms (in this extreme form) is itself taken to be a symptom. The alternative, that clique-formation is an *inevitable* consequence of spaceship living, whether or not there is a colonial situation, has not been examined.

8   Both Riches and Lange (whose material is incorporated by Riches) found only two cliques, at any one time, in the settlements where they lived. More comparative data are needed before drawing any conclusions on the number of cliques in small settlements.

9   In Frobisher Bay, whites' opinions about Inuit are less uniform than they are in the smaller settlements, and opinions about white policy towards the Inuit can be markedly divergent (though usually only expressed within clique boundaries).

10   There is still important work to be done on the meaning and tolerance, as well as distribution, of friendship among whites-in-the-Arctic.

11   Briggs (1976) describes one of the numerous ''games'' by means of which Inuit teach their children appropriate interpersonal motivations and values, and by which they continually test their progress toward the achievement of emotional control. She quotes one mother as saying: ''A person who can't control himself isn't worthy to live.''

12   Among sources which support Lange's thesis and which illustrate its relevance to the meaning Inuit place on kinship, see Guemple (e.g., 1976). For a discussion of consensual role behaviour outside the Inuit culture, see Chiaramonte (1971) and Paine (1975).

13   Having demonstrated how autonomy and consensual relations are both upheld in Inuit society, Lange leaves us wondering about the place of competition, bargaining and secrecy, as well as about the difference between secrecy and privacy in Inuit culture. He suggests that information is ''nearly a free resource''; but here one hestitates to agree with him, for two reasons. First, information may pass from person to person very slowly, or not at all, for fear that the information might threaten the personal autonomy of certain individuals in the community (Freeman, personal communication); in other words, the reason here is not a selfish hoarding of information. But secondly, why is one not to suppose that on other occasions, information *is* hoarded?

14   For a discussion of the bureaucrat role, see Weber (1947) and Etzioni (1964), and for the patron role, Wolf (1966) and Paine (1971).

15   Sociologically, then, a verdict of 'bushed' is quite different from a local diagnosis of cabin fever (see earlier discussion), and much more complex. Sampath (1975) describes conditions of cabin fever from the sociological point of view advanced here. It is not clear to me from Abbott and Kehoe (1972) and Atcheson (1972) what the difference between bushed and cabin fever is in terms of psychiatry. Still needed is research concentrating upon the fact that verdicts of bushed occur in a social context where there are also intra-white cliques and a private set of white norms *contra* the public set.

16   It is appropriate to acknowledge here the help I drew from Memmi's *The Colonizer and the Colonized* when thinking about the place of ambiguity, and in particular of the colonizer, in a colonial situation. (I came to this book from reading Koster, 1972.)

References

ABBOTT, A. P. and J. P. KEHOE
   1972 ''Mental Health Practice in the Yukon.'' *Canada's Mental Health*, XX(1).

ADAMS, C.
1971 "Flexibility in Canadian Eskimo Social Forms and Behaviour: A Situational and Transactional Appraisal." In Lee Guemple (ed.), *Alliance in Eskimo Society*. Proceedings of the American Ethnology Society, University of Washington Press.
1976 "An Assessment of the Reliability of Informant Recall." In Milton M. R. Freeman (ed.), *Inuit Land Use and Occupancy Project*, Vol. 2. Ottawa, Department of Indian and Northern Affairs.

ATCHESON, J. D.
1972 "Problems of Mental Health in the Canadian Arctic." *Canada's Mental Health*, XX(1).

BATESON, GREGORY
1968 Chapters 7 and 8 in J. Reusch and G. Bateson, *Communication: The Social Matrix of Psychiatry*. New York, W. W. Norton.

BOON, JAMES A.
1974 "Anthropology and Nannies." *Man* (N.S.), 9(1).

BRIGGS, JEAN
1968 *Utkuhikhalingmiut Emotional Expression*. Ottawa, Department of Indian Affairs and Northern Development, Northern Science Research Group, 68-2.

BRIGGS, JEAN
1974 "Eskimo Women: Makers of Men." In Carolyn Mathiasson *Many Sisters*. Glencoe, Ill., The Free Press.

BRIGGS, JEAN
1976 "Morality Play: Inuit Style." Paper presented to the American Anthropological Association.

BRODY, HUGH
1975 *The People's Land: Eskimos and Whites in the Eastern Arctic*. Aylesbury, Penguin Books.

BURCH, ERNEST S.
1975 *Eskimo Kinsmen: Changing Family Relationships in Northwest Alaska*. St. Paul, West Publishing Co.

CHIARAMONTE, LOUIS J.
1971 *Craftsman-Client Contracts: Interpersonal Relations in a Newfoundland Fishing Community*. St. John's, Institute of Social and Economic Research, Memorial University of Newfoundland.

DOUGLAS, MARY
1966 *Purity and Danger*. London, Routledge and Kegan Paul.

DUNNING, R. W.
1959 "Ethnic Relations and the Marginal Man in Canada." *Human Organization*, 18(3).

Eskimo
1958 Quarterly Magazine. Churchill, Oblate Fathers of the Hudson Bay Vicariate.

ETZIONI, AMITAI
   1964 *Modern Organizations*. Englewood Cliffs, Prentice-Hall Inc.

FRIED, JACOB
   1963 "White Dominant Settlements in the Canadian Northwest Territories." *Anthropologica*, (N.S.), 5(1).

GANS, H. J.
   1962 *The Urban Villagers*. New York, The Free Press.

GATHORNE-HARDY, J.
   1972 *The Rise and Fall of the British Nanny*. London, Hodder and Stoughton.

GOFFMAN, ERVING
   1961 *Asylums*. New York, Anchor Books.

GUBSER, NICHOLAS J.
   1965 *Nunamiut Eskimos: Hunters of Caribou*. New Haven and London, Yale University Press.

GUEMPLE, D. L.
   1976 "The Institutional Flexibility of Inuit Social Life." In Milton M. R. Freeman (ed.), *Inuit Land Use and Occupancy Project* (vol. 2). Ottawa, Department of Indian and Northern Affairs.

HONIGMANN, J. J. and IRMA HONIGMANN
   1959 "Notes on Great Whale River Ethos." *Anthropologica*, 1.

HONIGMANN, J. J. and IRMA HONIGMANN
   1965 *Eskimo Townsmen*. Ottawa, Canadian Research Centre for Anthropology, Saint Paul University.

KOSTER, D.
   1972 "Ambiguity and Gossip in a Colonial Situation." Unpublished M.A. Thesis, Memorial University of Newfoundland.

LANGE, P. A.
   1972 "Social Flexibility and Integration in a Canadian Inuit Settlement: Lake Harbour, N.W.T." Unpublished M.A. Thesis, University of British Columbia.

LANTIS, MARGARET
   1966 "The Administration of Northern Peoples: Canada and Alaska." In R. St. J. MacDonald (ed.), *The Arctic Frontier*. Toronto, University of Toronto Press.

LAUGHLIN, WILLIAM S.
   1968 "Hunting: An Integrating BioBehavior System and its Evolutionary Importance." In Richard B. Lee and Irven DeVore (eds.), *Man the Hunter*. Chicago, Aldine.

LEACH, E. R.
   1964 "Anthropological Aspects of Language: Animal Categories and Verbal Abuse." In E. J. Lennenberg (ed.), *New Directions in the Study of Language*. Cambridge, Cambridge University Press.

MEMMI, ALBERT
1965 *The Colonizer and the Colonized*. Boston, Beacon Press.
PAINE, ROBERT (ed.)
1971 *Patrons and Brokers in the East Arctic*. St. John's, Institute of Social and Economic Research, Memorial University of Newfoundland.
PAINE, ROBERT
1975 "An Exploratory Analysis in 'Middle-Class' Culture." In E. Leyton (ed.), *The Compact: Selected Dimensions of Friendship*. St. John's, Institute of Social and Economic Research, Memorial University of Newfoundland.
PAINE, ROBERT
1976 "Two Modes of Exchange and Mediation." In Bruce Kapferer (ed.), *Transaction and Meaning*. Philadelphia, Institute for the Study of Human Issues.
PARSONS, G. F.
1970 *Arctic Suburb: A Look at the North's Newcomers*. (Mackenzie Delta Research Project, Bulletin No. 8.) Ottawa, Department of Indian Affairs and Northern Development.
PETRIE, M. K.
1974 "Factors Affecting Native Employment North of '60." Ottawa, Department of Indian Affairs and Northern Development (stencil).
SAMPATH, H. M.
1972 "Migration and Mental Health of the Non-Eskimo in the East Arctic." Paper presented to the Third International Conference on Social Science and Medicine.
SAMPATH, H. M.
1975 "The Bushed Syndrome: Environment and Mental Health in the Canadian Arctic." Paper presented at the Canadian Psychiatric Association Annual Meeting, Banff, Alberta.
SHIBUTANI, TAMOTSU
1966 *Improvised News: A Sociological Study of Rumor*. New York, The Bobbs-Merrill Company, Inc.
VALLEE, F. G.
1962 *Kabloona and Eskimo in the Central Keewatin*. Ottawa, Department of Northern Affairs and Natural Resources, NCRC-62-2.
VALLEE, F. G.
1967 *Povuugnetuk and its Cooperative. A Case Study in Community Change*. Ottawa, Department of Northern Affairs and Natural Resources, NCRC 67-2.
WEBER, MAX
1947 *The Theory of Social and Economic Organization*. London, The Free Press.

WILKINSON, DOUG
1959 "A Vanishing Canadian." *The Beaver*, Spring Volume. Winnipeg, Hudson's Bay Company.
WILLIAMSON, ROBERT G.
1968 "The Canadian Arctic, Sociocultural Change." *Archives of Environmental Health*, 17(4).
WILLMOTT, W. E.
1960 "The Flexibility of Eskimo Social Organization." *Anthropologica*, 2.
WOLF, ERIC
1966 "Kinship, Friendship, and Patron-client Relations in Complex Societies." In M. Banton (ed.), *The Social Anthropology of Complex Societies*. ASA Monograph, No. 4. London, Tavistock Publications.

Some Qualities of Inuit Social Interaction*

Philip Lange

6

INTRODUCTION

The point of departure of this essay is the notion of social flexibility, whose importance in the understanding of Inuit society has already been discussed or noticed by several social anthropologists (Briggs, 1970; Graburn, 1969; Guemple, 1970; Honigmann, 1959; Willmott, 1960). What I want to show is, first, how flexibility as a principle of social action subsumes, at least in the Inuit case, two other crucial notions: creative action and consensual relations. I also want to draw attention to both the deeply-imbedded place that the notion of flexibility has in traditional Inuit culture, and its enduring place as an adaptive and integrative mechanism in contemporary Inuit society. Present-day Inuit society is – even at the level of local settlements – encapsulated in many respects by the society of white North America, and it is largely through their own modes of flexibility that the Inuit are able to retain some 'Inuit' patterns of interaction with each other, thereby maintaining their side of the ethnic boundary that runs between them and the local whites.

My field work at Innarulik impressed upon me the high degree of tolerance the Inuit afford each other regarding dissimilar means of achieving approved ends, as long as the different means are equally effective. Thus, in this essay, "flexibility" refers to the prevalence of situations in which no strong social preference is exerted, or even shown, by the community for any one of several feasible courses of action.[1] As Honigmann (1959:120) noted, flexibility does not suggest complete permissiveness. After all, it is concerned with alternatives of means and not of ends, and therefore does not mean an irregular, haphazard, and unstructured social milieu, as Stevenson (1971:4, 8) believes. Nor should the recognition of the important place of flexibility in Inuit life blind one to the presence of its opposite principle, inflexibility. This is present in a culture whenever it is an indisputable fact that certain behaviour is required and no alternatives are allowed, or when certain behaviour is strongly disapproved of. In the Inuit case, one kind of behaviour which is most commonly and inflexibly rejected is that which would restrict an individual's sense of autonomy.

Willmott (1960), in particular, clarified the effects of Inuit flexibility by

*Excerpted from the author's unpublished master's thesis, "Social Flexibility and Integration in a Canadian Inuit Settlement" (University of British Columbia, 1972), and revised (ed.).

describing specific areas of Inuit culture (family organization, kinship terminology, community organization, and recreation) and the effects of the flexibility observable in the activities of those areas. Beginning with the household, the basic social unit, he notices that the essential needs which it serves (food, sex, emotional support, sleeping space, and so on) are often satisfied elsewhere. There are a wide range of family types, and adoption is an important means of household recruitment. Kinship terminology is frequently non-specific and is more "appropriate to the nature of the personal relationships" between the persons in question than to genealogical position, and that kin terms are used between unrelated people (*op. cit.*:51). Willmott also describes how Inuit community organization has varied from that of small flexible bands without clearly marked leadership, to stable camps with quite powerful leaders, to settlement living without long-term leadership (*op. cit.*:49, 51, 52–4).

The question all this raises for Willmott is the relation between Inuit flexibility in social organization and the integration of the various levels of their society: "For if patterns of behaviour are not standardized as values ..." he asks, "what produces a solidarity and integration in the society, in the local group or in the family?" (*op. cit.*:57).

Inuit adaptation to changing circumstances includes creative action. This aspect of flexibility is of particular concern in this essay and the following proposition is examined: (i) Inuit social flexibility allows/promotes creative action, (ii) out of which arise consensual relations, and (iii) it is upon these consensual relations that the integration of the society endures even in a changing situation. One should add that the operation of the principles of flexibility/creative action/consensual relations, themselves, induce a situation of continuing change at any, or all, levels of Inuit society.

I use the word 'creative' in a rather limited sense as denoting the re-combination of elements already present in a situation (or imposed upon it) into new configurations. My meaning of 'integration' follows that of Landecker (1950:40), who develops Smend's approach to integration as "the constant unification" of the members of a group. When speaking of consensual relations, I have in mind those of mutuality and voluntariness between a particular person and one or several others. As is well-known, it is on this (loosely-termed) individual, as opposed to group, level that Inuit society on the whole demonstrates institutional sophistication and subtlety, and the 'steering' effect of this lower level of relations upon the other will be apparent in several places in this essay.

An implication of my thesis is that among the Inuit there is no interpersonal relationship whose initiation, content, and continuance can be taken for granted – not even that between mother and child, let alone between adults.

Children

Probably the most convincing evidence as to the fundamental value of the consensual mode among Inuit is imbedded in the relations an infant or child has with its mother and other persons. Pre-Christian central Inuit beliefs held that a child in the process of being born sometimes refused to emerge from the womb until its correct name-soul was recognized. With difficult births, the midwife or mother called out the names of various deceased relatives whose souls could be eligible for rebirth. When the correct soul was identified, the child would begin to come out of the womb. Thus, even an individual's identity was not assigned by others but was manifested by the newborn itself (Balicki, 1970:200). In the namesake-giver and -receiver relationship (*saunik*) as described by Guemple (1965), the namesake-giver is chosen by the child's parents before its birth, as is the ritual sponsor (*op. cit.*:469). But the newborn also participates in the relationship: just as the sponsor initiates his relationship with the child by the gift of a layette, so the newborn reciprocates, from the Inuit point of view, by choosing some clothing for his ritual sponsor. Various pieces of clothing are placed near the child and whichever he grabs first is given to the sponsor.

In these ways, the Inuk infant participates socially in its own birth and this first event in its biography is marked by rituals of consensus. Similarly, a mother's love for her child is not a given but depends on whether rapport is established between the two.[2] A mother's love can be adversely influenced by many factors. One of these is separation from the child at birth or soon after, as it is believed that this can prevent a child from arousing love in its mother. Several women at Innarulik each had a child to whom they were apathetic or even hostile. They explained that it was because they and their child had been separated for too long at the hospital. Also, some babies are considered inherently unlovable because of their appearance, voice, or other reasons (Briggs, 1970:317). Once these children begin walking and playing outside, they become objects of pity because of their ragged clothing, their being left outside or without candy and soda-pop treats shared by their siblings. If a white berates a mother who neglects one of her children, she will sometimes answer, "Well, it's like this, I just don't like him!" (*ila! iqianammat*): or literally, "Because he/she arouses disgust in one, really!" Yet, my observations of six such children indicate that they all have harmonious relationships with their peers and with older people: they are open, expressive, and reciprocate socially.

There are several ways in which these children are integrated into the community. One adult may take on a protective and cherishing role, offering the child tidbits of meat, tea and bannock, or affectionate gestures when all the other adults present ignore the child. No one is assigned to do this and as far as I know it is neither approved nor disapproved, but results entirely from the protective feelings aroused by the child (who is able to reject the advances of the adult if it wishes). Such a child may also attract the attention of a protective older child who will make sure the other gets his turn, or he may draw attention to a special ability of the young child, be it singing, animal imitations, dancing, or sexual pantomines, thus securing his share of audience approval. In addition, Innarulik Inuit informally divide themselves into age sets so that all children spend much of their time in the company of their peers – people who will be important to them all their lives.

Adoption, of course, has an important place in Inuit society; it appears that besides children, both adolescents and adults are frequently adopted so that in some Inuit groups, as much as half the population have been adopted in their lives (Guemple, 1970: 18). It is significant that this occurs in a society where all kinship relations have a strong consensual side. On the one hand, kinship (including adoptive kinship) has to be validated through time by personal contact or it ceases to count; a sibling relationship is likely to lapse after a period of about ten years without personal contact, and with distant kin it happens in less time. This is not because a person forgets his kin, but simply "because I have not seen him (her) for a long time": *takqani akuniaaluk takungnginnama.* Guemple (1970:39) says that uncontacted relatives at Great Whale River and the Belcher Islands are called by kinship terms but are not considered real relatives. On the other hand, it is in Inuit society that an adopted person may belong to his new family while maintaining affectionate relations with his (her) natural parents all the while.

The large number of adopted children among the Port Harrison Inuit, "the relative ease with which children are passed from one family to another, and the apparent lack of personality damage to children," led Willmott (1960:57)[3] to wonder how an Inuit child gains his sense of personal identity, and how the child learns to understand his relationships with other persons. The evidence that has been presented here speaks to the existence of a fundamental association of Inuit identity and socialization with consensual relations, beginning at birth. The process is continued into adult life, as I now want to show.

In Work

There are twenty-eight economically active male[4] Inuit at Innarulik: seven are full-time wage-earners – one as an R.C.M.P. constable, two as H.B.C. clerks, and four work for the Department of Public Works (DPW). Two men have regular part-time wage employment, one as caretaker of the school and the other as the Shell Oil agent. The other nineteen men carve, hunt, trap, and take short-term wage labour whenever it is available. This diversity of occupations has not become a vehicle of prestige differences within the Inuit community – even though the men who have regular (full- or part-time) jobs almost always have credit at the Bay, in contrast to those who depend on carving, hunting, and trapping. *Prima facie*, one might suppose the explanation to be that this diversity of occupations is account-able by the Inuit as an artifact of the Euro-Canadian presence in their settlement. Such an explanation is inadequate, however, if one considers the differences in personal style and exploitative strategy *within* the same occupational group, and finds that these differences carry equal prestige as long as they are equally effective. Most striking is the importance attri-buted to competence in hunting: two men who are skilled hunters enjoy equal prestige even though one may be a top-notch carver and the other a poor one.

Two general reflections concerning this attitude should be mentioned before proceeding further with the descriptive material. The first is that it may be missing the point to slot the males of Innarulik into a particular job in an occupational structure. Rather, most of the men distribute their labour in time and space between a number of resources, each man making fine distinctions – that are simultaneously ecologic, economic, and social – with reference to a greater number of alternatives (that is, niches) than ever is apparent to a resident white. In aggregate, the process results in consid-erable overlapping between the occupational programmes of individuals. The second general point is that the notion of prestige appears to be less helpful in understanding Inuit behaviour (both etically and emically) than are the notions of flexibility, consensus, and creativity. I return to this notoriously difficult problem of prestige in the last section of the essay; meanwhile I wish to present more data concerning the domain of work.

On the non-wage labour side of the ecology and economy at Innarulik, my data indicate that the expenses of the skidoo are so high in relation to the returns from the seal skins or fox furs harvested, that hunting and trapping can be considered only as a source of cheap and nourishing meat, and not of cash profit.[5] As a result, a hunter-carver who hunts by skidoo works his way – perhaps slowly, but inevitably – into debt. Eventually his debt will be such that he is denied credit, and then the only way to restore his position is through scarce part-time wage work or by making and selling carvings; these men, then, *carve to hunt*. All but two of the nineteen men mentioned try to resolve the problem in this fashion. The remaining two have made a radical response: they concentrate on carving, only hunting incidentally for meat (for their own consumption) and skins. One might say these men *hunt in order to carve*.

One of the two men who concentrate on carving is a stranger to the area and has no kin in the settlement outside of his household. He specializes in smooth-faced abstract solids with delicate engravings of arctic animals and Inuit in fur clothing. His walrus tusks with engraved hunting scenes are always in demand. One of the best engravers in the eastern Arctic, he finds a ready market for his work at the local H.B.C. store, among the resident whites, and at the co-operative store in Frobisher Bay. He enjoys the few friendships he has with whites, and makes no attempt to sell carvings to private individuals.

The other man who principally carves, and hunts only sporadically, flies frequently between Frobisher Bay and Innarulik to sell his carvings. His wife and children live in Innarulik, participating fully in community life there among their many kinfolk. A flight into the settlement often brings the husband in for a quick visit with his family and a supply of large soapstone lumps from his cache. He returns to Frobisher on the same flight. Alternatively, he will spend a few weeks in Innarulik, socializing, hunting, and carving. His large massive sculptures with rounded forms and little detail are seen as 'real art' by whites, commanding good prices and a ready market at the Frobisher Bay co-operative store. While in Frobisher Bay he lives with kin.

The two men who work part-time, the Shell Oil representative and the school caretaker, both have jobs which pay approximately the same; however, these jobs occupy them but a couple of days each week and for the rest of the time each man pursues his livelihood with a distinctive strategy and style. The responsibilities of the Shell Oil representative are selling gasoline and other fuels, and topping up the stove oil tanks that supply each building. He feels that he should stay fairly close to the community because of his job, and so he does not make as many trips to Frobisher Bay to sell carvings, as other men do; but when he can get away he has many large carvings to take with him. He also puts his other resources, such as available time and cash, to effective use in hunting. A good example of this occurred during a two-week period in which overall, few seals were taken. All of the hunter-carvers were going out daily, but because most of them were already in debt, they went only as far as necessary to get to potentially productive areas. In this way they got in as many trips to the seal grounds as was possible out of their remaining credit. One March morning, the Shell Oil agent left early, and for a long time his tracks were the only ones in the soft deep snow. (The snow discouraged most of the others from going as they were still hunting beside the seals' breathing holes and deep snow made it almost impossible to find the holes, let alone hear the seals come up.) About nine o'clock that evening, the agent returned with five seals – almost as many as had been taken all week by the other men. Having enough cash for a large outlay of gasoline, he headed thirty miles west along the coast to an area much richer in seals than the Innarulik area, where he could hunt by the edge of the sea ice.

The school caretaker, on the other hand, hunts like the other men and frequently takes carvings to the Frobisher Bay co-operative. His uniqueness lies in his behaviour with the whites at Innarulik. Because he has a government job, he considers the white government employees his co-workers and visits them at least one night per week. He seems to enjoy socializing with whites more than most Inuit do. Also, his friends or acquaintances among the whites provide a market for his carvings, which are often quite detailed and greatly admired. Most interesting is the way in which he regularly utilizes the mail, putting his white friends to use as translators and/or helpers, in order to earn money in ways which no other Inuk in the community does. For example, by mailing his skins and furs directly to the fur auctions in southern Canada, he earns twice as much as he would from the H.B.C. Because of his friendship with the whites and because of his liking for dealing through the mail, the area administrator often asks him to carry out special requests arriving from various places, such as that from an Ontario mosquito repellent manufacturer for several barrels of polar bear and seal oil. Some of his contacts also came through his brother who was on the N.W.T. Council.

The job performances of the full-time wage workers are remarkably uniform (and their employers express satisfaction),[6] but there are considerable differences in hunting-trapping and carving skills, and in job utilization. The oldest, steadily employed man is in his late fifties and works on the D.P.W. municipal services crew. He is quite well-off, since his ample income is augmented by his retirement pay from long years of service as a R.C.M.P. special constable. He never carves. A strong and vigorous man, he is so keen on hunting that he sometimes hires another older man to work for a day while he goes hunting and/or checks his trapline. Although his full-time work prevents him from getting as many seals as the full-time hunters, he runs a long trapline (even in poor years) and checks it each Saturday, or during the week if he has hired a replacement for that day. As a result, he ranked twenty-second in terms of the number of seal skins traded and was the second most prolific trapper of foxskins.

This man has two sons who also work on the D.P.W. municipal services crew. The eldest, like his father, does not carve, and he usually hunts on a Saturday. The younger brother, however, both carves and hunts with unusual energy and commitment. He may come home from a full day's work and carve until bed-time. He sells his carvings to the local whites and to the co-operative in another settlement. Because he sets a faster pace and feels held back by frequent tea breaks, he often hunts and travels alone.

There are other examples, but those presented are sufficient to show that Inuit flexibility regarding work demonstrates (1) creativity in the sense of diversity of work modes – or of 'solutions' one might say; and (2) the norm of consensus in that the various solutions of individual Inuit are accepted as legitimate and reasonable by the community. Interesting supportive data are found in friendships between men who visit each other frequently and enjoy each other's company as equals. I can think of six cases in which a man has a different occupational arrangement and material standing from those of his friend. For example, one man possesses a large, new outboard motor and a new skidoo, and a carpet, console stereo, and washing machine in his home, while his friend has but an old outboard motor, an old skidoo, and only the furnishings given everyone by the government. But in all six cases, the friends are reasonably proficient hunters. The lesson here is that adequate hunting ability qualifies a man for egalitarian friendship with men who are more prosperous than he.

Dissemination of Information

In matters concerning ecology and economy at least, information among the Inuit at Innarulik is nearly a free resource. It seems to be offered without a return appearing necessary, but in fact, the recipient makes available such information as subsequently comes his way. The following incident, recorded when I was accompanying a man on a spring seal hunt is an example of Inuit 'good form': "[My friend] had just entered an area of cracked ice (where seals are likely to be found) when he saw someone skinning a seal. We went over and were soon tasting raw tidbits of seal. [My friend] asked if there were any seals around and he was given explicit advice ... in terms of direction and distance ... where there were two groups of seals basking. He set off and he got one from each group ..."

I find this particularly significant in view of several factors. The man who gave the directions had not finished hunting for the day, so that the information he gave to the other hunter reduced the number of seals immediately available to himself. Moreover, the men were hunting primarily for the cash or credit received for the seal skin and only secondarily for some meat. Nor were the men friends (nor opponents wishing to make up). In the days of intensive trapping when people used to live in scattered camps, a free flow of this type of information was likely functionally adaptive, not only for each camp but for each household in a camp; for most game could be hunted with greater effectiveness by more than one man (the exception would be stalking seals basking on the ice), and then it was shared throughout the camp. But today, meat is shared throughout the settlement only when large game (walrus or whale) is taken. Moreover, the hunters see themselves as pursuing with greater difficulty fewer and fewer animals.

Out of the twenty-five households, only one is outside this network of information. In my opinion, the explanation for the persistence of the system has to do with the critical interdependence of Inuit upon themselves as *the* group of social and cultural reference (see later discussion). This has become all the more important and accentuated with the intrusion of whites into their settlements. Thus it is that when an Inuk has to choose between disappointing and even angering a white, or being negatively sanctioned by just one other Inuk, let alone the entire settlement, he will invariably choose the former. For example, when a white asks for a large carving and the carver finds that all his soapstone is too small, rather than borrow stone for this purpose, even from a close relative, he will refuse the request. This situation is maintained in the face of significant material changes in life-style. For one thing, the functional (material) interdependence of all households and individuals has decreased now that food, fuel, and clothes are available through the white agencies in exchange for skins, fur, or labour, or evidence of destitution. Secondly, some Inuit are able to obtain more goods and services from the whites than are others.

There is, then, a strong cognitive interdependence (and hence cum-municative interdependence) among the Inuit even though reasons for a 'functional' interdependence (as perceived, for example, by whites in the settlement) seem less compelling than before, and even though there is now a material differential between them that could be divisive. What is impor-tant to the Inuit of Innarulik is common membership in a moral community; it is the maintenance of its precepts that I want to consider next.

Personal Autonomy

The precepts of the Inuit moral communtiy can be understood in terms of flexibility also. The flexibility principle has a great deal to do with preserv-ing the personal autonomy of the individual. However, Inuit also recognize that they cannot escape dependence on others or the need to assist others who depend on them. Our treatment of autonomy, then, must take into account the value that is placed upon co-operation, which can be under-stood in terms of the distinction that Inuit make between helping and meddling. Meddling is the giving of aid when it is not wanted: it is imposed help; it is not consensual as it is not mutually evaluated. Rather, meddling deprives – or threatens to deprive – an individual of his (her) autonomy and is therefore negatively sanctioned. Helping, on the other hand, is the giving of aid to a person who wishes it; because it is co-operative and consensual it does the least damage to the autonomy of the person requesting the help. Refusal to help is as negatively sanctioned as meddling; gossip, ridicule, and ostracism are, in both cases, the common modes of sanction.

Certain behaviour that has almost no significance by white standards might carry serious overtones of assertiveness and encroachment for the Inuit; for example, sitting too close to the front of a sled when travelling, or walking towards the harnessed dogs are both acts that are likely to be interpreted as attempts to take control of the dog team.[7] Inuit scruples about not helping until receiving a signal for help is something that has been misunderstood, I think, in much of the earlier literature on Inuit (for example, Lyon, 1824:25–6; cf. Briggs, 1970, *passim*). Perhaps a seemingly trivial example from my own field experience will help to illustrate the point. On my first seal-hunting trip, the skidoo pitched over rough shore ice and the towline to the sled broke, leaving the sled and myself stranded. Running up to the rope, I tried to pull the sled towards the smooth ice while my hunting companion just stood watching me ineffectively pull and strain. I smiled in an embarrassed way and continued alone in my vain hauling. Finally I said, "I can't" (*pigunnangngillanga*), at which he instantly grabbed hold. Inuit themselves may signal a request for help – although perhaps it is as much a matter of granting permission to help as requesting help – by making an oblique statement about the difficulty of the task at hand: "because this can make one tired" (*taqanagunnanmat*); or simply by a look right into the face of the other person, perhaps with a lift of the eyebrows (signifying "yes").

Flexibility, as we said at the outset, does not mean complete permissiveness; nor should the important place of flexibility in Inuit life blind one to the presence of its opposite principle. What is important to recognize is that in order to protect the positive value of personal autonomy, the Inuit are inflexible in their rejection and condemnation of meddling. Personal autonomy tempered with interpersonal co-operation is, then, supported through the conceived opposition between helping and meddling.

Now, the value of personal autonomy (with co-operation) is associated with the idea of the community being an open one – not necessarily open to Inuit from elsewhere, but equally open to all Innarulik Inuit. I think it is proper to regard this as a moral value, or as an attribute of the Inuit notion of a moral community; the value of economic behaviour, for example, is made accountable to it. In this connection I was able to recognize two more norms of positive behaviour, namely, interpersonal amiability and the sharing of information. Amiability is supported by a rejection of anger, a characteristic that has been considered at length by Briggs (1970) for the Back River Inuit and that I hope to look into further at Innarulik. My point at present is that amiability is an important, perhaps essential, quality of an open community, and anger has to be rejected as harmful and even destructive to it. For although the flexibility principle, *per se*, can make it easier to cope with anger and enmity, by allowing the 'dropping' of an offending party and taking up with someone else (a common recourse among nomadic Inuit), to do so in a settled community would turn it into something less than an open one, in the sense used above. Similarly, along with the practice of sharing information, there is the inflexible rejection of hoarding information – at least of an ecologic or economic character.

COPING WITH THE WHITES

Next, I want to consider the place of these Inuit principles of social interaction (flexibility/creative action/consensual relations) in Inuit-white relations. Equal account must be taken of the way whites perceive the Inuit and of the way Inuit manage their relations with whites. It is also worth reminding ourselves at the outset that – in the perception each group has of the other – Inuit-white relations have both involuntary and voluntary aspects.

Perceptions

Armed with a reading knowledge based on Farley Mowatt or Peter Freuchen, a typical white arrives in Innarulik anticipating to find a happy, smiling race of Orientals.[8] In addition, the horror stories of the popular press and the warnings of well-meaning friends have him so terrified of the weather that if he arrives in winter, he is sometimes afraid of getting frostbitten while going from the plane to his quarters. The first few days are sometimes spent in fear of a 'whiteout' – intense cold which would restrict him and others to their quarters, leaving him to fend for himself. He realizes that under such conditions, in such cold, if the furnace were to go out, his very life would be in danger. On the other hand, his first few experiences with "the Eskimos" are tantalizingly friendly, his first exploratory smiles and hellos meet with even broader smiles, and a few Inuit point at themselves and say their names. The new white is anticipating to get to know this hardy, friendly race; that they are able to survive in such a climate makes him respect them without ever having known one of them.

Soon, however, he is advised by the other whites that the weather is not all that formidable, and then begins a process of enculturation to the "real way things are up here", or, as Vallee (1967:105) says, the "old Hands" teach the "New Hands." Most of the Old Hands have complete contempt for the Inuit, maintaining that they were once a strong, self-reliant people but now just laze around and try to get welfare; they are considered to be childish and to waste their money on non-essentials such as candy and pop. Furthermore, many Old Hands consider "Eskimos" dishonest, recounting stories of broken trust, hard-driven bargains, and other alleged betrayals. Now the New Hand begins to wonder if he had figured out the "Eskimos" correctly. But whatever his decision regarding his relations with them, he now knows that he will only be silenced for expressing positive attitudes towards them, for there are sure to be Old Hands present who, with their greater experience, are only too willing to correct his ignorance. One thing is certain: whereas before he expected only good from Inuit, he is now alerted to negative qualities as described by the Old Hands.

For the Inuit, by contrast, there are many different kinds of white men, not just in terms of their work (or lack of it: some are obviously rich although they do very little work), but also in their personalities; some are always laughing, joking, and enjoy dancing, whereas others are gruff and never happy, and some are generous while others are stingy beyond belief –

especially since they obviously have more than they need. The various adventures with these strange men furnish many stories that are heard by children who, up to a certain age, have seen the white man only from the safety of their mother's parka hood. By the time the child has reached the age when he (she) must have dealings of his own with whites, he possesses an extensive body of folklore on the subject. It is important to remember that, whereas a white typically begins interacting with Inuit with little prior knowledge of them, any Innarulik Inuk does so as part of a group which has had critically important economic and social dealings with whites for at least a hundred years. Traditionally, the H.B.C. store was the place where Inuit encountered whites. They came into the settlements from their camps, where only fellow Inuit were seen and where only their own language was spoken. Although the whites were often frightening, what could not be disregarded was that they had control of the trade goods which the people had to have. Whites were frightening because they got angry easily, and they were all very strong-willed and had to have their own way: in fact, they all had the bad characteristics of children.

So we see that members of each culture perceive the other's behaviour as childish. The Inuit are quite frank on this score and have freely admitted to various investigators that they felt this way (Rasmussen, 1931:128; Briggs, 1970). On the other hand, I heard only one white openly say that he considered "Eskimos" childish, and yet this idea was implicit in much of what was said about them. Whites frequently said that Inuit were improvident, lacked a sense of time, lacked foresight, were self-centred, and cruel to each other and to animals.

To be more precise, Inuit were seen to exhibit a syndrome that can be described as that of "cunning children": improvident and careless, and always looking for an opportunity to take advantage of the white man. These sentiments were expressed with bitterness or anger by seven of the twelve agency whites who were stationed at Innarulik at some point during my stay there; only four of them ever expressed any positive evaluation of the Inuit (one expressing both views). It is possible that the term "childish," or something akin to it, was avoided because it could be construed as racist; also, my presence as a student who was not obligated to any of the agencies might have made them cautious.

Behind the tendency for members of the two cultures to regard each group as childish, there are significant differences in the way each culture handles relations across the ethnic boundary. The whites of Innarulik, for their part, frequently rejected – typically after only a few months' acquaintance – the Inuit as a whole, considering them to be a people not deserving respect: any one fault in an individual Inuk seemed to disqualify him from being appreciated by the whites. One well-thought-of (by whites) Inuk did something that left his behaviour open to several valid alternative interpretations; from that moment he was judged as avaricious, and more to the point, this instance was used as proof that "You just can't trust these Eskimos."

By contrast, the Inuit attempt to hold in check any stereotypic characteristics when dealing with individual whites. Indeed, the criteria that Inuit use to judge local whites seem to be consistent with those they use when judging other Inuit. It is even hard to say whether the cultural standards they apply to whites are different from those applied to unknown or unrelated Inuit, or to those Inuit considered a bit odd and potentially frightening or dangerous if not treated delicately. At all events, there is certainly no evidence from Innarulik that Inuit there have a group stance *vis-à-vis* whites as individuals.

In accordance with this behaviour, then, Inuit avoid (that is, postpone) close relations with a white who is a newcomer to the settlement until he has been there long enough for them to learn what kind of person he is. As he becomes known, individual Inuit will come to know whether, and on what basis, they can interact with him. It would almost certainly be a dyadic relationship, *on the basis of a dyadic mutual consensus, and not in terms of the occupational role of the white.*

An indication of the prevalence and importance of this kind of relationship among Inuit is seen in the fact that despite years of contact with different varieties of agency personnel, Inuit frequently take their problems to the white whom they know best rather than to the agency representative responsible for dealing with that particular problem. For example, people came to me with problems about their children's schooling or about lumber owned by the government. Those Inuit who liked the H.B.C. manager went to him for treatment of fairly serious injuries; yet he had little more than a first-aid kit whereas the acting nurse had an extensively equipped office. By going to the person whom they preferred, Inuit were clearly functioning within a dyadic consensual framework and not within a role framework.

Communication

The individual Inuk depends little on special information extracted from whites. For one thing, a white who has any information he considers of vital interest to Inuit usually calls a meeting; for another, if a white passes on information personally, it is likely to spread rapidly among the Inuit. Thus the opportunity to trade furs, skins and carvings, to perform wage labour, and to collect social assistance almost never depends on privileged information.

By contrast, whites depend on information obtained from individual Inuit for even a minimal performance of their jobs, and certainly for job promotion. For example, the Settlement Manager must know the people well enough so that he can make decisions concerning social assistance allotments and work assignments. It would be a poor H.B.C. manager who was not aware of alliances and divisions within the community, as well as of everyone's economic potential, reliability on the job, and other such traits. The missionary should know the spiritual and carnal histories of his parishioners.

The H.B.C. manager and the R.C.M.P. have Inuit assistants: a chief clerk and special constable, respectively, who speak good or excellent English. What is important is that each is likely to stay in his job over the years while his white superior frequently gets transferred or leaves. The assistants, then, are able to supply the new man with such information as helps him fulfill his job almost immediately upon arrival. However, the white who does not keep up good relations with his assistant soon finds that important information source drying up. With the exception of the H.B.C. chief clerk and the R.C.M.P. special constable, Inuit definitely avoid giving information to little-known whites even about something as apparently innocuous as the weather.[9]

Individual whites who want information about people usually carry on in the manner of anthropologists: they are friendly and good to the people, attempt to joke, and to show themselves as good fellows. Yet anyone who acts like this is only doing as have dozens of whites before him, and it would be strange if Inuit – who are such perceptive observers of behaviour – did not realize what was going on. These data-seeking activities are carried out on a personal, rather than group level.

One common information-eliciting device, in particular, misfires when applied to Inuit. It is the trading of gossip – general information and personal details of one's own and others' lives (Paine, 1967) – as a sign of rapport. On the assumption that the same process 'works' among Inuit, many whites advance information of the type that *they* want reciprocated. Thus, a teacher who wanted information on marriage and morals told a young Inuk about the conditions upon which young whites sleep together and then paused, waiting for his friend to reciprocate. There was no response. He went on to relate the history and decline of arranged marriages and again paused, again in vain. The usual reaction of an Inuk to these pointed revelations is an embarrassed silence, with avoidance of eye contact.

Occasionally, a white offers an Inuk information as a token of friendship and indication of trust. However, such information never concerns another white who is part of the settlement situation, or who could possibly become part of it. This 'white rule,' as we might call it, applies as equally to one's enemies and opponents among the whites as to friends and supporters. A definite barrier is raised here which attempts to shut out Inuit from even apparently innocuous information about whites. This barrier has much to do with the white expectation that Inuit as a group are not worthy of respect and trust; as a stereotypic expectation it is justified, or fulfilled, by actions on the part of Inuit which the whites consider unethical. In fact, Inuit are criticized for behaving in many of the same ways that the whites do: trying to get as much as possible out of their transactions (in cash, goods, or services), drinking, committing adultery, and so on. As part of the maintenance of this boundary, whites themselves expect each other "to refrain from excessive drinking, overt sex play with Eskimo women, swearing, off-colour stories, and so on *in front of the Eskimos*" (Vallee, 1967:105; emphasis added). Local whites also cooperate in trying to prevent any of their number from forming friendships or romantic ties with Inuit.

Thus, should any Inuk and white become friends, they are likely to face not only the run of misunderstandings arising from cultural differences between them, but also the prejudice of the white community as well (cf. Brody, this vol.). As the prejudice feeds on the misunderstandings, so these are treated by the local whites (in general) as supportive proof that "You just can't trust those Eskimos." Once more, then, we find the whites building up their own expectations of mistreatment by Inuit.

There are also Inuit-white misunderstandings that follow from simple breakdowns in cross-cultural communication outside the field of friendship. Genuinely painful crises occur on both sides. One example would be when a baby dies and the Inuit feel that the whites (perhaps particular agencies) did not take care of it, while the whites feel that the baby's parents were criminally negligent. Other crises in Innarulik that left one or both parties mystified or bitter stemmed from teaching the children American Indian myths: the teacher was completely unaware of the resentment felt by the children's parents. On the other hand, the effort to initiate a swimming programme often left the teacher resentful: although the children were interested, they "forgot" to come. (Their parents were worried about drownings and prevented them from attending.)

Another factor reinforcing the boundary between whites and Inuit, besides white deprecation of Inuit, is the 'missionary' stance commonly taken by whites. Vallee (1967:129) notes from Keewatin that almost all whites see their self-imposed role and image as working to "change at least some features of Eskimo behaviour and bring them into line with his or her conception of the desirable person." At Innarulik this role was unquestionably accepted by eleven of the twelve agency whites; only one seemed to be sufficiently uncertain about such efforts to talk about his doubts. As already noted, there is a reciprocal force towards boundary-maintenance on the Inuit side, based on their sentiments of interdependence as members of a moral community.

CONFRONTATIONS AND INTEGRATION

In conclusion, I shall look at some situations of confrontation involving the Inuit of Innarulik for elements of consensus and personal autonomy in their behaviour even when under duress or when faced with disagreements among themselves. It is also in this context that questions of leadership and prestige may be usefully broached. By this route we reach the conclusion we began with: that through consensual relations the integration of Inuit society endures even in a changing situation.

Confrontation with Government

Sometimes, Innarulik Inuit confront a government official who has flown into the settlement to present a plan (or a change in the procedures of an agency). Typically, he arrives with a plan that has already been formulated by his superiors, believing that he needs only the tacit approval of Inuit – about which there should be no problem. Such was the belief of the government co-operative organizer who, soon after arriving, came to ask a favour: would I mind helping to get the co-operative started; it would simply be a matter of working a couple of hours a month? (It was because of my experience in trying to establish fishing co-operatives in Brazil that he felt that I would be useful.) I agreed, and he requested that I come to the meeting that afternoon in the schoolhouse.

Only two other white people were present at the meeting: the area administrator and the co-operative organizer himself. There were two 'groups' of Inuit: the five members of the co-operative committee and those who performed municipal services for the D.P.W. The translator was the chief clerk at the H.B.C. Several Inuit present belonged to both groups. The government official began by explaining what he had been doing and why he had been delayed in coming to see them about the co-operative which they wanted to start. The Inuit committee head thanked him for coming and said that they still wanted to have the co-operative. Then the government official explained that I would be available to help both them and the government with matters that could be handled by mail. This announcement was met with blank faces.

Next he told them that the first problem in starting the co-operative would be to get the initial capital, but his chief had thought of a very wise plan and now he wanted to know what they thought of it. It would work like this: the government would give the co-operative the lump sum that paid the yearly salaries of all the D.P.W. municipal service workers. Carvings would be bought from the people with this money and then sold to distributors; thus the money would be used twice, both to give the co-operative its initial capital and then to pay the salaries of the D.P.W. workers. He quoted the lump sum available in this way and asked the Inuit what they thought of the idea.

After a silence of about a minute, the youngest Inuk there (except for the translator) said in his own language "perhaps it's not enough." The others said "perhaps so" and began calculating the sum of their yearly earnings. In the midst of the discussion, the official asked the translator what was being said. He did not reply until several men each summed up their incomes and compared them with the sum being offered – which was about three-fourths of what they earned. With agreement among the Inuit the translator said, "Oh, they say it's not enough, that they all together earn [X] amount." The official then asked each Inuk what he earned and calculated his own total. They were right. He said, "Well, uh, I don't feel it's right to lower your men's wages. I'll have to talk this over with my supervisor and contact you as soon as it's straightened out." He asked if there were more questions. There were none and he adjourned the meeting.

This example shows how ably Inuit improvise strategy in an egalitarian manner and without leadership, a process which constantly occurs while men are hunting. Present at the meeting were the Inuit heads of the community council and the Innarulik Housing Association, another man considered by the whites as the Inuit leader, and another who could be outspoken in public meetings. Yet none of these attempted to influence the others, none took initiative, no one was asked what he thought, or was in any other way consulted. The young man who first mentioned that the lump sum was perhaps too small is well-liked by all, but is certainly not a leader. One should also note that the interpreter kept silent, on his own understanding of the situation, until a consensus had been reached among the men, despite pleas for translation by the official.

Confrontation with "Eskimoness"

So often I heard Inuit children jeer at another child who had dirty ears, saying in English "He *very* dirty, *very* Eskimo"; or they would ridicule a child who said *puua* instead of "four": "He *very* stupid, *very*, *very* Eskimo." One is led to consider what the likely implications would be of deprecatory behaviour among members of one's ethnic group. This is another topic for further study. Meanwhile I draw attention to the following two alternative and opposing modes of explaining group membership. The one is that an Inuk orients his behaviour to a generalized Inuit group so that if he rejects "Eskimoness," it means that he will ignore those who persist in embracing Inuit values. Guemple (1970:186–90) and Lubart (1969:42–5) say that this has already happened with many Inuit women who yearn for a Euro-Canadian lifestyle through unions with white males.

The other explanation is the one followed in this essay; namely, that Inuit integration is maintained through mutually consensual dyadic relationships. This being so, it is likely that an Inuk could reject some characteristics of "Eskimoness" and still participate fully in long-term reciprocal relationships with other Inuit (cf. Kleivan's discussion of Greenland, 1969–70). These persons would constitute his reference group. I see much to support this view even in the behaviour of the girls in Innarulik and Frobisher Bay who sought white boyfriends and husbands. They reject Inuit clothing (in favour of American Indian or Euro-Canadian dress), arranged marriages, and much correct Inuit behaviour besides. Yet they still take pride in speaking their language on occasion, frequently visit friends and relatives – including some who are "traditionalists," and they also exchange work and food with those Inuit they like. Unlike Guemple and Lubart, I saw none who completely reject their heritage.

Prestige and leadership

As we said, little can be taken for granted, *a priori*, about any Inuit relationship – be it between mother and child, or among peers – and the high degree of consensus in their enduring relationships is a consequence of the high order of flexibility over the content of these relationships. It is important that this be borne in mind when considering Inuit prestige and leadership, for these qualities are awarded and recognized in a strictly personal way and on the basis of the same logic of interpersonal relations as we described in connection with helping as opposed to meddling. This means that the prestige and leadership of an individual should not be (and is not, generally speaking) felt by another person as something imposed upon him; there should be no threat to the personal autonomy of another person.

Weyer (1932:212–13) cites all of the following pre-1930 sources as saying that central Inuit leadership is associated with the opinions of one or more older, capable men: Birket-Smith (1929:259), Boas (1888:173), Hall (1864:316), Hawkes (1916:110), Mathiassen (1928:209), Rasmussen (1927:283), Rink (1887:27) and Turner (1887:101). More recent sources with a similar interpretation are Honigmann (1965:234) and Vallee (1967:201–04); Willmott (1960:63–69) adds that ownership of large boats is a leadership prerequisite at Port Harrison. Damas (1963:184) and Graburn (1963:17–19) stress these three prerequisites of leadership: being head of a large kin group, owning a Peterhead boat (or trap boat) and personality.

Although these attributes are often relevant to leadership among Inuit, I do not believe that they of themselves explain its basis. For example, in Innarulik there is an older man who is head of a large kin group; he also owns the only Peterhead boat, and he has a vigorous personality. Yet he is not a leader. On the other hand, another man with a smaller boat is definitely leader of the camp people, who are a much smaller kin group. The missing part of the explanation is to be found in a later statement by Graburn (1969:48) to the effect that a leader among Inuit is heeded only as long as he benefits his followers (in support of this view, see Spencer, 1959:152–3). The difference between the two Innarulik men is that in the settlement situation, the various assets of the older man cannot be of much common benefit (certainly not moreso than in the case of several other adult men there), whereas in the camp situation, the knowledge and direction of the man who is leader are of direct benefit to his kin group there.

One further point arises out of this. The Inuit leader functions in the context of an intermediary role – not simply between Inuit but between Inuit and natural resources and events: he leads people to the best hunting grounds, he leads them out of danger, hunger, and so on. The obvious connection this suggests between leadership and distribution of resources throughout a local group or band is a valid one. It should not be a matter of surprise, then, that the Inuk who has accumulated for his own use an unusually large share of luxury articles from the white world is not accorded special prestige on that account (though the local whites may believe he is); he may be 'in the lead' but as he does not lead his fellows into, say, prosperity, he does not enjoy their deference.

NOTES

1 Webster's New Collegiate Dictionary gives several meanings of "flexibility" that describe the Inuit: "yielding to influence; capable of responding or conforming to changing or new situations."
    Honigmann (1959:119) was the first to analyse Inuit society in terms of its flexibility, which he defined as "... a relaxed mode of procedures and tolerant attitudes towards demands of living." Graburn (1969:47–8), on the other hand, presented quite a different view of Inuit society to the one in this essay.
2 In the Central Inuit dialects, the sentiment "I love you" is phrased as *naklinaqtutit*: "one is caused to love you" ("you arouse love").
3 Willmott (1960:50) found the adoption rate at Port Harrison to be 16% for children under 15, and some of these were serial adoptions, with a child going from one household to another; at Innarulik, in 1969, the adoption rate was 13.1%, almost unchanged from the 12.5% found in 1960 by Graburn (1963:16).
4 Unfortunately, I have little information at this time of writing of women's activities at Innarulik.
5 This statement is based on the costs of a skidoo, its parts and gasoline (with an average consumption of 2 gallons per hour at $1.15 per gallon) compared with earnings from sealskin and fox fur harvests (per hunter, per month) collected from the H.B.C. in Innarulik.
6 It is interesting to note that the whites' unfavourable stereotypic judgements of Inuit do not prevent them from acknowledging their Inuit employees as being good workers on the job.
7 Personal communication from Mrs. Minnie Freeman (the Killam Project Arctic Seminar, autumn, 1969).
8 The following description is based on my own observations, my conversations with new arrivals, and on Vallee (1967:105, 111–12).
9 This contrasts with the openness and directness which Rasmussen (1927:22–4) and Fleming (1965:126) often encountered: within minutes of meeting, native persons would begin telling them their life stories, and speak of their joys and sorrows, even of their philosophy of life.

References

BALIKCI, ASEN
1970 *The Netsilik Eskimo*. Garden City, New York, The Natural History Press.

BIRKET-SMITH, KAJ
1929 *The Caribou Eskimos*. Report of the Fifth Thule Expedition 1921–1924, vol. 5. Copenhagen.

BOAS, FRANZ
1888 *The Central Eskimo*. Reprinted in 1964 by University of Nebraska Press, Lincoln, Nebraska.

BRIGGS, JEAN
1970 *Never in Anger. The Portrait of an Eskimo Family*. Cambridge, Harvard University Press.

DAMAS, DAVID
1963 *Igluligmiut Kinship and Local Groupings: A Structural Approach*. National Museum of Canada, Bulletin No. 196, Anthropological Series No. 6, Department of Northern Affairs and National Resources.

FLEMING, ARCHIBALD L.
1965 *Archibald of the Arctic*. Toronto, Saunders of Toronto, Ltd.

GRABURN, NELSON H. H.
1963 *Lake Harbour, Baffin Island. An Introduction to the Social and Economic Problems of a Small Eskimo Community*. Northern Coordination and Research Centre, Department of Northern Affairs and National Resources, Ottawa.

GRABURN, NELSON H. H.
1969 "Eskimo Law in the Light of Self- and Group Interest." *Law and Society Review*, 4(1):45–60.

GUEMPLE, D. L.
1965 "Saunik: Name Sharing as a Factor Governing Eskimo Kinship Terms." *Ethnology*, 4(3):45–60.

GUEMPLE, D. L.
1970 *Eskimo Adoption*. St. John's, Institute of Social and Economic Research, Memorial University of Newfoundland.

HALL, C. F.
1864 *Life with the Eskimo*. Edmonton, M. J. Hurtig Ltd. (reprinted 1938).

HAWKES, E. W.
1916 *The Labrador Eskimo*. Memoir 91, Geological Survey of Canada, Anthropology Series No. 14, Ottawa.

HONIGMANN, JOHN J. and IRMA HONIGMANN
1959 "Notes on Great Whale River Ethos." *Anthropologica*, 1:106–21.

HONIGMANN, JOHN J. and IRMA HONIGMANN
1965 *Eskimo Townsmen*. Ottawa, Canadian Research Centre for Anthropology, Saint Paul University.

KLEIVAN, HELGE
1969–70 "Language and Ethnic Identity: Language Policy and Debate in Greenland." *Folk*, 11–12.

KLEIVAN, HELGE
1969–70 "Culture and Ethnic Identity: On Modernization and Ethnicity in Greenland." *Folk*, 11–12.

LANDECKER, WERNER S.
1950 "Smend's Theory of Integration." *Social Forces*, 29:39–48.

LUBART, JOSEPH M.
1969 *Psychodynamic Problems of Adaptation – Mackenzie Delta Eskimos*. Ottawa, Northern Science Research Group.

LYON, GEORGE FRANCIS
1824 *The Private Journal of Captain G. F. Lyon of H.M.S. Hecla, During the Recent Voyage of Discovery Under Captain Parry* (reprinted 1970). Barre, Massachusetts, Imprint Society.

MATHIASSEN, P.
1928 *Material Culture of the Iglulik Eskimos*. Report of the Fifth Thule Expedition, 1921–24, vol. 6, Copenhagen.

PAINE, ROBERT
1967 "What is Gossip About? An Alternative Hypothesis." *Man*, 2(2):278–85.

RASMUSSEN, KNUD
1927 *Across Arctic America*. New York, G. P. Pitman's Sons.

RASMUSSEN, KNUD
1931 *The Netsilik Eskimos: Social Life and Spiritual Culture*. Report of the Fifth Thule Expedition, 1921–24, vol. 9, Copenhagen.

RINK, HENRY
1887 *The Eskimo Tribes*. Medelelser om Grønland, vol. XI.

SPENCER, R. F.
1959 *The North Alaskan Eskimo: A Study in Ecology and Society*. Bureau of American Ethnology, Bulletin 171. Washington.

STEVENSON, DAVID
1971 "The Social Organization of the Clyde River Eskimos." Unpublished Ph.D. thesis, University of British Columbia.

TURNER, LUCIEN
1887 *On the Indians of the Ungava District, Labrador*. Transactions of the Royal Society of Canada, V, section 2.

VALLEE, FRANK
1967 *Kabloona and Eskimo in the Central Keewatin*. St. Paul University,

Ottawa, Canadian Research Centre for Anthropology.

WEYER, EDWARD M.

1932 *The Eskimos, Their Environment and Folkways.* (Reprinted 1969.)
Hampden, Conn., Shoestring Press.

WILLMOTT, W. E.

1960 "The Flexibility of Eskimo Social Organization." *Anthropologica*,
(N.S.), 2:48–59.

Legacy of Tutelage: Divided Inuit*

Evelyn Kallen

7

INTRODUCTION

The village of Sikuvik is located in the eastern high Arctic approximately 2,000 miles north of Toronto – considerably above the tree line and well above the Arctic Circle. The terrain is permanently frozen and when the winds sweep across the winter darkness, temperatures can drop from 40 to 60 degrees below zero.

The modern settlement of Sikuvik dates back to the 1930s when a Hudson's Bay trading post was established to serve the dispersed camps of the region. Sikuvik remained an outpost service settlement until the 1960s when a variety of factors precipitated the large-scale movement into the village of much of the dispersed Inuit population in the region. First among these was the decreasing viability of a subsistence hunting and trapping economy in the face of the increasing demand for consumer products. When a short-lived market for seal skins collapsed after 1964 (Crowe, 1969:74–78), there was a strong economic reason for families to move to Sikuvik, for there they received government cheques from the Administrative Centre, and could purchase goods from the Hudson's Bay store. In addition, in 1960, the first federal day school was established at Sikuvik and many families responded by moving into the settlement to be near their children. However, what became the major factor was a large-scale house-rental scheme set up by the federal government in 1965. Within one generation the domestic environment of the eastern high Arctic Inuit changed from one of tiny snow-and-ice-huts in winter, sod and canvas huts in summer, fuel oil lamps, and communal sleeping platforms covered with caribou skins, to one of prefabricated houses with electricity, oil heating, and separate bedrooms. The housing scheme precipitated drastic changes in almost every aspect of Inuit life, changes which greatly increased Inuit dependency upon the Euro-Canadian.

Consequently, the Inuit have become very much a "people under tutelage" (Honigmann, 1965:157), a people living within communities initiated and controlled largely by the Euro-Canadian (or *kadlunat*, the modern white man). One purpose of this essay is to document the divisions which occurred among the Inuit as a result of this tutelage; the other purpose is to

*Excerpted from an unpublished manuscript, and revised (ed.).

consider how, within the constraints of these divisions, individuals try to establish and maintain positions of influence in their community and possibly beyond it.

Inuit and Euro-Canadians in Sikuvik
Especially since 1965, most decisions at the community level have emanated from the following agencies: the Anglican Church and mission, the Roman Catholic Church and mission, the Government Administrative Centre, Settlement Council, Community Development Fund, Housing Association, the Hudson's Bay Company store, the co-operative store, government day school, nursing station, Royal Canadian Mounted Police, the local newspaper, Scouts and Guides associations, and the Inuit Cultural Association (*Innumarit*). Without exception, these are all Euro-Canadian creations; with only three exceptions, they are still (1973) run along Euro-Canadian lines and controlled by Euro-Canadians (as opposed to Inuit); the exceptions are the Inuit Association, the co-operative store and the Anglican mission, which are missionary creations – two Roman Catholic and one Anglican – run by the Inuit along somewhat more traditional, kin-based, co-operative lines. These associations are, in purpose and design, more convergent with traditional Inuit ways than are the other Euro-Canadian Institutions: they emphasize cultural survival and they offer the Inuit opportunities for active participation in community affairs without such imposed constraints as Euro-Canadian rules of procedure (whose introduction into Settlement Council meetings is the source of much misunderstanding and misgiving).

All agencies provide a limited number of wage-work jobs, thus affording some opportunity locally – albeit at a low level[1] – for economic participation in the Euro-Canadian world. However, given the decline in hunting and trapping activities, as well as the increased demand for consumer goods, the need on the part of the Inuit Sikuvik (approximately six hundred Inuit as opposed to forty Euro-Canadians) for wage-work far exceeds the available opportunities. Moreover, in this contact situation characterized by a long-term scarcity of resources, the local representatives of the agencies, usually Euro-Canadians, bestow favours when they provide employment or welfare: they are local patrons of Inuit clienteles.[2]

It can be appreciated how this *economic* dependency of the Inuit upon Euro-Canadian patronage seriously impedes the ability of the Inuit community to generate leaders, including those who could act effectively as middlemen in political negotiations with Euro-Canadian agents and agencies. Thus, the Inuit are in a position of *political* dependence too. Although Sikuvik is officially self-governing (as of April, 1971), ''resolutions' passed by the Settlement Council have recognized status only as recommendations which must be forwarded to the appropriate agency of the Territorial and/or Federal Governments for approval; and at that level, in the Euro-Canadian scheme of things, the local Inuit have still less political influence. Ultimate decision-making in the political sphere remains an Euro-Canadian prerogative.

Besides dependency, divisiveness characterizes the community. The local representatives of the agencies provide a powerful Euro-Canadian 'presence' in the community; yet their spheres of influence, and their transactions with the Inuit, often overlap. The agencies are placed, to a varying extent, in competition with each other. Moreover, the personal values of individual agents, as well as the institutional values of the different agencies differ, even markedly. Thus, shortly after its establishment, the Inuit community became divided into clienteles and fragmented along lines of acceptance and rejection of particular values and particular patrons.

Relations between the two ethnic groups of the village are limited as most of their dealings with each other are within the formal contexts of the agencies. Socially, Euro-Canadian gatherings rarely include Inuit guests.[3] This social segregation is reinforced by residential segregation; Euro-Canadians live in separate blocks of houses – the large houses with large water tanks, plumbing, fine furnishings, and a year's supply of food. In contrast, the Inuit, for the most part, live in small, over-crowded dwellings, with tiny water tanks, no plumbing, meagre furnishings, and a day-by-day supply of food obtained largely through traditional economic pursuits (hunting and fishing).

A further reinforcement of this pattern is the preferential treatment typically accorded a Euro-Canadian by many Inuit. The customary 'courting' of Euro-Canadian patrons by their Inuit clienteles is currently arousing resentment among growing numbers of Inuit – especially the more acculturated youth, who claim that the Inuit are being discriminated against by their own people on racially-defined grounds. For example, complaints about water and ice delivery by the (Inuit) co-operative have been lodged by two young Inuit in the local newspaper (January, 1972); Euro-Canadian water tanks are filled regularly by the co-operative while the Inuit are often compelled to cut their own blocks of ice in order to fill theirs. Such episodes not only reinforce ethnic boundaries but also the divisiveness among the Inuit.

'Parallel' and 'Alternate' Systems: Kadlunamuit and Traditionalists

Indeed, transactions with Euro-Canadians in Sikuvik quickly led to the emergence among the Inuit of two polarized status systems. The one guided by a transitional ideology may be termed the *parallel* status system (parallel to the Euro-Canadian world), whereas the one with a traditional ideology may be termed the *alternate* status system (alternate to the Euro-Canadian world).

Within the alternate system, hunting ability is the ultimate measure of a man's status, and the excellent hunter provides the primary role model. Thus, the traditional camp groupings which have moved to Sikuvik within the past few years still retain their forms of organization, including patterns of co-operation and leadership. For example, related families may live in separate houses but their members continue to co-operate in subsistence activities; women continue to sew and make clothes together and men to hunt and trap together. Even more importantly, these families continue to share their food and goods and to place a high value on co-operative activities and sharing. The recognized leaders of these previous camp communities form an informal council of elders; it is they who are the patrons within the alternate status system.

In contrast, among the Inuit who have acquired some fluency in English and have received some training in Euro-Canadian occupational skills, a growing number are interested in Euro-Canadian ways. For instance, some prefer wage work to hunting and trapping, while others wish to combine the two kinds of occupation; when opportunity allows, they seek Euro-Canadian jobs. Their transitional ideology generates the parallel status system in Sikuvik, and they are known as *kadlunamuit* (literally "people of the white man") (Vallee, 1962).

Whereas the political strategy of the traditionalists is one of encapsulation – the withdrawal from all but the necessary minimum contact with whites – in order to reduce the loss of traditional ways, the transitionalists or *kadlunamuit* seek both to penetrate Euro-Canadian political and economic institutions and to ensure, in the private domain, the continuity and integrity of alternate Inuit institutions.[4] It should be noted that some *kadlunamuit* are excellent hunters and trappers as well as skilled wage-workers, and seem to experience little or no difficulty in shifting from one economic pursuit to the other. In economic terms, they tend to be the most successful persons within the community, taking advantage of both kinds of economic activity as the opportunity arises. Some of them are permanently employed in full-time wage-work for Euro-Canadian agencies, but none of them are full-time hunters and trappers as are the traditionalists.

The *kadlunamuit's* long-term strategy in transacting with the Euro-Canadians focuses on acculturation as a means of penetrating public Euro-Canadian institutions. Yet they shift tactics as the situation demands, sometimes allowing a Euro-Canadian to act as patron, at other times seeking to alter the distribution of power, privilege and prestige. The particular tactic adopted depends both on their immediate interests and on the assumed (or stated) goals of whatever segment of the local Inuit population they happen to be representing at the time.

It should be emphasized that the processes we are describing have not resulted in two distinct Inuit communities; nor is it true that a given individual operates solely within the sanctions of only one of the two status systems. In fact, most Inuit fall somewhere between the two, priority being given to one or the other as the situation demands. Nor has the presence of a Euro-Canadian reference group yet resulted in changes in ethnic identity: even the most acculturated Inuit in Sikuvik still tend to identify and be identified as Inuit by Inuit and Euro-Canadians alike.

'Marginal' Youth

However, there are between 50 and 60 young Inuit in Sikuvik, between the ages of 17 and 24 years, whose personal and social status can be considered marginal.[5] They have all spent considerable time (nine months of the year, for about eight to ten years) away from home at residential schools. In many ways, these youth (of both sexes) appear to be in limbo between the divergent worlds of the traditional Inuit and of the Euro-Canadians. Nor are they *kadlunamuit*.

Torn between the expectations and demands of these two worlds, they are highly ambivalent about their own values, goals and behavioural standards. Moreover, their long absences from home have left them with insufficient skills to participate effectively in either of the two worlds. For example, some of the young men can hunt and trap only with a great deal of assistance; thus they lose face and prestige as hunters and, indeed, as men within the traditional status system. At the same time, the training they may have received, say, in carpentry at a northern Euro-Canadian vocational school, usually leaves them at a level of expertise below that of Euro-Canadians. One result seems to be that they become bored, dispirited and restless, shifting from job to job. Some continue to search for new opportunities through adult education and vocational courses. Frustration quickly reappears, however, when they are unable to find jobs commensurate with their newly acquired skills, and to gain a feeling of self-fulfillment outside their work situation.

Given sufficient encouragement and support from Euro-Canadian patrons (employers, teachers, and others), some of these youth would probably go south at the first opportunity were it not that – for the present, at least – loyalty and obligations to family and kin keep most of them within the community and subjected, at least in part, to the traditional sanctions of the alternate system.[6] Because they have not yet made their final choices about jobs and marriage, these marginal youth are also without recognized adult status within both status systems. Those who eventually choose to remain at home permanently may, as adult members of the community, become more concerned with preserving distinctive Inuit ways and skills. Some of them, undoubtedly, join the ranks of the *kadlunamuit*. At present, however, their political reference group is clearly Euro-Canadian, and this means looking for Euro-Canadians (as patrons) to act on their behalf.

Anglicans and Catholics

Even prior to the movement of the Inuit into permanent settlements such as Sikuvik, conversion to Christianity divided them into Anglicans and Roman Catholics, resulting in separate camp communities and strong discouragement of inter-denominational marriages. These early divisions have increased their salience in the contemporary settlement at Sikuvik. From its beginning, the population was divided into two clusters, centered around the Catholic and Anglican missions at opposite sides of the village and in approximately the same numbers. But now there is also an increasing measure of socio-political segregation on the basis of religious denomination.[7] This has serious implications for the handling of political transactions in Sikuvik.

The Settlement Council and affiliated Euro-Canadian agencies are officially run along democratic, Euro-Canadian lines; nominations and elections are held annually, and any permanent resident of Sikuvik (Inuit or Euro-Canadian) is eligible to stand for office. However, the religious division between Anglicans and Catholics was always recognized unofficially and an attempt was made to have a roughly equal representration of Anglican and Catholic members on the council. Moreover, almost all questions of importance to the Inuit community are decided or handled by the council and agencies, and then relayed to the various segments of the community by Inuit middlemen (close kin, other relatives, and friends). In effect, decisions made by elected representatives – the official political leaders in the parallel status system – are 'bent' by these middlemen to reflect the different and sometimes conflicting claims, strategies, and goals of one or the other of the two religious segments. In these ways, denominationalism has become the source of political factionalism, between Anglican and Catholic, at both levels of the community and in both of its status systems.

Denominationalism and the Youth

Denominationalism in Sikuvik has had severe repercussions among the youth; in particular, it exacerbated parent-youth conflict. The seeds of this conflict lie in the young people's desire for privacy and autonomy in decision-making, at least in social relationships with their peers, and the adults' refusal to accept the legitimacy of this newly acquired (Euro-Canadian) peer-group need.

Until two years ago, Sikuvik youth had their own club, holding meetings and 'teen' dances at the community hall. As a Euro-Canadian-inspired organization, the youth club was officially designed for all the Inuit youth in the settlement. But the club and its dances were stopped by an action of the Settlement Council, largely influenced by the powerful Anglican canon. The canon's objection to the youth club, and in particular to the dances, was overtly expressed in terms of his personal version of both Christian and Inuit morality: the club and dances contravened the traditionally accepted norms which prohibited tactile contact between the sexes, particularly between unmarried couples, in public. The dances also broke the midnight curfew rule imposed upon young people – who even turned off all the lights and danced in the dark. Not surprisingly, a number of pre-marital pregnancies were attributed to the influence of the club and the dances.

Yet the most important reason for the canon's objection was covert: he realized that the club and its dances would lead to Anglican-Catholic friendships, dating (indeed mating) and, inevitably, marriages – a pattern frowned upon by the leaders of both faiths, but especially by the Anglican canon. A pre-marital pregnancy, in itself, did not really present a severe problem: for if the couple were of the same faith, they could easily be persuaded to marry in accordance with the traditional Inuit custom of arranged marriages between families. A problem presented itself only when a pregnancy occurred as a result of Anglican-Catholic intimacy.

Support for the canon's stand came from adults of both religious communities, and the motion to terminate the club and the dances was passed by the Settlement Council amost unanimously. Some of the parents were so opposed to the club and the dances that they reportedly tore their ballots in half and voted "no," twice. Since that time, social relationships between young people of the two denominations have become less frequent; although some crossing of religious boundaries continues covertly, Anglican-Catholic marriages are rare.[8]

LIMITS OF LEADERSHIP

It is against this background of Sikuvik as a multiple-fractured 'constituency' that one must view the efforts towards the exercise of leadership; to this end I wish to sketch two pairs of case studies, beginning with the two religious leaders.

Catholic Priest and Anglican Canon

In recent years, there has been a marked shift from Catholic to Anglican dominance in the political sector in Sikuvik. In large part, this is an outcome of the different strategies employed by the Euro-Canadian Roman Catholic priest and the Inuit Anglican minister. Both men have served as formally elected members of the Settlement Council almost from its establishment in 1967.

For nearly twenty years, the Catholic priest dominated the local political scene because of his effective bargaining power within the Euro-Canadian world. He was the 'power' behind the organization and growth of the Inuit co-operative store, the settlement day school, and *Innumarit* – the Inuit cultural centre. Not surprisingly, it was his *persona* that provided the community with its most persuasive Euro-Canadian role model: he thus served as the prime acculturative force in the Inuit community.

A major factor behind his eventual political demise[9] lay in one of the unanticipated outcomes of his forceful transactions in the educational sphere. The priest used to place considerable emphasis on formal education of the young and, accordingly, had exerted strong pressure upon his congregation (Catholic parents) to send their children to residential (Catholic) mission schools. Much to the dismay of both priest and parents, it was especially the graduates of these schools who ended up in the ranks of the marginal Inuit youth. The Catholic parents began to put the blame for the "youth problem" on the priest – and on the whole "bundle of Euro-Canadian values" (Paine, 1971:6) that the priest and mission school purportedly represented.

In response, the priest reversed his strategy and began to de-emphasize acculturation to Euro-Canadian ways and to emphasize preserving Inuit ways. (Most dramatically, he assumed the leading role in a new project: the building of a centre for the preservation of traditional Inuit artifacts.) This new policy reduced Inuit opposition, but it failed to prevent the erosion of his political power at the same time as that of the Anglican minister (now canon) increased.

Unlike the Catholic priest, the Anglican minister, an Inuit, exerted no pressure on his congregation to send their children away to school, but left the decision to the parents themselves. As a result, fewer Anglican than Catholic Inuit youth have been educated away from home; most have received their formal education at the territorial school in Sikuvik. Yet, though the ways of these Anglican youth are somewhat more convergent with their parents' ways and views than those of Inuit youth educated away from home, the difference between these two groups of youths is small. The more highly acculturated youth are currently providing powerful role models for both their Inuit peers educated in Sikuvik, and for the younger children, Anglican and Catholic, now attending the territorial school in the settlement.

The Anglican canon, painfully conscious of the growing influence of marginal youth in Sikuvik, has taken a firm stand against any further "corruption" of traditional Inuit values (associated by the canon with

Christian values) by the adoption of southern Canadian ways. He has, accordingly, been in the forefront of the current community-wide efforts directed towards fostering, preserving, and strengthening those aspects of Inuit tradition deemed crucial for ensuring a strong and positive sense of ethnic identity and commitment on the part of Inuit youth. Because the canon, *as an Inuit*, expresses a firm commitment to Inuit values, he is trusted by all the Inuit in Sikuvik, Anglicans and Catholics alike, when he speaks as an 'insider.' Given the current political climate in Sikuvik, this community-wide trust has largely contributed to his increasingly powerful position as political leader.

The long-term political strategy of the Anglican canon is essentially a traditional one: recruitment of support from extended family members and kin on the basis of loyalties and obligations generated within the traditional (or alternate) system. Because the Catholic priest is an outsider (ethnic status) and unmarried (religious status), he cannot count on either family or kinship networks for support. The Anglican canon, on the other hand, has a large and rapidly expanding extended family from whom he recruits political support. All three of his sons are Settlement Council members and one (re-elected March, 1971) has been chairman for the past three years. In addition, the canon and one of his sons are elected members of the housing association, and at one time or another have been active members of almost every council and agency in Sikuvik.

The increasing political power of the Anglican sector is reflected in the fact that in 1972, the only Catholic representative elected to the Settlement Council was the Catholic priest himself (unofficially, however, the priest quickly co-opted one or two more Catholics as representatives as soon as the elections were over). Similarly, a disproportionate number of new houses within the settlement have, over the past two years, been erected on the Anglican side of the community, although the perceived and actual need is greater on the Catholic side.

But it is important to remember that as yet most Inuit are politically unsophisticated in Euro-Canadian terms, and are generally apathetic – notwithstanding their dependency on favours from local patrons – towards the official and parallel political structure of the village. Attendance at Settlement Council meetings is low,[10] and those who do attend participate little. It is therefore absolutely crucial to any aspiring Inuit political leader to be able to corral support through the traditional or alternate system. It is here that the canon has the advantage over the priest as he uses his sons and other members of his large extended family as middlemen in negotiations within as well as outside the village. The canon himself is able to hold himself aloof from all but the most necessary contact with Euro-Canadians: rather than courting them for their influence, he makes them come to him –

and even then he refuses to use his rather poor English, insisting on an interpreter. Secondly, he is able consistently to play the role of churchman and advocate of traditional Inuit-and-Christian values.

Henry, a Kadlunamuit; Peter, a 'Marginal'

Henry, one of the canon's sons, became chairman of the Settlement Council in 1973 and occupies an institutionalized middleman role between Sikuvik residents and the Territorial Government, as well as between the whites and the Inuit in Sikuvik. From his point of view, success in this role is determined primarily by his ability to appeal to Inuit as a fellow Inuit who represents their common interests, and secondarily by his ability to appeal to the Euro-Canadians as a "fellow Canadian." This path led him to demonstrate a concern with both the protection of traditional ways and the wishes of Euro-Canadians.

How effective is Henry as a political leader and middleman? He purports to represent the entire community, but more often than not he represents only the Anglican sector of a fragmented community. Even there his authority and influence are qualified: on the one hand, he is regarded as "the Anglican canon's son" and precedence is given to the father, as the minister; and on the other hand, the traditional and informal, but powerful, council of (Anglican) elders curtails his power.

The Catholic sector does not recognize Henry as spokesman for their interests, although he can enlist their support on some community-wide issues. The marginal youth deny his ability to represent them in any way. This lack of support from the youth who speak English more fluently and have more formal education than the kadlunamuit poses a serious political threat not only to Henry, but also to any other political aspirant among the kadlunamuit.

Henry is similarly hampered in his role of middleman by the local Euro-Canadians' belief (generally supported by the Inuit) that it is they, rather than the Inuit chairman of the Settlement Council, who should make the decisions. For what is required, in their opinion, is skill in Euro-Canadian ways of viewing and doing things. Henry is in still greater difficulty in his dealings with the political and governmental bureaucracies outside Sikuvik. Thirty-five years old, he has no formal education. (His expressed educational aspirations are directed towards the younger generation of Inuit rather than towards himself.) He speaks English poorly and often uses an interpreter.

In sum, Henry lacks not only the requisite skills for penetrating the Euro-Canadian political circles, but also the vital support of his own community. He 'represents' an economically dependent, politically divided, unsophisticated, and largely apathetic constituency, most of whom neither understand nor care what he is doing outside the community. Thus, he has been unable to rally the voting support of his community as a whole; in 1971 he ran for political office in the Northwest Territories and was defeated by the opposing Euro-Canadian candidate.

Peter, on the other hand, is a young Catholic with grade 10 education and considerable proficiency in English. Twenty-two years old now (in 1973), he worked for the Canadian Broadcasting Corporation in Ottawa between the ages of seventeen and nineteen, but returned to Sikuvik because of "homesickness" and an expressed inability to adjust to a totally Euro-Canadian environment. In Sikuvik, he attends adult education classes and works, part-time, as a clerk in the Government Administrative Centre. Since his return home, Peter has been the principal person representing the interests of the marginal youth in dealings with both Inuit and Euro-Canadians in Sikuvik. He was president of the original (but now defunct) youth club and is now president of a new youth club called the *Pittau* (meaning "worthy") Club.

The *Pittau* Club is the result of a strategy of compromise between the demands of the marginal youth for an exclusive club and the continued refusal of the adult Inuit community to concede legitimacy to this demand. The compromise was the creation of a club which benefits the "whole community" and provides social and cultural activities for all ages: open houses with games, music, and refreshments, a programme of traditional arts and crafts, money-raising activities such as rummage sales – but also 'teen' dances with rock music once a month and on special occasions such as Christmas and New Year.

From the beginning, the proposal for the new club received support and encouragement from the adult education teachers in Sikuvik. This led the adult Inuit community to assume that the club – to be housed in the Adult Education Centre – would come under the moral scrutiny and guidance of the teachers, unofficially at least. The proposal for the club initially met with considerable informal community support, but it was still voted down (60 to 40) at a meeting of the Settlement Council, largely because of the expressed opposition of both the religious leaders. Nevertheless, the teachers' support and Peter's strong leadership enabled about ten youth, all enrolled in the adult education programme, to organize the club on their own. Despite the formal opposition of the Settlement Council, and increasing informal opposition of the adult Inuit community, the Pittau Club is flourishing with about one hundred paid-up members (membership fee: $1.00 per annum).

From the point of view of the majority of adult Inuit, Peter and his fellow 'marginals,' by initiating and operating the club on their own – and in direct opposition to the Settlement Council – are not only flaunting the traditional authority of elders within the alternate system, but are also threatening the authority of the elected leaders within the parallel public institutions of the settlement. Accordingly, they are labelled "trouble makers," "radical upstarts," and "Kadlunat hangers-on." This opposition, clearly, is not based solely on "Christian, moral grounds." The club is designed and operated in accordance with modern, Euro-Canadian norms rather than traditional, Inuit ones. Role models for *Pittau* Club members are readily provided by the adult education teachers: a newly married couple from southern Canada, who are only slightly older than most of their students (and younger than some) and whose expressed attitudes and behaviours are clearly compatible with the aspirations of marginal youth. It is not surprising, therefore, that the adult Inuit community and the two religious leaders increasingly oppose the club as prejudicial to traditional Inuit ways, norms, and sanctions.

SUMMARY AND CONCLUSIONS

Domination and control by Euro-Canadians, coupled with power struggles between their various agencies, have been the principal sources of fragmentation of the Inuit community. This is evidenced by religious divisions, generational divisions, and inherent conflict between the co-existing parallel and alternate status systems. An overriding consequence has been Inuit inability to take concerted political action; when the community is faced with an issue, several strands of division are always likely to become entangled in it. Nevertheless, it has been possible to separate several group strategies and goals, including the local Euro-Canadians.' The following is an attempt to summarize them.

Until recently, the Euro-Canadian strategy was clearly one of dominant conformity – on the paternalistic assumption that their ways and skills were superior to the Inuit ones. Accordingly, the process of acculturation was begun without regard for the loss or erosion of traditional Inuit ways. Today, however, counter-pressures generated within the adult Inuit community itself have forced a shift (officially sanctioned at the highest levels outside the community) towards the preservation of selected aspects of Inuit tradition. That notwithstanding, however, the Inuit are still expected and, in fact, still urged to acculturate within the parallel (Euro-Canadian) institutions.

It is the strategy and goals of the Inuit traditionalists that diverge most from those of the Euro-Canadians. Indeed, they attempt to isolate themselves from all but the most necessary 'contact'; this means they desist from assuming the political role of middleman. Nevertheless (as has been pointed out), they exert considerable influence on political decision-making in Sikuvik through the alternate status system. Their strategy may be viewed as one of encapsulation, and it is to this end that they oppose the parallel status system with the alternate one.

The *kadlunamuit* occupy the middleman role between the two ethnic populations and the two status systems; they are the transitionalists. While they clearly recognize the political and economic dependencies of Inuit on the Euro-Canadian world, they also respect the alternate system and the Inuit elders. Attempting to operate within the sanctions of both systems (and wishing to increase their status simultaneously in both), their strategy may be viewed as pluralistic; they also tend to be the peacemakers across the ethnic divide. Yet the instance of Henry suggests that his attempt to play middleman compromised his ability to achieve the firm status of 'leader' within any one segment of the community. Whatever he might do, Henry's political influence as chairman of the Settlement Council was likely to be stunted by forces emanating both from within and outside his local community.

The 'marginals' in the community tend to be the conflict-makers between the adult Inuit community and the Euro-Canadians. They realize that their efforts to effect broad changes in the direction of Euro-Canadian norms are perceived as flaunting Inuit traditions and as challenges to the authority of the elders. But they are also aware that within the traditional *cum* alternate system, there is no option for young people, and no chance of a compromise with the writ of the elders. In response to this perceived impasse, they centre their efforts upon winning 'friends' and support from among the local Euro-Canadians.

Yet one is bound to add that their present position is not without ambiguity. For they do actually support, in principle, their elders' goal of ensuring the continuity and salience of Inuit ethnicity; it is simply that they do not believe this goal will be furthered by "clinging to old-fashioned ways." Like some of their Euro-Canadian friends, they view Inuit ways as 'museum culture' to be cherished as remembrances of past days and ways – perhaps providing important ethno-historical 'roots,' but otherwise inappropriate for the twentieth century.

Returning to the traditionalists again, they are not at a standstill; indeed, they are gaining ground in some respects. For instance, since the blame for the alleged youth takeover of the *Pittau* Club was assigned to the Euro-Canadians, or at least to the influence of Euro-Canadian social institutions, the adult Inuit community, Anglican and Catholic alike, has adopted a policy of screening and limiting Euro-Canadian input into the community. For example, in 1972, following a rash of controversial articles documenting the views of marginal youth, the local newspaper was taken from the school teachers by the Settlement Council. Until its demise a year later, allegedly because of lack of funds, the newspaper was far more 'traditional' in orientation than ever before.

Inuit adults are making a concerted effort to revitalize interest in their language, as currently spoken and written (syllabic alphabet), and educational texts created by Inuit authors and artists have already replaced some of the Euro-Canadian ones. Inuit elders now come to the school to teach traditional technology such as sewing, building snow-houses, carving, and others; in the spring of 1974, the entire school, including teachers and pupils, undertook a caribou hunt. At the same time, a new secondary and vocational school has been actively opposed, partly because it is located in Frobisher Bay (which has a bad reputation among Inuit elders), but also because of the youthfulness of the teachers and counsellors and their alleged inability to discipline the children properly. Only a handful of students from Sikuvik (four in 1972, and three in 1973) have been allowed to enroll (ed. note: see Koster, this vol.)

As a postscript, one notes the possible influence on Inuit self-consciousness and on politics in Sikuvik of the official Canada-wide Inuit organization, *Inuit Tapirisat*. Although it is mainly *kadlunamuit* who seek to take concerted action through this organization, its 'national' platform appears to be carefully designed to include the more important claims of the traditionalists also, and even of the 'marginals' (Inuit Tapirisat of Canada, 1972). While it provides an important 'laboratory' for the acquisition by Inuit leaders of sophisticated Euro-Canadian political skills, it is also exerting an integrative influence at the local scene. For instance, that Henry, the chairman of the Sikuvik Settlement Council, is an active member of *Inuit Tapirisat* helps to buttress, if only in a small way, his credibility in Sikuvik. Similarly, the blurring of Anglican and Catholic lines in Sikuvik, if only in the public domain of the settlement's political life, is connected with the emergence of a local consciousness of *Inuit Tapirisat*.

NOTES

1   Most Inuit are employed as "assistant to" Euro-Canadians: they are assistant teachers, assistant constables, assistant electricians and carpenters, or assistants in manual labour such as construction, garbage collection, water delivery, and so forth.
2   Usage of the terms "patron" and "middleman" follows that of Paine (1971:8–21).
3   Here I am referring to invited guests; some Inuit often do drop in on those Euro-Canadian patrons who do not actively discourage them from doing so.
4   It is for this reason that I do not characterize them simply as modernists, as this term would suggest too sharp a dichotomy between them and the traditionalists.
5   A "marginal" category has also been identified by Anderson (1971); see also Fried (1963:57–67).
6   It is perhaps pertinent to note that Sikuvik is, *by choice*, a 'dry' community. Inuit are required to obtain permission from five members of the Settlement Council before they can bring alcoholic beverages into the community. In this way, a high degree of control over alcohol consumption is exercised from within the settlement itself. 'Home brew', however, is occasionally produced in both Inuit and Euro-Canadian households. Nor is it unknown for Euro-Canadian patrons who have a large supply of alcoholic beverages on hand to 'lend' a bottle of liquor to an Inuit. Restrictions upon importation of alcohol do not apply to the Euro-Canadians so that counter pressures favouring alcohol consumption are generated by them as are role models in connection with alcohol use and abuse.
7   Because the Inuit of the Sikuvik region constitute a closely related kin grouping, there is still some traditional sharing in decision-making between members of the different religious denominations, especially among the elders within the alternate status system.
8   In pre-Christian times, marriages were arranged from among a wide range of near and distant kin in neighbouring camps; if a marriage failed, it could be dissolved at will by either

partner. With conversion to Christianity, arranged marriages persisted, but two new limitations were imposed: denominational endogamy (Anglican or Catholic), and permanency of
marriage. The first measure cut in half the number of prospective marriage partners, but
subsequent natural population increase has restored the proportions. The real constraint
flowing from denominational endogamy as reported by young people is that familiarity with
peers of the same religious sub-community decreases their mutual attractiveness as marital
partners: they tend to regard each other "almost as brothers and sisters." Compounding this
problem are the current difficulties (and expense) of travelling the long distances between
settlements.

At present, youth are postponing marriage beyond what had traditionally been considered
the proper age (14 or 15 years for girls, about 20 years for boys). However, under increasing
pressure from parents and the religious community, most young people succumb by the age of
24 or 25 and enter into "forced marriages" – the label which the youth have put upon arranged
marriages. The incidence of marital problems and separation, however, is high. At the time of
this study, 3 arranged marriages had led to separation, but the strong religious (Anglican and
Catholic) prohibitions against divorce effectively blocked any attempts to adopt this solution.
9   The Catholic priest has since left the community because of pressures exerted upon him by
the upper echelon of the Oblate hierarchy. At present, he is attempting to establish an
experimental "traditional and Christian community" with two extended families outside the
settlement.
10   Continuing appeals by the chairman of the council for better turn-outs and more active
participation are cited in the local newspaper for 1971–73.

References

ANDERSON, E. O.
   1971 *Eskimo Ethnic Identity: A Synthesis of Problems and Approaches*.
   Anthropological Series No. 11, Department of Anthropology, University of Toronto.
CROWE, K. J.
   1969 *A Cultural Geography of the Northern Foxe Basin, Northwest
   Territories*. Ottawa, Dept. of Indian Affairs and Northern Development.
FRIED, JACOB
   1963 "White Dominant Settlements in the Canadian Northwest Territories." *Anthropologica*, 5(1):57–67.
HONIGMANN, JOHN and IRMA HONIGMANN
   1965 *Eskimo Townsmen*. Ottawa, Canadian Research Centre for Anthropology, Saint Paul University.
Inuit Tapirisat
   1972 *Inuit Tapirisat of Canada*. Ottawa, Information Canada.
PAINE, ROBERT
   1971 "A Theory of Patronage and Brokerage." In R. Paine (ed.), *Patrons and Brokers in the East Arctic*. St. John's, Institute of Social and
   Economic Research, Memorial University of Newfoundland.
VALLEE, FRANK
   1962 *Kabloona and Eskimos in the Central Keewatin*. Ottawa, Canadian
   Research Centre for Anthropology.

'Why is *He* Here?': White Gossip*

8

Ditte Koster

BACKGROUND

The Approach

On the Nordair plane from Montreal on my way to Frobisher Bay, I sat next to an elderly American couple. They told me that they were going to visit their married daughter whose husband, a former missionary, had been in charge of a government department for about a year. Stationed in Frobisher Bay, his territory consisted of the whole Baffin region, and he had spent the first few months travelling to the different settlements to familiarize himself with local conditions. My acquaintances expressed the hope that he would not stay in the north too long but find a position closer to home where he could settle down with his family.

At Frobisher Bay airport, I observed the greetings, introductions and back-slapping among the people who met upon landing. "Are you coming or going?" was a well-used phrase. This question was often answered with extensive itineraries describing how many settlements had been, or were to be, visited in a certain number of days or weeks. New arrivals were quickly whisked away in private cars to the hotel or the homes of residents. One recognized the old-timers[1] by the fact that they greeted some of the Inuit standing about: exclamations about "how nice it was to see them again" were met with smiles but few words. Women's *amauties* (parka hoods) were peeked into to admire the new baby, little children had their ears pulled in a friendly fashion, and men were invited to "a beer sometime."

In the months to follow I often went to the airport to see new people come in or see others off. The Ikaluit Eskimo Co-operative, the craft shop above the airport hall, did a brisk business on the days that planes left for Montreal. It was fun to see people leave, clad in their colorful parkas and sealskin boots, loaded up with carvings, Eskimo dolls, mittens, purses, and the like. I could not help but think that they were going back to a world where they would be recognized as arctic experts, often regardless of how long or short their stay "up north" had been.

My observations on the plane, at the airport, and my first weeks in town led me gradually to the focus of my work. Conversations with other Euro-Canadians reinforced my belief in the relevance of my interest in the

*Excerpted from the author's M.A. thesis, "Frobisher Bay: Ambiguity and Gossip in a Colonial Situation" (Memorial University of Newfoundland, 1972), and revised (ed.).

readily observable, and entirely obvious fact that many people from various social and cultural backgrounds mingled in Frobisher Bay. I became particularly intrigued by the professional newcomers in town; their views of social reality of Frobisher Bay – and how they acquired these views – became a major object of my attention. How did this educated, middle-class, and highly mobile or transient group of civil servants adapt to their new social environment? How did they – indeed, did they? – establish relationships with each other and with the old-time Euro-Canadians and the Inuit who were already there? How did they explain Frobisher Bay to themselves and to one another?

Approaching these questions theoretically by way of McHugh (1968), Mead (1970), Paine (1967), and Shibutani (1966), among others, I looked to the pervasive themes of gossip among the Euro-Canadians for one possible answer. Gossiping is one phenomenon that cannot fail to strike a visitor to the community. Another is the apparent defensiveness of many Euro-Canadians about their living there. A natural assumption is that the two phenomena may be related; this is what I shall try to demonstrate in this paper.

Both Paine (1967) and Shibutani (1966) emphasize the communicational aspect of gossip. Gossip, says Shibutani, ''... is restricted to small local groups in which members are bound by personal contacts and concerns the private and intimate details of the traits and conduct of specific individuals'' (1966:41–2). For Paine, ''... a working definition of gossip would include 1. talk of personalities *and* their involvement in events of the community, 2. talk that draws out other persons to talk in this way'' (1967:283). In other words, the gosspier wants both to receive and to disseminate information, to project or protect individual or group interests.

In Frobisher Bay it was found that in some cases, the content of gossip was a good index of peoples' values and attitudes, whereas in other instances, the content hid these. As they gossiped, people made guesses, declared hunches, and elicited indications from others about the probable significance of events and personalities. On some occasions, gossip was inconsistent with peoples' beliefs and actually conflicted with their behaviour. At all times, however, the content of the gossip was related to the function, and my reporting of the content, in this essay, is directed towards illuminating its possible functions. The obvious way in which gossip was used was for getting information from others; however, much gossip was used for more subtle purposes than that: it could be a camouflaged means of sounding out others with reference to a certain matter or person; it could attempt, indirectly, to transmit a particular point of view which, if necessary, could be retracted (it is difficult to withdraw from a position openly stated[2]); or, it could indicate to others a point of view held by the gossiper in the hope of altering theirs.

The Bureaucratic Setting
In the last decades, administration in the Canadian north has expanded enormously. The present system is complex and many-faceted, and includes the bureaucracies of both the Federal and Territorial Governments. It has considerable impact on the native people. Most of the territorial public service positions are held by non-native officials originating outside the territories. Their task is to establish and provide administration, communication, education, transportation, medical and welfare services. In addition, Euro-Canadians represent Federal Government and private industrial interests that control renewable and non-renewable resources of the country. Increasingly these people are newcomers to the north and many remain only for a few years.

The system does not offer adequate and satisfying employment to many native people. The bureaucratic superstructures erected by both governments demand knowledge, skills, and attitudes towards work that native people are believed not to have mastered sufficiently. Also, some of the professional organizations and labour unions require qualifications that many native people are unable to meet. Thus, at present the non-native sector provides most of the supervision while the native people continue to perform the manual labour. Consequently, much economic and political power remains concentrated in the hands of an ever-increasing number of non-native *and* transient "job-holders," while a powerless subservient native proletariat is being created.

Beginning with a modest thirty officials in 1967, the Territorial Government now employs several thousand people, and the various federal departments employ an even greater number. Official employment figures for May 31, 1974, listed a total of 2,732 approved positions in the Territorial administration (of these 435 were vacant at the time). Employed on that date were 579 teachers, 254 other school personnel, 146 employees engaged in municipal services and 1,318 other employees on staff (Report of the Task Force on Personnel Policy and Management, Government of the Northwest Territories, August 12, 1974). The 1,318 staff positions (excluding educational and municipal service personnel) mean that there is one civil servant per 29 people for a total of approximately 40,000 inhabitants. Recently, the turnover of Territorial personnel has averaged 27 percent a year. According to the same report, the employment of Inuit, Indian, and Métis people in the Territorial public service "has never exceeded 21%." Most of the native people presently employed have been recruited through special programs such as the Interpreters Corps, Classroom Assistants and Teacher Training programs, Hire North, and various apprenticeship programs. Only occasionally is a native person employed at a managerial level.[3]

Frobisher Bay

As a result of its unique development from an American airbase during World War II to the administrative centre of the Baffin region, Frobisher Bay has a heterogeneous population. In 1971, the population of the hamlet was approximately 2,300, of which 1,000 were non-native residents. Most of the latter were transient civil servants:[4] many were relatively young, middle-class, and generally beginning their professional careers. Their transiency, occupation, housing, living standard, and life-style did not allow much opportunity for learning and experiencing Inuit culture. Few of them were able to communicate in the Inuit language. Their interaction with the Inuit was largely limited to on-the-job situations in which the latter were usually the clients, patients, workers, or students. Knowledge about the Inuit, as individuals and as a culture, was thus derived from occupationally-specific contact, from books and films, as well as discussions and story-swapping with other Euro-Canadians.[5]

Since 1941, the Inuit population of Frobisher increased gradually as a result of both in-migration and natural population increase; a large part of the present population originated in Cape Dorset, Lake Harbour, and Pangnirtung. The identical attraction of the affluence displayed at the airbase and the desire for employment and educational, medical, and religious services were the predominant migration-stimulating factors. As it became clear that the settlement had limited opportunities for employment, insufficient housing, and scarce game resources, some families returned to their home communities. In 1971, there was a considerable transient Inuit population including patients of the regional hospital, some of whom stayed at the transient centre or boarded with friends or relatives on an out-patient basis. Dissatisfaction with life in Frobisher stemmed also from home sickness and many social problems such as drinking, gambling, prostitution, and racial prejudice.

That Frobisher Bay's dubious reputation was widespread among the Inuit became clear in 1971 with the opening of the new regional high school intended to serve students from the Baffin and Keewatin regions. Education authorities had expected an enrollment of four hundred students. However, parents, as well as some community councils, refused to send their children, and from the Keewatin region only ten students arrived. The total enrollment was 275 students, including 55 Inuit and 64 Euro-Canadian youngsters from Frobisher Bay.

A generalized comparison between the two ethnic groups residing in Frobisher Bay in 1971 illustrates some pertinent cultural and socio-economic differences and disparities. The Euro-Canadians were relatively young, middle-class, and trained or experienced in the particular jobs they held; they thought of themselves as professionals and were career-oriented, working within the different government departments and each reporting to his own headquarters in Ottawa or Yellowknife.

Euro-Canadians were physically healthy (having passed requisite medical examinations), well-housed, and well-nourished. Few were unemployed. Their orientation was toward southern Canada or another country of origin (only one non-native person was known to have been born in the north, in the Mackenzie region). Many people maintained close contact with the south, telephoning frequently, subscribing to newspapers from their home communities, eagerly awaiting mail, and keeping track of airline schedules. Some rented their houses in the south while they were away for "a year or two." One man's wife and children remained in England while he worked in Frobisher Bay; he visited them during Christmas and summer holidays. Most people took their holidays in the south or overseas, some sent their children to be educated there, and some women went south to have their babies. In short, their past as well as their future were outside the N.W.T.

The Inuit population of Frobisher Bay was relatively young too, but included old and disabled persons. Many lived in sub-standard overcrowded housing, and health, diet, and education standards were far below the national averages. The population included second- and third-generation settlement dwellers as well as those who only recently abandoned camp life. There was thus a wide spectrum of acculturation manifested in different life-styles, opportunities for and attitudes toward wage employment, and aspirations for the future. Coming from different areas, Inuit in Frobisher Bay spoke different dialects and belonged to different religious denominations, although the majority were Anglican. Whereas the older generations clung to narrow kinship or regional affiliations, the younger people formed groups based on interests, experience, and present- and future-oriented aspirations. A locally recognized generation gap had been created, which generated much conflict and unhappiness within Inuit families. Some Inuit were permanently employed by government or private agencies and were recipients of the same salaries and fringe benefits accorded Euro-Canadians; however, many of them were not in that position. Some were employed on a part-time basis as "casuals," while others were seasonally employed or permanently unemployed, and consequently receiving social assistance of some kind.

Gossip in a Colonial Situation

Clearly, circumstances in Frobisher Bay represent those of a colonial situation; indeed, for non-natives, going "up north" is like going "to the colony."[6] Some implications of this situation are revealed in the place that gossip has in the life of the Euro-Canadians in the town.

First of all, it appears to be a colonial situation replete with problems and ambiguities. One is immediately struck by the defensiveness of many Euro-Canadians about their presence in the town. There was a general concern about the reasons some stayed while others left, and for coming "up north" in the first place. I observed many people, especially newcomers, who felt they had to explain and justify their coming. They also frequently evaluated, and conjectured about, other peoples' reasons and motives (see *Being 'Up North,'* below).

Symptomatic of this unrest among the Euro-Canadians were tales about the terrible isolation, the mediocrity of government personnel, and charges of favouritism and nepotism: "Competition for public service positions are a sham; people hire their friends by phone"; or "the wives of important officials have first choice of the easy secretarial positions," and so on. Then there is the popular white myth about "being bushed."[7]

The remarks quoted above reflect a situation, locally perceived, as one in which there is a lack of useful information through formal, legitimate channels of communication, or as one where the information available through these channels is unreliable, contradictory, or open to conflicting interpretations. It may be expected (cf. Paine, 1970; Shibutani, 1966) that supplementary communication channels, such as rumour and gossip, will be employed to reduce the stress arising out of the ambiguous situation.

One heard many complaints about the apathy and lack of leadership of native and non-native residents alike. Some people aired their views publicly in letters sent to the local newspaper, as the following excerpts illustrate.

You are right about the apathetic attitude of this town and I for one can envision no change for a long time. This town is composed of people who WANT the best of everything – all for nothing. ... The people here deserve nothing except each other. ... This town has given me nothing but regrets for 15 months. I count every day lost. ... I'm leaving Frobisher in the near future and I only hope that I can fit into the world again after being away from it for so long (Eastern Arctic Star, January 11, 1971).

I have noticed that other peoples' needs and feelings are not much respected in this town. The only thing that seems to count is to have as much fun as *you* can (Eastern Arctic Star, February 22, 1971).

Here note should be taken of how Frobisher Bay qualifies only marginally as a "community" in the accepted sense of there being shared sets of values and well-established norms of behaviour that are more or less adhered to. On the contrary, it is a haphazardly-selected conglomeration of ever-changing job-holders from various national and socio-cultural backgrounds, who have dissimilar values and whose occupational philosophies and activities are also dissimilar or conflicting. Accordingly, I believe that few Euro-Canadians considered themselves as *we Frobisher Bayers*, but rather as *we non-natives*, and in particular as *we teachers*, *we nurses*, and so on. This, too, affected the gossip among the Euro-Canadians (see *The 'Sorting-Out' Period*, below).

I also learned that Frobisher Bay has had a negative press lately and that many residents were upset about the "unscrupulousness' of southern journalists who stayed in town for a few days. At the hotel bar, they picked up some gossip and then wrote devastating articles about "that terrible place," usually referring to crime, alcohol, and prostitution. Relatives of residents who read these stories sent strongly-worded letters "to get the hell out of there."[8]

It was frequently mentioned that the Territorial Government judge, Justice William G. Morrow, had recently called it "the cesspool of the north ... the lousiest place in the territories." He was referring not only to the physical appearance of the settlement, but also to the high rates of alcohol consumption and the many criminal offences committed under the influence of liquor. Emergency meetings were held by the recently formed Frobisher Bay Chamber of Commerce, The Royal Canadian Legion and the Frobisher Bay Executive of the Northwest Territories Public Service Association: protests were mailed to the judge as well as to the Commissioner of the Northwest Territories.[9]

The ethnic dimension of the colonial situation in Frobisher Bay undoubtedly throws its shadow across relations *within* the Euro-Canadian community – adding its contribution to the pervading sense of ambiguity and unease. Living with an Inuit family most of the time while conducting research among the Euro-Canadians, my own experience of the 'two worlds' was vivid. When I set forth every day to observe and interact with Euro-Canadians, I felt that I was crossing an invisible boundary demarcating two different ways of perceiving and acting out reality. In comparing my own experiences with other Euro-Canadians in Frobisher, especially with some old-timers and men who were married to Inuit women, my impression of the existence of two worlds was confirmed. They told me, as did indeed several Inuit, that many of the adult Inuit were consciously withdrawing from the overpowering, loud, aggressive, and competitive presence of the Euro-Canadians, especially since the latter usually did not stay long enough for the Inuit to find out if they were "good" persons. Although physically present at some of the events organized by Euro-Canadians, such as bingo games and bake sales, psychologically, the older Inuit were not "with it," I was told. Yet the younger generation of Inuit, including some with secondary education, were very much in evidence. In fact, they were becoming increasingly vocal and critical of what was happening in the north, while at the same time emulating some of the Euro-Canadians' behaviour and practices.

It is possible that more Euro-Canadians, dissatisfied with the southern way of life, will align themselves with Inuit native rights groups, or at least attempt to support them. This will increase polarization among Euro-Canadians and result in a more overt and vocal 'white backlash.' As it is, a situation approaching mutual avoidance has become more pronounced in recent years. It was mainly among the teenagers that one saw social interaction between Inuit and Euro-Canadians. Much of this socializing, however, seemed to take place in neutral places, such as the high school, the coffee shop and the cinemas, but not in the parental homes. Some of it took place in the apartments of young Inuit or 'liberal' Euro-Canadians.

Viewed from our present interest in the behaviour of Euro-Canadians and how they define their situation in Frobisher Bay, what is most significant about this ethnic dimension are Euro-Canadian perceptions of the popularly called "Eskimo problem." Few Euro-Canadians in Frobisher Bay can say that they "know the Eskimos," since each works in his own professional area and, as stated, social interaction between the two ethnic groups was slight. Not only does the work arrangement determine to a large extent which group of Inuit, or which individual Inuit, a person will come into contact with, but it also tends to influence – in accordance with the profession of the person – his perception of the Inuit community, and hence his attitudes towards it.

However, Euro-Canadian perceptions of the "Eskimo problem" differed independently of professional boundaries. Particularly evident with regard to the question of how Inuit should be treated, or what their future is to be, were the contrary viewpoints of the assimilationists and the integrationists. The former were likely to say, "Of course the Eskimos are losing their culture; they have to if they want to make it." The integrationists, on the other hand, were not sure about the values and benefits of western civilization; they were inclinded to say: "We are here to motivate them to start doing things for themselves." A particularly divisive question was that of perceived benefits *contra* detrimental effects of welfare and what influence it had on Inuit sense of identity, self-worth and responsibility.

But perhaps most significant of all was the tendency to make the problems of Frobisher Bay synonymous with the "Eskimo problem." When a committee (The Coordinating Committee of Social Problems) was formed in 1970 "to bring together local personnel working in different capacities, each of which might have a bearing on identifiable social problems within the community of Frobisher Bay," *all* the problems identified and discussed by the committee were "Eskimo."

ANALYSIS

The 'Sorting-Out' Period

I was told that the period between September and Christmas is when gossiping is at its highest, September being the month when many newcomers, especially teachers, arrive in town. This was described as "the sorting-out period." Newcomers meet each other and the old-timers, opinions are offered and received on a great variety of matters, including peoples' reasons for coming to, staying in, or leaving the town. It was at this time that the quality of life was evaluated, when people took stands, and took note of other people's positions on controversial or sensitive issues. Newcomers were socialized into current attitudes, values, practices and modes of behaviour considered appropriate by those already in Frobisher Bay – within the Euro-Canadian world as well as in relationships with the Inuit community. Specific individuals of both ethnic groups would be singled out as examples of what the speakers meant, serving as models or as examples "to stay away from."

Both old-timers (see note 1) and newcomers were interested in this communication game; old-timers asserted and protected vested interests in professional and social spheres as well as their 'ins' with the Inuit community, while newcomers made known the status and influence they brought with them from the outside. In turn they received indications of how much rank and power would likely be accorded to them locally. They had to discover, often through gossip, who was important in Frobisher Bay, and what constituted their power and influence. I was told by several people that snap decisions are often made during the first few weeks in town, decisions which proved to be crucial for the rest of an individual's stay.

Newcomers let their wishes and needs be known regarding the existing social networks, while old-timers indicated which newcomers were allowed to join in-groups and what the membership entailed in terms of behaviour and attitudes; some newcomers were excluded from certain existing groups because of things they had done or had said during the initial period. In some cases this process was so ruthless that a few people said, a few weeks after their arrival, that they would "never make it," and intended to leave as soon as possible. In connection with this, it should be mentioned that the orientation programmes conducted by the administration take place in the north after recruitment. Most departments, however, have no formal orientation programme, leaving many officials quite unprepared when they start work.

The general frontier *camaraderie*, which Wilkinson (1959) referred to, has disappeared from Frobisher Bay, as evidenced by many residents and as experienced by myself. Old-timers often nostalgically recall "the old times when things were so different" and when "people were friendly and helpful." I was told that, "There is no hospitality anymore" and that the former sharing of resources and services was now absent. In many cases this change was attributed to the growth of the settlement and especially to "too many strangers, transients, and civil servants." Often, I made a point of asking people about their neighbours or a specific local personality, and would find they were not acquainted since they belonged to different occupational or social groups. However, these same people usually would relate some information about the neighbours, which they gleaned indirectly through gossip and which was not always complimentary.

In this respect, Frobisher Bay was a strange mixture of large- and small-town atmospheres. It depended on the newcomer's personality as to whom he met and how quickly he established contacts. Whereas some people exchanged greetings after having seen one another only a few times, others treated Frobisher Bay as a large town, not acknowledging a person unless properly introduced. This was a striking feature of 'high rise' apartment living: some residents knew almost everybody on their floor and visited back and forth, often leaving doors open to indicate that visitors were welcome; others would not greet their neighbours even when they met in the elevator.

Much of the gossiping was situational, either brought on by a certain event or chance meeting: gossip could be picked up in the Commissary, the coffee shop, in the elevators, or by joining a group of secretaries at lunch. Other chance opportunities arose if one happened to meet an acquaintance while picking up one's mail at the post office, or when being driven home, or attending a bingo game, and so on. The gossiping was influenced, however, by the particular experience which the individuals brought with them, and depended on such situational contingencies as whether a person felt that he had to interact with many other people to gather information, or whether he believed himself to possess sufficient knowledge to perform his occupational duties and satisfy his private needs.

In Frobisher Bay, as elsewhere in the western world, there was a belief that women gossiped more than men; men were thought to discuss, whereas women gossiped. This may partly have been due to the fact that few women had senior positions in the various government departments and thus were likely to have less inside information. The stenographers and typists, on the other hand, formed a 'grapevine,' transmitting information from one department to another. Wives of employees, who did not work themselves, depended on information their husbands brought home – and this would then be fed into another grapevine among the wives.

Parties were another source of gossip. Generally, a great deal of liquor was consumed and people tended to speak more freely. One of the reasons for the excessive alcohol consumption among Euro-Canadians in the north might well be that the various socio-cultural backgrounds and the high personnel turn-over necessitated making new acquaintances and friends constantly, and drinking at parties was a means of facilitating and accelerating social interaction. Also, perceptions regarding shared feelings of isolation, frustration, and culture-shock may prompt people to rely on gossip more than they would in their home environments. Alcohol helps to accomplish this.

One may regard much of the social interaction, including the partying and the drinking, as well as the necessity for frequent gossip, in the light of Vallee's analogy (1962:98): "The Kabloona form a community rather like one formed by passengers of a long cruise; they are in intimate contact with one another for a period, but are always aware that this contact is likely to be broken once the fellow-passengers leave the ship." On the cruise, people make snap judgements about one another. They know little about one another's background or plans for the future, and thus they exchange confidences and discuss events and personalities, knowing the relationships will end soon. Under those circumstances, some conventional social barriers might be broken down, especially when people are reacting to one another's discomfort and frustrations, as is the case in Frobisher Bay. I was told by several people that, "although we work together now, who knows who will be here next year, and what it will be like then?" Others said that, "so-and-so is quickly working himself out of a job and I just hate to think of whom they will be sending in next." Several people mentioned that it became very lonely in the north after a few years because, "one loses one's friends so frequently." One woman repeatedly told me that her decision to resign at the end of the year was based on the fact that the friends she had made in previous years had all left and she wished not to invest more energy and emotion in making new ones. This point was stressed by others, especially single people, who had lived in Frobisher Bay for a number of years. They reported making friends, "often with the help of partying, drinking, or joining social clubs," in whom they were not really interested. The high psychological cost led some to say, "It is extremely difficult to remain human in an inhuman situation."

Being 'Up North': Financial Reasons

As previously stated, many people, especially newcomers, justified their reasons for being in Frobisher Bay; and it was in this connection that frequent evaluations and conjectures were made concerning other peoples' reasons and motives. Reasons attributed to others were usually couched in negative terms, often with a somewhat moralistic overtone. They seemed to fall into three major categories: financial, professional, and personal; together, they formed an important *genre* of gossip.

The reason ascribed to a person – although originally perhaps no more than a loose conjecture – was likely to become accepted as a virtual categorization of the whole of that person. If, for example, a professional reason were attributed to someone, that reason, with all its implicit assumptions, was often felt to *explain* that person. I found little perception of a possible change in peoples' reasons for being in the north, and there seemed to be a tendency to view others in unidimensional terms.

In the financial category of reasons, some of the most common statements were: "They only came here for the money," "he is here to make a stake," or "he had debts and had to make some money quick." The implication was that once these financial goals were met, the people would return to the south. Indeed, many people quite openly stated they were in Frobisher Bay "for the money," intending to save as much as they could so as to settle down in the south. Some of their goals were quite specific: a farm in Ontario, a trip around the world, retirement funds, or the estab-lishment of a private business. The north seemed to offer these people a better opportunity to satisfy their material needs than a comparable period working elsewhere would, especially because "there is nothing here to spend money on anyway." (These were often also the people who com-plained most bitterly about the high food prices since they wanted to avoid spending their salary on daily necessities as they would have done in the south.)

A woman who had lived in the western Arctic for many years remarked upon the differences between residents of the two regions. She found that people in Frobisher Bay "don't spend their money like in the west. There they enjoy life, they buy things, charter planes and, in general, try to have a good time." She was amazed at the number of wives who were working. A common goal of working couples was to bank one of the salaries, and a favourite pastime was to guess the amount people took with them when they left; staggering amounts of $20,000 and $30,000 were mentioned. Some were believed to play the stockmarket via long-distance telephone, whereas others were thought to make their fortunes playing poker. In addition, there were moon-lighters who sold insurance on a part-time basis, worked in the hotel kitchen at night or tended the bar. Some wives tried to supplement their husbands' incomes by running small businesses in their homes selling Avon cosmetics, providing hair-dressing services, or run-ning small boutiques.

I was told a supposedly authentic story about a professional couple who came to the Baffin region on a one-year contract with the specific intention of earning sufficient funds to enable each to go his own way upon divorce. They were employed in a small community where there were few other Euro-Canadians. The personal problems between them were magnified by the isolation, however, and they had to be flown out before their year was up.[10]

Being 'Up North': Professional Reasons

Professional reasons, also attributed to others, were surrounded by a certain amount of uncertainty. Since the Territorial Government took over, there has been considerable job insecurity among some employees. I was given the impression that "in the old days of the Federal Govern-ment," firing was almost unheard of. Once one had a northern position,

one's future in the civil service was secure; the worst that could happen
was an unwanted or undesirable transfer. In 1971, however, the Territorial
Government was felt to be "tightening up."[11]

This situation was compounded by the new ideology of "obsolescence"
first expressed by Jean Chretien, Minister of the Department of Indian
Affairs and Northern Development (now Indian and Northern Affairs), in a
speech to the Yellowknife Board of Trade on November 10, 1969 (Lotz,
1970:148). For a number of years, the Commissioner and other Territorial
officials referred to this ideology in their speeches across the Territories.
The ideology's stated goal was "to have 75% of all staff positions in the
territories filled by local residents by 1977" (Canada Year Book, 1970–71).
For example, at a community meeting in Grise Fiord in November, 1971,
Commissioner S. M. Hodgson said, "This means that every Settlement
Manager who is now employed by the government, has to work himself out
of a job and that local people have to be trained to take over." The fact that
the terms "local people," "northerners," and "native people" were used
interchangeably left some ambiguity in the minds of Euro-Canadians,
especially since few knew whether the ideology had become official policy
or the programmes through which it was to be implemented.[12]

The most common professional reason attributed to others was, "He
couldn't find a job in the south" – a comment on both rising unemployment
in southern Canada as well as the supposed deficient capabilities of the
person in question. Either an individual's qualifications were thought to be
unacceptable for employment in the south, or his work record was such
that the north was the only place left for him: "This was all he could find."
Non-Canadians were sometimes singled out in this respect since it was
believed that their degrees or diplomas were not valid in most provinces. I
met several non-Canadians who admitted this fact; the province of Newfoundland and the Northwest Territories were the only places in Canada
where they could practise their trade or profession without retaining or
rewriting examinations.

Furthermore, it was recognized that a few years of "arctic" or "cross-
cultural" experience could be valuable for some careers. In those cases, a
number of years in northern service was viewed as a calculated move and a
stepping-stone in a career culminating outside the Territories. Transients
in Frobisher Bay were sometimes also perceived as "on the way up in the
system," since a transfer to another settlement in the north usually meant a
promotion.[13] Some of these judgements were reserved for men married to
Inuit women; it was thought they had an unfair advantage over others
because "nobody can fire *them*." The belief was that by "marrying native" some men assured themselves of job security. Inter-ethnic marriages
were sometimes described as "political moves" on the part of the men
attempting to entrench themselves in the bureaucratic system. Also, it was

said that most Inuit women were not able, or not willing, to adjust to life in the south and hence, their husbands were condemned to a life of exile. Opinions of some Euro-Canadians were quite strong on this point; I was told that, "These women are dragging their husbands down"; or "They can't have anything in common." Some marriages were perceived as "irresponsible" and the men "married for sex only."

Being 'Up North': Personal Reasons

The third category of reasons attributed to others included perceptions of problems and troubles that allegedly had driven people to the north. The reasons mentioned were marital problems, a criminal record, alcoholism, an irregular work record, and so on. In general, these people were perceived as escapists who, under other circumstances, would not have dreamed of going north. Often an unhappy or unstable background of some kind was assumed or documented, and these people were believed to be running away from difficult situations, from certain people, or just because "they had to get away from it all." If one believed what was being said in Frobisher Bay, there must have been hundreds of people who came "to dry out," and a few hundred more with unhappy marriages or broken love affairs.

Reasons attributed to single women were often sexual in nature. It was said that they came "to find a man," or they were "running away from a man," while others were believed to have come "to have a good time." Implied was the belief that supervision and social sanctioning of single women was much less restrictive in the north; that single girls, especially those from rural areas, found the newly found freedom so overwhelming that "they go haywire." Whereas local matrons felt threatened by the presence of single females, men travelling through town as well as local male residents were quick to take advantage of the situation. Single women who were disinclined to drink, flirt, and occasionally avail themselves as sexual partners were likely to have a difficult time and to find their social life limited. Reasons for coming north attributed to girls and single women of any age were seldom professional or financial; it was said that by going north, women "put themselves on the market." These views were shared by male and female residents.

Besides escapists, Frobisher Bay was believed to have a number of drifters who travelled because they failed "to fit in anywhere." It was said, however, that they "can give a few years of very good work." Although they didn't like to stay in any one place for too long, they were respected because they were "independent." I met a few men who openly stated, "I never stay anywhere longer than a year." Some of these were believed to have come north in the hope of working at a responsible job, but with little supervision and no "bureaucratic hassles." I was told, "These are the ones who don't like anybody breathing down their neck." As one employer explained, they were hired regardless of their unstable employment records, mainly because their mobility had given them a certain detachment and apparently helped them shed some of their ethnocentrism. They were thus believed to suffer less from culture shock and to be able "to take things in their stride" without identifying too intensely with the local situation. They were also less likely to be "idealists" or "Peace Corps types who want to change everything overnight."

People in the idealist category, a few of whom were said to be in Frobisher Bay, usually provoked strong negative reactions from the other Euro-Canadians. Those who had been overseas with Canadian University Services Overseas, or belonged to a fundamentalist religious denomination, for example, were often placed in this category and were said not to last long in the north, the reasons being two-fold: 1) either they were ostracized to such a degree that their situation, professionally as well as socially, became untenable; or 2) they could not resolve the conflict between their ideals (these usually included variations of "helping the Eskimos" or "helping the Eskimos help themselves") and the realities of a colonial bureaucratic system that did not support them in the way they desired and, according to them, in the way the situation warranted. It was said that such people "set their expectations too high," "didn't understand the local situation," and became too impatient and disillusioned. One individual said to me, "I'm going to leave. The problems are so immense and nobody really wants to solve them. So why stay?" These people were sometimes called "Eskimo lovers" (this term has gained the same negative connotation as "nigger lover").[14]

Old-timers[15]

The perspective on much of this material can be sharpened by further considering how old-timers viewed life in Frobisher and what they made of the newcomers. It was especially in professional matters that antagonisms arose between old-timers and newcomers. Old-timers viewed many recent arrivals somewhat as interlopers: their professional ethics and goals, their impatience to get a job done, and their ignorance (and sometimes disinterest) of the country and the people were likely to destroy the delicate balance between isolation and commitment which some of the old-timers had achieved. The attitude of many old-timers was summed up in the following way: "We have seen them come and go. Usually they don't stay long enough anyway to implement the policies and programmes they propose." Their resentment is understandable if one remembers that they have to live with the results of mistakes made by transients, especially the many unanticipated results of experimental programmes initiated by newcomers, without proper consultation, soon after their arrival.

One old-timer, in Frobisher Bay since 1964, told me, "I don't know the teachers this year". My impression was that he was telling me that he had seen so many teachers passing through during previous years that he could no longer be bothered to concern himself with them. His wife knew only the teacher of her school-age son. She was equally disinterested in the others and said to me, "Oh, they are all the same anyway. They are here for the money and if they can't hack it anymore they'll leave." Both these people were vitally concerned with the town, but tended to associate with other residents of some years' standing. Old-timers generally did not take newcomers seriously before they managed to get through their first winter and return after their first summer holiday. Then it was said: "Perhaps they will do, after all."

Some old-timers, in fact, may have been threatened by many of the newcomers, with their up-to-date degrees and higher qualifications. Also, newcomers tended to criticize what they failed to understand, to point out things which "should have been done long ago" or which "could have been done better." Old-timers would say, "Let them stay for a while and they'll find out what it's really like", or "they'll pipe down after a while." I was told, "People are not committed to Frobisher Bay as a community where they plan to stay and bring up their children. The result is that they only take but don't put anything back in." Some of the old-timers would like to see the town, and the north generally, develop in certain ways, and they often have vested interests in this process. But they see transients assume control and impersonal agencies increasingly take over their former responsibilities. Some told me, "Frobisher Bay is getting too large ... We can't keep our eyes on what happens anymore."

The annual spring exodus, when people leave for good or take their holidays in the south, was described as "a real strain on those who stay behind." Some said that the high personnel turnover was "offensive." These feelings were intensified among those old-timers who would have liked to leave themselves, but could not. With rising unemployment in Canada, many people found it difficult to obtain positions elsewhere equal in rank and salary to those they held in the north.

As old-timers themselves were quick to point out, a long stay in the north does not necessarily imply commitment or dedication to the region or the people. Indeed, when listening to them, I often heard charges of "stagnation," "becoming parochial," "being bushed," and "out of touch with the world." Some actually disliked living in the north but saw no chance of getting out; alternatively, salaries were high and they decided "to stick it out as long as possible." A couple who had lived in a small settlement for several years and were in their first year in Frobisher Bay reported a sense of stagnation: "We don't really care anymore about what happens in the rest of the world. Listening to news is an effort and we hardly read our newspapers." About other old-timers they remarked, "After a while, all you meet are others in the same boat. They have lost interest, even to do a good job. Similar sentiments were expressed: "Just go along, save your neck, that's the way to survive here," and "Just drink with the boys and you'll be O.K. here."

Not surprisingly, old-timers appeared to some newcomers as "those sad people who have given up competing." They were thought to be "unable to make it in the south"; I heard that "They came when the going was good; they wouldn't be able to get a job now if they applied for it," implying their inferior capabilities as well as the fact that they seemed to be "in a rut" and had "given up." Some newcomers, therefore, felt it best not to overstay in the north lest the same fate overtake them.

CONCLUSIONS

It is true that one seldom heard *positive* reasons for being in Frobisher Bay attributed to *others*: when people reflected or gossiped about motives one rarely heard that a person may have come because he really wanted to, or because he was interested in the country and its development, the people, and so on. Barger (1972:9) noted of the Euro-Canadians in Great Whale River: "the whites appear to possess a somewhat tenuous self-esteem. A sense of guilt and insecurity indicates some negative self-judgement and lack of self-assuredness. Frequent judgement and condemnation of others might reflect an outward projection of a tenuous self-image."

If this was so in Frobisher Bay, and I do not know whether it was, the usual negative reasons attributed to others may have reflected attributes and motives the individuals questioned in themselves, and thus may have been conscious or subconscious rationalizations of their own motivations for being in the north. One person told me shortly before I left: "O.K., if you want me to be really honest, I would have to say that I was fired from several jobs down south. I just couldn't take anymore and didn't know where to turn or what to do. ... So I came here." Although not equally frank, several others indicated similar sentiments when discussing their past.

Most striking in Frobisher Bay was the pervasive ambiguity experienced by many Euro-Canadians, especially in the occupational sphere (adult education, local government and economic development officers, teachers, social workers, and so on). I found a general confusion about the goals and objectives of government policies and programmes. It was often said, and sometimes supported by evidence, that superiors held varying or even conflicting interpretations of the priorities and the problems – and how they should be tackled. Morale was often low. Many individuals did not seem to have a clear idea of their positions and roles within the bureaucratic system, or they were unhappy with the duties they appeared to have been allocated. Levels of authority and channels of decision-making were often perceived to be unclearly defined, and departmental as well as individual responsibilities were sometimes uncertain. Adequate job descriptions were lacking and communications within and between departments were poorly developed and the source of a great deal of frustration.

It was generally believed that many of the decisions and judgements officials were required to make depended on an intimate knowledge of the Inuit, but it was recognized that such knowledge was difficult to obtain in Frobisher Bay. The lack of easy communication (often conducted with the aid of untrained interpreters or children), little informal social interaction and mutual understanding of basic belief and value positions resulted in doubts, unease, and suspicion, and consequently in cynicism. Furthermore, despite the conflicts among the Euro-Canadians, there was a conscious effort to maintain "white solidarity" *vis-à vis* the Inuit. This was often verbalized, and sometimes explained in terms of "having to set an example." For this reason, social withdrawal was frowned upon – especially if it involved relations with Inuit people (visiting, drinking, or sex). This kind of behaviour earned a person the label "bushed."

It was also said that because of culture shock, a public servant "begins to earn his keep" only after about a year of adjustment. Furthermore, pertinent files were often not available or easily obtained locally because previous ones were stored in Ottawa and current ones were often sent on to Yellowknife. These factors, together with the short tenure of many of the officials, usually without a period of overlap between incumbents of positions, led to many bitter complaints about the lack of relevant information and local knowledge needed to fulfil occupational duties adequately.

The prevalence and quality of gossip, then, should come as no surprise; in fact, as I hope I have shown, gossip in a town such as Frobisher Bay is eminently predictable.

But there were those who did not gossip. For example, the school staff-room was deliberately avoided by some teachers. I think they did so for two reasons: they did not *require* the information which was transmitted and they did not *want* to share information in their possession with others. The same applied to other individuals, both newcomers and old-timers, who avoided places in town where they knew gossip sessions would likely be held.

There *were* people who gave genuine positive reasons of their own for being in Frobisher Bay. I met or was told of several people who seemed to have made a successful adjustment to their new environment, who found their jobs interesting and rewarding, who enjoyed the social life, and who saw that their future was (at least, the near future) in the north, although not necessarily in Frobisher Bay. "I can't visualize myself living anywhere else anymore," said one. Another told me, " I really like it here. It is not like in Montreal or Toronto where nobody looks you in the eye. Here, when I walk into town, I'm greeted all the time, and I know everybody." Another said, "You find out that the things you were used to in the south are not all that important after a while, and there is so much to compensate for them."[16]

Not surprisingly, these persons and the non-gossipers, by and large, were the same individuals. They told me that they were usually too busy with work, sports or hobbies to bother about going to parties to gossip. They did not frantically seek to gather or disseminate information, since they had established well-functioning communication channels – channels that often included members of the Inuit community, a fact which they did not always publicize.

NOTES

1   Old-timers, as perceived in Frobisher Bay and used in this paper, is a relative term; it is a situational rather than an absolute description. In some cases, a 'second-year northerner' might be perceived as an old-timer by a newcomer, but not by other old-timers. Generally, people with five years northern experience or more were considered old-timers. Occasionally, an old-timer is referred to as "someone who was here five minutes before I was."
2   See Paine (1970) on "signed" and "unsigned" messages.
3   This has long been a contentious issue, with the government placed uncomfortably between demands of native people and the "white back-lash." For example, on June 20, 1974, the Commissioner stated that, "The Executive has identified two positions specifically for native people. This is not to discriminate against anyone, but to be sure that native people are in the Executive Offices" (Council of the Northwest Territories Debates, 53rd sessions, 7th council, p. 149). The next day, he said that lack of education and training were the reasons that not more native people held senior positions in government, but also that, "Various other people, particularly the Brotherhoods ... are able to offer senior positions ... to people that we would be delighted to have in the senior levels of our governments, or working up through the middle levels" (op. cit., p. 217). One of the native councillors, however, pointed out that the two proposed positions were, in effect, clerical, "and that the job entails getting statistics in the field on certain things that might have to do with native people," and asked whether the government would "reconsider the fact that only clerical positions are being made available" (p. 219). The Commissioner took "the question as noticed."
4   In the Eastern Arctic, unlike the Mackenzie District, there are as yet no stable, non-government, white residents (the "petits blancs" in colonial parlance).
5   This had led to a rather confused situation with out-of-date stereotypes about "the real Eskimo" because many of the books and films emphasize traditional culture. The lack of social contact means that many Euro-Canadians were unaware of present Inuit life-styles.
6   For statements about the Canadian Arctic as a colony, see Ferguson (1971), Jenness (1968), Smith (1971), and Vallee (1971), among others; for useful general analyses of colonialism see Mannoni (1956) and Memmi (1967). Numerous cross-cultural parallels between colonialism in the Canadian north and in, for instance, British and French Africa are quite evident from a reading of Fallers (1965), Mercier (1965), and O'Brien (1972). Also, see Tanner (1964) for an illuminating description of the role of gossip among white administrators in colonial Tanganyika.
7   "Being bushed" was explained as "a feeling of being locked in, of being imprisoned with the walls closing in on you. You just have to get out or go crazy." Getting out means leaving the north, either totally or for a long holiday. Implied in the concept is that the bushed person

is no longer responsible for his actions, and that he no longer conforms to the respectable middle-class image most Euro-Canadians seek to maintain. A girl who, because of promiscuous behaviour, had been the subject of much malicious gossip, suddenly received the label "bushed." Immediately people pitied her and said, "She doesn't care anymore what happens to her. She should leave." It also seemed to be possible to arrive bushed, but how, I never really understood.

8   Cf. Finnie (1948:194) for similar incidents in the Western Arctic.

9   This happened some time after Prince Philip's visit when he let a remark slip about "this garbage heap."

10   According to informants in Yellowknife (in summer of 1974), the financial reason has decreased because present salaries in the north are alleged to be not much higher than in the south, whereas the cost of living is considerably higher in the north. I was told by several senior officials that it is now very difficult for the Territorial Government "to maintain a competitive position in the Canadian labour market." The 435 job vacancies are partly related to this.

11   At the same time I was also told that, because of recruitment and removal expenses, the administration did not encourage frequent or detailed supervision and inspection of employees – thereby hoping that they would remain in the north.

12   Asking about the fate of the ideology in Yellowknife (in summer of 1974) I was given to understand that it had died "an unofficial death" and was not referred to anymore in polite company. The employment figures presented at the beginning of this paper testify to its spectacular lack of success (cf. note 3).

13   The structure of the administrative system itself appears to make frequent transfers inevitable, particularly for purposes of promotion within the system. Senior officials are often transferred "to take care of a difficult situation." Also, until recently, official policy stated that employees were to be removed after five years in any one settlement, presumably to counteract over-identification with the particular inhabitants and their problems and needs, and to maintain official impartiality and impersonality, considered to be essential and desirable features in western bureaucracies.

14   It is uncertain how effective they could be in bridging the gap between the two ethnic groups. They tended to receive such strong condemnation from other Euro-Canadians that they succeeded mainly in separating themselves from them.

15   See note 2.

16   These people enjoyed in common certain features of life in the north: a peaceful rhythm of life and lack of tension, a beautiful landscape and unpolluted air and water, a good standard of living, close family relations and satisfying face-to-face interaction with others who enjoyed the same things. When mentioning these positive aspects, they did not, as did many others, dwell on what was unavailable. The felt deprivations of Euro-Canadians are too numerous to mention here. They contained the common themes of lack of choice and variety: little choice in selecting one's housing, entertainment, food and clothing, and the lack, as well as rapid change-over, of like-minded people from among whom to choose friends. I do not, however, want to minimize the very real physiological and psychological stresses involved in adjusting to a new, often-called "extreme" environment such as the Arctic (cf. Stillner and Stillner, 1974).

References

BARGER, W. K.
   1972 *Ethnic Character and Culture Change. The Eskimo and Cree of Great Whale River; a Working Paper.* Chapel Hill, North Carolina, Department of Anthropology, University of North Carolina.
Canada Year Book
   1970–71 *The Canada Year Book*. Ottawa, Bureau of Statistics.

Council of the Northwest Territories
1974 Council of the Northwest Territories Debates, 53rd Session, 7th Council. Ottawa.
FALLERS, LLOYD A.
1965 *Bantu Bureaucracy*. Chicago, University of Chicago Press.
FERGUSON, JACK
1971 "Eskimos in a Satellite Society." In J. L. Elliott (ed.), *Native Peoples*. Scarborough, Prentice-Hall Inc.
FINNIE, RICHARD
1948 *Canada Moves North*. Revised Edition. Toronto, Macmillan of Canada.
JENNESS, DIAMOND
1968 *Eskimo Administration: V. Analysis and Reflections*. Montreal, Arctic Institute of North America.
KOSTER, DITTE
1972 "Frobisher Bay: Ambiguity and Gossip in a Colonial Situation." Unpublished M.A. thesis, Memorial University of Newfoundland.
LOTZ, JIM
1970 *Northern Realities: The Future of Northern Development in Canada*. Toronto, New Press.
MCHUGH, PETER
1968 *Defining the Situation*. Indianapolis, Bobbs-Merrill.
MANNONI, O.
1956 *Prospero and Caliban: The Psychology of Colonization*. London, Methuen.
MEAD, GEORGE H.
1970 "Self as Social Object." In G. P. Stone and H. A. Farberman (eds.), *Social Psychology Through Symbolic Interaction*. Toronto, Ginn.
MEMMI, ALBERT
1967 *The Colonizer and the Colonized*. New York, Beacon Press.
MERCIER, PAUL
1965 "The European Community of Dakar." In P. L. Van Den Berghe (ed.), *Africa: Social Problems of Change and Conflict*. San Francisco, Chandler.
O'BRIEN, RITA C.
1972 *White Society in Black Africa: The French of Senegal*. Evanston, Illinois, Northwestern University Press.
PAINE, ROBERT
1967 "What is Gossip About? An Alternative Hypothesis." *Man* (N.S.), 2:278–85.
PAINE, ROBERT
1970 "Informal Communication and Information Management." *Canadian Review of Sociology and Anthropology*, 7(3).

SHIBUTANI, TOMATSU
1966 *Improved News. A Sociological Study of Rumor.* Indianapolis, Bobbs-Merrill.
SMITH, DEREK G.
1971 "The Implications of Pluralism for Social Change in a Canadian Arctic Community." *Anthropologica*, 13(1–2):193–214.
STILLNER, VERNER and MARIANNE STILLNER
1974 "Adaptational Experiences in an Extreme Environment." Paper read at the Third International Symposium on Circumpolar Health, Yellowknife, NWT.
TANNER, R. E. S.
1964 "Conflict within Small European Communities in Tanganyika." *Human Organization*, 23:319–27.
VALLEE, FRANK
1962 *Kabloona and Eskimos in the Central Keewatin.* Canadian Research Centre for Anthropology, Ottawa.
VALLEE, FRANK
1971 "Eskimos of Canada as a Minority Group." In J. L. Elliott (ed.), *Native Peoples.* Scarborough, Prentice-Hall Inc.
WILKINSON, DOUG
1959 "A Vanishing Canadian." *Beaver*, Spring:25–28.

Neighbours in the 'Bush': White Cliques*

9

David Riches

INTRODUCTION

Social scientists who go to the Canadian Arctic are often challenged by Euro-Canadians there to spend less time studying the Inuit and more time studying the whites. Conspicuous among whites in northern settlements is their tendency to group into cliques, and in accepting their challenge to 'do something on the whites' I offer an analysis of this behaviour below.

It will be suggested that in the small, isolated, northern settlements, where visiting is the recreational preoccupation, cliques arise in order to exercise retribution over adversaries in disputes. Since this hypothesis raises some definitional problems, a brief discussion of the sociological characteristics of cliques and fractions seems appropriate.

Cliques and Fractions

Although cliques have frequent mention in sociological literature, they are usually dealt with in relation to – and often subsidiary to – other types of coalition, particularly factions. They have no consistent definition, although the one offered here appears to be fairly representative:[1] cliques are small informal groups which, without formal leadership, intensively interact in the sharing and conservation of certain purposes, opinions, or life-style. Factions, by contrast, are informal groups recruited by a specific leader for the purpose of exacting maximal spoils from a political contest (for example, Firth, 1957:292; Nicholas, 1965; Boissevain, 1968:551; Bailey, 1969:52–4). Thus, factions are clearly purposive and emerge to fight political battles. Cliques, however, are more formally defined and their purpose vague. Indeed, many authors offer a purely formal definition; for instance, Homans sees a clique as a group whose "interactions with one another are more frequent than they are with outsiders or members of other sub-groups" (1951:133). Although cliques may in various circumstances have "many bases" (Goffman, 1959:84) or functions, a consideration of their most typical social linkages would suggest, nonetheless, that they often fulfil a common *general* function in the social process as well.

Most cliques have in common an association of individuals who are not linked by structural directives, or if they are so linked, they interact on

*This essay draws inspiration from an unpublished manuscript on white cliques by Philip Lange; the author and the editor wish to acknowledge Mr. Lange's generosity.

occasions not specified by such directives. In the latter instance, Smith notes that when kin are co-members of a Grenadian elite clique, they are selectively recruited from a wider range of equally close relatives (1965:59). I suggest, therefore, that however these cliques are bounded – whether through common age, school, colour, language, place of work, or shared political or economic interests – and to whatever extent they are engaged in a wider social arena as cores of factions (Nicholas, 1966:66; Smith, 1965), or in ellicit economic exchange (Goffman, 1961:245), cliques arise in satisfaction of people's inclinations towards private relationships and identification with private groupings.

This view stems from the work of Wolf (1966) and Paine (1969) on friendship, the relationship through which clique association is most often expressed. Privacy in a social relationship means here that "the relationship may be established and maintained independent of reference to the various group-derived statuses of the individuals. It also means that particular individuals may choose whether or not they will communicate to others the content and the norms of conduct of the relations between them" (Paine, 1969:513). The clique is thus typically "the carrier of an affective element, which may be used to counter-balance the formal demands of the organization, to render life within it more acceptable and meaningful. Importantly it may reduce the feeling of the individual that he is dominated by forces beyond himself, and serve to confirm the existence of his ego" (Wolf, 1966:15). It is precisely its privacy that allows the clique its extensive range of (private) purposive activity.

In contrast to cliques, factions are public organizations designed to exploit or influence situations in the public arena. They are mobilized, as far as possible, along existing structural ties (and hence on the basis of existing obligations); for political success – especially if in a fight or an election (Nicholas, 1965:57) – is determined largely by numbers recruited, and recruitment will prove expensive if based only on bribes or on the promise of later material reward (Bailey, 1969:52). Cliques, as we have seen, cannot utilize structural ties; they are unlikely, therefore, to exploit the familiar symbols and rituals that organizationally bind structurally-linked individuals. Since they are not directed towards action in the public arena, cliques are unlikely to recruit support through the promise of spoils from group participation in this arena. Rather, cliques typically achieve an identity by the continued and frequent interaction of their members, the logistics of which inevitably limit their size.

The Setting

Anurivik, a small settlement in Canada's Northwest Territories (NWT), arose as a result of government socio-economic development of Inuit communities during the 1960s; by 1970, about 160 Inuit lived there permanently and their livelihood was oriented mainly towards hunting and fishing. Most of the adult whites – there were no more than ten at any one time – were government employees: administrators, resource development officers, school teachers, nurses, and mechanic/power plant operators; non-government whites included the manager of the Inuit co-operative and researchers (social scientists). Missionaries, Hudson's Bay Company (HBC) managers, and Royal Canadian Mounted Police (RCMP), commonly resident in similar settlements, were absent in Anurivik. Sometimes, one individual simultaneously held several of the positions listed above. All the positions required some interaction with the local Inuit and, with the exception of researchers, involved the instruction of particular skills.

Anurivik is extremely isolated. Since it lacks an airstrip, it is cut off from the outside world (bar the occasional emergency helicopter) for about four months of the year: in the fall, when the sea ice is freezing, and in the spring, when the ice is thawing and dissipating. Recreational facilities for whites are limited and offering mutual hospitality in each other's houses is the main pastime. The turnover of white personnel in the Canadian Arctic is high,[2] particularly in isolated settlements; in one, Lange (this vol.) met 22 adult whites over a 10-month period but only 11 at any one time: In Anurivik, there were 17 people over 18 months, but only 10 at any one time. Few whites in government employ stay more than 18 months.

Since their jobs are mainly concerned with the Inuit, whites seldom interact at work; nevertheless, the positioning of their houses, and often their place of work, put them under continual surveillance of one another. This, together with their small number, their intensive rate of free-time visiting – virtually every evening of the week and most of the week-ends – result in their awareness of the most intimate details of one another, probably to an extent that would be reserved for 'best friends' in the southern Canadian culture from which they have come.

It is rare for whites to visit regularly Inuit (although Inuit frequently visit whites). When whites arrive in the north, they usually have intentions of breaking down the cultural barrier between themselves and the Inuit; in practice, most find it too difficult. At best only superficial Inuit-white friendships develop. The occasional white who does manage to develop a deeper relationship risks being described, behind his back, as "going native."[3]

Despite the appearance of extensive visiting among Anurivik whites, this visiting is markedly selective. A particular individual will visit certain others regularly – and these we call his clique mates – while consciously avoiding the remainder. The local or folk explanation of this situation stresses the inevitability of tensions ("Here we are cooped up for the winter with only a dozen other whites ... it's no wonder tensions de-

TABLE 1

Chronology of Anurivik Whites

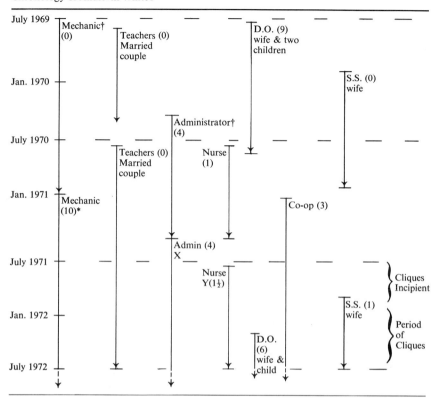

Key: Years of previous northern experience are bracketed. Spouses present are specifically indicated.

D.O. – resource development officer

Co-op – manager of Eskimo co-operative

S.S. – social scientist

†these two men shared a house for three months.

*most of this man's northern experience was gained in defence establishments and therefore under conditions markedly different from those in an Eskimo settlement.

velop."). However, this explanation is questionable, as it may be merely a rationalization. The most obvious evidence for this latter view is a two-year period (from July 1969 to July 1971) during which cliques did *not* emerge, in spite of a comparatively slow rate of personnel turnover. In contrast, another six-month period was one of virulent clique activity. The Anurivik chronology (Table 1) illustrates the two contrasting periods and also helps eliminate possible causal factors of its particular cliques, such as the presence of non-working women (with or without children), or the sharing of a residence; nor were sexual jealousies found to be contributing causes in Anurivik.

As the chronology suggests, individuals X and Y were the 'catalysts' of clique formation. However, it must be emphasized that other persons were equally active participants once the cliques had emerged. What is significant about the 'catalysts' is that they were poorly adapted to life in a small arctic settlement: The norms peculiar to this society will now be considered.

SOCIAL NORMS

Old-timers and Newcomers

A number of social norms – those which we call the public norms – have emerged among whites in northern settlements as a result of the special exigencies of isolated arctic life. Historically, most of these norms evolved under earlier conditions strikingly different from those today. It is therefore possible that some of these norms are no longer appropriate, generate conflict, and are at the root of clique behaviour. At all events, it is useful to make a distinction between the old-timers – whites who came north more than ten years ago, before the proliferation of government settlements and services – and the newcomers – those who have come north within the last ten years to implement these services.* The old-timers were representatives of the three traditional white agencies of the Arctic: the Church, the HBC and the RCMP. They lived in exceedingly small groups at trading and mission posts which had rudimentary facilities and very tenuous aircraft and radio connections with the outside world. Although Inuit would only occasionally visit these posts to trade or to collect welfare, the style of life of the old-timers was supposedly one of adaptation to the arctic environment, particularly in becoming adept at Inuit customs, skills, and language; indeed, many old-timers were lured to the Arctic by the promise of just this style of life (for example, by HBC recruitment advertising). The old-timers' social patterns seemed relatively well-adapted to maintaining harmony among groups of perhaps two to four persons in extreme isolation; visiting was comparatively infrequent and social behaviour characterized by relative formality and reserve. It is possible, of course, that this formality was a cover for antagonisms which had to be suppressed because of the participants' vital dependence on one another.

Despite the vastly improved amenities in northern settlements in recent years (communication and housing are obvious examples), the newcomers are, in marked contrast to the old-timers, non-adapters to the Arctic; they stay a comparatively short period of time and while there, seek to replicate

*Cf. Koster, this vol. (ed.).

a southern Canadian style of life in their settlement. A particular feature of their behaviour is how they seek compensation – for the isolation and lack of recreational facilities – by intensive visiting.

Public Norms

Newcomers no longer need the old-timers' presence in their settlement (and there are none in Anurivik) in order to learn the public norms of arctic community life; this task is taken care of by orientation courses before coming north. Although such 'orientation' is subsequently often found to be irrelevant to a person's specific job in a specific settlement, it nevertheless introduces the newcomer to the public norms of northern community life.

All the public norms verbalized by whites in Anurivik refer to the isolating circumstances of arctic life. All evidence shows that these norms are well-internalized, and when a person does not observe them in daily behaviour, he usually has an explanation – indicating his own awareness of his deviation. One set of public norms derives from the general values of hospitality and neighbourliness. New arrivals to the settlement are usually offered lodging in a white's house, or will be loaned equipment to tide them over the difficulties of moving house. Similarly, since the settlement's retail outlet is unlikely to cater to all their southern-style needs, there is extensive borrowing between whites. Other public norms derive from the value of tolerance. Whites are enjoined to get along together and to tolerate personal idiosyncracies. Occasionally, social and psychological fears and tensions arising from the settlement's isolation will result in a white becoming 'bushed.'* The symptoms of this vary, depending on the personality of the individual concerned. They may become manifest in reclusiveness, excessive drinking, or in an irrational detestation of the settlement and its Inuit inhabitants. A 'bushed' person may become the subject of gossip (though never to his face), but efforts will be made to visit him and draw him into group activities; he will certainly not be ignored. Indeed, whites often remark how a person's strange behaviour is tolerated far more in the north than it would be in the south.

A third set of public norms concerns co-operation in work for the benefit of the community and its Inuit inhabitants. Such co-operation is usually diffuse since whites largely perform their jobs independently of one another.[4] A white is

expected to co-operate with the other kabloona [whites], to seek their guidance – particularly if he is a [new arrival] – and to mix with the others in social activities. Like the other kabloona, he is expected to be a good example to the Eskimos, to refrain from excessive drinking, overt sex play with Eskimo women, swearing, off-color stories, and so on, in front of the Eskimos.

*Cf. Koster, this vol. (ed.).

He learns that he must maintain the appearance of solidarity with other kabloona, even if he is at odds with some of them. For instance, he learns that disputes between kabloona are not to be argued out in front of the Eskimos. With the latter he is expected to be friendly but not overtly intimate: some social distance must be maintained (Vallee, 1967:105).

Private Norms

In contrast to the well-internalized and verbalized public norms, whites in Anurivik are also influenced by a number of private norms that are inferred rather than verbalized. In many situations these norms flatly contradict the public ones.

Given the isolation, and hence, social closure of small arctic settlements, it is fruitful to examine these norms on the basis of an analogy between whites in the arctic and inmates in a total institution. Of course, since a white's life in an arctic settlement is neither regimented nor formally administered (cf. Goffman, 1961:11), the analogy is not perfect; nevertheless, the intensive verbalization of public norms might constitute a substitute for such regimentation. In addition, on entering the settlement, whites may experience considerable "modification" (*op, cit*.:31–3) as their personal privacy is assaulted by the persistent staring and inquisitiveness of the Inuit. Such "regimentation" and "mortification" may conspire to threaten the whites' "prior conception of self" (*op. cit*.:40). Certainly in the closed society of the arctic settlement, a premium is put on "removal activities" (*op. cit*.:67), such as the yearly trip to the neighbouring township for a conference with colleagues from other settlements, an activity that is "sufficiently engrossing and exciting to lift the participant out of himself, making him oblivious to himself for the time being to his actual situation" (*loc. cit*.).

But while in the settlement, whites develop what Goffman calls "secondary adjustments," behaviour that "provides [them] with important evidence that [they] are still their own man, with some control of [their] environment" (*op. cit*.:56). These secondary adjustments – the private norms of settlement life – are essentially southern-Canada-orientated. Basically, they constitute (1) either a refusal to lose southern Canadian values in spite of their incompatibility with the public norms of northern life; or (2) through preparing-to-return-home behavioural orientations, the norms provide an indication of the non-identity of the whites with arctic life.

Thus, the first private norm states that *hospitality should be reciprocated in a balanced manner*, and not in the generalized manner (to use Sahlins' 1965 terms;) demanded by public norms. Each white family keeps a mental ledger of hospitality extended and owed. One woman was heard to say: "We've had 'A' here for a meal three times, yet not once has he invited us in return."

A second category of private norms derives from the fact that most northern whites are aware that they are priviledged to be working among what are popularly the most exotic of Canadian ethnic groups. Thus, quite a few describe the rigours and customs of the Arctic in articles to local newspapers back home (and the Inuit are becoming increasingly irritated by being the unpaid subjects for the whites' incessant photography). As a result of this particular kind of awareness (which, we submit, stems from continuing identity with southern Canada), whites have two desires – for Inuit artifacts (such as clothing, animal skins, and carvings) and for a knowledge of (as opposed to a proficiency in) Inuit customs and language. Yet such artifacts and information are in short supply, and as a result, three important private norms emerge. The first disallows the monopolization by a single person of any one artifact. The second discourages the inflation of prices payable to the Inuit for the artifacts; a newly-arrived white will have no idea of the value of Inuit-produced goods, but on enquiry, will find out from other whites that there is a going rate – often too little, considering the time taken for the manufacture of the goods.

The third norm, arising from the desire for information, is the assertion that knowledge about a settlement accrues in direct proportion to the time spent in the settlement. If, for example, there were old-timers in a settlement, it is they who would have the greatest knowledge of Inuit customs in general, and of the idiosyncracies of the local Inuit population. As a result of their more intensive contact with the Inuit people, social scientists are particularly vulnerable to criticism in respect to this norm, and if they bandy about their knowledge too much and too soon, are liable to be branded by the other whites as upstarts.[5] However, the few social scientists who have worked in the north for a long time and have experienced considerable hardships in their study are almost revered.

Others also fall afoul of this norm, especially those who suffer from "previous settlement-itis": the need to compensate for newness to a settlement – and hence low pecking order on the knowledge scale – by incessant talk about a settlement previously lived in. This is found particularly annoying when opinions and hypotheses about the previous settlement are applied uncritically to the new one. Each settlement is proud of its uniqueness.

A third group of private norms arises from the whites' work situation. All the whites in Anurivik were specialists, and in southern Canada, could expect institutionally-supported deference from others. However, some of the circumstances of life in a small arctic settlement today – in particular the intensive scrutiny of each other's work performance – tend to heighten sensitivity and apprehension over the delivery of this expected deference; and private norms have been developed to preserve and enhance the inviolability of the specialist. Other people's meddling, interference and informing are the anathemas from which a person must protect himself; I shall consider each briefly.

Charges of meddling are usually traced back to the crusading or vocational approach to Inuit welfare and behaviour demonstrated by a small minority of whites, the so-called 'do-gooders.' While the majority of whites perform the work required of them adequately but minimally, the 'do-gooders' are likely to over-exert themselves and, perhaps, step outside their specific job requirements. They overact on occasions when the majority may be said to underact, and they are likely to be accused of breaking the norm against meddling.*

It is especially when he gives orders to another white that a person will be charged with interference; his misdemeanour may be no more than invoking an official arrangement of hierarchy in a local cultural context, when – because each expert tends to be responsible to his own government or private agency outside the community – this should be left as unexpressed as possible. Thus, a mechanic would likely resent being given orders about his machines; the district officer would not appreciate being told when to set his seal nets by an administrator who, although the senior person in the community, had no specialized knowledge of such equipment. Like the skipper of a Norwegian herring boat *vis-à-vis* his crew (Barth, 1966:7), a wise administrator would translate such a "relationship of command ... into a voluntary relationship of leadership and acceptance."

Apprehension over informing arises because, although each white in a settlement might be a specialist, his promotion prospects may nonetheless be influenced by others in the settlement. His 'boss' is many miles away in the regional township, and finding it difficult to assess the work of his man in the field, he is likely to take note of any reports that emanate from the settlement. Such information is typically gleaned from whites who are based in the regional town, but who circulate, spending no more than two months in surrounding settlements – perhaps substituting for a man on holiday, or giving courses to the Inuit.

The regional town for Anurivik is itself relatively small; it has a white population of about 700, with perhaps 150 people working in government departments directly concerned with Eskimo development and welfare. The whites who are sent out to visit settlements are thus likely to be acquainted with (and beholden to) the heads of most of the government departments concerned. Accordingly, it is not unusual for them to be asked to secure information about particular whites in the settlements they are to visit; certainly they will be asked whenever a complaint against a particular white (by another white, or by an Inuit) has been lodged, this occasionally being the reason for their visit. Obviously the easiest method is for them to

*Cf. discussion of "meddling" in Lange, this vol. (ed.).

TABLE 2

Summary of Private and Public Norms

PUBLIC	
derived from:	*manifest in:*
hospitality and	helping out (generalized
neighbourliness	reciprocity)
tolerance	social inclusion
co-operation	white solidarity
PRIVATE	
derived from:	*manifest in:*
domestic resource	balanced reciprocity
conservation	
egalitarian access to	ownership of and pricing of
arctic 'credentials'	Eskimo artifacts; knowledge
	hierarchies
professional competence	inviolability of the specialist;
and authority	'playing it by the book'

secure the information from fellow whites in the settlement, many of whom will *not* be reluctant to gossip about a person whose work performance, or other aspect of his conduct, has been an annoyance. Thus, there is some tension between whites in a settlement lest the third norm of the work situation be broken: not to inform on another's job performance. Jobs requiring the least specialized knowledge – such as administration or the management of a co-operative – are the most vulnerable to informing, since opinions about the way they should be performed are the most easily held by non-incumbents.[6]

The tensions between whites in their performance of job roles (because of potential accusations of meddling, interference, or informing) are controlled by *a general overall norm* of 'playing it by the book.' This norm is the implicit subject of many conversations in which the execution of certain tasks in borderline situations, on the basis of what is laid down in employers' instructions to employees, is intensely discussed. The existence of this norm does not preclude conscientious fulfillment of job requirements, nor co-operation in particular tasks, provided such co-operation is agreed upon. It does, however, occasionally encourage a 'pass-the-buck' attitude; for example, when an unpleasant situation can be avoided by all whites on the grounds that it is someone else's duty (or right) to deal with it.

CLIQUE FORMATION AND MAINTENANCE

Social Control

The contradictions between public and private norms (see Table 2) are the inevitable source of many of the disputes in Anurivik, and this situation directs our attention to the means of social control that are available.

There are no formal adjudicatory institutions in small arctic settlements; there are few structurally-directed obligations to restrain disputants, for there are very few formal relationships between whites; yet casual avoidance of a deviant person is quite impossible. Thus, in default of other methods, the standard retaliatory procedure to alleged norm-breaking in Anurivik is deliberately to deny a highly valued social gratification – that of visiting and being visited. Such attempts at ostracism, I maintain, are responsible for the formation of cliques.

That social interaction is highly valued by whites as an end in itself is quite evident in their fear of being "left out of things." For when a person is left out – for example, from a snowmobile expedition – he may be considerably piqued, even though it is known that he is not particularly fond of snowmobiling; the efforts of the group to allay his fears may be quite elaborate. It should also be noted that, because of the emphasis on visiting, whites lose interest in their hobbies (if they have any), even though the opportunity to develop hobbies is emphasized in recruitment advertising.

As stated previously, the public value of tolerance requires that a white's personal idiosyncrasies be ignored. Even if a person persistently abuses a norm of interpersonal behaviour, many northerners will tolerate the abuse and avoid retaliation for a longer period of time than they would in the south. However, each individual does have his breaking point.

This process of social control may be seen in the following two cases and the retaliatory action that was taken in each.

Case 1: the polar bear skin. The first polar bear skin of the new hunting season had been bought by Bill, and Jim declared his interest in the next one. When a second bear was killed, Jim began negotiations with the Inuit hunter with the apparent blessing of Bill. However, Jim did not know that Bill had been asked by a person in another settlement, where polar bears are scarce, to buy a skin on his behalf. This person was prepared to pay a price well above the going rate. So when Jim was about to make his transaction, Bill suddenly stepped in and offered an extremely high price for the skin which, since Jim was not prepared to bid higher, the Inuit accepted.

Bill had clearly broken two private norms: firstly he had monopolized a rare artifact (he had two skins now – though one was not for himself – and Jim none); secondly, he had inflated the local price for bear skins. Subsequently, all Inuit hunters demanded his high price. Bill justified his behaviour according to a public norm: he had contributed to the well-being of the Inuit, and hence the settlement, by securing the best possible price for a skin.

Case 2: the redirected plane. A settlement was expecting two airplanes, the first from the regional township to collect a mechanic, the other from another settlement to deliver freight. It was known that there was a sick child in the nursing station, but the nurse had not declared her intention of sending him to the hospital in the regional township on one of the expected planes. When the plane from the regional township arrived, it could not land because of bad weather and had to return without the mechanic. The other plane, however, managed to land later in the day. The administrator met the plane and asked the pilot if he would take the mechanic and sick child to the regional centre; and he sent a message to the nurse to radio for clearance for sending a patient on a plane not normally chartered by the medical authorities. Later the nurse condemed the administrator for making arrangements on her behalf: "It's my duty to arrange the evacuation of patients and if I had wanted Johnny to go out, I would have met the plane myself."

From the nurse's point of view, the administrator (an over-reactor) had meddled in her affairs, and had not 'played it by the book.' A non-expert acting on her behalf had symbolically challenged her competence. But had she confronted the administrator, he would have claimed that he acted in the spirit of the publicly held value of co-operation between whites.

At some point, an aggrieved person may find an alleged norm-breaker's behaviour intolerable and become a plaintiff seeking to have public opinion support his views. Both Jim and the nurse did so. To do so, however, is dangerous because he cannot be sure of the reaction of other whites, who in supporting him, might have to ignore public norms. If possible, he will present his point of view as being consistent with both public and private norms. In case 1, Jim maintained that the price paid for the bear skin was, considering its size and quality, unrealistic for any NWT settlement, and that the Inuit had been done a disservice by Bill's purchase in that they would now expect prices that no one would be prepared to pay. In case 2, the nurse maintained that since Johnny was not particularly unwell, his family had been done a disservice by his unnecessary evacuation.

The support of public opinion is vital to a plaintiff if he seeks to ostracize his accused – the standard form of social control. For in the context of the intensive social interaction that exists among the whites, the only way to ensure, unilaterally, the avoidance of one individual is the hypothetically undesired path of avoiding all. (There was a case of an individual who followed this path for a short while, voluntarily ostracizing himself without presenting his case to public opinion.) So neutral whites must be informed that the plaintiff prefers to be visited rather than do any visiting himself, for in following the latter course, he would risk meeting the person he sought to avoid.

The position of the alleged norm-breaker is equally delicate. He may not even realize that he has broken a private norm. He may only discover his alleged transgression when informed by a neutral white who is, however, affectively closer to him than to the plaintiff; the plaintiff himself, in these early stages, is unlikely to confront the wrongdoer, as by so doing he would proclaim his own deviation from the public value of tolerance. Sooner or later, however, there will be a number of unambiguous signs by which an individual can perceive that he is the subject of displeasure: if both of the principals are together in a third person's house, the plaintiff will ignore the other, or even leave; or if in the plaintiff's house, the offender will not be offered refreshments, even when others are being served; or if the offender invites the plaintiff to his house, the invitation will be refused.

Whether or not he eventually learns of his supposed error, the alleged transgressor will feel hurt by the plaintiff's behaviour – which is, of course, quite in contradiction to the public norm of hospitality – and will search his mind for incidents in which the *plaintiff* had broken northern norms, but which he, himself, ignored in the interests of keeping the peace.

Mobilization of Support

The principals in the dispute have thus emerged. Both can probably justify their behaviour as consistent with northern values; both are probably unrepentant; reconciliation is now virtually impossible. In attempting now to ostracize one another, each is likely to use one of four strategies to solicit the support of other whites in the settlement.

(1) *Exploitation of affective ties.* One of the principals might say to another person: "If I come to your house and find so-and-so (the other principal) there, I'm afraid I won't be able to stay." If, as the speaker hopes (and perhaps knows), this person feels affectively closer to him than to his opponent (and especially if that person considers the speaker's point of view justifiable), it is likely that he will join in making the other principal unwelcome in his house.

(2) *Setting one's opponent against "all" others.* One principal might criticize another and end up by saying to him: "Everyone feels like this about you." Now, it is quite likely that "everyone" did find fault with this person and, like all whites, he was gossiped about behind his back. But probably "everyone" had no intention of allowing him to know of their criticisms, perhaps because they merely believed his behaviour to be idiosyncratic, perhaps because they did not believe his norm-breaking to be serious enough to warrant retaliatory action. They are now embarrassed that their feelings have been made public, and yet, not easily able to deny them, they find themselves considered by the principal they criticized to be supporters of the other principal who made their criticisms public.

(3) *Use of patronage.* There are important implications for clique support recruitment if one of the principals holds a job which allows him the dispatch of many favours. The mechanic holds such a job; his specialized knowledge is in short supply in a small arctic settlement and his goodwill is often sought by other whites when their snowmobiles or outboard motors need repairing. To opt for the opposing group to the mechanic can thus be a considerable sacrifice for a non-mechanically-minded white. In Paine's terms (1971), the mechanic is a dispenser of patronage; if he wishes, he may choose whether or not to provide resources for the other whites (his clients) on the basis of the attitudes they adopt.

The dispenser of patronage *par excellence* is the administrator: as the government's general representative in the settlement, he is involved in many ways with the welfare of every government-employed white there; moreover, as the senior person in the settlement, some of the other whites are directly accountable to him for certain aspects of their jobs: the mechanic is one of these. Not surprisingly, then, the administrator-mechanic relationship is commonly a sensitive one in northern settlements; it can also be understood in terms of the patron-client model. Not only are these individuals both patron and client to one another on different occasions, but also – and more significantly – they each uniquely threaten the other's dominance (through patronage) over the remainder of a settlement's white population. The situation is represented diagrammatically below (Fig. 1) where A and M are the administrator and mechanic, respectively, and a, b, c, x, y and z are other settlement whites whose opportunity to offer patronage is limited; the direction of the arrows indicates the hierarchical dimension of a patron-client relationship.

Figure 1

I suggest that the formal (hierarchical) aspect of their relationship (because the mechanic is accountable in his job to the administrator) is relatively unimportant as a basis for the tension between them, although it is undoubtedly an irritant of it, especially from the mechanic's point of view, and the tension may be verbalized in terms of it: 'What does he know of my machines?.'[7] Rather, the important feature is that the two are rival patrons. Corroborative of this is the fact that the tension is far less in evidence in the other cases of job accountability to the administrator (the resource development officer, for instance). These other jobs carry little patronage potential.

(4) *Alliance through common interest*. An important component in the formation of cliques in Anurivik was the bond of alliance between two or more individuals who were simultaneously attempting to ostracize, or were being ostracized by, a common third person or group of people. This is an almost inevitable behavioural response in a triadic situation where two equally weak individuals are ranged against someone stronger (Caplow, 1968:2). We return to this point later.

Waverers

At any moment in its life cycle, a clique will have its principals (who are not necessarily the original principals), who single-mindedly pursue clique purposes, and the waverers, who express uncertainties about these purposes. The latter are likely to include new arrivals canvassed by the opposed cliques; they may have nominally aligned themselves but they still seek validation of 'their' clique's point of view before finally committing themselves to it. The fate of waverers is either to be drawn more tightly into their clique's activities or to be rejected.

The main method of inclusion is to make the waverer aware of the opposing clique's gossip (particularly when it is about him) – in contrast to the non-clique situation when such gossip would not be discussed. In the clique situation, however, confiding gossip to the waverer normally serves to arouse his anger and then to draw him into clique activity. Since members of opposed cliques normally avoid one another, information of what one clique is saying about members of the other must be passed between the cliques by individuals who are members of neither. Those persons who are on short official visits and are thus likely to be naive about the local clique situation, may be the unwitting transmitters of information, not realizing that (in the clique situation) their gossip is no longer confidential. (These same persons may also be courted by opposing cliques for a show of strength.)[8]

Besides waverers, individuals who wish to remain 'neutral' (always but a few) and to deny the existence of cliques in the settlement may also serve as transmitters of information between cliques. But the waverer who, deliberately or inadvertently, passes information is in a precarious position, liable to be sucked into one of the cliques. For the information he passes will either have been deliberately leaked by one clique in order to "subvert" another – that is, to capture some of its support, perhaps by discrediting its principal (Bailey, 1969:91–2) – or else it will be a betrayal of confidence. In my experience, the second instance occurred more commonly, but except when subversion misfires, both result in a lessening of the cohesive strength of one of the cliques.

The aftermath of the bear skin case suggests that the clique that suffers in this way is likely to reject the waverer who passes information. Bill (who finally bought the skin) was kept aware of Jim's intentions by Fred, a waverer who was close to Jim. In fact, Bill's success was partly due to the information he received. Jim, however, who assumed that he had spoken to Fred in confidence, received little information about Bill's intentions in return. Later, when Jim was in open dispute with Bill, red told him that he had known that Jim would have little chance of purchasing the bear skin. Henceforth, Jim treated Fred with extr me suspicion and when cliques began to solidify around Bill and Jim, Jim rejected Fred for his earlier behaviour; Fred joined Bill's clique, despite the fact that his affective tie with Bill was formerly weak.[9]

The Non-joiners

Most waverers, and even avowed neutrals, tend to find life uncomfortable if they attempt to socialize with both cliques and they end up being repelled from, or pulled towards one clique or the other. But there are certain 'types' of individuals who are able to sustain a position of comfortable neutrality.[10]

First, there is the 'popular personality' who refuses to recognize the existence of cliques, even when clearly being aggravated by an individual's norm-breaking behaviour. His view is that "I shall invite whomever I like to my house, no matter what their opinions about each other may be," and because of his popularity he is, in fact, frequently visited by both cliques. But such a situation forces rival cliques to watch his house closely to see who is visiting before they themselves visit, and each clique will tell him their opinions of the opposing clique. Yet, the 'popular personality' comes the nearest of any positive agent to diminishing the power of cliques.

Another non-joiner is the 'infrequent visitor' who keeps his interactions with other whites to a relatively low level and is thereby relatively invulnerable to a strategy of ostracism on the part of cliques. One such individual in Anurivik was fortunate enough to have a number of Inuit friends with whom to spend leisure hours. But even whites accepted him because he reserved his opinions about clique matters and appeared not to betray information (however, people tended to be more reticent in his presence). Behind his back he merely suffered mild criticism for "going native."

There is only one non-joiner whom the whites in Anurivik do not seek to recruit to their cliques. He is the missionary. It is not his periodic absences from the settlement that account for his unique treatment; the explanation lies in the attitude of whites towards ostracism – the behavioural basis of clique formation. Whites perceive ostracism diffusely as a means of social control over an individual who, as Lange's informants put it (1972:55), "did wrong ... and he knows he did ... and is too ashamed to come around." The implication is that only a failure to repent bars the individual from a return to the fold. The faults of the individual who "did wrong" may then be listed and put down to personality (idiosyncratic) failings, and/or public norm deviance, or private norm deviance; the first two often rationalize accusations of failing to respect private norms that are either poorly perceived as norms, or else are perceived as contradictory to (and thus, less morally right than) public norms. The point I wish to make is that ostracism, even though privately legitimated in terms of social control, is contrary to the public value of tolerance. In Anurivik, whites only reluctantly recognize their grouping behaviour as that of cliques. The presence of the missionary should symbolize the correctness of public values; to confront him with the notion of ostracism becomes immediately a symbolic admission of anti-social attitudes. Hence, in his presence, even if in a private setting, both clique behaviour and clique talk are *lèse-majesté*.

Clique Symbols

Because of the idiom through which they are made manifest, that is, through intensive private visiting, Anurivik cliques, we maintain, carry the seeds of their potential self-destruction. With regard to this we must qualify Homans' statement (1951:133): "The more frequently persons interact with each other the stronger their sentiments of friendship for each other are apt to be"; and also Caplow's (1968:4): "... the presence of an antagonist increases one's affection for a friend... ."

Clique behaviour offers clique-mates more opportunities for scrutinizing one another's behaviour and personality and for detecting deviations from public or private values (particularly private values). The alliance is put under considerable strain. This state of affairs is likely when a clique has emerged solely on the basis of shared opposition to a common antagonist. In Anurivik, for example, one individual in such an alliance soon realized that as he got to know the other party better, this person was not behaving according to the fundamental public value of co-operation for the benefit of the settlement and its Inuit inhabitants. Over time, this clique developed serious tensions, but maintained a united public front for as long as it considered its alliance a valuable ostracizing strategy.

Important counterweights to internal dissention are the rituals and symbols characteristic of cliques. Behaviour in inter-clique ritual is so blatantly contrary to public norms that considerable clique-binding emotion is released by it. If a person, while entertaining his clique-mates, were visited by someone from another clique, the visitor would be coolly received, not offered refreshments, and might even hear one of his clique mates directly abused. His response would more likely be subdued than aggressive. Similarly, at festivals – Thanksgiving, Christmas, and Easter – when traditionally all whites in a settlement assemble for a lavish dinner, rival cliques may prefer to hold their own separate celebrations, as experience may have shown them the impossibility of 'healing the breach' even for such occasions.

The symbols of clique behaviour are of two types. The first denotes what Bateson (1935) describes as "symmetrical differentiation" between two groups. These symbols constitute items of behaviour which the opposed groups evaluate similarly, and are used on an *intra*-clique basis; examples are commodity sharing and reciprocal hospitality (practised by all cliques but never extended across clique lines).

The second type of symbol arises out of the principle of "complementary differentiation" (Bateson, 1935) and operates on an *inter*-clique basis: certain items of behaviour are aspired to by one clique, but denigrated by the other, and this in turn leads to different behaviour. The most important symbol of complementary differentiation is drinking (cf. Lange, 1972:58). Drinking is a preoccupation among almost all non-teetotal whites in the Arctic, particularly when alcohol is in short supply or when its arrival by airplane is imminent. Yet, typically, if one clique emerges as heavy-drinkers, another will wish to be known as moderate drinkers. Other complementary symbols were encountered (in a two-clique situation): one clique extolled the joys of arctic life, while the other emphasized its detestation of it; in inter-clique encounters, the one was verbally aggressive and the other passive.

Cliques in Public

Although cliques may never be publicly acknowledged, it is not uncommon for clique behaviour to spill over into a public arena. On occasions when all whites must gather – such as meeting planes, going to movies and community meetings with Inuit – clique divisions are quite evident (as is also symmetrical differentiation). Clique-mates joke and fool with each other and with neutrals, but studiously ignore the opposed clique. When a visitor, usually a minor government official, arrives in the settlement, he will be introduced to the clique-mates of the person who first meets him; others will have to introduce themselves. Visiting whites, as well as the Inuit population, soon discover where clique lines are drawn.

However, when a public situation specifically demands adherence to public norms of behaviour, clique lines will dissolve. During formal meetings with Inuit, for example, rival whites will behave in an exaggeratedly reasonable manner to one another, hoping to demonstrate their co-operative attitudes.[11] Similarly, when a senior government official, such as the regional director or the commissioner for the NWT, makes an inspection visit to the settlement, the whites will present a united front, affirming for him the unity that is expected of them. It is rare (though not unknown) for complaints to be made to officials about the conduct of other whites in the settlement (cf. Dunning, 1959:119); such complaints, of course, imply an admission of failure to fulfill the public values of tolerance and co-operation, and may be taken as indicative of the unsuitability to arctic life of the complainant himself.

Cliques and Inuit

Inuit in Anurivik perceive a white's duty in the north to be "to help the (native) people," and most of their criticisms of whites are thus based on their failure to do this. Indeed, elsewhere in the Arctic, Inuit have occasionally been successful in persuading the government to remove a white whom they thought not to be doing beneficial work. Clique behaviour is generally not perceived by Inuit as constituting an abrogation of whites' duties towards them; indeed, cliques tend to work more for their benefit. In the first place, behaviour of whites towards Inuit may be seen as symbolic of their attitude to public values. Thus, although they may not recruit Inuit into their cliques, they seek to legitimize their stance (which they see as morally correct with respect to public values) by behaving reasonably towards the Inuit. To do this, they exploit their control over the resources Inuit desire: the administrator may supply a family with an electric stove cast out from a white's house, or the teacher might suggest using the school for a community dance.[12]

Secondly, there is a psychological dimension in behaving kindly toward Inuit, particularly for whites in a minority clique: as donors of largesse, they may persuade Inuit to think kindly of them, and thereby find some compensation for their rejection by the opposing clique. Inuit acceptance of their gift is made to symbolize to some extent their 'rightness' in the inter-clique dispute. (For example, one white in a minority clique began to distribute candies to the children before each movie, his supply being at that time the last remaining in the settlement.)

Occasionally, Inuit are sucked into inter-clique disputes. A bilingual girl was once asked to communicate a clique message over the radio to another settlement so that a particular white, who might hear the message (the radio was in his house), would not understand it. Her father was later resentful; he described inter-clique behaviour as that between enemies (*akirariit*). In Inuit culture, ostracism may be used as a strategy of social control (Briggs, 1970:285 ff.), but it will constitute a conspiracy of the community *as a whole*; the victim has little chance of support. Furthermore, disputes and feuds were, in general, resolved by the separation of rival parties; clique in-fighting was unknown.

But if Inuit consider a white's behaviour as being seriously contrary to their expectations, they may assume that members of the clique opposed to this person will sympathize with their complaints and perhaps work with them to pressure the government for his removal. This did come to pass in Anurivik, but the attempt backfired, as the government accused the whites of influencing the Inuit in their opinions.

CONCLUSIONS

In the 'pre-development' era (before 1958), conflict among whites generally arose out of ambiguities in an authority structure wherein a number of different specialists perceived themselves as incumbents of equivalent status positions (Dunning, 1959; cf. Paine, 1971:99–100). By the early development era (1958–65), this situation had been partially rectified;

however, whites would come into conflict with each other because of inconsistencies in function, values, and overall aims of the agencies and government departments which they represented (Vallee, 1967:122). By the early 1970s when Anurivik was being studied, most of these ambiguities and inconsistencies had been ironed out. Yet it is my impression that conflict among whites was at least as prevalent as it had been previously, and was particularly manifest in disputes between cliques.

The *raison d'être* of cliques, it has been argued here, is to exercise social control over an individual whose alleged behaviour is deviant. Since the principal form of social gratification among the whites is visiting, it follows that social control will involve a denial of this gratification, or in other words, ostracizm. But such attempts can be effective only if others co-operate. Accordingly, the principal disputants compete to gather such co-operation from their fellows.

With this in mind, let us return to the distinction between clique and faction with which the essay opened. In fact, the rival groups in Anurivik, even though not strictly political in purpose, were in certain respects of form and function reminiscent of factions. For example, they were geared to influencing situations in the public arena – something which cliques are not meant to do. On the other hand, the usual formal definitions of cliques aptly describe these rival groups of Anurivik. Here is a case, then, where cliques act as factions. Why this is so is explicable through the special situation of these tiny, 'closed,' white communities. The very nature of social control in the community, operating as it does through the idiom of visiting, demands a high rate of exclusive interaction within each group; and secondly, the size of the rival groups is always small because of the small size of the community itself.

From two different points of view, therefore, the selective interactions observed in Anurivik are both cliques and factions. Yet however they are described, a final problem remains: that of schismogenesis. As Bateson (1935) observes, there is the danger that when two groups become progressively differentiated through rivalry, the whole system, of which they constitute the parts, will break down. We must look, therefore, to forces counteracting this tendency. I suggest that the turnover of whites in arctic settlements serves this purpose.

The motives of the government and other northern employers for sponsoring this turnover are not altogether clear; petitions from restless employees certainly provide an impetus for it. However, it is an extremely adaptive policy in that it appears to be the sole important force for (temporarily) destroying cliques. In our experience, quiescent periods in clique activity occurred when a clique principal was on extended leave; and a particular clique grouping disappeared altogether when the principal terminated his contract or was transferred to another settlement. Sometimes it was not long before new clique alignments emerged; nevertheless, for a short time, peace reigned.

NOTES

1   See Boissevain (1974:174), Homans (1951:135), Goffman (1959:84), and Smith (1965:58–9).
2   Vallee (1967:104) discusses some interesting implications of this turnover.
3   Social scientists appear to be exempt from this charge as their work is perceived as being explicitly concerned with *researching* native customs.
4   An exception is, for example, the administrator and the co-op manager co-operating in assigning welfare, in that the manager informs the administrator, who distributes welfare, of the financial circumstances of a potential Inuit recipient.
5   Vallee (1967:111–12) draws attention to upstarts: for him, they are new arrivals who too readily attempt to initiate ideas or services.
6   Whereas most whites consider each other's roles in the settlement worthwhile, many judge the social scientist's role negatively. The value of his accomplishments is assumed (in some cases justifiably) to be slight or non-existent, or he is thought to actually damage the settlement. Because he lacks a clearly defined role in the community, and because his 'boss' is inaccessible, he is the most vulnerable of all whites for being accused of meddling or informing. Whites are often on their guard when introduced to a social scientist and their suspicions probably contribute to the frequently expressed concern that social scientists' findings should be more widely circulated among whites working in the north.
7   The formal aspect of the administrator-mechanic relationship can, however, exercise such constraints on a mechanic that he 'plays safe' in intra-settlement politics. Once, when cliques emerged as a result of the administrator's controversial behaviour, the mechanic who had criticized the administrator behind his back, aligned himself with him in a minority grouping, rationalizing, "I have to work with him."
8   Occasionally, Inuit may innocently reveal one clique's activities to another clique, though as mentioned later, their recruitment to cliques is not sought.
9   Fred's (the waverer) intentions here are unclear: when he gave information to Bill he knew that the relations between Jim and Bill were already near breaking point. Possibly he anticipated the eventual clique situation and decided that Bill offered him better patronage. However, he persistently claimed that he deplored the "pettiness of it all."
10   These types are also described by Lange (1972:55) from Lake Harbour.
11   But in private work situations, clique lines will be redrawn and rivals will obstruct one another to the extent that is permitted by work norms: "The next time you leave those windows open and the pipes freeze, you can phone the regional township and get a *proper* plumber to repair them."
12   The difference between this situation and the one recognized by Dunning (1959) from an earlier era is noteworthy: no longer is competition for leadership of the native community a dominant feature of settlement life; indeed, with the plethora of Inuit community organizations today, all controlled by the administrator, such competition is not feasible in most cases.

References

BAILEY, F. G.
   1969 *Stratagems and Spoils*. Oxford, Basil Blackwell.
BARTH, FREDRIK
   1966 *Models of Social Organization*. Occasional Paper of the Royal Anthropological Institute, 23. London.

BATESON, GREGORY
1935 "Culture Contact and Schismogenesis." *Man*, 35:178–83.
BOISSEVAIN, JEREMY
1968 "The Place of Non-Groups in the Social Sciences." *Man* (N.S.), 3:542–56.
BOISSEVAIN, JEREMY
1974 *Friends of Friends: Networks, Manipulators and Coalitions*. Oxford, Basil Blackwell.
BRIGGS, JEAN
1970 *Never in Anger*. Cambridge, Harvard University Press.
CAPLOW, T.
1968 *Two Against One: Coalitions in Triads*. Englewood Cliffs, New Jersey, Prentice-Hall Inc.
DUNNING, R. W.
1959 "Ethnic Relations and the Marginal Man in Canada." *Human Organization*, 18(3):117–23.
FIRTH, RAYMOND
1957 "Introduction." In R. Firth (ed.), *Factions in Indian and Overseas Indian Communities*. British Journal of Sociology, 8:4.
GOFFMAN, ERVING
1959 *Presentation of Self in Everyday Life*. New York, Doubleday & Co.
GOFFMAN, ERVING
1961 *Asylums*. New York, Doubleday & Co.
HOMANS, GEORGE C.
1951 *The Human Group*. London, Routledge & Kegan Paul.
LANGE, PHILIP
1972 "Social Flexibility and Integration in a Canadian Inuit Settlement." Unpublished M.A. thesis, University of British Columbia.
NICHOLAS, R.
1965 "Factions: A Comparative Analysis." In M. Banton (ed.), *Political Systems and the Distribution of Power*. A.S.A. Monographs 3, London, Tavistock Publications.
NICHOLAS, R.
1966 "Segmentary Factional Political Systems." In M. J. Swartz, V. W. Turner and A. Tuden (eds.), *Political Anthropology*. Chicago, Aldine.
PAINE, ROBERT
1969 "In Search of Friendship: An Exploratory Analysis in Middle-Class Culture." *Man* (N.S.), 4:505–24.
PAINE, ROBERT
1971 "A Theory of Patronage and Brokerage." In R. Paine (ed.), *Patrons and Brokers in the East Arctic*. St. John's, Institute of Social and Economic Research, Memorial University of Newfoundland.

SAHLINS, MARSHAL
   1965 "On the Sociology of Primitive Exchange." In M. Banton (ed.),
   The Relevance of Models for Social Anthropology. A.S.A. Mono-
   graphs 1, London, Tavistock Publications.
SMITH, M. G.
   1965 *Stratification in Grenada*. Berkeley, California, University of
   California Press.
VALLEE, FRANK
   1967 *Kabloona and Eskimo in the Central Keewatin*. Ottawa, The Cana-
   dian Research Centre for Anthropology.
WOLF, ERIC
   1966 "Kinship, Friendship and Patron-Client Relations in Complex
   Societies." In M. Banton (ed.), *The Social Anthropology of Complex
   Societies*. A.S.A. Monographs 4, London, Tavistock Publications.

The Settlement Manager: Ambivalence in Patronage 10

Hugh Brody

Inuit throughout Canada are being economically and ideologically incorpo-rated into mainstream life. Dates at which this incorporation began vary from region to region; degrees to which the process has been completed are not uniform. The irregularities of northern history, however, are under-written by the uniformity of what might be termed the structural features of change. Moreover, in the most recent period, when government decisions applied throughout the entire Northwest Territories (and in some measure apply also to Arctic Quebec), even the historical disparities have been consolidated. The most recent attempt at incorporation is political: the attentions of missionary, trader, doctor and teacher have been followed by those of administrator and local government programmes. The main pur-pose of this essay is to look analytically and critically at the social context in which political incorporation is made real. The empirical emphasis will be on the relationship between one Settlement Manager and his dealings with the Inuit of one small settlement.

I

Understandably enough, social scientists and others often suggest a crucial discontinuity between the pre- and post-administrative eras, between the time when missionaries, traders and RCMP were alone responsible for the Inuit, and recent times when administration is exclusively in the hands of government agents and specialized departments. A number of reasons underly this suggestion. Firstly, the formation of a federal department with special responsibility for the north gave relative continuity and uniformity where there had been variety. Secondly, continuity and uniformity were achieved with the help of vastly improved communications. Thirdly, the entry of government was marked by large-scale investment in northern services: it was felt that men had to be encouraged to go to these remote locations, and encouragement had to take the form of high salaries and high living standards. Thus arose a white community which was marked off from the Inuit by its elaborate material life. Fourthly, the entrance of government inevitably disturbed a balance of power and influence that had grown over some decades between non-government agencies and their middlemen in the north.

These changes were everywhere apparent to northern old-timers, whose laments even now can be heard across the Arctic, laments for the great times when individuals could make decisions, when northern whites "knew the people" – when "the government" was not effectively there. It was a time when it was allegedly possible to live in the north with a measure of freedom, freedom compounded out of unique conditions, special duties, clear purposes, and distance from meddlesome overseers of any kind. This independence is said to be in striking contrast with modern day subordination to bureaucratic administration, even in the High Arctic.

Discussions of the Canadian north which emphasize this discontinuity between the pre- and post-administration periods do reflect what many white northerners and some Inuit say about changes they have lived through in the past thirty years. What they do not emphasize, however, is the extent to which the development of white/Inuit relations have followed a single path between the day of the missionary, trader and RCMP, and the day of the local administrator: all have sought to change the Inuit, and in realizing these changes have successively dominated them. The subordination of the Inuit to white agencies was not diminished by the entrance of Federal and Territorial Governments. Differences existed, of course, between some of the ways and purposes of the individual agencies, and changes have meant that one or another agency has lost some of its influence and freedom of action. As far as the Inuit are concerned, however, these shifts in the balance of local white power have not changed the structural relationship. Whites have dominated the Inuit, and continue to do so.[1] Specifically, this domination has a pattern common to all the agencies: Inuit have come to depend on (or become convinced that they depend on) goods which only whites can dispense. This applies as much to the beneficence of a Christian God as to a gun or anti-virus vaccination.

In the literature dealing with white incursion into the Inuit world, Helge Kleivan's (1966) study of Labrador stands out. Perhaps the Moravian Brethren were more anxious to reform the details of life among Labrador Inuit than other missionaries, but they embody the principles of the activity. The traditional spiritual leaders of the Inuit became objects of remorseless criticism. Missionaries sought to undermine their influence in every family. Customary social practice, from sexual life down to the very minutiae of games, were attacked. Conversion was encouraged by trade, medical benefits (a specific case of competition with their shaministic role), threats and tireless exhortation. Conversion tended to involve a move from camp life (under the influence of traditional social authority) to settlement (under the influence of the new church).

Similarly, the Hudson's Bay Company's interest in Labrador fox skins led to widespread social changes, and rapidly to pathetic dependence upon the trader. "All in all, it is no exaggeration to suggest that the economic dependency of the Inuit upon the Company increased in step with the poverty in the 1930s and onwards" (Kleivan, 1966:135). Summarizing,

Kleivan quotes another writer on the "economic serfdom" of relationships between Inuit and Hudson's Bay Company traders (*loc. cit.*). Perhaps it is also no exaggeration to speak of moral serfdom to the mission. The RCMP's presence in the north has received less critical attention, but there is sufficient evidence to suggest that their role was similar. Milton Freeman's discussion of Grise Fjord, for example, provides one case in point (1971:34–55).

In the 1950s, when administrators began to arrive in the settlements, they came partly to organize the provision of a number of services. Indeed, one reason for their arriving at all lay in a feeling that the time had come to make sure that all Canadians, even those living in places and ways apparently far beyond the mainstream of national life, be recipients of services such as welfare, education and adequate medical care. In some settlements, government officials took over the administration of welfare from men whose lack of experience in such matters had resulted in much antagonism. In other settlements, where credit at the Hudson's Bay store was the only local source of emergency relief, the new administrators introduced the first systematic provision of welfare. Furthermore, the new administrators (at first under the title of Northern Service Officers) were specifically concerned with expanding the economic base of each community. One author introduces his study of an Arctic Quebec community with a sense of new beginnings at that time: "In 1959, the people of George River went through an intensive period of social change . . . the impetus for change came from the Government of Canada's programme of social and economic development and had two main objectives; first, to gather the scattered Eskimo people together in settlements for administrative efficiency and to complement social services already existing in the rest of Canada, and second, to improve and organize the economy based upon the formation of Eskimo co-operatives. George River, in 1959, became the first of these communities" (Arbess, 1966:1).

Early administrative endeavours may, therefore, lead us to expect significant reformation of Inuit/white relationships. It would perhaps appear that exploitative agencies were being displaced by supportive ones. In time, however, if not always from the start, the government agency exhibited similarities to, rather than differences from, other agencies. This is brought out analytically by simply noting that an appointed administrator was a patron *cum* broker (cf. Paine, 1971) in much the same way as the Hudson's Bay Company or missionary. In the words of another theorist of patronage and brokerage, he "may distribute patronage to a small minority and yet keep his position: for his removal depends on the outside agency, and public pressures against him for biased distribution of favours must coincide with the dereliction in his formal duties if the outside agency is to be persuaded to dismiss him" (Mayer, 1966:168). The government administrator, like other local patron/brokers, is installed by officials in the south who define purposes in relation to needs *they* have perceived. Corresponding to the analytical points is the broad configuration of Inuit attitudes. All whites tend to be seen as coming from one overall agency, and all tend to be vested with the same limitless reserves and powers. Individuals may be more or less helpful, but politically relevant distinctions between various agencies have not been conceptualized.[2] Thus, the social position of the Northern Service Officer combined with the way in which Inuit understood the collective role of whites, giving added continuity to the pre- and post-administrative period.

Yet the social and material lives of the Inuit, even in the remotest parts of the Eastern Arctic, have changed significantly since the arrival of Northern Service Officers. Elements of the southerners' material culture had already become incorporated into Inuit life. Trade relations had been built on new technological devices, and demanded new hunting routines. I have already mentioned the leadership and settlement patterns which were implicitly and explicitly encouraged by missionaries. Similar trends were urged by the administrators: dispersed populations were encouraged to come together to form fewer but larger communities, which were easier to administer and for which medical and educational services were more conveniently and less expensively provided. However, the administrators, armed with their ideas of economic self-sufficiency, at least encouraged trapping for the fur trade (which turned subsistence into a money economy), or sought to establish entirely new activities (which involved new technology and often nurtured new social relations).

By the time a form of government had been granted to the Northwest Territories as a whole, many of these changes had brought into existence a new kind of Inuit settlement that by 1970 had become the norm. This is most often, and quite poignantly, noted by the absence of symbols essentially Inuit. Gone are the dog teams, snow houses, the seal oil lamps; here and there remains a camp where a traditionalist or two stoically hold out against pressures to move. But even they do not wear inner skin parkas: their clothes or the material for their clothes are for the most part bought at the Bay. The stereotyped image of the traditional Inuk has given way to a contemporary one, with a set of new symbols: it is said that the snowmobile is as derelict as it is ubiquitous; only astonishing mechanical skill compensates for entirely inadequate maintenance. We are told that goodwill is everywhere, but that local councils are less effectual than they might be, that the duties of councillors are guided by short-run pleasures rather than longer-term goals. It is said that the shyness of Inuit is endemic and results in a strong tendency for whites to become isolated. We are warned that the young Inuit have no place and little thought for their community; the future is accordingly uncertain. Liquor creeps up from the south, threatening to engulf everyone.

It is hardly necessary to remark that such stereotypes as these are results of the distances they lament, themselves a result of other changes that have taken place. Whites tend to look at Inuit across a vast distance through ideologically distorting mirrors and impermeable language problems, living in their own sub-community and according to their own middle-class style. In most cases, it is with remarkable naivety that settlement whites become troubled by this distance, and become perplexed at the excruciation of the many Inuit that do come into occasional contact with them.

These stereotypes are held in one form or another by many of the whites who are now living or working in northern settlements. Some of the views are absurd, but virtually all are focused on problems. They reflect a growing feeling that all is far from well among the Inuit, and that problems in Inuit/white relationships are becoming tainted with that air of insolubility which characterizes inter-racial difficulties far to the south.

Besides the above changes, the Territorial Council is pushing forward a local government programme. The Northern Service Officer has gone as has his successor, the Area Administrator; today there are Settlement Managers. Among other more traditional functions, the Settlement Manager's job includes responsibility for the advancement of local councils. He is expected to encourage local initiative, supervise the elections, and prepare the route to greater local autonomy and influence. If Inuit councils show that they have the right understanding, follow the proper procedures, and altogether exhibit an on-going ability to maintain institutions of local government without special supervision, then a settlement can be granted hamlet status.[3]

Thus, at a time when most whites who have first-hand experience with Inuit communities are troubled and even alarmed at the quality of life in the settlements, the impetus towards political incorporation is gaining strength. This is no coincidence: our democratic institutions may no longer be seen as panaceas for all social ailments, but they are still widely thought to be minimally necessary conditions for that self-respect and collective assertiveness which, in themselves, are held to be solutions to *some* social ills.

II

Richard Travis arrived at Fort John in midwinter.[4] He was the settlement's first manager, but not the first administrator. Although attitudes towards the first administrator, an industrial development officer, had been critical, his enthusiasm and goodwill inspired a general confidence in the possible achievements of his successor. When Travis arrived, therefore, he received a fulsome welcome. The Inuit noted his kindly appearance, commented favourably on his readiness to shake hands all round, and on his strong build.[5]

Indeed, the first weeks passed happily enough. The large suspended basement house where Travis lived was much visited, and often he and the Inuit men played games together. There was much laughter. Since Fort John has been one of the poorest communities, recurrently enduring privation until quite recently, such socializing gave rise to high expectations among the people. A Settlement Manager, they knew, controlled welfare payments and other subsidies and represented their needs and wishes to the government. Their needs and wishes being numerous, Travis was naturally expected to offer a great deal of new or augmented support. Fort John Inuit were, even then, under no illusions about their dependence upon southern munificence.

When Travis arrived there was a council already and a clearly defined group of leaders (who were all, but one, members of the council). In addition, there were a number of men who were conspicuous for their outspokenness. In fact, Fort John, according to many northern whites, was distinguished for the confidence with which its residents expressed their views. Certainly the council did not hesitate to voice criticisms and express anger. Nevertheless, the majority of Fort John people insisted that they needed help from the whites, a need that was perceived partly in political terms: the council and co-operative could be strengthened if, and only if, whites provided information and taught the skills necessary to run the new institutions. The Inuit community had come to believe that these institutions could significantly enhance their lives and livelihoods, and they looked to Travis, in particular, to help them.

These signs of development need some explanation. Fort John was among the last Inuit communities to come to the attention of white Canadians. Its housing, educational and medical services were among the last to come into effect. Although the dire need for welfare was evident to northern officials in the 1940s, payments came much later than that, and were administered first by people who lived over 70 miles away, and later, by a school teacher whose competence in the matter was doubtful. Impoverishment and sporadic hunger thus continued until the late 1960s, while the hungry became increasingly aware of possible government support. The industrial development officer regularized welfare payments, and finally confirmed people's entitlement to government support. By that time, however, Fort John hunters had discovered that neighbouring settlements had far less difficulty in receiving support, and had come to feel that they had been treated unjustly. This sense of injustice, combined with the greater need for support among the Fort John people, probably gave rise to some of the assertiveness *vis-à-vis* southerners that already characterized Fort John when Travis arrived.

By the same historical token, welfare payments were a delicate matter. From the first, Travis determined to reduce the scale of what he saw as welfare dependence. Indeed, he measured his success by the size of the Fort John welfare budget: the smaller it was, the better he felt he was doing. During the first weeks, he tried to discover the men who depended on welfare but who could be depending on another resource. He managed to encourage some men to carve soapstone in order to earn enough to support their families (or to lose their claims to welfare payments). At first it appears that his strategy against welfare dependence did not arouse much antagonism. In the early spring he left Fort John for seven weeks, during which time he visited other settlements, and attempted to learn a little of the Inuit language.

It was during his first absence from Fort John that I got to know Richard Travis. Immediately striking was his enthusiasm for his job and the optimism with which he looked forward to working with the Fort John community. Less apparent, but more troubling, was Travis' intense concern with organizational matters; he insisted upon casting a net of exact arrangements around others' activities, and tended not to notice the small signals put out by those who were irritated or mildly troubled by his ways. He seemed to have become strangely inured to the subtleties of interpersonal relationships. By and large, he was able to overcome this flaw in his personality by virtue of other qualities: he was *always* willing to organize, was not afraid of hard work, and showed much generosity. Moreover, he was always in a good mood – all qualities which are much appreciated in settlement life of the far north.

But it was clear that Travis was profoundly antagonistic towards welfare. First, he regarded welfare as 'money for nothing,' and subscribed to some of the most conventional moral views: anyone who lived off handouts was in danger of chronic and irreversible moral decrepitude. A man on welfare, he felt, was liable to lose all self-respect, all dignity, and all interest in work. (The exceptions were made clear, and included the old and the sick.) Secondly, he tended to idealize the traditional Inuk because the traditional Inuk was able to look after himself in that hard climate with a minimum of material support. Obviously, an Inuk that lived on welfare stood out in stark contrast to that ideal. For Travis, a man was more a traditional Inuk, at least morally, if he scraped together a living by carving and doing occasional wage labour, than one who sought welfare in order to survive as a hunter and trapper. When it was suggested that welfare payments were the only recourse for many Inuit, even for men who were entirely healthy in body and mind, and that maybe these men should be allowed to judge for themselves what they needed by way of support, Travis became extremely indignant.

Arguments about welfare are common enough in the Canadian Arctic, and the issues tend to repeat themselves a thousandfold. Hence Travis' opinions were not unusual, and the positions he adopted (given the configuration of attitudes and opinions of other northern whites) were not *prima facie* unsubstantial. Indeed, he was able to urge his position on others with much coherence.

Although I did not know how Travis interacted with Inuit in his professional capacity at this time, in a purely social context, he was cheerful and always ready to communicate, even though there was virtually no language in common. Also he was interested in hunting and fishing, which provided important points of contact. He was always ready to join Inuit on their hunting trips and was quite prepared to accept their leadership. Once again, all these are good qualities not common among whites. Perhaps the most important element in Travis during this period was also the most general: he was anxious to learn from and be friendly with the people he met. As an administrator, this translated directly into his apparently sincere hope that he would indeed be helpful.

Some four months later, I visited Fort John and our discussions continued. Travis talked about his position in Fort John, about the way his administrative role was now working itself out, and how he foresaw the settlement's and his own future – emphasizing what he saw as his successes. Welfare payments were much lower and were amenable to even further reductions. The village itself was cleaner and tidier than it had ever been. A number of individuals were doing strikingly well in jobs after having been dependent on welfare. According to Travis the community council was functioning well, and the councillors were rapidly assuming much greater control of settlement affairs. Most of this information was explicitly contrasted with what Travis saw as his predecessor's bungling.

In these conversations, it was troubling to notice the degree to which Travis adopted a proprietary attitude towards the people of Fort John, as evidenced in sentences such as: "I have a boy doing really well down in Winnipeg"; "I'll send my longliner over to fetch them"; "my mechanic is no damn good at his job." The boy was a Fort John Inuk attending school, the ship belonged to the community co-operative and was entirely at its disposal, and the mechanic was an employee of the Territorial Government with functions quite separate from those of the Settlement Manager. Furthermore, it was obvious that the Inuit had more or less ceased visiting Travis except for a specific purpose, and even on those occasions, visitors tended to stay in the office and appeared nervous of entering the living-room. In the first few encounters I witnessed between Travis and Fort John men, it was impossible not to notice the somewhat assertive, almost domineering manner Travis adopted. When anxious to overcome the language difficulty, he tended to raise his voice and simplified his English by baldly stating instructions. It seemed that Travis' willingness to be friendly despite language and cultural difficulties had evaporated.

In the following months I heard many Fort John Inuit talking about their Settlement Manager. Confidence in him was extremely low. It was said that he refused welfare to people who needed it, while supporting others who were already adequately provided for by their immediate families. People remarked that Travis thought he knew who was and who was not receiving support from their families, and would not listen to those Inuit involved. Furthermore, it was repeatedly pointed out to me that only local hunters could assess hunting possibilities; yet Travis sometimes refused welfare to a hunter because he (the white man) was sure that hunting possibilities were good. ("He looks out of his window, and sees all sorts of birds flying about, and says to an Inuk: there is good hunting out there, go and hunt, you are not going to get any welfare this month when there are many birds so close to the settlement. But birds do not stay and wait for the hunter. They come and they go again. The Settlement Manager cannot know when the hunting is good by looking out of his window. If he had to live by hunting he would know better and would not say such things.")

A second complaint centred on Travis and the co-operative. Although the co-operative does not officially fall within the Settlement Manager's responsibility, the two institutions inevitably impinge on one another. The Fort John people were convinced that Travis did not wish to help the co-operative and specifically remarked on the extent to which he found objections to the co-operative directors' proposals and plans. Again and again I was told that Travis had nurtured rivalry and opposition between the government and co-operative. This was contrasted most unfavourably with Travis' predecessor, who had offered every support for the co-operative, even to the extent of placing government facilities and equipment at their service.

A third complaint concerned Travis' manner. He was said to be "boss," forever seeking to demonstrate that he and no one else was the boss. Evidence for this criticism came from all areas in which he repeatedly objected to local people's suggestions. But it came also from more personal or idiosyncratic traits: he was inclined to shout, to become angry suddenly and fiercely, to disregard the arguments or objections of community councillors or members of the public, and he generally behaved towards the Fort John people as if they were children. It was claimed that his behaviour revealed that "he does not want to help the Inuit." Often these reflections on Travis' character and ways received fullest expression in the light of his changed behaviour. A number of men insisted that his very appearance, his facial structure, had altered since he first landed in Fort John. ("When he came here he was friendly, he was smiling. I thought: how good that this new Settlement Manager is going to help us. He shook hands with us all. Then later I saw him, and his face had changed. He was not handsome any more. His nose had become much bigger.'') Astutely enough, the Fort John people often commented on the extraordinary extent to which whites often change when they come into Inuit communities. So striking is this phenomenon, that some men have developed theories about the patterns of such change. With reference to Travis, one such theorist told me that whites who are all smiles and enthusiasm when they first come are the ones who most surely and darkly become troubled, angry, and the first to become anxious to leave.

By the end of Travis' first year in Fort John, relations between him and the community council began to reach a crisis point. Criticism of the Settlement Manager was beginning to rub off on his interpreters who became reluctant to translate for him. The chairman of the council, Isaac Tullik, was also the main interpreter, and he confided to me his despair. Since he passed along all Travis' most important decisions and translated the official rebuttals of one or another council plan, many people in the community began to think of their council chairman as hand-in-glove with their Settlement Manager. This was much aggravated by the nature of the dual role: as interpreter, Tullik first said things which confused and annoyed the community, and then as a comparatively sophisticated man and as council chairman, he tried to explain why Travis was saying, or was obliged to say, the things he did. As the tensions increased between the community and Travis, so Isaac Tullik's job became unendurable. Moreover, he came to dislike Travis keenly, and found the inevitable contact with him very disagreeable. As his troubles increased, so he tried to identify himself with the faction of the council most hostile to Travis. However, the public, the non-council but outspoken people who concerned themselves with Travis and his ways, remained suspicious of Tullik and somewhat hostile to him.

During this time, Travis himself became increasingly tense and more abrupt in his dealings with the people in general and the council in particular. At successive meetings, he became angry and defensive. Councillors complained that it was becoming exceedingly difficult to talk with him. At one meeting, when his interpreter asked Travis to explain a point, he angrily ordered the interpreter to translate exactly what he had said. When the interpreter insisted that he could not make sense of the English, Travis became indignant and simply reiterated the order. The interpreter told the public that he could not make sense of what was being said, and the hiatus in proceedings was then overcome by Travis' belief that this was the translation he had been demanding. At another point in the same meeting, Travis remarked that he agreed with some of the old people, who had been lamenting undisciplined tendencies among the younger people, and that he had spoken to some of the young people about these matters. At this point an elderly man, who usually refrained from public speaking and was in no way an ally of the established critics, commented: "I do not believe what you say, because what you say is never true. But if this time you are speaking the truth, then I thank you, because what you say is right." Towards the end of the meeting, in response to a speech about welfare that Travis had just concluded, one man stood up and demanded, "I want to ask you one thing: what the hell are you doing here?" He did not wait for a reply, but added scorn to insult by walking directly out of the meeting.

Travis reacted to gestures of this kind by criticizing the leading critics and discounting them as incorrigible trouble-makers who fed on the misunderstanding and gullibility of the people. He continued throughout these difficulties to affirm privately his faith in and affection for the people as a whole, while beginning to express the antipathy he felt towards various individuals. By this process, he discounted the seriousness of the criticisms themselves, and never even began to try to come to terms with what was actually going wrong with his position in the settlement. Rather, he entrenched himself and even dignified himself by explaining the situation in terms of his having to bear the harsh responsibility for teaching the community and its leaders what self-government was and was not all about. Conciliation or concessions would, by such explanation, be tantamount to dereliction of duty. It began to seem that even good manners or honest endeavour towards coherent discussions could be taken as signs of that weakness which rapidly turns into incompetence.

As these attitudes in the Settlement Manager became more and more evident to the councillors, so they intensified their pressure on him to give ground. Isaac Tullik came to find his job utterly unbearable, as did the chairman. At a public meeting, the chairman explained that it was impossible to continue working with Travis, that he had come to realize how the burdens of his many roles were making him worry and lose sleep. The question was put to the vote, and only three people – all closely related to Tullik – agreed that he should resign. (Although Travis was at the meeting, he did not understand what was happening, and nobody offered to translate for his benefit. Afterwards, he revealed that he 'understood' that the community was voting for the person who would be the dog-catcher in the settlement.) Influenced by the scale of this support, the troubled chairman agreed to reserve his decision until the next council meeting. At the same time, he indicated that he wanted to ask a government officer in Churchill to come to Fort John and help them through this crisis.

Shortly after this meeting, the council met again with Travis, but walked out after three minutes; the council decided that they would not talk with Travis again until the officer from Churchill came. For a number of days

Tullik tried unsuccessfully to get in contact with a particular local government officer whom he trusted and who had become well-liked in Fort John. When a message did reach him by way of someone who had to travel from Fort John to Churchill, it is said that the reaction was unsympathetic; officials in Churchill were convinced that all was going smoothly in Fort John, that Travis was doing a good job. Eventually, the radio-call reached Churchill, and the government officer said that he would come as soon as possible. But his schedule was very full, and he never did come. The passage of time was the only balm that eventually eased the crisis, aided by the pessimistic resignation which Fort John Inuit adopted *vis-à-vis* the world of white officialdom and their own embodiment of it. The less resigned, more vehement critics found some hope in a meeting between councillors and administrators, which had been scheduled for that fall, and which was supposed to provide an opportunity for discussing and resolving the difficulties that the local government programme was encountering in the settlements. That meeting never took place.

    Shortly after the final council meeting, Travis left Fort John for approximately two weeks. As he left, a rumour reached him that in another settlement, in another administrative region, two whites – the Settlement Manager and the mechanic – had been attacked and beaten by local men. Like most northern rumours, this one turned out to be false. But, also like many northern rumours, it had a ring of truth; Travis was clearly affected by it, and it led him to talk about his own situation in a new way. In the last conversation we had together that autumn, Travis asked himself for the first time what he was doing, raising the possibility that he was making bad decisions and exciting justifiable opposition. He glimpsed the dangers of his position once they had been translated into the idiom of physical violence. He raised the ultimate (and essentially symbolic) question: was anything being gained by the Inuit of Fort John as a result of his work there? It seemed possible that he might regain some of the good humour and balance that had characterized his behaviour during his first winter and spring in the Arctic, that he could return to Fort John in a spirit of reconciliation.

    During the second winter, the community council again began meeting with Travis, and the welfare issue calmed down. Travis went on a few hunting trips with some of the men. However, some bad feeling arose out of the official visit of the commissioner for the NWT, who tended to be isolated from the Fort John people by social activities in the Settlement Manager's house. One or two violent episodes erupted: once, Travis found it necessary to punch one of his critics in the face, and on another occasion, a man decided to go and shoot Travis, but was prevailed on by his family to stay at home. Both these episodes involved drunkenness. It would appear, therefore, that social quiet and the functioning of the community council were managed at the cost of some degree of repression. Critics were quieter because they sensed that little or nothing could be gained by the sort of criticism expressed the previous summer. The harmony was uneasy and, ultimately, unreal.

During the spring and summer, Travis' situation once again changed in important respects. He was now living with his wife, who came to the north for the first time. Isolated and lonely for her children, she soon became antagonistic towards Fort John and its people. She felt that the Inuit had been given too much, and regarded the northern whites as under-appreciated people who had given and sacrificed much in order to help the unlettered primitives. Against that backdrop, Travis' views appeared rela-tively moderate. Yet his criticisms were now turned on the community as a whole. He felt that Fort John Inuit would not regard the settlement as their own place for which they should be actively responsible. He lamented the absence of that community spirit which inspires people to work hard for the general good of all. Instead, he argued that the men expected high wages for work which should be done on an essentially voluntary basis. He also claimed that Fort John people were reluctant to seize initiatives for them-selves, but were concerned with what he held to be petty and private demands for more money.

Behind this complaint against the community lay a more general impati-ence with the bureaucracy that employed him. In the course of his eighteen months in Fort John, Travis had grown cynical about the policies and intentions of his superiors and during that spring and summer, his cynicism turned into outright hostility. The sources of all his troubles with the Fort John people lay in the policies of Yellowknife and Ottawa: he charged the policy-makers with ignorance of northern conditions, with failing to adapt policies to the special needs of northern peoples, with over-emphasis on educational services, with hiring teachers and mechanics whose experi-ence was insufficient and whose natural abilities were even less. More generally, he felt that the administrators in the larger centres acted without that modicum of consistency which makes the work of a Settlement Man-ager possible; they continually changed their minds, their policies, and their directives. Moreover, it was his view that at every turn they wasted money.

Throughout the spring and summer, it was evident that Travis' critics had become more numerous and their complaints more damning. Yet their readiness to articulate those complaints to him at public meetings had become much less. The community had reached a consensus about their Settlement Manager: the sooner he left the better it would be. Some of the more articulate men had begun to raise the possibility of hamlet status, for then Travis would probably have to leave. This view was expressed by the community at a public meeting in late July.

Travis was informed of the purpose of the meeting and he was asked to attend and voice his opinions. The first hour was taken up by speeches directed against Travis; the condemnations were fierce, turning on his personality as much as on his role. All the difficulties that had been endured *vis-à-vis* his functions were brought up against him. Once again, nothing was translated for Travis' benefit. During the denunciations he sat slightly to one side of the public, playing with small children. Towards the end a woman pointed out that Travis could not understand the things being said. One of the councillors replied that he couldn't understand anything anyway, so there was no point in bothering with interpretation. These exchanges were followed by a speech from a councillor in favour of hamlet status. But a vote was taken, and the suggestion was opposed by a proportion of 3:2.[6] The meeting moved on to a number of smaller issues, and after almost two hours Travis was finally asked to speak.

Travis spoke against the bad ways of the children, who had been breaking windows in the school, had damaged the small dock on the shore, and had even thrown one or two rocks at the government truck. This was translated to those present, but the interpreter did not translate the comments or discussion from the floor into English. So Travis spoke into a curious void: he was denied access to the effect his words might have been having. Then he elaborated on an argument that I had heard him use, less directly, at a number of other encounters with the Fort John community. It ran: school windows are very expensive because special glass has to be used; in fact, each pane costs $15; now, the community will have to pay for damage to the windows, will have to find $15 for every broken pane; this will come about indirectly: the government will run short of money because it has to pay so much money for new windows, and because it runs short of money it will have to economize in other ways; therefore, money will not be available for Fort John houses, and people will have nowhere to live or at least have houses which are in exceedingly bad condition. When he came to the end of these warnings, there was no reply from the public – a dearth of response that was merely given emphasis when a Fort John hunter followed Travis' speech with a statement of his intention of using a boat which had been left lying on the beach for some years. This statement was not translated into English. That said, the chairman of the council closed the meeting.

Shortly after this meeting a rumour began to circulate in Fort John to the effect that Travis wanted to leave. It eventually became an open secret that he wanted to leave not only Fort John, but the Northwest Territories altogether. The secret was open because Travis began to devote much working time to filling out application forms for jobs in southern Canada. The news was attended by two more changes in the local government situation. First, even the more assertive councillors and critics began to withhold expressions of disgruntlement, and found greater ease in so doing. Secondly, Travis himself began to express more openly and vehemently his complaints against the local government programme. There is a strong, if unwritten, rule to the effect that whites should not criticize one another to the knowledge of Inuit. Travis, albeit very selectively, began to break this rule. On one occasion, he announced to his interpreter that as far as he, Travis, was concerned, the new local government programme was "a crock of shit."

Travis left Fort John at Christmas, just two years after arriving there. I do not know what he felt when he left, but the people there were certainly pleased to see him go. The last summer had been marred by a severe shortage of gasoline. Supplies had run out in the spring and only a few men could hunt as they wished between spring and late summer, when the ship finally delivered new supplies to the co-operative stores. During much of that time, government supplies of gas were not exhausted, and many people felt that Travis was refusing to sell those stocks to hunters who needed it. Every time Travis was seen using his canoe and engine, criticism flared anew. When Travis explained the importance of the services which had to be kept going and which would need fuel throughout the summer, he was usually discounted as a liar. At the end, Travis' distance from the people of Fort John was so vast and so evident that even he discussed it. In accounting for the problem, he remarked that it was not possible to have friends among the Inuit, simply because it was essential not to appear to have favourites. Thus, in speaking of the gap between himself and the people he was supposed to be helping towards political autonomy, Richard Travis encapsulated the vast distance between his situation on leaving and his intentions on arriving.

III

Before turning to an analysis of these events, it is necessary to indicate where Fort John criticisms of Travis were without foundation. He was not the liar he was made out to be. Nor did he wish to subvert the co-operative or undermine the authority of its directors. His attitude to welfare payments and the moral horrors of welfare dependency was rigid and conservative, but he did not wish to see families hungry. The moral failing attributed to him was not so much real as a direct outcome of an abrupt and unsympathetic manner. If he had a moral flaw, it was self-righteousness, heightened by an exaggerated confidence in his own judgements. Also, the criticism and complaints directed against him were often obscure in their expression; discovering their meanings involved patience and preparedness to decipher an unfamiliar idiom. It was easy enough for Travis to misread such criticisms, and mistakenly categorize them as misunderstandings on the part of the Inuit. And it was not easy for him to have patience and time when burdened by apparently endless paper work. Therefore, when little troubles turned into major crises, the hostility had accumulated and chances of proper communication were correspondingly diminished. Moreover, Travis was a man who from previous experience or by disposition was not likely to find communication through confrontation anything but difficult. So it came about that he was suspected of hoarding gasoline for no good reason – because no one was likely to listen to the reasons he gave. In fact, he had offered all the gasoline he could spare to the co-operative, holding government reserves at the lowest level he could risk.

The welfare problem was in large part an inheritance. Provision of welfare to the needy had been characterized for over a decade by inconsistency and capriciousness. Inuit in the region can remember receiving less than fifty cents as a monthly welfare cheque. They also remember a series of humiliations administered to those seeking help from a former teacher who was responsible for welfare: men were kept waiting in an anteroom, were told not to talk while waiting, not to sniff too loudly, and were treated to long moralizing perorations on the twin subjects of welfare money and indolence. At one time, welfare was in the hands of officials who lived sixty miles from Fort John. It is recalled that during that period, the officials' interpreter became so unpopular among Fort John people that he eventually became literally sick with worry and left.

In the light of this background, it is not surprising that every move and every decision made by Travis was regarded with suspicion. The Inuit anticipated that he would continue the established tradition of welfare officers, and so their reactions to his decisions were, as far as he could see, not commensurate with the decisions themselves. He did not know the history of welfare officers' dealings with the community, and was not in a good position to discover it.

As well as these local and individual reasons for some of the difficulties, there remains the intrinsically problematic nature of a Settlement Manager's functions. These difficulties (which are in effect institutional) were occasionally amenable to Travis' own analyses, and some of them were stated coherently by him in retrospect. These institutional considerations not only urge a more sympathetic view of his professional fortunes, but also offer much insight into the workings of the local government programme as a whole.

IV

A contradiction is to be found at the heart of much administrative endeavour in the Canadian eastern Arctic. There is a thesis which runs: Eskimos are in need of such and such material provision. Therefore, we (the whites) must provide them. Yet the Eskimos should not have everything done for them (by whites) because dependence of that kind is morally and socially corrosive. Moreover, unqualified provision by whites to Eskimos presupposes that, in all cases, whites really do know what Eskimos need. And that is at odds with conceptions of political and social development expected from all other Canadian citizens. Therefore, Eskimos must be encouraged to do things and control their affairs themselves. It follows that political institutions must be created and local leadership encouraged. Then and only then, the argument runs, will it be possible for Eskimo communities to achieve a proper degree of self-determination and influence over the quality and cause of their lives, which is the acknowledged right of all citizens.[7]

This argument is presented to the Eskimos by way of encouragement; they are told that participation in local government will result in the shift of control from whites to Eskimos. In other words, it will redress the balance of domination. In practical terms, the message is clear enough: if you (Eskimos) adopt these political ways, constitute the necessary electoral bodies, demonstrate adequate leadership qualities, and accomplish all this by following a number of uncomplicated procedural rules, then the things we (whites) control will pass into your (Eskimo) hands.

All the evidence at my disposal points to the conclusion that Inuit, in the eastern Arctic at least, received this idea with enthusiasm. Alongside the development of schooling, nursing stations, as well as the ubiquitous administrative presence, many Inuit were anxious to reform circumstances and reverse a number of trends. It happened, therefore, that a leader or a council, or perhaps an individual, requested a change. It was in the nature of things that requests for change were concerned with important aspects of community life: one or another family should be given welfare; liquor laws should be changed; prices at the store should be lowered; a particular white should leave the settlement; young people at residential schools in far-away towns should not be allowed to go to bars. In all these examples, the Inuit were told that such issues were beyond their range of jurisdiction. Community councils could not decide liquor laws, nor could they interfere with rules governing children in residential schools.

Thus, administrators are in a curious position. On the one hand, they are telling the Inuit communities that every effort is being made to give them responsibility for their own affairs. On the other hand, they insist that much of what the Inuit regard as their own affairs are not included in the sphere of Inuit responsibility. Verbally, encouragement is given to the Inuit to try and take power; yet in practice, Inuit discover that they remain powerless in a vast range of crucial matters, and anything more than the trimmings of social life are to remain solidly under white domination. Therefore, local government programmes – in some measure inspired by a sense of the subordinate status of the Inuit – create or accelerate that retreatism which local government programmes are especially aimed at obviating. Settlement Managers have the unfortunate role of translating this irony into everyday political realities. The irony is not lost on the Inuit.

The problems of Settlement Managers and other administrators can be formalized as follows:

1. Prescriptive context in which the administrators work: "Inuit must take over roles and responsibilities presently in the hands of whites."
2. Inuit agree: "Acts should be changed."
3. Administrator (in his educational role): "*You* cannot change acts; that is not part of your possible authority."
4. Recurrence of 2 and 3 undermines 1.
5. Administrator is identified with negation of 1.[8]

Of course, the contradiction originates in confusions about areas of responsibility and authority, which also create a second and converse difficulty. Whites in the settlements have their own ideas about the possible provinces of Inuit responsibility. Teachers, for example, feel that getting children to bed at night is the responsibility of the parents; Settlement Managers feel that apportioning the settlement budget is the responsibility of the community council. Sometimes the Inuit do not agree, or consider that they do not have the requisite skills and expertise. The tendency to leave the whites with difficulties can be intensified either by retreatism in the wake of recurrent difficulties with white authority, or by resentment against whites for maintaining their dominance, or merely by an impression that, in effect, the entire settlement is a white creation and should be duly organized by whites. In Fort John a number of older people considered that the need for an administrator had grown alongside the difficulties which beset the community. A woman told me: "We are in a fog. The whites have led us into this fog, and it is their job to lead us out again." Attitudes towards the school were similar. The institution, the rules governing it, and what was taught were the creation of whites; so the whites should continue to bear the responsibility for its daily routine as much as for the problems it caused. Given the extent to which a settlement, physically, ideologically, and economically, is a creature of southern intrusion, it is not surprising that many Inuit automatically assume that whites will bear many of the costs.

Travis, like other eastern arctic administrators, was bedevilled by those difficulties. In the terminology elaborated by Paine (1971) and others, the Settlement Manager is archetypally a broker. Behind and above him stands the government patron. But his position in the community is so central and his influence so considerable, that he is inevitably something of a patron himself. Paine remarks that an aspiring patron ideally "offers items and services that are new to the culture, thereby actually creating the need for his commodities" (*op. cit.*:14). "What distinguishes the patron from his client is that only values of the patron's choosing are circulated in their relationship" (*op. cit.*:15). Since a Settlement Manager is also a controller of information – an important potential service – he can dispense patronage simply by disseminating information selectively. Moreover, as a hirer of men, he can choose a labour force with an eye to asserting a patron role. The most important of Paine's observations is probably that the roles of patron, broker, client are dependent "upon the situational context for their recognition" and "may be embraced alternately or even in combination by the same person" (*op. cit.*:21). It is worth asking to what extent the difficulties of a Settlement Manager are amenable to analysis in terms of confused or uncertain patron/broker role positions.[9]

At the outset, it must be recognized that subjective factors are of real importance. A broker or go-between can, in a Canadian arctic settlement, project himself as a patron. There are resources with which he can substantiate this projection, and there is a background of relatively little knowledge (compounded by language differences) against which exaggerated aspirations to patronage can avoid detection. Furthermore, there is that tradition of white subordination and dominance which has been built by men who seemed to be patrons. This subjective element will naturally vary from individual to individual, from Settlement Manager to Settlement Manager. But the objective circumstances make it possible, indeed probable, that any administrator will be seen as a patron, even if he is not personally inclined to emphasize that aspect of his status and functions. In the past, whites have tended to be perceived by Inuit as a single power with unified objectives. By the same token, individual functionaries are likely to be seen in a context of overall white domination (and therefore as part of a monolithic white patronage), rather than in an intricate hierarchy of institutional arrangements. This means that an administrator who sought to be perceived by his settlement only as a broker or as a go-between would have to disengage himself from the patron role by dint of self-conscious effort. *Ceteris paribus*, he will be thought of as a patron at least as much as a broker.

It is possible that Travis was untypically interested in appearing to be a patron. Initially, he may have felt attracted to the position of Settlement Manager by the opportunities it offered for a patronage role. Certainly he tended to identify the fortunes of Fort John with his own endeavours and initiatives, and he was gratified and rewarded just insofar as his ideas or suggestions were accepted. Correspondingly, Fort John people were inclined to expect patronage, and certainly hoped, thereby, they would be able to secure those changes in their community that they wanted; the patron, it was hoped, could be lured and persuaded into dispensing favours according to local aspirations. Perception of the Settlement Manager in a strong patron role was thus based on that reciprocity which so essentially characterizes the patron/client relationship. It need hardly be added that it also yielded continuity with a history of white/Inuit contacts.

As Travis' position became complicated by the community's rejection of his ideas and suggestions, so he asserted his go-between role. Still more important, it was in the role of broker or go-between that he vetoed suggestions made by the local council. More generally, the function of a Settlement Manager does centre on the purveying of rules that emanate from government: delimiting possible Inuit authority, demarcating responsibility, as well as effecting changes in these are done outside the settlement. Equally, the decision to pursue a policy of political incorporation in the settlement is not within the province of a Settlement Manager's authority. These comparatively trivial observations do indicate the intrinsic brokerage of the Settlement Manager's position. No matter how effectively local councillors denounce such policies or demarcations, irrespective of how accurately they expose contradictions or errors in the fiats of governments, the administrator to whom these arguments are directed is in no position to take practical heed of them. Such are the real limits to his patronage. In reply to the critics, he can only affirm his go-between role: yes, it may be that such and such are problematical rules, but they are nonetheless rules, and it is his job to enforce them. He is acting under orders.

The circumstances in Fort John would be in no way bizarre were it not for the fact that Travis had given the impression of being a patron. A sudden assertion of limited brokerage is therefore likely to be seen as dishonesty, at worst, or sheer humbug, at best. So it happened repeatedly, as relations between Travis and the community deteriorated, that Travis was charged with using the rule book only when it suited him. More seriously, they charged that what suited him was preventing them from doing the things *they* wanted. In essence, they denied him the right of appeal to his limited role as a mere go-between. In this way, the trap that threatens to seize a Settlement Manager, that can easily isolate him behind a wall of suspicion and resentment, is laid in part by the nature of his position. To a limited extent, the trap can be lessened by self-conscious self-definition as go-between, in defiance of the historical and institutional elements which urge patronage. The danger is that the trap is made deep and dark by any personal tendency on the part of a white administrator to enhance his prestige by encouraging those aspects of the situation which suggests he *is* a patron.

Establishment of a local government system is aimed at shifting power from outsiders to insiders, or by corollary, it is aimed at obviating some of the worst consequences of persistent domination by outsiders. The trap then lies in the limited degree to which such an objective corresponds to reality. In the case of the Canadian Inuit, dependence upon white society alongside vulnerability to governmental decisions in the south, is not ultimately relieved by achieving hamlet status. Inuit will remain a tiny minority in the total electorate, and a weak pressure group in the context of an advanced industrial society. It thus follows that a Settlement Manager, *qua* broker or go-between, is no more able to eliminate the fundamental relationship between Inuit and the south than an elected council chairman. The *limitation* of patron/broker analysis, therefore, may be discovered in the light of larger relationships than those which exist exclusively within the settlements themselves.

It is as well, therefore, to return to the starting point of this discussion. It was argued at the outset that there has been an essential continuity in white/Inuit relationships over the past fifty years of eastern arctic history. Political incorporation has followed economic and ideological incorporation in the latest attempt at changing the social and economic life of the Inuit to a form which is thought to harmonize with Canadian society as a whole. The aim of this political incorporation is expressed by the Settlement Manager who, in the idiom of the contemporary north, "works himself out of his job." The underlying argument here is that this aim achieved, the continuity will remain. Settlement Managers, such as Travis in our example, are caught in the problematic, and this is the price for continuity. It may be suggested to the people of the far north that their social and economic formation is to become more their own affair, but the separate development that such a suggestion implies is not at present being countenanced by the patrons who make the rules. There certainly is room for economic and political developments which could give reality to some of the stated objectives of national policy towards Canadian Inuit and Indians alike – fatalistic staring into the Medusa face of industrial society is no more justifiable than it is helpful. Unfortunately, these developments appear to be neither secured nor even encouraged by the attempt at political incorporation implicit in the present urge towards local government.

Yet continuity in the history of white presence in the Arctic is at the level of overall southern objectives *vis-à-vis* Inuit communities and culture. Discontinuity can be found in Inuit reactions to those objectives and, accordingly, to individuals and institutions representing those objectives in the settlements. Although Inuit throughout the eastern Arctic note without hesitation their dependency upon the society and government to the south, they are also beginning to add hostility to dependency. The direction and form of this hostility was expressed to me by an Inuit woman in Fort John:

Some of the people are still doing whatever the government officials and the white men tell them to do. Maybe that is why government officials think that the people are stupid, because people here sometimes do things for the government even though they are against them. So I think that in the future this should be done: the people here should just decide to go ahead. If the co-operative or the council want to do something, and not do things *this* way or *that* way, or want to quit doing something, then we should just tell the government to stop coming here because they aren't really trying to help. The people should tell the government to go away and try and fool people somewhere else.

NOTES

1   It is possible that competitiveness between the various white agencies has aggravated the tendency towards domination, since agencies indicate their effectiveness to one another by making their influence over the Inuit population very apparent.
2   This is, of course, likely to vary from settlement to settlement, but it is a generalization strongly supported by my own findings in the Canadian eastern Arctic.
3   Some hamlets do not have settlement managers.
4   All the names in this section are altered in order to preserve anonymity. Fort John is in fact a small community in the eastern Arctic; Travis came to Fort John more or less directly from work in the south. He was of a youthful middle-age, and arrived at Fort John without his family.
5   This and some of the following information came from reminiscences, many of which were long and detailed. I have no reason for doubting their validity.
6   Rejection of the proposal is not surprising, given the extremely negative attitude in the community towards the problems of the settlement. Since the Fort John Inuit as a whole felt that whites should deal with the problems they had created, it is impressive that rejection of immediate application for hamlet status was by so narrow a margin.
7   This view is reinforced by that fashionable concern with ethnic cultures, especially with the exotic Eskimo, as well as by that equally fashionable rejection of western culture and technology. A false inference is all too easily made from the establishment of local government for the preservation of things essentially 'Eskimo.'
8   In broader terms, of course, the entire white or southern society is identified with negation of 1.
9   Paine elaborates on (*op. cit.*:6) the distinction between broker and go-between in terms of manipulation or processing of messages or instructions: the broker is a less faithful purveyor of the patron's rulings than is the go-between. Thus defined, both roles are ideal types. It is indeed hard to imagine how, in practice, a true go-between could exist. Certainly a Settlement Manager is more of a broker than a go-between, even if he should, in theory, be as much of a go-between as possible. In this discussion, therefore, I use the terms go-between and broker almost interchangeably, but am conscious that the distinction between them is analytically useful.

References

ARBESS, S. E.
    1966 *Social Change and the Eskimo Cooperative at George River, Quebec.* Ottawa, Department of Northern Affairs and National Resources (NCRC 66-1).
FREEMAN, MILTON
    1971 "Tolerance and Rejection of Patron Sales in an Eskimo Settlement." In R. Paine (ed.), *Patrons and Brokers in the East Arctic.* St. John's, Institute of Social and Economic Research, Memorial University of Newfoundland.

KLEIVAN, HELGE
1966 *The Eskimos of Northeast Labrador. A History of Eskimo-White Populations, 1771–1955*. Oslo, Norsk Polarinstitutt.
MAYER, ADRIAN C.
1966 "The Significance of Quasi-Groups in the Study of Complex Societies." In M. Banton (ed.), *The Social Anthropology of Complex Societies*. A.S.A. Monograph, 4. London, Tavistock Publications.
PAINE, ROBERT
1971 "A Theory of Patronage and Brokerage." In R. Paine (ed.), *Patrons and Brokers in the East Arctic*. St. John's, Institute of Social and Economic Research, Memorial University of Newfoundland.

The Canadian government has recently encouraged Inuit and Indians to embrace settlement associations in the hope that small kin-based groups will be cemented into larger communities with heightened control over their own affairs (cf. Balikci, 1959; Arbess, 1966; Vallee, 1967). However, these institutions have usually fallen (initially, at least) under the domination of Euro-Canadian advisers – though not without disputes as to how they should be run.

The objective of this essay is to present a case study of the processes by which this kind of domination can be achieved, and to identify the bases of the disputes that ensued in this particular instance. The scene is the co-operative in the small, isolated, Inuit settlement of Port Burwell, off the northern tip of Labrador (in the NWT), where the Canadian adviser, the development officer (DO) and the Inuit members became engaged in a struggle for its control, even though the decision-making rights had been legally given to its members.

It is argued that the key to the adviser's designs for power, as well as the contradictory strategies of Inuit and government officials in formulating and discharging co-operative policy, were based on three sets of highly-prized community ideals. Their simultaneous realization proved to be an impossibility.

I

The Setting
In the late 1950s, the Ungava Bay coast of New Quebec was the prototype area for planned regional Inuit socio-economic development. Piecemeal government attempts to relieve northern natives from the material and psychological miseries of an economy perched precariously upon fur trading and underwritten by relief rations had failed until then in this area and others (Findlay, 1955; Evans, 1968). It was now proposed that administrators, development officers, teachers, and nurses be sent to the north in droves to lure Inuit from the primitive nomadism they had pursued during the decades of the 'contact era' (cf. Helm and Damas, 1963) as wards of traders, missionaries, and policemen (RCMP), and to install them in settlements replete with schools, nursing stations, power plants and prefabricated houses.

As an area for regional development, Ungava Bay was propitious. It is rich in resources along different segments of its 500-mile coastline; of particular note are the stands of timber (around Fort Chimo and George River) and the large numbers of seal and fish around its headlands (near Port Burwell). It was believed that with improved (government-loaned) technologies and the encouragement of economic relations *between* communities, the Inuit economy of the area could be considerably diversified (cf. Dunbar, 1952). Indeed, since development began fifteen years ago, *per capita* Inuit income has increased five times or more throughout the area.

Yet the development of the resources of Ungava Bay has succeeded only in the headland communities; paradoxically, these are the areas that traders and missionaries abandoned decades ago because of their isolation and inaccessibility. Today (1970), deep in the Bay, a thousand or more Inuit live largely by wage labour, welfare, and weekend hunting and fishing. Off the northeast headland, on Killinek Island, the 150 Inuit of Port Burwell (27 households) enjoy flourishing seal, cod and char fisheries, eiderdown collection and handicraft industries based on local products.[1] The consumer and producer co-operative around which the community focuses (and to which all 84 adults belong) paid off its $6000 loan long ago, and in early 1970, when I arrived for a year's fieldwork, it was renowned for its financial success.

Though many are immigrants from larger settlements around Ungava Bay and from the Labrador coast, the Inuit of Port Burwell remain comparatively unsophisticated. Their isolated settlement is costly to service – by plane from Fort Chimo or from Frobisher Bay on Baffin Island – and for this reason it is not often in contact with the larger administrative townships which enjoy (or suffer) a more hectic Canadian style of life. The half-dozen or so resident Canadians – the DO, the school teachers, the nurse, and the mechanic – are concerned that 'traditional' Inuit life-styles remain unspoilt in an area where the exploitation of 'traditional' Inuit resources is still possible. Little money circulates in the community, and most co-operative transactions are discharged through credit-debit accounting. The co-operative's retail order of southern Canadian luxuries is restricted by limited capital, so that three or four months after the annual ship delivery in August ('sea lift'), little other than basic necessities remain in stock.

Prior to 1970, for ten years, the Port Burwell co-operative had apparently been successful and tranquil, though dominated by Canadian advisers. But during 1970, when administrative jurisdiction of Port Burwell passed from Fort Chimo to Frobisher Bay, circumstances changed, partly because of increased government interest. The Inuit began to argue, covertly, about and against co-operative policy. The basis of the argument and eventual confrontation with the government rested on three crucial sets of ideals.

Conflicting Ideals
Set I. These particular ideals stress the co-operative's provision of economic services, and are those which government officials presented to the Inuit to encourage their participation in the institution. A lecture course designed to give Inuit information about co-operatives states the ideals succinctly: ... "the co-operative is to serve its members. In some cases, that may mean trying to sell whatever the members have produced for the highest price possible in order to give the members more money for their effort. In other cases it may mean trying to supply members with food and other things that they need for as low a cost as possible. As the people themselves who are interested in these services are the ones who make decisions, the group's interests are always safe" (Sprudz, 1966:20).[2] With such ideals, certain organizational requirements were propagated, notably a more expanded social network and a greater allegiance to institutionalized (elected) leaders than the Inuit were familiar with from the 'contact era.'

Set II. These ideals stem from the co-operative's function as a business institution; they revolve around the notion of profit, meaning that minimally the annual income should exceed expenditure.

Set III. These ideals demand the fulfillment of traditional Inuit values which (notwithstanding modification since contact with Europeans) still stress egalitarianism in wealth and power, and particularistic relations of kinship and neighbourhood – among whose principal obligations is the provision of succour in times of need.

The introduction of the second set of ideals made the Inuit aware of the jargon of market economics. "Profits," "shares," "capital investment," and other concepts were added to a Euro-Canadian economic vocabulary that hitherto had been restricted (in this sphere) to two words vital in dealings with H.B.C. traders: "credit" and "debt". (Both are included in a single concept, *akiliksaq*; literally, that which requires payment.) The new concepts are still but hazily understood by most Inuit.

To encourage acceptance of the co-operative, many Canadians have stressed the similarity of its "co-operativism" (Worsley, 1971) with the co-operation demanded in techniques of traditional hunting (cf. Q-book:286; see also Vallee, 1964:46). But I doubt, as do J. and I. Honigmann (1965:233) and Graburn (1971:116), that the Inuit appreciate the similarity. The social arrangements of co-operatives are hardly akin to those of any traditional activities. Co-operative distributions, whether of dividends, credit, or commodities, cannot be likened to traditional distributions of game in which the securer shares his spoils with unsuccessful hunters; moreover, the co-operative distributes non-perishable goods which, customarily, Inuit keep instead of share (animal pelts, for example).

Furthermore, translations of concepts such as "profits" and "shares" into Inuttitut are imprecise, inconsistently used, and rarely refer explicitly to traditional ideas of social organization or handling and distributing resources.[3]

Worsley (1971) and the contributors to *Two Blades of Grass* (particularly Dore) have discussed at length issues that concern the interaction of traditional social systems and the organizational imperatives of co-operatives. They are of the opinion that however suitable a foundation a traditional system apparently provides, it will inevitably contain elements "dysfunctional" for co-operative development. For example, the cohesiveness and egalitarianism of many traditional communities refer usually to small groups, and would likely imply factionalism in the wider community that a co-operative would normally embrace (Dore, 1971:52).

The Development Officer

The DO had a crucial role in the Port Burwell co-operative. His overall position in the community corresponded with Worsley's conservation officer in an isolated northern Saskatchewan Indian community, who was a "multiplex bureaucrat at low level; face to face with his clients interacting with them as a total personality; with considerable latitude and autonomy; working for 'decolonization' goals (which frequently conflict with his own or other officials' technical jurisdictions, functions, training, and interests), these goals being [based upon] socialist democratic values" (Worsley, 1964:388). Within such a position, the Port Burwell DO devised a job strategy for himself which had significant implications for government-Inuit economic relations.

Specifically, the Port Burwell DO had a dual task. He had to oversee the co-operative, especially its retail store, and he had to experiment with, and instruct the Inuit in, new techniques of harvesting resources. The relationship between these two activities, coupled with his emphasis on the former one, determined much of his role strategy. Let me illustrate by comparing our DO's strategy with that of the DO in George River in Arctic Quebec.

According to Arbess (1967:124), the George River Inuit wanted to obtain extensive credit from their co-operative store, and applied pressure on the young Inuk manager to grant them this. However, at a meeting with senior government officials, the Inuit were told that their debts were far too large, and that they should go to their DO for welfare assistance to help pay them off. In reply, the Inuit, taking advantage of the DO's absence from the meeting on account of illness, claimed that the debts accumulated over the previous year precisely because they had been refused welfare. This the DO later denied, stating that the debts arose from the purchases of expensive luxuries. Nevertheless, the senior official's view was that the Inuit complaints had some justice, and welfare payments were subsequently increased. In blaming the DO for their debts and indicating that they needed a higher *level* of welfare payment, George River Inuit managed to manipulate officialdom. Arbess argues that the DO's conflict with the Inuit arose because he had given priority to resource development, restricting welfare so as to encourage the Inuit to involve themselves in this development. Yet, the monetary yield from harvesting natural resources was itself insufficient for Inuit needs.

It is of obvious analytic importance that the DO in George River had control over the distribution of welfare, as did the Port Burwell DO. Yet he emphasized a different aspect of his job: he was principally concerned with controlling the financial fortunes of the co-operative and ensuring an annual profit (cf. Set II ideals). If extra welfare were required, he would distribute it, even though he shared the George River DO's opinion that too much welfare induces laziness among Inuit hunters.

The strategy of the Port Burwell DO may be appreciated from three inter-related perspectives:
(1) Control of the co-operative's finances offers a greater probability of success than experimentation with new resources or harvesting techniques with which unpredictable environmental factors are likely to interfere.
(2) Success in terms of profit-making is highly regarded by the Euro-Canadian public to whom the DO's superiors in Frobisher Bay are ultimately accountable for their expenditure on the co-operative scheme.
(3) The DO, like most government employees in small arctic settlements, was little committed to his settlement. He sought to demonstrate his abilities to his superiors as soon as possible and to achieve promotion to another settlement.[4]

Co-Operative Monopoly
It is common in the Canadian north, as in Port Burwell, for a DO to perform secretarial and treasurer duties for an Inuit co-operative. But it is the board of directors, elected from the membership, who are empowered by law with all the co-operative's decision-making; if the DO is not a member (and the Port Burwell DO was not), he is in a position to offer advice only; he cannot even vote on proposals. Despite this, the Port Burwell DO managed to fulfil his strategy of controlling the financial fortunes of the co-operative, even though his policies often ran against what the Inuit perceived as their best interests. The DO was successful, in part, because the Port Burwell co-operative enjoys a monopoly in the handling of goods that enter and leave the settlement, with one exception mentioned below.

Theoretically, a trading monopoly can set its retail prices at any level. If prices are low, then the overall profit it desires can be achieved through comparatively low payments for the produce it buys; alternatively, if retail prices are high, producers can be paid correspondingly more. Now, the Port Burwell co-operative, as a retail outlet, faced *potential* competition from mail-order houses offering a variety of goods at reasonable prices (by arctic standards), particularly hunting equipment and clothing (this is the exception to the co-operative monopoly). Thus, it might have been expected that the co-operative would set its retail prices at a low level in order to compete with the mail-order firms, and then pay its Inuit members lower prices for skins, fish, and handicrafts.

In practice, this occurred only partly. Until mid-1970, the prices Port Burwell Inuit received for their produce were low in comparison to those paid to Inuit in other settlements. Overheads were also kept at a minimum, for example, by soliciting free labour for building co-operative amenities, and by paying low wages to the store clerks. Yet the prices of retail goods were high (20 to 33 percent mark-ups over prices at George River or in the mail-order catalogues).

The first factor concerning the high retail prices was the high wholesale costs faced by the Port Burwell co-operative because of its isolation and small clientele; the George River co-operative was advantageously placed in both these respects. The second factor is the *actual* lack of competition. The nearest trading outlet to Port Burwell is the co-operative at George River, 140 hard-travelling miles away. Competition from the mail-order catalogues failed to materialize as the Inuit of Port Burwell made little use of them. I believe the isolation of the settlement was the principal deterrent, as orders often took up to three months to arrive; secondly, few Inuit in Port Burwell (unlike those in less remote settlements) had the skills to order for themselves and had to approach a Euro-Canadian for help – often an awesome task that could involve a cross-examination of the individual's financial circumstances. I do not think that the shortage of cash in the settlement was much of a factor here: it is true that the Inuit were aware of the cash shortage but, as a later discussion of their attitude to debt will indicate, it would have been out of character for them to be discouraged from ordering for this reason. Only when parcels arrived (some months after the order was placed) did a search for the cash to complete the transaction begin, and usually be found – from savings put 'under the mattress,' from lucky gambling, or through exchange with Euro-Canadians. Nor did the DO deliberately restrict the amount of money in the community, nor in any other way attempt to hinder the Inuit from mail-order purchases.

Later, quantitative data are presented that suggest the Port Burwell co-operative could neither pay competitive prices and wages to its member producers and workers, nor set competitive prices on its retail goods, *and* make a profit. Until 1970, it had enjoyed profits largely by exploiting its near-monopolistic privilege, since only a monopoly can sustain uncompetitive prices and survive as an enterprise.

Adjustments of Control

The Port Burwell co-operative effectively and efficiently secured its profits. It did so in part because the total yearly value of goods held as retail stock could be roughly matched with the community's total annual income. This balance was attained through the regular operation of four interrelated adjustments, all initiated by the DO; in effect, they constituted his economic control of the co-operative's finances. But it should be stressed at once that his motivation for making adjustments appeared to me to stem largely from his impressions of the co-operative's current – rather than long-term, or yearly – fortunes, impressions that came from a periodic scrutiny of the co-operative's ledgers which give details of the current credit status of each member.

Two of the adjustments involved altering the community's income: (1) increased production could be brought about, and (2) the amount of welfare distributed could be altered. Probably because success in hunting is partly dependent on factors outside an Inuk's direct control, such as availability of resources, luck, weather, and hunting skill, the community as a whole was never urged to hunt 'harder;' but those whom the DO considered lazy, were. These Inuit might be refused welfare and told to procure seal skins instead, or to make handicrafts and trade them at the store. However, no one was persistently refused welfare. Since no able-bodied hunter received welfare before 1968, this sanction was comparatively recent.[5]

Thus, welfare was also used to augment community income. During parts of the year (especially winter), when hunting was slack, the DO would write out welfare cheques for all the household heads other than the few who held regular part-time jobs in the settlement. On these cheques, he would specify the goods for which the welfare credit could be exchanged – usually for food, clothing, or fuel. He did not investigate the circumstances of each recipient as a welfare officer is supposed to do. Had he investigated, he would certainly have found that each *was* in need. But the willing distribution of welfare reflected primarily his *perceived needs for the co-operative*. This is confirmed in the DO's remarks about the new administrator, who arrived in May 1970, to take responsibility for welfare: the DO hoped the administrator would be tolerant of Inuit requests for welfare; otherwise "it might be bad for business, especially in the winter." The offering of casual jobs or welfare boosts to Inuit who had accumulated almost unassailable debts reflects similar concerns.

The remaining adjustments involved altering the amount of retail goods available for purchase: (3) extra goods could be ordered from southern

Canada, and (4) the sale of the goods could be restricted. Because sea-freight charges were cheap, most of the retail goods were shipped to the settlement once a year in summer. However, without consulting the Inuit, the DO would occasionally place orders with southern distributors (with whom the Inuit were unable to communicate) for small quantities of goods to be flown to the settlement at much higher freight charges.[6]

Restrictions on the sale of retail goods applied to all whose debts exceeded $150. Periodically, the DO would post a list of these members and, theoretically, they would then be disallowed further purchases unless they made payments into their accounts (ideally from sealskins and carvings; in practice just as often from welfare cheques). Later I will show that the day-to-day operation of the restrictions was unsuccessful because it had to be delegated to young Inuit store clerks. But the sale of large items was carefully controlled by the DO. Twice he recalled washing machines because he figured that the families who had been allowed them on credit would never pay for them; and the very expensive snowmobiles, outboard motors, and canoes were allowed only to those who held half the required payment in their accounts, though this rule was waived for the few regular wage-earners. One young man had his snowmobile confiscated when he lost his job, and it was returned only three months later, after he had accumulated half the skidoo's cost. (The board of directors concurred in this decision.)

The choice of two or three adjustments usually available to secure the same end provided the flexibility that undoubtedly contributed to the DO's success in controlling the co-operative's finances. Each adjustment has its limits: if the amount of welfare being dispensed becomes excessively large, a DO may be obliged to submit an explanation to his superiors; if the sale of goods from a store is overly restricted, Inuit are perhaps denied goods they legitimately need. Often two or more adjustments have to be applied simultaneously.

Furthermore, the DO of an isolated arctic settlement with a very small Canadian population may be expected to try to maintain harmonious relationships with the Inuit. Therefore, he would be more inclined to make adjustments which would increase income levels and goods available rather than restrict them. For example, if community income were in excess of the value of goods available, he might prefer to order more goods than cut back on welfare; and if community income were less than the value of goods available, he might increase welfare rather than restrict purchasing. These were usually the Port Burwell DO's strategies.

Symbols and Rituals
Occasionally, the DO was forced to make adjustments that were unpopular with the Inuit (for example, the fourth one listed above). Furthermore, he

also had to sustain the low payments to producers and store employees, and the high prices of retail goods (which were partly set by more senior government officials), since only at these levels could the co-operative secure its profit. To do so, the DO consistently had to be able to overrule actual or potential opposition (or counter-suggestions) from a board of directors legally entitled to alter payments and prices. Due largely to Port Burwell's isolation, Inuit knowledge of prices and payments in other settlements was still limited in early 1970. This meant that there was little opposition to the prices and payments of their own co-operative; what opposition there was, the DO suppressed by exploiting the power in certain symbols and rituals.

The content of the symbols related to the Set II ideals (see above), extracted out of context, were presented independently as undeniable absolutes; for example, "the essentiality of profit," "the virtue of credit," and "the sin of debt." The evocation of a symbol by the DO would indicate whether a proposed course of action was desirable or undesirable, since each symbolized what was "good for" or "bad for" the co-operative's financial "health." Thus, to a director's proposal that some tinned food be ordered to relieve the monotony of eating seal meat throughout the long winter, the DO's response was that the co-operative could not afford it; if the food were ordered, he said either the co-operative would "not make a profit" on the purchases, since the members would have no money to buy the food, or, if buying were allowed on credit, the members would merely "go further into debt." No extra food was ordered.

Various rituals on the part of both the directors and the rank and file, obscured the extent of the DO's control over the co-operative; instead they helped to create the impression that the ideal roles of the directors (as decision-makers) and the DO (as adviser) were being exercised. The annual general meeting (A.G.M.) of the co-operative, in which the board of directors (prompted by the DO, or visiting government officials) stumbled through a full-scale share-holders' meeting attended by every member, was one such ritual.[7] The monthly board meeting between the DO (or government official) and the directors was another: it stressed that Inuit were *participating* in decision-making over their economic affairs; in fact, because of their subservience to the power of the symbols, the directors seldom made any decisions. When they did, they invariably consulted someone with more knowledge – the DO – to check that their proposals would not jeopardize their co-operative's "good health." With their initiative heavily dampened, the directors appeared not so much apathetic as indecisive and uncertain. In other settlements, Canadian advisers to co-operatives, whether they were DOs, RCMP constables, or missionaries, apparently found it necessary to exercise similar control or veto power over Inuit decision-making (see, for example, Arbess, 1966; Freeman, 1971; Vallee, 1967).

II

Dissatisfaction and Action
The effectiveness of the symbols was related to the incomplete grasp that the Inuit had of the complexities of the concepts implied in the Set II ideals. Also many of the co-operative's unfavourable prices and payments – which the symbols were no doubt invoked to support – had gone unquestioned because of the people's inadequate comparative knowledge. However, with decreasing isolation through cumulative contact with the outside world (visiting relatives, hospitalization, going south to take courses, and so on),[8] Port Burwell Inuit were becoming more aware of the extent to which they were economically underprivileged. By mid-1970, they knew that hunters in the neighbouring settlement were offered higher prices for their seal skins, that retail goods in Fort Chimo were cheaper, that a clerk's wages in Port Burwell were little more than half what should be expected. Set I ideals, they perceived, were going unrealized.

The dismay engendered paralleled that of co-operative members (Inuit) on St. Lawrence Island, Alaska, who were told that by joining a federation they would enjoy cheaper retail goods; but having joined, prices later rose (Hughes, 1960:172–8). In Port Burwell, in 1970, it was especially difficulties over debts that aroused the people's frustration and ire – which, however, were diffusely expressed (sometimes in drunken rages) and not articulated by the directors; as far as I know, the DO was never aware of their frustration. Failure to produce an organized community response, even at that time, is probably accountable to the ambience of submission effectively promoted by those symbols and rituals described in the foregoing pages (not to mention the legacy of submission from the paternalism of the 'contact' era).

Although the Inuit were aware that dissatisfaction could and should be voiced during meetings, complaints were never made at the meetings I attended, or read in the minutes. Indeed, before September 1970, the only complaint was made by the senior store clerk who threatened to leave her job unless her wages were improved. The DO hastily consulted officials in Ottawa, and the girl's wages were raised. She is the only Inuk in Port Burwell capable of handling the co-operative's book work, and the government is anxious for Inuit to fill such positions of responsibility.[9]

However, after September, numerous changes were introduced in co-operative policy, all of which helped eliminate Inuit economic dissatisfactions. These happened in connection with the promotion of the DO to another settlement; thus the agent who reinforced the power of the symbols for the co-operative's 'health' was removed, and the effect of the symbols began to decline among those (notably among the store clerks) who had worked most closely with the DO. After his departure, the DO's responsibilities were divided: the assistant took charge of hunting projects, the senior store clerk of the duties of secretary and treasurer, and the new administrator, who arrived in May 1970, of welfare and general administration.

The DO having departed, the directors were encouraged by the members to award increases of up to 50 percent for skins and furs traded into the store; only then did prices in Port Burwell approximate those being paid by the H.B.C. in Lake Harbour, a settlement of similar size on Baffin Island (Philip Lange, personal communication). Also after the DO's departure, both store clerks secured the directors' agreement for wage increases of about 25 percent. Retail prices in the store were reduced: on one occasion, the administrator's suggestion for a 50 percent mark-up on a shipment of clothing was overruled, and a 33 percent mark-up substituted; on another occasion, the vice-president, claiming to have consulted all other directors, instructed the junior clerk to halve the retail prices for flour and Grenfell cloth (the material for the outer layer of the Inuit parka). The clerk did as asked but later expressed her horror: "He doesn't understand; it's because he's got so much debt himself." However, the vice-president was one of the more sophisticated men in the community; I believe he *did* realize the effect the cuts in prices would have on profits. But I suspect that, in the general trend to improve payments on skins, he was persuaded to order the cuts by the consumers – whom he lacked the authority to overrule according to traditional values (Set III ideals). In this respect it is significant that he failed to consult one man: the government interpreter and newly-appointed DO. This was almost certainly a deliberate gesture so that later he would not be compromised by his employers who might say to him: "Surely *you* knew the effect these cuts would have on profits."

The administrator was invited to 'he director's meetings, at which price alterations were made. But, unlike the DO, he had no specific responsibility for the co-operative: he was its adviser just as he was the adviser on a variety of issues, from starting a bank account to filling in an income tax-return form. With five years experience in various N.W.T. settlements, he in fact appreciated the justice of some of the economic improvements. However, he baulked at the proposal that payments for white fox pelts be raised from ten to eighteen dollars to give parity with Baffin Island prices. Though he himself had once claimed that some H.B.C. stores on Baffin Island were paying twenty-five dollars for the best white fox pelts, he had misgivings about the effects of an 80 percent price increase on the Port Burwell co-operative's finances, and he recommended a more modest increase. When I left Port Burwell in January 1971, trappers were receiving fifteen dollars for these pelts.[10]

The Escalation of Debt
Inuit behaviour following the DO's departure reflects a realization of the Set I ideals requiring a co-operative to give economic service to its members. But they were realized in a novel way – through the escalation of debts. Although this happened at the time of the DO's departure, there were more important causes. The first among them was the government's decision, in March 1970, to expand the co-operative's business using the profits of past successful years. The expansion, however, merely involved increasing the amount of goods in retail stock, and took no account of the essentially static nature of the community's income at this time. In fact, in the months preceding the shipment in August 1970, poor ice conditions had been responsible for reduced hunting and fishing activities, and when the goods arrived, most Inuit were less well-off than at corresponding periods in previous years. The second factor in the debt-escalation was a population decrease during 1969–70: in early 1969, 175 Inuit lived in Port Burwell, but by September 1970, there were only 143 (of whom 13 were infants born after April 1969).[11]

In September 1970, therefore, there were (relative to other years) fewer Inuit and less money, but more goods. In itself, this situation was still insufficient to account for the escalation of debts. Had purchasing of goods been controlled, the excess that the community could not afford might have been held over for the succeeding year. However, the store clerks ignored the departing DO's instructions to refuse thirty persons further credit (because each owed in excess of $150). They were young girls in their early twenties, who found it difficult to make demands on the older members of their community – such as to trade in handicrafts or sealskins – rather than run up larger debts. The senior clerk admitted, "I get scared of these people." She used to say, "A director should be in the store everyday to enforce these restrictions." However, I doubt whether a director would have been much more successful than she, especially as two of the directors had large debts themselves. The directors' efforts in restraining the purchase of large items – the sole task concerning debt-restriction they inherited directly from the DO – were singularly unsuccessful. When a young man with a part-time job and a small wage was allowed by a clerk to take a new outboard motor (worth $800) on credit, the co-operative president said, "he might have to return it," for the man had a debt of $100. However, the man was never approached and the outboard never returned.

In a small isolated community in which traditional notions of authority were weakly developed, and in which social relationships remain largely particularistic, it is hardly surprising that difficulties in the universalistic control of debt arose (in the absence of a Euro-Canadian supervisor). Other writers have described similar problems from other social settings, particularly with reference to village shopkeepers (for example, Bailey, 1964; Benedict, 1964) and Canadian Indian co-operative managers (Worsley, 1964:385).[12]

Inuit reluctance to control debts was in evidence even in the days of the DO when the daily restriction of credit-buying was already then delegated to store clerks; two elderly non-producers had, back in 1968, each accumulated more than a $500 debt. But because retail goods had always roughly matched the community's income prior to 1970, the total debt had never been high; in *November 1970*, however, with an increase in goods and a decreased population, as well as the store clerks' lack of authority, the community's debt to their co-operative had risen to $24,000 from a *March 1970* level (apparently acceptable to government officials) of $7,000.[13] Many individuals owed between $500 and $1,000. Since most were hunters with yearly incomes of less than $2,000 (including welfare), these were considerable sums.

Earlier, I interpreted the alteration of prices and payments for produce, wages, and retail goods as a situation in which the Inuit exercised Set III ideals (based on traditional values) to suppress Set II ideals (of the co-operative as an economic institution), so that the co-operative could provide economic services (Set I ideals) to its members; I believe a similar interpretation should be given to the escalation of debts. Thus, to demonstrate that debt escalation indeed comprised an extraction of economic service, it is necessary to consider the Inuit attitude to debts in general.[14]

Attitudes to Debt

Three variables are pertinent here:

Variable 1 focuses on the degree to which the symbol "taking (too much) debt is bad" (because it endangers the co-operative's 'health') impinges on an individual's decision-making over debt. The symbol might have a great, moderate, or negligible (a, b, or c) impact. It is realistic to assume that all Inuit have internalized this symbol to some extent; traders introduced them to the credit/debt concept sixty years ago, and the Inuit word for debt, *akiliksaq*, "that which requires payment," suggests an appreciation of the debtor's responsibilities.

Variable 2 refers to the extent of an individual's concern for his future earning potential. This concern might be obsessive, moderate, or negligible (a, b, or c). Whereas the first two variables refer to the individual's state of mind with respect to moral and rational aspects of a person's economy, *variable 3* is an objective assessment. It refers to the accuracy with which a person estimates his future earning potential, whether it be too conservative, reasonably accurate, or overly optimistic (a, b, or c).

The following examples, all recorded after the DO's departure, illustrate how an individual's rating can be assessed for each variable. Example A is of a regular wage-earner who was never in debt. Indeed, lest he go into debt, he arranged to pay for a snowmobile in two installments, since a single wage cheque was insufficient to cover its total cost. This and other behavioural considerations would label him 1a/2c/3b. Example B is of a man who had a part-time job. He and his wife (who had a negligible income) each accumulated a debt of $1,000, yet he showed little concern. He considered that a job ($150 per month) was a virtual guarantee of financial solvency. His rating is 1b/2b/3c. Example C is of an elderly man who did a small amount of hunting. He was little concerned with a debt of $500, and even asked if he might buy a new canoe priced at $700. His rating is 1c/2c/3c.

Analytically, the three variables can be separated; but from the perspective of an individual, each will in some way affect the others. This is particularly the case with the two subjective variables, especially when one of them rates high (a); however, the actual effect may not be predictable. For example, an individual who rates 'a' for variable 1 may consequently be extremely concerned about his future earnings (as in example E below); yet he may be equally casual about them. Apparently, other dependent variables may be involved, and case A suggests that 'actual income' may be one of these.

An explanation for the different levels of debt tolerance of Port Burwell Inuit, as indicated by their different ratings, may be found in their varying personal experiences. Inuit with an 'a' rating for variable 1 seem to be those who have worked most closely with the DO; for example, the store clerks and board of directors (example A is a former director). Of course, '1a' ratings do not actually preclude a large debt; two of the present directors (who both rate '1a') tolerate unrealistically large debts because they are rated 'c' for variables 2 and 3. Involvement with Euro-Canadians, and employment by them, especially in the regional settlements from which some of the Inuit have emigrated, might account for 'a' ratings in variables 2 and 3; Euro-Canadians, who are lured to the Arctic by high wages and prospects for saving, are typically concerned with their finances and sometimes take pains to indoctrinate the Inuit. However, there are exceptions to this hypothesis, and clearly, receptivity to Euro-Canadian advice would probably also influence Inuit ratings.

Circumstances may not allow an individual to have a smaller debt than his 'maximal debt tolerance,' and he may therefore experience anxiety. One divorced woman (*example D*: 1a/2b/3b) had to support two children alone. By the end of 1970, she was considerably worried; her purchasing requirements were larger than her small income allowed, and her debt had risen to a level greater than she could comfortably tolerate. In contrast, another woman (*example E*: also 1a/2b/3b) kept her debt at a level she found acceptable; for when her needs exceeded her meagre income, she would use the food and other commodities that her more affluent unmarried sons and daughters had purchased.

A wide range of debt tolerance and anxiety are thus experienced by the Inuit of Port Burwell. Yet, their opinions of the debts of others are all fairly uniform. They acknowledge that whereas large debts are not to be desired, they may be necessary when legitimately needed goods have to be bought. Children's requirements must be satisfied; these include not only the year's supply of clothing, but also the attractively displayed and pleasant-tasting tinned foods, soft drinks and candies that are plentiful in the store for the three months following 'sea lift.' Indeed, the whole family 'needs' store food to alleviate the monotony of eating seal when caribou and fish are scarce. Hunters must buy equipment and spare parts, and they may have to go into debt to do so; and if their hunting is successful, they must share their spoils with relatives and neighbours, as Inuit obligations require.

When an Inuk is thought to have too great a debt, it is because he is considered to be purchasing in a socially unacceptable manner. Then the general comment is that "debts like that are bad for the co-operative;" thus, the following derogatory remark about one young man: "*There's* a single man, with no snowmobile, outboard, or canoe, and he has a debt of seven hundred dollars." The ultimate in disgust was expressed of a woman who, instead of making skin boots for her four children, bought four pairs from the store (where they were awaiting shipment to the south as handicrafts) that cost her one hundred dollars.

It appears, therefore, that there are both self- and community-imposed (mainly by gossip) restraints on owing debts. Yet, those Inuit who have large and growing debts are usually considered to be satisfying reasonable needs – an opinion shared by the store clerks, even though their position is exploited for these needs (of others) to be fulfilled. Thus, regarding the satisfaction of needs, debt escalation may be interpreted as a fulfillment of Set I ideals.

Quantitative Data and the Sets of Ideals
Quantitative data show quite clearly that the co-operative at Port Burwell could not be run to satisfy both Set I ideals (as interpreted by Inuit) and Set II ideals (as interpreted by the DO), given the co-operative's comparatively small annual business. Before September 1970, hunters in Lake Harbour were earning about 60 per cent more (or $3,600 per year, according to the Port Burwell rate of production) for seal skins and fox furs than were Port

Burwell hunters. Had Port Burwell store workers been employed in any other arctic settlement, they would have received 100 percent higher wages (or, between them, an extra $4,000 per year) for doing similar work. Thus, an extra $7,600 per year was needed prior to September 1970, to give co-operative members in Port Burwell economic parity with members in most other settlements. Even if the producers and workers, who would have received this extra income, had spent it at the co-operative's store, only 20 percent of it ($1,500) would have been recovered by the co-operative as profit from the extra retail purchases. While the DO was in the community, the co-operative appeared to make an annual profit of $5,000 to $8,000. Thus, had the extra non-recoverable $6,100 been paid to producers and workers, this profit would have been all but eliminated over a period of years;[15] furthermore, there would have not been a profit had a hypothetical reduction of the high retail prices been considered in these calculations. I have heard it argued that if a good profit is achieved, the hunter is compensated for the low prices paid him when he receives his dividend from the profit, the dividend being based on the amount of sales and purchases he made during the year. However, based on a $6,000 profit, the best hunter could not get more than a $200 dividend. Yet he could have earned an extra $200 in just two months in the fall harp-seal fishery had he been paid more for the skins he produced.

In addition to the Set I ideals that require the co-operative to give service to its members, there is of course a reciprocal requirement for members' loyalty and responsibility: "Each time you buy or sell somewhere else, you are hurting your own business" (*We Co-operate*:5, 1969). A situation, as in December 1970, in which a quarter of the co-operative's capital assets was tied up in debts, suggests that the Inuit were evading their responsibilities. However, had they received higher payments and wages in past years, an equivalent material income would certainly have been achieved without the accumulation of as much as $24,000 of debts.

Epilogue and Conclusion
At the time of the DO's departure, there was a marked change, in the Inuits' favour, in the operative ideals of the Port Burwell co-operative. But there was an abrupt reversal in December 1970, when government officials in Frobisher Bay decided that a Canadian manager was needed to work full-time for the co-operative because they had heard from the administrator that "Annie (the senior clerk) cannot control the debts." They rationalized the appointment by recalling that the board of directors had requested it two years before in imitation of several other Inuit co-operatives. The request had been rejected then on the grounds that, if granted, progress towards full Inuit responsibility for their co-operative would be retarded.

No doubt the government wished the co-operative to render economic service just as the Inuit wished it to make a profit. But the covert argument between government and Inuit as to which of these ideals would have to be sacrificed had now developed into a full-scale confrontation. The government had introduced a special resource, to which it alone had access, into the arena of negotiation in an attempt to enforce its own point of view. The picture is now, at least, clearer. When the government speaks of "Eskimo responsibility" in local economic affairs, it means responsibility in accordance with Set II ideals.

NOTES

1 Per household income of Port Burwell Inuit from the trade of all these products and from wage labouring (permanent, though part-time, jobs are available to a half dozen Inuit only) ranges between $1500 and $4000. Lower-income Inuit receive welfare in periods of slack hunting.
2 Excerpts from this course (held in Churchill, Manitoba) were reproduced in the leaflet "We Co-operate" which is printed in English and Inuit syllabics, and circulated to all members of arctic co-operatives.
3 For example, 'shares' are *ilangiutiguti* (literally, the part put by for someone, from the root, *ila*, meaning part or partner); the "distribution of dividends" is *tuniuqqaijuq* ("he gives several of them," from the root, *tuni*, meaning "give") or *akguijuq* ("he distributes"), a word of wide compass which describes the dealing of playing cards as well as traditional sharing of game (Schneider, 1966).
4 Historical context must be invoked to explain the different strategies of the two DOs in Port Burwell and George River. The Port Burwell co-operative had a reputation for financial success almost unequalled among arctic settlements when its present DO took his job in 1969; however, the George River DO took his job in 1963 when the co-operative scheme was still young, an unknown quantity, and offering no such precedents to influence decision-making.
5 At about this time, some hunters began to invest in snowmobiles. These machines then cost up to $1000 per year to buy and maintain, and their introduction into the Inuit economy may have been the principal factor necessitating welfare payments.
6 Occasionally, when hunting equipment was in short supply, an Inuit director would radio an order for replacement stock to the Inuit manager in Fort Chimo. Such introduction of extra goods into Port Burwell stemmed from the requirements of the Inuit population, and cannot therefore analytically be linked with the extra goods that the DO ordered in accordance with his estimation of the *co-operative's* needs. However, since the radio was located in the DO's house, he was in a good position to veto the Inuit orders if he felt that they were unrealistic and might be detrimental to the well-being of the co-operative.
7 It is the ideal rather than actual behaviour of the directors at the A.G.M. that is recorded in the minutes.
   The five directors of the co-operative were those who were the best hunters, had best grasped the concepts of the Euro-Canadian world, and who came nearest to achieving relationships of equality with government officers.
8 During 1970, 47% of the adult population visited another settlement; quite a few made two or three visits.
9 The commissioner for the N.W.T. stated that "the early programme of (co-operative) development is designed ... to ensure that full management and responsibility for the affairs of Eskimo co-operatives is placed in the hands of the membership just as soon as the people are fully capable of taking them on" (Canada, 1962).
   This girl was educated in a comparatively sophisticated settlement on the Labrador coast; her family and one other from the same settlement are socially somewhat isolated in Port Burwell.

10   A year later, in January 1972, the price was reduced to $10, reflecting a decreased demand for the pelt on southern markets. Seal skins, however, were sustained at their new levels.

11   Most of those who departed from Port Burwell did so to reactivate kinship ties in other settlements and/or to escape the violence resulting from the drinking that had arisen in the community over the past year or so. Economic difficulties were not *directly* responsible for their leaving.

12   Dore (1971:56–7) stated this problem more generally: if the universalistic rules of the co-operative are applied, he who applies the rule (the young store clerk) will likely suffer animosity from the petitioner (an elderly Inuk) to whom the rule is applied; but, on the other hand, if a particularistic claim is allowed, those who are not in a position to make similar claims (for example, those Inuit younger than the store clerk), may withdraw their interest in the co-operative. The general solution of the Port Burwell clerks was to accept the claims of all.

13   The traditional arrangement of arctic trader and Inuk trapper involved the trader outfitting the trapper on credit at the commencement of each season (Graburn, 1971). However, the debt quoted here does not reflect a similar arrangement since there are three earning seasons of roughly equal importance at Port Burwell (spring: eiderdown collecting and sealing; summer: fishing and sealing; fall: harp seal fishery) with the possibility of earnings throughout the year.

14   I think Hughes is at fault when he says: "the store ... is an area in which the old Eskimo sentiments concerning immediate sharing of goods ... clash directly with ... a system that establishes a continuing financial obligation for goods bought on credit" (1960:177). As we said, store goods, in general, have become identified with traditional goods that were *not* normally shared.

15   Prices paid by the H.B.C. fluctuate with market demand, whereas prices paid by the Port Burwell co-operative over the past 10 years have been much less sensitive. It might accordingly be argued that since Lake Harbour payments quoted here are from a year in which the H.B.C. were paying high prices for skins and furs, in other years, when the H.B.C. payments were lower, the Port Burwell co-operative has compared more favourably than the calculations suggest. However, according to figures given by Brochu (1971), the pre-1970 payments of the Port Burwell co-operative for ringed seal and white fox (though not for the less important red fox) have always been so low that every year (except 1966–67 for ringed seal), H.B.C. posts in New-Quebec have been paying higher prices to Inuit and Indian hunters. Indeed, for several years, the H.B.C. was paying higher prices than in 1970. The non-fluctuation of Port Burwell payments would not appear to invalidate my calculations.

References

ARBESS, S. E.
1966 *Social Change and the Eskimo Co-Operative at George River, Quebec*. Ottawa, Department of Northern Affairs and National Resources (NCRC-66-1).

ARBESS, S. E.
1967 "Values and Socio-Economic Change: The George River Case." Unpublished Ph.D. dissertation, McGill University.

BAILEY, F.
1964 "Capital, Savings and Credit in Highland Orissa (India)." In R. Firth and B. Yamey (eds.), *Capital, Savings and Credit in Peasant Societies*. Chicago, Aldine Publishing Company.

BALIKCI, ASEN
1959 "Two Attempts at Community Organization Among the Eastern Hudson Bay Eskimos." *Anthropologica*, 1:122–135.

BENEDICT, B.
1964 "Capital, Savings and Credit among Mauritian Indians." In R. Firth and B. Yamey (eds.), *Capital, Savings and Credit in Peasant Societies*, Chicago, Aldine Publishing Company.

BROCHU, M.
1971 "A Preliminary Study of the Establishment of Equalisation Prices for the Pelts of Fur-Bearing Animals in New Quebec." *The Musk Ox*, 9.

Canada
1962 *Council of the Northwest Territories*, debates. Ottawa.

DORE, R.
1971 "Modern Co-operatives in Traditional Communities." In P. Worsley (ed.), *Two Blades of Grass*. Manchester, Manchester University Press.

DUNBAR, M. J.
1952 "The Ungava Bay Problem." *Arctic*, 5:4–16.

EVANS, J.
1968 *Ungava Bay: An Area Economic Survey*. Ottawa, Department of Indian Affairs and Northern Development.

FINDLAY, MARJORIE C.
1955 "A Study in Economic Development for Ungava Bay Eskimos." Unpublished Ph.D. dissertation, McGill University.

FREEMAN, MILTON
1971 "Tolerance and Rejection of Patron Sales in an Eskimo Settlement." In R. Paine (ed.), Patrons and Brokers in the East Arctic. St. John's, Institute of Social and Economic Research, Memorial University of Newfoundland.

GRABURN, NELSON H. H.
1971 "Traditional Economic Institutions and the Acculturation of Canadian Eskimos." In G. Dalton (ed.), *Studies in Economic Anthropology*. American Anthropological Association, Special Publication.

HELM, JUNE and DAVID DAMAS
1963 "The Contact – Traditional All-Native Community of the Canadian North." *Anthropologica*, 5:9–21.

HONIGMANN, JOHN J. and IRMA HONIGMANN
1965 *Eskimo Townsmen*. Ottawa, Canadian Research Centre for Anthropology.

HUGHES, C.
1960 *An Eskimo Village in the Modern World*. Ithaca, N.Y., Cornell University Press.

Q-Book
1964 *Quajivaallirutissat*. Ottawa, Queen's Printer.

SCHNEIDER, L.
1966 *Dictionnaire alphabético-syllabique du lange Eskuimau de L'Ungava, et Contrées limitrophes*. Quebec, Laval University Press.
STRUDZ, A.
1966 *Co-Operatives: Notes for a Basic Information Course*. Ottawa, Canadian Research Centre for Anthropology.
VALLEE, FRANK G.
1964 "Notes on the Co-operative Movement and Community Organization in the Canadian Arctic. *Arctic Anthropology*, 2.
VALLEE, FRANK G.
1967 *Kabloona and Eskimo in the Central Keewatin*. Ottawa, Canadian Research Centre for Anthropology.
WORSLEY, PETER
1964 "Bureaucracy and Decolonization: Democracy from the Top." In I. L. Horowitz (ed.), *The New Sociology: Essays in Honour of C. Wright Mills*. New York, Oxford University Press.
WORSLEY, PETER
1971 *Two Blades of Grass*. Manchester, Manchester University Press.

Leaving the Nursery?

Robert Paine

12

What escape is there in future from the constricting logic of Inuit-white relations as described in these last chapters? Before attempting an answer let us bear in mind that most of the research took place between 1968 and 1971.

Relentless Reciprocity (1968–71)
The phrase "relentless reciprocity" was used to assess relations between colonizers and the colonized in another part of the world (J-P Sartre in Memmi, 1965), and it captures much of the essence of Inuit-white relations as we have described them. On the one hand, Inuit can no longer be regarded simply as a burden on the Canadian government and taxpayer, since they are now a source of employment for a large number of Canadians. On the other hand, although there are signs that Inuit are impatient with white paternalism, at the same time they are worried about what would happen to them should the whites get up and leave one day – they are worried that this could happen (Brody, 1975; Freeman, 1976).

This sense of an enveloping reciprocity – unsought, unexpected and even resisted by some Inuit – helps explain the degree of resignation among many Inuit, as well as whites, in the midst of a situation that could otherwise be construed as one that promises changes. In obvious respects, the situations of Inuit and whites are different, but their reciprocal relations also put them in a common situation, and from that perspective, what difference does it make to Inuit, one may ask, whether they are the "wards" or the "clients" of whites (see Ch. 5)? Similarly, many whites may be disillusioned with their part in the 'northern experiment,' but what difference does that make to those for whom being in the north is just another job? Of course, these things do matter to many Inuit and many whites, but then, what resources do these persons have with which to do battle? Very few.

It is true that Inuit were sometimes able to put pressure on white administrators at the local level: the essays by Brody and Riches describe what may justifiably be called Inuit confrontations. But what was finally won in both these cases – or whether anything was won – is not clear. A particular administrator loses a battle and leaves the settlement, but when his replacement arrives does he concede to the Inuit the ground that his predecessor lost? There is good reason to doubt it.

Nor can it be forgotten that whites still appeared to be assisting the Inuit, and not exploiting them or repressing them; for this helps to maintain the *status quo* in many ways. Most important of all is that white tutelage is so intrusive that it is difficult for Inuit to maintain a perception of self which is independent of the white man and his culture, or independent of situations of white help. This help is made to seem (for both whites and Inuit) all the more necessary because of the application of white norms of public administration. In the regional centres, such as Frobisher Bay, the social scale is probably too large and life too anonymous for the Inuit role system (Chs. 5 and 6) to be effective. But this role system is also officially disregarded in the many small settlements; it is thought to be anachronistic in the modern context of local government. If acceptance of the Inuit role system would, as is feared, make life more complicated for the white administrators in the small settlements, for the Inuit, it would do much to restore their confidence in the 'white' government's professed intentions on their behalf. As it is, the Inuit role is present but 'underground.' One result of this is that the dilemmas in which whites find themselves in their dealings with Inuit may themselves be taken as confirming the need for the continuance of 'nannies.'

Yet the "rigid," "hierarchical" and "bureaucratic" (Zariwny, 1973: 87) procedures by which government is still exercised in the arctic settlements themselves contribute to the difficulties encountered. On the one hand, the potential contributions of many Inuit are lost, and on the other, the white administrator finds himself 'tied to the book.' Of course, even while so tied, he is invested with a degree of absolute power such that he may (from the Inuit point of view) "arbitrarily stop, modify or delay any initiatives" that come to him from his local advisory council of Inuit (Girard and Gourdeau, 1973:154). But the paradox in this situation is that it is perhaps these local administrators who have the least resources to *change* things. Not only are the non-conformists among them taken out of the north, but also the reward system within the white administration moves one up *and out* (of the smaller settlement, or from the north altogether). The frequency with which whites are moved to new postings within the north is also an obstacle in the way of any white who wishes to earn the confidence of the Inuit in his community, no less than it is for Inuit who wish to share with him the handling of their local problems.[1]

"The Land is Ours ..." (1971–   )
Thus far, then, we find only reasons for supposing that the constricting logic of Inuit-white relations will continue indefinitely. But we have directed attention to the possibility of changes initiated from the white side only; in fact, Inuit-white interaction is more likely to be modified as a consequence of new kinds of relations among Inuit themselves. Such

relations have begun to emerge with increasing strength in the most recent years. We may begin by noting this assertion of Brody's (1975:206): "Today parents are determined to try to salvage their authority, and therefore to redeem their future; they feel that they are personally and culturally threatened and they are unwilling to resign themselves to material or psychological dependence upon their wayward and frightening children. They are becoming hostile to dependence upon the young as they are to dependence on the Whites."

Possibly of still more far-reaching significance are indications of a new world view among Inuit, centred upon the concept of *kabloonamiut*. In the 1950s, it signified "settlement people" as opposed to "camp people" or *nunamiut* (cf. Ch. 2); at that time the terms did not carry connotations of different Inuit views of whites and their culture. But such views became attached to the terms,[2] and the *nunamiut* values are interpreted by Kallen (Ch. 7), for example, as implying "withdrawal from all but the necessary minimum contact with whites." Whereas *nunamiut* values are "conservative," *kabloonamiut* ones are "progressive"; whereas the one set of values leads to an uncompromising cultural stand, the other set is more pragmatic and conciliatory. The *kabloonamiut* value system accepts Euro-Canadian institutions at the same time as it calls for the continuation of Inuit ones. *Kabloonamiut*-oriented action, then, does not preclude patron-client relations with whites; yet it seeks to alter the traditional distribution of "power, privilege and prestige" between whites and Inuit (Kallen).

Today, precisely because it addresses itself to the bicultural aspect of settlement life, as the *nunamiut* value system does not, the *kabloonamiut* ideology is generally the politically persuasive one. The principal problem for an Inuit politician is to demonstrate that he is able to put Inuit content into the institutions that are modelled on Euro-Canadian ones; in other words, he has to make them into institutions that "parallel" the Euro-Canadian, while remaining Inuit (Kallen). Success in this venture can make the politician the power-broker between whites and Inuit – including even many of those wishing to hold to their *nunamiut* ideology. Thus, in Kallen's village it is around the minister of the Anglican Congregation, an Inuk with the prestige and power of a white-derived office, that a new basis for Inuit self-identity at the community level is emerging. It rises above the divisions in the community (though not entirely without factional conflict), divisions that are there as legacies of white tutelage. One notes, for example, that there is also a Roman Catholic congregation in the community: its priest, however, is non-Inuit and his political influence has been reduced markedly in recent years.

It is no accident that another local leader in the same community attempted to make *Inuit Tapirisat* of Canada (I.T.C.) his political forum. This national Inuit association was founded in 1971, and an early policy statement (Inuit Tapirisat, 1972), we find an overarching rationale of Inuit co-identity very similar to the *kabloonamiut* ideology. The first three aims of I.T.C. relate to the pressing need for the organization and integration of local Inuit communities at the national level: (1) to expand effective communication among Inuit; (2) to unite them; and (3) to develop effective leadership to represent them. The fourth and fifth aims concern the Inuit language, traditional culture, and social institutions: (4) to help promote the Inuit language and culture as a viable means of participating in Canadian society; and (5) to promote dignity and pride in Inuit heritage. The sixth and seventh aims have to do with the needs of Inuit *vis-à-vis* Euro-Canadian institutions: (6) to assist Inuit in their right to full participation, and a sense of belonging, in Canadian society; and (7) to promote public awareness of the issues concerning Inuit.

The problem of the local politician is to persuade his community that as a source of support, I.T.C. is an effective alternative to the local government agencies, and that as a source of power, I.T.C. can help a community in confrontation with these agencies. It is because much of I.T.C. thinking is derived from the level of the local community – in contrast to white-directed local government – that the association is able to work as an active political force. However, its efficacy at the local level varies and cannot be taken for granted. There are several reasons for this, the first among which is that I.T.C. has been Ottawa-oriented from its inception. It is not that I.T.C. is in league with Ottawa (nor do we have in mind here the political control which the Federal Government is sometimes said to exercise over I.T.C.); on the contrary, Ottawa is the public adversary of I.T.C. and *this* has meant a diversion of a great deal of I.T.C. energy and thinking to dealings with (and in) Ottawa. Secondly, the most important work of the I.T.C. – certainly that which has most caught public attention – has been with land settlement claims (Cumming, 1977): the citation at the head of this section is from a speech by the first president of the I.T.C., Tagak Curley; but it cannot be assumed that this issue, or the way it is handled (a number of I.T.C. field workers are themselves non-Inuit), necessarily finds a politically responsive chord in each settlement. Thirdly, as a 'Pan-Inuit' organization for Canada, I.T.C. inevitably faces periodic regional disillusionment, if not with its policy, then with its strategy; instances include the separate land claim presented by the Committee for the Original Peoples Entitlement (C.O.P.E.).

I do not explore this matter further here (with the exception of Kallen's study, the I.T.C. had little place in the research of the different settlements in the East Arctic – itself a datum of interest) except to say that the problem raised by the I.T.C. is one of the organizational level of ethnicity. This *was* an important issue for the research of Labrador communities and it is the focus of discussion of the next chapter. Meanwhile, it is reasonable to suppose that already there are changes in the political and emotional climate in the East Arctic from that encountered by this volume's researchers and writers.[3] Looking back over the first section of this chapter, then, one may question whether "resignation," for example, has not already become less appropriate as a characterization of the Inuit view of their future. By the same token, Inuit acceptance of whites being there to help them – so important to the maintenance of the *status quo* – is now a matter of tortuous (as well as sceptical) evaluation by an increasing number of individuals. Not only is there a *public* political life for an Inuit élite, there are Inuit-dominated political occasions even in the smaller settlements. One also notes the reports of the way Inuit (individuals or groups) circumvent the bureaucracy to gain direct access to the minister. A route available to a few public servants besides the one to the commissioner, it erodes the "absolute power" of local administrators. The other characterization of Inuit-white relations, "relentless reciprocity," might still be in force; however, in view of other changes in the political and emotional climate, this may now imply an increase in Inuit ambiguity, and in the seriousness of ambiguity for them – something that we had grounds for minimizing in Chapter 5.

Whites; 'Why are we here?' (1971–   )
The colonial mould of the typical East Arctic settlement is not impregnable and snatches of the talk of changing times are heard there. But the talk itself belongs to a political life beyond that of the settlement. The question is what significance does politics at that level have for the handful of whites in individual settlements? Although this must be left here as a question, we have been able to document much of the relevant background. The evidence in our chapters accumulates around one point: the sense of failure that whites have had of themselves. This seems true whatever the motive that took them north:[4] they failed as frontiersmen, they failed as liberals, and they failed in their efforts to reproduce southern life. Those who went north for the money saved some, but lived for the day when they could leave (see Ch. 8). Now, if the changing political and emotional climate is not able to lighten the white burden of failure, one can at least expect that the sense of failure in the future will be differently derived. At the time of our research, it was closely connected with the simplistic view of tutelage possessed by government (of which the Honigmanns were the academic apologists; see Ch. 5). Since then, if only because of Inuit (elite) political activity, the government has in one way or another surrendered a number of the premises on which that tutelage was based. The sense of failure also had to do with the personal predicament in which whites were placed by the public ideology of northern service agencies that operated as if the only 'problem' population in the north was the native, and not the white (Ch. 5);

this is becoming de-mythologized (Ch. 3). These same factors help to explain how whites were able to continue for so long in their tutelage roles, apparently without comprehension of Inuit aspirations. Today, however, Inuit 'messages' are being delivered loud and clear (for example, in the *Nunavut* Proposal and the Berger Inquiry testimonies). In addition, there are now Inuit politicians, as well as white, and there are articulate and determined whites in the Inuit 'camp.'

Before any reliable conclusions can be drawn about the future of Inuit-white relations, further research must be done. Suppositionally, one may argue thus: as the earlier dichotomy between whites and ''Eskimos'' is rendered a good deal more problematic (for the whites), and as it becomes increasingly possible for individuals to de-mythologize their 'white' code of public behaviour (Ch. 9), so whites are presented with the chance of changing their tutor role (with its patronage philosophy) to that of consultant. But will that chance be taken? Even if it is, Inuit-white relations still depend on political decisions at the macro-level. Will Ottawa's approach to her north change significantly? Dosman (1975:219) and perhaps many others believe that there is only the remotest chance of this happening. But his view is based on an examination of the Canadian government's record in the north with respect to the politics of oil. Hopefully, this is too limited an examination (as an examination it betrays tendencies of self-fulfilling conclusions: Dosman himself becomes fascinated by Ottawa's fascination for oil). It may be quite unlikely that Ottawa will change its policies in that field, but what of its wish and ability to change its social (cultural) policies? May not the 15,000 Inuit have the ecologic and cultural space they need for their own purposes at the same time as Canada has its oil revenues? Naively put, perhaps, yet this is the kind of question that Canadian culture would teach us to ask and to respect. There is here, as well, a responsibility for social anthropologists in Canada to research, one which should be within its capabilities.

NOTES

1   Until recently it was official policy to limit postings to a maximum of 5 years. This ruling was intended as a means to prevent whites from ''getting too involved''; i.e., making friends and perhaps taking sides in the local community of Inuit, so that they can no longer be ''objective'' (personal communication of a R.C.M.P. officer to Jean Briggs).
2   But now without reference to two discrete groups of people; as Vallee (1962:135) was careful to point out, the *nunamiut/kabloonamiut* distinction refers to ''continuous rather than dichotomous'' criteria, and Kallen, too, emphasizes that the distinction has not resulted in two separate Inuit groups in the community of her study. Cf. Correll (1976) on Inuit -*miut* terms.
3   I am grateful to Ms. Ditte Koster for drawing my attention to this, and for her help with several of the points that now follow.
4   Though in retrospect their northern experience may be mythologized as *the* adventure of their lives.

References

BRODY, HUGH
1975 *The People's Land: Eskimos and Whites in the Eastern Arctic.* Aylesbury, Penguin Books.
CORRELL, THOMAS C.
1976 "Language and Location in Traditional Inuit Societies." In M. M. R. Freeman (ed.), *Inuit Land Use and Occupancy Project*, vol. 2. Ottawa, Department of Indian and Northern Affairs.
CUMMING, PETEA A.
1977 *Canada: Native Land Rights and Northern Development.* Copenhagen, INGIA.
DOSMAN, EDGAR J.
1975 *The National Interest. The Politics of Northern Development, 1968–75*, Toronto, McClelland & Stewart Ltd.
FREEMAN, MILTON M. R. (ed.)
1976 *Inuit Land Use and Occupancy Project* (3 vols.). Ottawa, Department of Indian and Northern Affairs.
GIRARD, G. and E. GOURDEAU *et al.*
1973 "Epilogue." In *Man in the North; Technical Reports: Education in the Canadian North.* Montreal, Arctic Institute of North America.
Inuit Tapirisat
1972 *Inuit Tapirisat of Canada.* Ottawa, Information Canada.
MEMMI, ALBERT
1965 *The Colonizer and the Colonized.* Boston, Beacon Press.
VALLEE, F. G.
1962 *Kabloona and Eskimo in the Central Keewatin.* Ottawa, Department of Northern Affairs and Natural Resources, NCRC-62-2.
ZARIWNY, A. R.
1973 "Politics, Administration and Problems of Community Development in the Northwest Territories." In N. Ørvik (ed.), *Policies of Northern Development.* Kingston, Department of Political Studies, Queen's University.

THE REGIONS OF THE NORTHWEST TERRITORIES

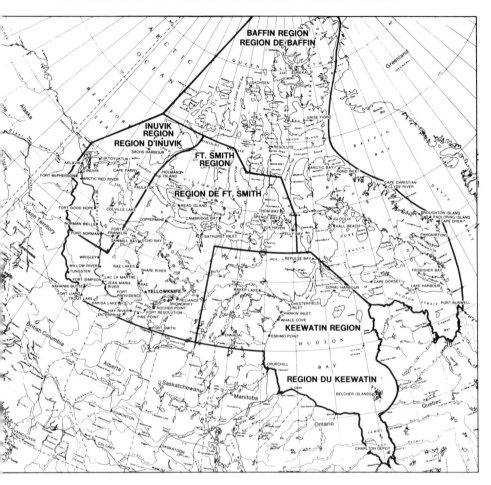

Source: *Canada's Arctic Today*. Annual Report of the Government of the Northwest Territories 1974. Yellowknife, Government of N.W.T. [1975].

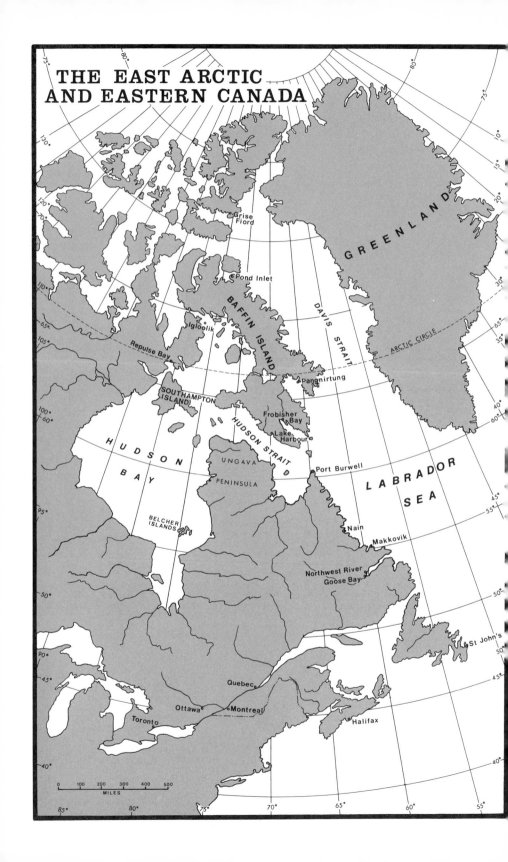

THE EAST ARCTIC AND EASTERN CANADA

GREENLAND

Grise
Fiord

Pond Inlet

BAFFIN ISLAND

DAVIS STRAIT

ARCTIC CIRCLE

Igloolik

Repulse Bay

Pangnirtung

SOUTHAMPTON
(ISLAND)

HUDSON STRAIT

Frobisher
Bay
Lake
Harbour

H U D S O N

UNGAVA

Port Burwell

LABRADOR
SEA

B A Y

PENINSULA

BELCHER
ISLANDS

Nain

Makkovik

Northwest River
Goose Bay

St John's

Quebec

Ottawa   Montreal

Toronto

Halifax

0   100   200   300   400   500
MILES

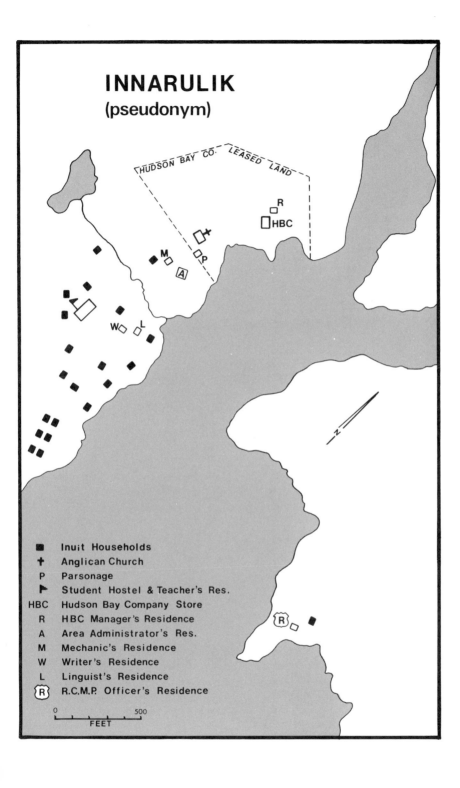

INNARULIK
(pseudonym)

HUDSON BAY CO. LEASED LAND

R
HBC

M
A
P

W L

N

Inuit Households
Anglican Church
P   Parsonage
        Student Hostel & Teacher's Res.
HBC   Hudson Bay Company Store
R   HBC Manager's Residence
A   Area Administrator's Res.
M   Mechanic's Residence
W   Writer's Residence
L   Linguist's Residence
R   R.C.M.P. Officer's Residence

0   500
FEET

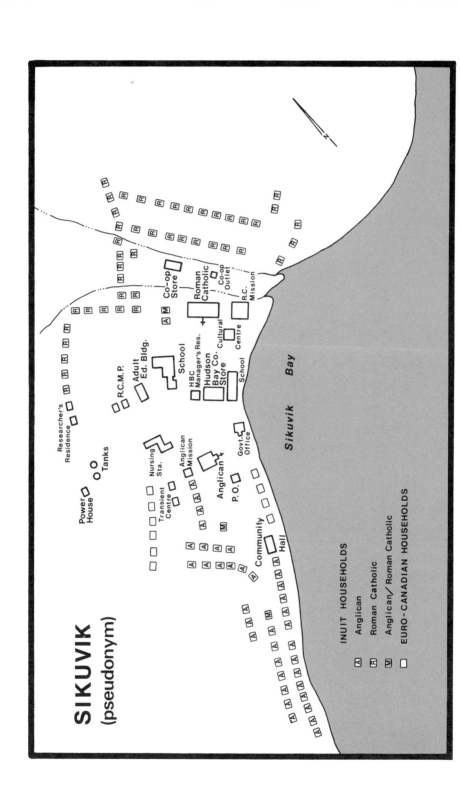

SIKUVIK
(pseudonym)

Researcher's Residence

Power House

Tanks

Co-op Store

R.C.M.P.

Adult Ed. Bldg.

School

Roman Catholic

Co-op Outlet

R.C. Mission

HBC Manager's Res.

Hudson Bay Co. Store

Cultural Centre

School

Nursing Sta.

Transient Centre

Anglican Mission

Anglican

P.O.

Govt. Office

Community Hall

Sikuvik Bay

N

INUIT HOUSEHOLDS

Ⓐ   Anglican

Ⓡ   Roman Catholic

Ⓜ   Anglican/ Roman Catholic

▢   EURO- CANADIAN HOUSEHOLDS

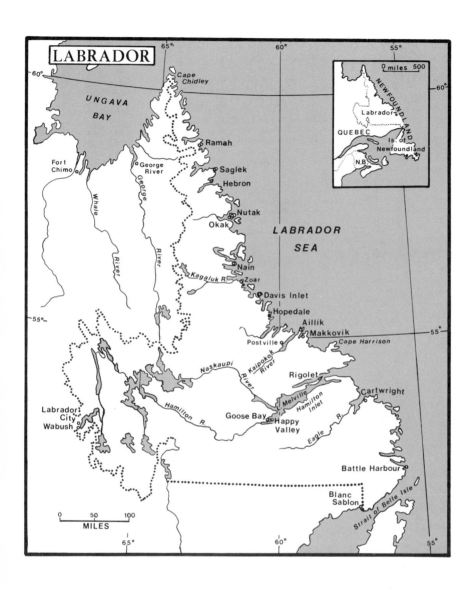

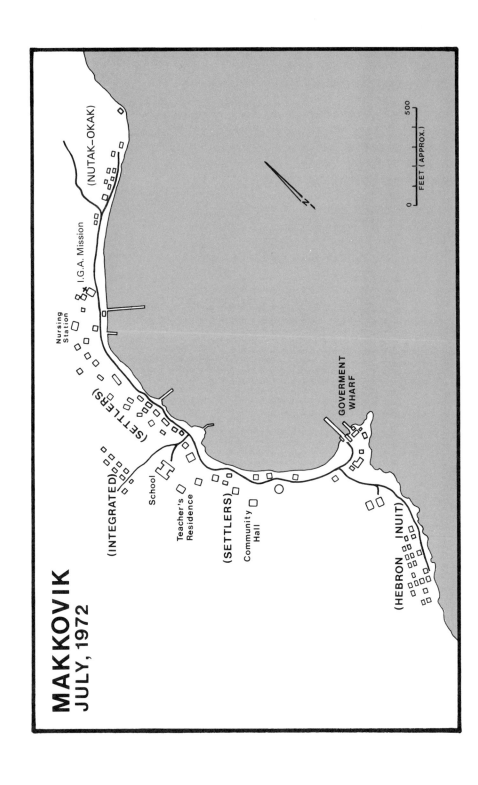

MAKKOVIK
JULY, 1972

(NUTAK–OKAK)

I.G.A. Mission

Nursing
Station

(SETTLERS)

(INTEGRATED)

School

Teacher's
Residence

(SETTLERS)

Community
Hall

GOVERMENT
WHARF

(HEBRON INUIT)

N

0   500
FEET (APPROX.)

NAIN

NAIN BROOK

R.C.M.P.

HOSPITAL

SCHOOL

BOARDING
SCHOOL

SCHOOL

THE CLUB

SNACK
BAR

STORE

STORE

STORE

N.S.D.
STORE

MORAVIAN
COMPLEX

FISH
PLANT

COMMUNITY
HALL

GRAVEYARD

GRAVEYARD

N

NAIN INUITS

INUITS RELOCATED FROM HEBRON AND NUTAK
(Including pre-resettlement individuals)

HEBRON OR NUTAK AND NAIN INUITS
(Marriages immediately after relocation)

INUITS AND NAIN SETTLERS OR OTHER WHITES

NAIN SETTLERS

OTHER WHITES

Case Studies from the Labrador Coast

Tutelage and Ethnicity, a Variable Relationship

13

Robert Paine

> "[C]ulture ... becomes not so much a super-organic
> thing *sui generis*, but policy, tacitly and gradually
> concocted by groups of people for the furtherance of
> their interests."
> *Wallace* (1964:28).

In introducing the chapters from Labrador that now follow, I want to examine the relationship between tutelage and ethnicity juxtaposed in this book as analytic concepts. Labrador presents us with a more complicated situation than the N.W.T. (see p. xi).

The ethnohistory of coastal Labrador occupies the next chapter, and so it is sufficient to note here the three most important ways in which the historical situation differs from that of N.W.T.: (1) there has been a Settler population in Labrador since the early 19th century, and although white, at least in origins, it constitutes another 'native' population alongside the Inuit (and the Naskapi Indians[1]); (2) The Moravian missionaries established themselves on the coast even earlier – in 1771; (3) finally, the population is not under the jurisdiction of the N.W.T. but under the Government of Newfoundland and Labrador. Whereas the Inuit population of the N.W.T. is about 15,000, the Inuit and Settler populations of the northern Labrador coast each number less than 1,000.

Culture and Ethnicity
Before we can begin our analysis, it is necessary to distinguish between the two words, culture and ethnicity. For by speaking of both, as we do, the latter may seem to be in danger of not having any meaning of its own. In my view, the meaning we give to ethnicity depends very much on our approach to the more general notion of culture. With this in mind, I wish to make two points concerning the relation of culture to *circumstances* and to *organizational levels*.

Few definitions of culture offered by anthropologists have been concerned with how a culture – or, more precisely, particular items of a
cultural repertoire – can be mobilized (and perhaps transferred in the
process) for the attainment of certain ends, which themselves may change
from time to time. Rather, "a culture" has too often been represented as
though it were a consistent, self-contained and autonomous corpus (of
"knowledge, belief, morals, custom" in Tylor's classic definition) that
provides a charter for normative behaviour.

Such an approach has little to say about the changing circumstances of
the people caught in this definitional net of "a culture" – even though it is
generally recognized that circumstances matter and are, by any definition,
changeable. By stressing the charter aspect of a culture we may, inadvertently, falsely assert *its* invariable validity or, at best, its validity as an
independent variable. This places a culture above the circumstances that
generated it and circumstances that may change it. By taking circumstances into serious account, however, our attention will be directed to
action, and thence to the ways in which a people use, mobilize, and perhaps
transform their culture for the attainment of certain ends – which need not
be only material. We can then observe how different parts of a culture are
selected for various purposes, at different times, and by different groups of
people within the culture. In short, we can observe the processes of emic
decisions about cultural priorities.

The view of culture that I am urging has been put the most forcefully by
Wallace (1964:28) in the citation at the head of this chapter: his choice of the
mildly irreverent verb "concoct" I take as a deliberate and salutory antidote to the usually hallowed language (and thought) in discussions of
culture. Geertz (1970:57) contributes to the antidote by urging a "control
mechanism" view of culture. This "begins with the assumption that human
thought is basically both social and public – that its natural habitat is the
house yard, the marketplace, and the town square" (*ibid.*).[2] Here we also
see the emergent relation between "a culture" and its organizational
levels. This is our second point and follows as a corollary of what we have
said about the importance of circumstances.

The case for the existence of levels of organization within a culture, and
their significance, I leave to the last part of this chapter; the point that I
want to stress here is that when writing about "a culture," anthropologists
(of all people!) too often neglect to specify which level of that culture they
are discussing. Here, the potency of the notion of charter leads us (again,
perhaps inadvertently) to unwarranted and misleading notions of cultural
holism. Thus, when we insist that a culture is more than the sum of its parts,
we may also be demonstrating an analytic unwillingness to separate the
parts, or to recognize that they may constitute several 'wholes': it is as
though we still resist the lesson learned from *The Political Systems of
Highland Burma* (Leach, 1954).

Turning now to ethnicity as an aspect of cultural activity, the task most consistently associated with ethnic symbolism is the construction of a self-image of a people that expresses the differences between themselves and others. On that all seem to be agreed: the selected traits are given "emblematic" status (Kennedy, 1976:14), and ethnicity refers to that aspect of culture that is mobilized in "boundary maintenance" (Barth, 1969:15). Forces of ethnicity, then, are likely to be forces of cultural *action*, and pursuing what we said about the higher abstraction, culture, the processes of emic decisions about cultural priorities constitute the domain of ethnicity within the cultural world. Accordingly, it is essential that we do not assume that either the "tokens" that are raised or the "boundaries" that are defended are beyond change – and even abandonment. More important still, we should avoid the assumption that ethnic symbolism, at any one time, will be of one piece. Rather, one may expect expressions of ethnicity among a people to differ with respect to the levels of organization within their culture.

There are two further points about ethnicity that I want to make before closing these introductory remarks. The first (Wadel, personal communication) is that anthropological writing stresses how "culture" teaches a people about their own world, neglecting to a large extent what a people learn about the worlds (that is, the cultures) of other peoples, and how they acquire and codify such learning. In my opinion, much of what is meant by ethnic processes and symbolism is addressed precisely to this task. Secondly, it seems to be widely (but loosely) accepted that people necessarily construct their own ethnic symbols; that they themselves select the emblems they venerate, and establish the boundaries, which we know, they defend.[3] This is particularly important for the interpretation of the data from Labrador, and leads directly to the critical question of the relationship between *tutelage* and ethnicity. It might seem as though the social forces of the two are necessarily opposed and would give rise to mutually exclusive processes, perhaps along the lines of the distinction between 'made for' and 'made by' decisions advanced in conclusion to Chapter 3. However, a review of cultural relations along the Labrador coast through recent historical periods will show how the relationship between tutelage and ethnicity is itself variable. Nor is it always one of opposition: Inuit ethnicity was, during one period, a creation of the Moravian missionaries rather than of the Inuit themselves.

The rest of this chapter is – in accord with its purpose – schematic, but rests principally upon the data in the subsequent chapters from the two communities of Makkovik and Nain, researched between 1962 and 1976. The first period, associated with the hegemony of the Moravian Mission from the early 19th century, illustrates a process that may be appropriately characterized as one of *ethnicity through tutelage*. The contemporary scene in northern Labrador is, by contrast, dominated by *ethnopolitics*:

dating approximately from 1970, its aims include the displacement of white tutelage. Overlapping these two, historically and structurally, is the intrusion of a N.W.T.-style of tutelage by the Newfoundland government: still persisting today, it dates from the early '50s. Its aim is to incorporate the native populations of the coast within the Euro-Canadian fold and the ordinary administrative and civic structures of the province.

Ethnicity Through Tutelage

During the long period of Moravian tutelage (see Kleivan, 1966; Hiller, 1971), the Mission was determined to keep the Inuit in Labrador alive as a distinct ethnic group; and the Mission went to particular pains to protect their wards against all other European contact along the coast. The mission influence destroyed (usually deliberately) a good deal of the pre-contact Inuit culture, but what was destroyed was systematically replaced and blended with the elements that were allowed to remain. In short, a new ethnicity emerged in which these wards of the Mission became Moravian Eskimos.

The different effects on Inuit ethnicity of Moravian tutelage and Canadian northern policy in the N.W.T. are plain. In the N.W.T., tutelage implied a dismantling of ethnicity as a source of inspiration for a people, and yet government agencies claimed that through this process, the Inuit would regain a sense of autonomy. A palpably spurious claim,.what was presumably meant by it was that through white tutelage, the Inuit might avoid stigmatization. In the Labrador case, however, tutelage did, paradoxically, ensure the Inuit a measure of cultural autonomy, in the sense of self-identity, as a group with a distinct culture. Yet the Moravians, too, based their tutelage on the conviction that "a people with a personality and culture like that of the Eskimo" could not do without it; so wrote the Honigmanns (1965:241) of tutelage in N.W.T. It is not difficult to find similar passages in Moravian writings about their "Eskimo" charges (cf. Kennedy, Ch. 14, this vol.). The Moravians also practised a rudimentary system of rewards for conformity to the behaviour they prescribed, and of punishments for deviation from it, similar to the one described by the Honigmanns as being part of tutelage in the process of socialization.

Although not as complete as it was in the case of the Inuit, a tutelage relationship was eventually established by the Moravians over much of the Settler population of Labrador as well. From such a position they came to exercise a controlling influence over ethnic relations *between* Settlers and Inuit. This stage of affairs, to which we return in a moment, continued well into the 1950s and '60s, during which time the Newfoundland government officially relieved the Moravians of many of their responsibilities for the coastal population. In 1951, a provincial Division of Northern Labrador

Affairs (D.N.L.A.),[4] was set up, and in 1954, the first of a series of federal-provincial agreements was signed for the funding of health, educational and other services in northern Labrador. In 1956 and 1959, respectively, the two northernmost communities of Nutak and Hebron were resettled, for logistic reasons, farther south. All in all, D.N.L.A. assumed a public, institutionalized role of tutelage, much along the lines of government in the N.W.T. (cf. Ch. 2), the intention being the replacement of the Mission (tutelage) with government (tutelage). However, the position that the Moravians had established in Inuit and Settler communities along the coast meant that in many respects it was the D.N.L.A. that was left with but a nominal tutelage role throughout the '60s, despite the material and political resources at its command.

We should note here that a consequence of the resettlement of Nutak and Hebron was to press Inuit upon Settlers, in the case of Makkovik, and Settlers and other Inuit upon Inuit, in Nain. Through this enforced 'heterogenization' of the coastal communities, Inuit-Settler relations were moved further into the domain of everyday life than they ever had been and, *pari passu*, the place of the Mission in these relations became all the more important.

Now, it is unlikely that the control – pre-dating World War II – that the Mission exercised in Inuit-Settler relations would have been possible simply through the Mission's own exertions. In fact, it rested quite as much on the way both native groups, but especially the Inuit, used the Mission in connection with the management of their separate group identities. Thus, "by separating the two groups for ritualistic and other activities, the Mission provided each with a context for the expression of their ethnicity" (T. Brantenberg, Ch. 16, this vol.); in short, "the Mission reinforce[d] expected ethnic differences" (Kennedy, Ch. 18, this vol.). The Mission, then, came to fulfil an important third-party role in Inuit-Settler relations – not one of cultural broker[5] but rather of buffer, and even of referee at times. It is probably because of this role that Inuit and Settlers have been able to remain in their own cultural worlds. Particularly noteworthy is that although these worlds are defined largely in terms of their conceptual oppositions to each other, they have been maintained – until recently – almost without confrontations between the two groups. Such confrontations as did occur led invariably to avoidance and increased distance between the groups.

These worlds have also persisted despite Inuit-Settler marriages in each generation, and this fact provides another important clue as to the nature of ethnicity along the coast. In stressing the separateness of the two groups, we approached the puzzle of ethnicity approximately from the vantage point of the ideal model that Inuit and Settler families themselves hold of ethnicity. This is a static and nicely balanced model, but one which the mixed marriages show not to be entirely true – at one level of reality at least. The element of choice of identity, Inuk or Settler, which these marriages give rise to, has also to be taken into account. From T. Brantenberg's discussion (Ch. 16) (which should be compared closely for differences in emphasis with Ben-Dor's description of Makkovik fifteen years earlier) the salient points are: (1) mixed marriages do *not* give rise to a mixed or intermediate group, and the proof for this is the absence of any 'intermediate' symbolism; (2) offspring of mixed parentage may identify either as Inuk or Settler, and even siblings sometimes choose differently; (3) it follows that, in practice, there is an absence of stratification between Inuit and Settlers, for if there were it would predetermine the ethnic allocation of the offspring of mixed marriages. The reason for there being no inter-ethnic stratification is surely to be found in the symmetrical opposition in which Inuit and Settlers, as groups, face each other. By and large, both exploit the same natural resources and have to contend with the same natural constraints; yet each group makes its separate adaptation. What this means in cultural terms is that each group has its own solution to problems they share in common, and draws its identity as a group from that solution. Therefore, it is to be expected that neither will admit there is merit in the ways of the other. Neither wishes to 'become' the other. So the ideal model of the people themselves is, after all, upheld by their own behaviour (and their circular reasoning) – even in the face of mixed marriages.

What is the content of the ethnicity that fills these symbolic worlds of Settlers and Inuit? Whatever the differences between Settler and Inuit ways of life when abstracted as systems of thought, as observed systems of behaviour, their two worlds separate at a micro-cultural level. "Inuit" and "Settlers" are, one may say, each abstractions of two semiological codes of the social structure of the northern Labrador coast. Much about these codes is closely associated with the micro-ecologic distinctions one can observe between the exploitative patterns of each group. Thus, typical diacritica of ethnicity include the way a person hunts seals, disposes of meat from the hunt, fuels his dwellings and prepares a meal. At another level, particular importance is attached to the place mission-related activities have in a person's life. Language competence (particularly among the children of mixed marriages) is not, of itself, a decisive ethnic marker; on the other hand, situational choices of language usage are very important as indicators of micro-cultural interpretations of role and, ultimately, identity.

In conclusion, it is the mixed marriages that should particularly catch our attention. The problem that has to be solved culturally and socially along the coast in each generation is the allocation of the offspring of these marriages to either of the two groups. Although there are structural constraints in many cases, there is also always a measure of individual choice

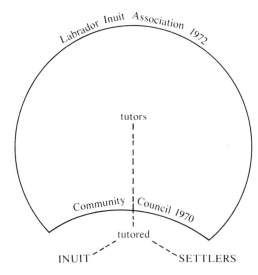

Fig. 1: *Ethnopolitics and the Replacement of the Tutelage Relationship*

in such a decision. It is here that one recognizes how the approach to ethnicity that has been described makes good sense. If it is to be possible for these persons to choose, then the alternative idioms of ethnicity must be based primarily on performance, and not on ascription alone, and they should be familiar to all – as they *are*. If we pressed the point and asked why the expression of ethnicity along the coast has little supportive institutional superstructure, the answer surely would be that this superstructure (with one partial exception discussed below) has been in the hands of others:[6] first the Mission and then the Government of Newfoundland.

Ethnopolitics

In April 1970, a community council was established in Makkovik, and in Nain in July of that year; then in September 1972, the Labrador Inuit Association (L.I.A.), a provincial branch of the national Inuit association (I.T.C.) was founded in Nain. These events mark the beginning of a new period in the relationship between tutelage and ethnicity along the Labrador coast; it is one in which relations between the two native populations begin to cross-cut those between tutor and tutored, eventually becoming the superordinate set of relations (Fig. 1). We use the phrase "ethnopolitics" as a shorthand conveyance of this process.

Ethnopolitics emerged despite considerable difficulties and resistance among sectors of the tutored population itself. Not only did ethnopolitics imply, in general terms, a revision of some of the basic cultural premises of life along the coast, it also forced both Inuit and Settlers to consider the possible effects of their own behaviour on their own interests. Inevitably it placed the question of identity, that is, of ethnic domains under debate among themselves. Until this point, both groups had only experienced a situation, under Moravian tutelage, in which the relation between behaviour, self-interest and identity was tautological. Each group had existed in ideologically closed systems.

Yet the inspirational source of this process, which we identify as ethnopolitics, was *not* ethnic self-consciousness on the part of Inuit and Settlers – neither as separate groups nor as an ethnic coalition. Instead, it was the realization that by incorporating their communities within the provincial system of local government, they would be eligible for provincial and federal-provincial community development grants and other amenities, which they might otherwise not receive (cf., p. 7). As this realization gradually spread through Makkovik and Nain, it became a matter of political controversy, in the course of which the ethnic context of Settler-Inuit relations was brought to the forefront.

In Makkovik, whence Inuit from northernmost Labrador had been resettled in the late '50s, the politically active among the Settlers began to 'court' the Inuit, departing dramatically from previous practice; it was feared that unless the Inuit in Makkovik were seen (by government) to be actively supportive of the community council, the village might have its share of the federal-provincial funding for "native" communities reduced or withdrawn. However, the Inuit sense of belonging to Makkovik was weak. They also interpreted the operations of the community council as supportive of Settler self-interests more than of their own, and as another instrument in the maintenance of Settler hegemony in the village. Accordingly, they were reluctant to oblige the Settlers politically. Indeed, a number of Inuit families left Makkovik at about this time, taking up residence in Nain. This was seen by the Settlers as seriously prejudicial to the future of their community, so much so that they themselves eventually took the step of gaining membership in the L.I.A.,[7] with the purpose of politically establishing their own status as that of "native" persons of Labrador.

Whereas in Makkovik the Inuit minority adopted a politically passive stance towards the introduction of a community council, the opposite occurred in Nain, where the Settlers are in a minority. Here, the advocates of the community council approached the Inuit of the Moravian council of elders, the one piece of institutional superstructure to which Inuit and Settlers had access during the Moravian period of tutelage. Settler membership in the council of elders, however, was only intermittent and, in 1970, there was not one Settler elder in Nain. The council of elders is traditionalistic and authoritarian, qualities that marked the leaders' early opposition to the community council. At issue were two different notions of community (the one secular, the other theocratic) and, because elders identified with the Inuit rather than the Settler culture, the differences were sometimes expressed in terms of Inuit versus Settler interests. Today, however, there is negligible political polarization on this basis, the main reason being the degree of cultural heterogeneity in present-day Nain, even among the Inuit themselves. No longer are all the Inuit in Nain *of* Nain, and issues raised in connection with the coming of a community council showed that the 'northerners' were resentful of the 'Nain hegemony' of the Inuit elders. Then again, some of the younger and politically conscious Inuit of Nain early recognized the council as a necessary institution for their community and for their own place in the community. Their position at this time was particularly intricate: although they wished to see changes in the traditional basis (Moravian Eskimo) of village authority, these could not be allowed to happen at the expense of Inuit *gemeinschaft*. Aware of the increased influence of Settlers in Nain, now that the community was being drawn into closer contact with the province, they also recognized that they themselves – as young Inuit – should take an active part in community politics. For them, then, balanced against the risk that the community council could become a Settler-dominated forum was the realization that it was only with a community council that Nain could hope to escape from a state of tutelage (in part Moravian and in part governmental).

In sum, the establishment of the community council in Nain was the first occasion whereupon Settlers and Inuit, first separately but eventually together, put the traditional relationship between ethnicity and tutelage under political examination; that is, they connected their common circumstances of tutelage with their traditional state of ethnic division: it became clear to both Settlers and Inuit that each needed the other politically. Although no more than a handful of the population was active politically, it proved sufficient to ensure the founding of the L.I.A. in 1972. As already mentioned in the discussion of events in Makkovik, Settler membership in the L.I.A. was accepted; indeed, the first elected chairman was a Settler from Nain. His father-in-law was the chief elder of Nain, and he was elected vice-chairman.

Transformation of Ethnicity, 1: Meanings

The ground that I have quickly covered is found in detail in chapters 18 and 19; my concern is to find a way to conceptualize the cultural process – for such it is – embedded in the recent events at Makkovik and Nain. As the relations between the native groups become superordinate to those of tutelage (Fig. 1), a transformation takes place in the meaning of ethnicity, and Wallace's classic discussion of culture brings us quickly to the heart of the matter (1964:1–41).

The transformation is from a situation in which Inuit and Settlers each depended on the construction of conceptual oppositions between them, to another in which they together work out a policy – hesitantly, at first, and with difficulty – for the furtherance of their common interests (cf. Wallace, *op. cit.*:28). Whereas the maintenance of ethnicity in the first situation depended to an extraordinary degree on what Wallace calls the "replication of uniformities" (*op. cit.*:27) (separate uniformities for Inuit and Settlers), the successful transformation of their relations to something beyond that depends on a process of "organization of diversity" (p. 28). Inuit and Settlers do not now expect of each other a sharing of "uniformities," but they do work together towards a relationship of "mutual prediction" (p. 29), of mutual understanding on selected issues. These become the issues of ethnopolitics, and the understanding achieved by Settlers and Inuit with regard to them becomes the basis of a shared ethnicity among them. Thus, the ethnic transformation along the Labrador coast is from an expression of differences between Inuit and Settlers to that of differences between coastal Labradorians (Settlers and Inuit together) and others – especially the island population of Newfoundland and other non-native residents along the Labrador coast. But the construction of emblems for this new ethnicity is problematic.

The nature of the problem can be appreciated by comparing, once again, the two situations of Inuit-Settler relations. In the earlier one, ethnic emblems had only to satisfy an internal logic: Inuit and Settlers were concerned, each in their own way, with demonstrating to themselves that they were different from each other. A self-validatory logic was quite sufficient for this purpose.[8] Today, however, Inuit and Settlers (together) wish to construct ethnic emblems for a political purpose whose accomplishment involves others besides themselves. Accordingly, they face the problem of getting the legitimacy of the emblems accepted by these other parties. It was for the purpose of securing native rights for themselves that Inuit and Settlers in the two Labrador villages joined forces in the L.I.A., using the Inuit emblem. But the inclusion of Settlers as Inuit still has to be accepted by the Federal and Provincial Governments, as well as the national Inuit association (I.T.C.), to all of whom the message (with its definitional claim) is directed. Here, self-validation is quite insufficient as the basis of ethnic logic.

Transformation of Ethnicity, 2: Organizational Levels

The new ethnicity is based on a pluralistic appeal. Yet it is a different pluralism to that which Furnivall (1944:304) coined in the phrase "[they] mix but do not combine"; Inuit and Settlers, on the contrary, now combine for specific purposes in public, even though they still do not mix much in private, and Inuit emblems take (political) precedence. Meanwhile, the domestic domain remains relatively unconstrained by the dictates of cur-

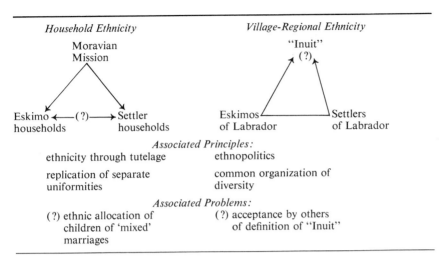

Fig. 2: *Ethnicity in Labrador: Two Domains, Two Organizational Levels, and Two Meanings*

rent ethnopolitics, whereas in the earlier period (of ethnicity under tutelage), the public markers of ethnicity were symbolically expressed in contrastive behaviour in the domestic domain, thus reducing ambiguity.[9] Today, there is a notable strain between the public and domestic domains, and perhaps for the first time, ethnicity in Labrador is a source of ambiguity in social relations. For the transformation of which we speak has led not to the replacement of the earlier ethnicity; instead, there are now *two* domains of ethnicity. Indeed, one may speak of two social constructions of ethnicity that exist side by side but at different organizational levels, and each imparts a particular meaning to ethnicity. With the help of figure 2, a finer delineation is possible of the differences between these two social constructions, and of the forces of strain and ambiguity between them and within each of them.

Household Ethnicity. It is here that ethnicity is constructed out of micro-cultural idioms that are themselves closely associated with micro-ecologic distinctions between Inuit and Settlers. Such a system of ethnicity is predicated on an absence of inter-ethnic transactions, and in Labrador, this is maintained in two ways. First, there is the influence of the Mission (see above); one should note that it was always with the Mission (instead of with each other) that each group had transactional relations. Secondly, there is the ethnic stereotyping by Inuit and Settlers of each other and of themselves, described in some detail in chapter 16. In sum, the behaviour of each group is as though it fears its ethnicity will be contaminated by close contact with the other; in Kennedy's phrase (this vol.), each is engaged in "holding the line."

Village-Regional Ethnicity. Here, ethnicity has been lifted to a higher social and cultural level. It encompasses village interests through Inuit-Settler participation in community councils, and regional interests through participation in the Labrador Inuit Association. This organization of ethnicity, far from precluding transactional relations between Inuit and Settlers, is dependent upon them. Whereas the forces of household ethnicity can be understood through the notion of "imperative status" (Barth, 1969), it would be a less appropriate conceptualization with regard to village-regional ethnicity where it is the strength of the L.I.A. as a political resource that matters. This may mean having a Settler as its chairman.

As Kennedy (1976:17) observes, these contemporary ethnic processes along the Labrador coast demonstrate how "the kinds of interests which a human group has in its past (and in itself) varies with the problems its members face in the present."[10] It is also in this connection that one notices how the organization of ethnicity at the level of village (and region) is an alternative to the mode of social incorporation urged upon coastal Labradorians by government agencies. Government efforts are directed towards incorporation within a provincial and southern context, whereas the Labradorians themselves have a Labrador orientation. Indeed, inter-ethnic populism has begun to flow from the new ethnicity, especially in Nain. These points are confirmed in A. Brantenberg's discussion of the school in Nain (Ch. 17): the pupils see their school (with its southern curricula, objectives, and notions of commitment and discipline) as marginal to their community, and not the other way around. A youth culture has emerged among the pupils which, combining modern idioms of expression and the traditional way of life, is "an adaptation *to* the local scene, and not away from it." At the same time, the youth culture in Nain demonstrates the latent ambiguity and contradiction in a situation where two social constructions of ethnicity persist: on the one hand, the youth culture does not discriminate between Settler and Inuit; on the other, the youth are still constrained to find spouses within their own group.

The emergent sentiments of populism have become a factor in the increasing determination of Inuit and Settlers to dispense with tutelage. Local positions of influence in the affairs of Inuit and Settlers are still held by whites; yet their role is now less that of tutor than of consultant, less that of 'missionary' and more of a politician seeking the support of a special constituency. Although patronage persists, its character as an inter-ethnic relationship is changing (cf. Paine, 1971). Ethnopolitics, anywhere, is likely to place special demands on the fundamental political skill of making the 'voice' of local constituents heard and making it matter in extra-local arenas. The following chapters will show how this is a complicated task of unusual delicacy along the coast of Labrador.

Conclusion

Besides attempting to de-mythologize ethnicity, I have tried at the same time to make our anthropological view of it more sociological. Earlier, Barth (1969:9–10) observed that ethnic boundaries, with associated processes of exclusion and incorporation, are maintained "despite a flow of personnel across them." The corresponding point made here is that people may re-draw (radically) their ethnic boundaries to correspond not just with their changing circumstances, but also with their changing perception of these circumstances. Barth's thesis led to the conceptualizing of ethnicity as an "imperative status" or one that "cannot be disregarded and temporarily set aside by other definitions of the situation" (*op. cit.*:17). At the same time as this catches the ambience of many situations of ethnicity, it can also contribute to the mythologizing of ethnicity. For by referring ethnicity to such an overordinate principle of overordinacy, one can be led to suppose that no questions remain to be asked – when in fact there are.

The idea of imperative status makes sense only when it is imperative in all and not just in some cases (if we settle for less than that, we deliver ourselves over to tautology). What, then, is the ethnographer to do when he comes across a situation that appears to be charged with ethnicity, and yet he is unable to determine an overordinate and invariable rule of behaviour (concerning ethnicity) such as would qualify as Barth's imperative status? Part of the answer is in the transactional process, underlying most social and cultural relations. We should not assume that ethnicity is above transaction.[11] This transactional component is evident along the Labrador coast even in the earlier period of ethnicity under tutelage, let alone in the contemporary period of ethnopolitics, and it has produced differences in the meaning of ethnicity (also with regard to the matter of its imperativeness). Furthermore, we found these differences related to organizational level, something which is to be expected on the basis of sociological first principles. For the task of any cultural activity is "to impose meaning upon experience" (Geertz, 1970:57), and we always expect to find levels of experience within a society.

NOTES

1   See Henriksen, 1973. The Naskapi population is centred in Davis Inlet and Northwest River, and is thus excluded from the ethnography of these chapters which deal exclusively with the Inuit and Settler populations of Nain and Makkovik.
2   Geertz's (*ibid.*) formula of culture includes the following: "... culture is best seen not as complexes of concrete, behavior patterns – customs, usages, traditions, habit clusters – as has, by and large, been the case up to now, but as a set of control mechanisms – plans, recipes,

rules, instructions (what computer engineers call 'programs') – for the governing of behaviour.
3   The anthropological record shows how such an assumption is intenable; that it is made at
all must be attributed to the degree of mystification which the study of ethnicity, as a domain of
culture, has attracted.
4   Later replaced by the Northern Labrador Services Division (N.L.S.D.)
5   Though the Mission undoubtedly undertook brokerage between the D.N.L.A. and the
coastal population.
6   I reject, as a possible answer to this question, the fact that both groups live under similar
natural conditions and have small populations. The anthropology of band societies, for
example, has demonstrated how small populations, even when they share similar natural
conditions, may construct separate cultural systems replete with their own superstructures of
cosmology and ritual, and even political organization.
7   Before joining the L.I.A., they had for a short period affiliated themselves with the
provincial Indian association, most of whose members are on the island of Newfoundland.
8   Cf. discussion of self-validatory logic and the associated phenomenon of "privatization of
meaning" in Paine, 1976.
9   Cf. discussion of ambiguity in Chapter 5.
10 Cf. discussion of tradition in Chapter 3.
11 I have found some support from Cohen: "To put it in the idiom of research, ethnicity is a
variable" (1974:xv). He pinpoints an important aspect of ethnicity among the Settlers and
Inuit of the Labrador coast today when he observes that "an individual can [only] manipulate
customs if he becomes part of [the] group, adopting its current major symbols. He cannot
manipulate others without being ready to be manipulated by them" (p. xiii). The Labrador
material demonstrates how manipulations pertaining to ethnicity can be allocated differen-
tially between separate levels of organization within the composite (polyethnic) society.

References

BARTH, FREDRIK
1966 *Models of Social Organization*. Royal Anthropological Institute
Occasional Paper No. 23. London.
BARTH, FREDRIK
1969 "Introduction." In F. Barth (ed.), *Ethnic Groups and Ethnic Boun-
daries*. Boston, Little, Brown & Co.
COHEN, ABNER
1974 "Introduction' The Lesson of Ethnicity." In Abner Cohen (ed.),
Urban Ethnicity. Association of Social Anthropologists Monographs,
12. London, Tavistock Publications.
FURNIVALL, J. S.
1944 *Netherlands India: A Study of Plural Economy*. Cambridge, University Press
GEERTZ, CLIFFORD
1970 "The Impact of the Concept of Culture on the Concept of Man." In
E. A. Hammel and N. S. Simmons (eds.), *Man Makes Sense*. Boston,
Little, Brown & Co.
HENRIKSEN, GEORG
1973 *Hunters in the Barrens: the Naskapi on the Edge of the White*

Man's World. St. John's, Institute of Social and Economic Research, Memorial University of Newfoundland.

HILLER, JAMES
1971 "Early Patrons of the Labrador Eskimos: The Moravian Mission in Labrador, 1764–1805." In Robert Paine (ed.), *Patrons and Brokers in the East Arctic*. St. John's, Institute of Social and Economic Research, Memorial University of Newfoundland.

HONIGMANN, J. J. and IRMA HONIGMANN
1965 *Eskimo Townsmen*. Ottawa, Canadian Research Centre for Anthropology, Saint Paul University.

KENNEDY, JOHN
1976 "Ethnic Groups in Process." Paper presented to The Association of Atlantic Anthropologists and Sociologists.

KLEIVAN, HELGE
1966 *The Eskimos of Northeast Labrador*. Oslo, Norsk Polarinstitutt.

LEACH
1954 Political Systems of Highland Burma. London, Bell.

PAINE, ROBERT
1971 *Patrons and Brokers in the East Arctic*. St. John's, Institute of Social and Economic Research, Memorial University of Newfoundland.

PAINE, ROBERT
1976 "Two Modes of Exchange and Mediation." In Bruce Kapferer (ed.), *Transaction and Meaning: Directions in the Anthropology of Exchange and Symbolic Behaviour*. Philadelphia, ISHI.

WALLACE, A. F. C.
1964 *Culture and Personality*. New York, Random House.

Northern Labrador: An Ethnohistorical Account

14

J. C. Kennedy

The topic of this chapter is the recent ethnohistory of northern Labrador, that portion of the Quebec-Ungava Peninsula bordered on the east by the Labrador Sea, on the west by the Quebec-Labrador boundary, on the north by Cape Chidley, and on the south by Cape Harrison. Attention is given primarily to the region's largest aboriginal population, the Inuit, as well as to the European settlers who emigrated to the north coast after 1800. My comments on the Montagnais-Naskapi Indians, the inhabitants of the Labrador interior, are limited as contemporary Indian communities are not represented in this volume.

The essay is divided into five parts. The first examines the important establishment of the Moravian Mission in Labrador and its effects on 19th century Inuit culture. Part Two describes the arrival of European settlers and the development of Settler culture. Part Three is concerned with 20th century population dynamics and their effects on contemporary settlement patterns. Part Four reviews recent administration, ideology, and economic development, and Part Five the history of health and health care in northern Labrador, as well as that of education, transportation, and communication services.

PART ONE: THE MORAVIAN MISSION AND 19TH CENTURY INUIT
CULTURE CHANGE

What is known about the human habitation of Labrador prior to the mid-18th century comes from two sources: archaeological evidence and the reports of early explorers. Archaeological excavations in the Straits of Belle Isle area reveal that Labrador's earliest known residents were coastal-dwelling Palaeo-Indians who apparently moved into the bay area by about 9000 years B.P. (before present) (McGhee and Tuck, 1975). By 4500 B.P., there were Archaic Indians at Saglek Bay and Sandy Cove (in Hamilton Inlet). Between 1800 and 1700 B.P., Dorset Eskimo peoples inhabited the coast north of Hamilton Inlet, a region occupied after 1450 A.D. by the ancestors of modern Inuit, the Thule Eskimo (Schledermann, 1971).

During the 17th and 18th centuries, contact between Thule peoples and Europeans along the south Labrador coast was characterized by hostility and treachery. The Inuit, lured south by curiosity and by a desire for

European trade goods, were unfamiliar with the procedures of western trade and are reported to have stolen what they could not obtain through barter. The response of European fishermen and traders was equal to the occasion: Inuit were shot on sight by the heavily armed and suspicious foreigners. The hostile nature of these early contacts with Inuit was the major reason for the establishment of the Moravian Mission.

Although there was considerable Euro-American involvement in the Straits of Belle Isle and south Labrador coastal areas during the 17th and early 18th centuries, extensive contact with the region north of Hamilton Inlet did not occur until the late 18th century. French, Portuguese and American interests in southern Labrador focused on summer fishing, whereas activities on the north coast consisted of, at least ostensibly, missionary work among the Inuit. As will be seen, more than two hundred years of Moravian tenure in north Labrador has meant far more than the supplanting of one belief system for another; the Moravians irreversibly altered nearly every aspect of Inuit society and culture in northern Labrador. The particular manner in which the Moravians developed their Labrador Mission contrasts with less successful missionary endeavours elsewhere, possibly explaining the relative absence of millenarian or revolutionary responses among the indigenous population. As Kleivan (1966), Jenness (1965) and Ben-Dor (1966) have written, the Inuit of north Labrador have become "Moravian Eskimos," and to this day, stubbornly defend their involvement, as they see it, with the Mission.

Permanent Moravian presence in northern Labrador dates to 1771, but certain background information, largely summarized from Hiller (1967) and Whiteley (1964), help place the Mission in perspective. Along with the Waldensians, the Moravian Church (Unitus Fratum – the Unity of the Brethren), is the only Protestant sect to claim pre-Reformation origins. Founded in 1457 in Prussia, the sect grew during the 16th century until it was forced underground during the Thirty Years War (1618–1648). In the 1720s, the surviving adherents of the faith moved to Saxony where they were given refuge, and where it was decided to initiate an international missionary programme in the West Indies, Greenland, the Philippines and other countries. The Greenland Mission, begun in 1733, enjoyed some success and provided a handful of missionaries (some of whom later served in Labrador) with a knowledge of *Inuttitut* (Inuit language) and culture.

The history of the Moravian Mission in Labrador can be discussed according to the following periods: 1752 to 1770, 1771 to 1804, and 1805 to the present. After establishing their Greenland Mission, the Moravians sought to expand west to Labrador. The first expedition to Labrador sailed from London in May 1752, sponsored by a British merchant house and led by J. C. Erhardt, a missionary who had earlier served in Greenland (Hiller, 1966). Their vessel, the *Hope* arrived at Sandwich Bay in July and sailed north to Nisbet's Harbour where, in early August, the missionaries assembled a small prefabricated house and planted a small garden. Several of the missionaries stayed behind with one year's provisions while Erhardt and others left Nisbet's Harbour for what is now Davis Inlet to trade with Inuit prior to returning to England. On September 11, three Inuit approached the vessel, stating that additional trade could be conducted at a place nearby. It may be assumed that Erhardt and his followers, satisfied with their accomplishments at Nisbet's Harbour, yet anxious to satisfy the interests of the expedition's sponsors, were encouraged by the prospect of further trade. In any event, Erhardt, the *Hope's* captain, and five crew members followed the Inuit ashore and were never again seen alive. After awaiting three days, the crewmen of the now undermanned *Hope* returned to Nisbet's Harbour where the four missionaries, who were to winter in Labrador, were picked up to help sail the vessel back to England.

The years between 1752 and 1771 were marked by continuous Inuit-European hostility and by increased efforts to curb such hostilities. Under the treaty of Paris (1763), Labrador came under British rule, intensifying interest in pacifying the region to facilitate trade and fishing. In 1765, several Moravians returned to Labrador to investigate the establishment of a mission, and also to act as intermediaries between the Newfoundland government and the Inuit (Hiller, 1967; 1971b). This time the missionaries, whose party included two former members of the Greenland Mission (Jens Haven and Christian Drachard) encountered over three hundred Inuit at Chateau Bay. Since first going to Greenland in 1758, Haven persistently sought to establish a mission in Labrador. In 1762, Haven convinced Palliser, the Governor of Newfoundland, that the Moravians were suited by intent and training to the task of pacifying Labrador. In 1764, Palliser drafted a document prohibiting cruel treatment of Inuit and entrusted Haven to present it personally. The following year, Palliser issued a proclamation declaring that the Moravians enjoyed full British civil and military protection and support. That same summer, the Moravians again travelled to Labrador where they again met and traded with Inuit. As in 1764, the exchange between the Inuit and Moravians was facilitated by the fact that the Inuit had travelled south to trade with the French. Without question, the curiosity that these 'Eskimo-speaking whites' (must have) created, together with the positive tenor of Inuit-Moravian contact at this time set the stage for the events to follow. Until 1765, Palliser had supported the Moravians, but their demand for 100,000 acres of land at all future mission stations caused him to ponder Moravian intentions. Reluctantly, Palliser conceded to the Moravian request, and in 1769, awarded land grants at sites that would not interfere with the British fishery.[1]

During the summer of 1770, Haven and several other missionaries arrived in Labrador and selected Nain as the site of their first mission station.

In August 1771, Haven and thirteen others arrived to stay. Several points should be noted about the early years of the Mission in Labrador. First, the Moravians began by attempting to suppress all aspects of the aboriginal culture that were considered objectionable and contrary to Christian beliefs. Initially, this involved undermining the credibility of the Inuit *angakok* or shaman, as well as the legendary figures of Inuit cosmology, such as Nerchevirk, Torngarsoak, and Superguksoak (cf. Hawkes, 1970, Taylor, 1974). Also prohibited were dancing, drumming, singing, as well as the public fora in which such "heathen" practices occurred. Cranz (1820:308), for example, notes Moravian apprehension when during the winter of 1777, a *kache* (an Inuit ceremonial house) or, as the missionaries called it, a "pleasure-house" was constructed near Nain. Another Moravian strategy was to transform, whenever possible, elements of aboriginal ideology such as the belief in a *torngak* or individual guardian spirit, into the Christian category of 'sinful behaviour.' Still other aspects of aboriginal Inuit culture such as polygamy and multi-family dwellings took longer to eradicate. Multi-family residences survived in some northern districts until the mid-19th century (Kleivan, 1966:42), and cases of polygamy were recorded until the early part of the present century (Gosling, 1910:283). The tenacity with which basic elements of Inuit culture persisted meant that many early converts were only nominally Moravian in conviction and life style. For their part, the early missionaries were cautious to baptize Inuit and, as Jenness (1965:14) states, they "judged faith by its works, not by the eloquence of its words, and they sternly refused to sprinkle the water of baptism on every individual who had learned to recite the Lord's prayer."

Secondly, as Hiller (1971a:86–8) has argued, the Moravians sought to create settled communities – religious and economic units which would insulate Christian Inuit from Euro-Americans on the one hand, and heathen Inuit on the other. Frequent references occur in the 19th-century Moravian records of their intention to create sedentary communities apparently modelled after agrarian-like European villages. The early Moravians underestimated the implications that sedentary mission life would have on the economy of the previously nomadic Inuit. After a few winters in Nain, it became obvious that unless Inuit were to become totally dependent upon the Mission, something which it could not afford, they must respond to the vargaries of seasonally available resources. This, in itself, implied a flexible settlement pattern. Also, the missionaries soon discovered that Nain was not a good hunting place and resolved that future stations must be established in locations capable of supporting larger population concentrations.

The second and third stations, then, Okak (1776) and Hopedale (1782), were both places which supported relatively large populations in the pre-contact period (Taylor, 1974:11–12). Holding to their goal of sedentary communities, yet more realistic as to its attainment, the missionaries established a pattern of periodically visiting converts at their outlying hunting and fishing camps, and encouraging Inuit to remain at the mission stations during winter. This pattern, which emphasized the religious calendar between Christmas and Easter, survives today.

A final point about the early years of the Mission concerns the ambiguities that it must have created among Inuit. To being with, what Inuit sought from the Moravians and what the Moravians sought from the Inuit were different. Moravians, of course, sought converts whereas Inuit most likely viewed the Moravians as representatives of a technology they needed. Secondly, the Inuit had no way of knowing how long the Moravians would remain in Labrador, particularly given that no whites had thus far remained in northern Labrador during the winter. Such uncertainty meant that the Inuit who allied themselves with the strangers were risking a great deal.

In short, I suggest that individual Inuit faced a profound dilemma: should they abandon allegiance with an established cultural system or opt to adhere (at least in part) to the new system proposed by the Moravians. The final chapter of this dilemma was not to be written until early in the present century, when the last groups of "heathen" Inuit, primarily in the Saglek region, were converted. Most Inuit, however, accepted the Mission during its first forty or fifty years in Labrador. The decision to convert was facilitated by a number of social constraints inherent in pre-contact Inuit society. Taylor (1974), for example, describes the pre-contact period as riddled with conflict, tyrannical shamans, wife stealing, murder, and so on. At least partially, the mission stations offered a haven from such hostilities, and it is possible that they indirectly caused the dramatic increase in Inuit population at the stations between 1788 and 1819 (cf. Kleivan, 1966:146–7).

I would emphasize that these three characteristics of the early mission years – the suppression of "heathen" cultural traits, the aim to settle and insulate communities, and the ambiguities created by the Mission's presence – should not be associated solely with the period from 1771 to 1804. Indeed, the Mission's goal to establish sedentary Inuit communities, insulated from intrusive influences, remains a persistent theme throughout its Labrador experience. My point is simply that these three characteristics are most evident during this early period.

Between about 1779 and 1804, a religious 'awakening' occurred, beginning at Hopedale (Cranz, 1820:312) and spreading to Nain and Okak. The reasons for this increased acceptance of the Mission are not clear, though it probably was caused by a combination of economic depression, the high degree of conflict among their people, and the realization that the Moravians had no intention of leaving Labrador.

The increased number of converts (cf. Jenness, 1965:14) prompted the

Mission to consider establishing additional mission stations. During the summer of 1811, a small party of missionaries sailed from Okak to the Koksoak River (the Fort Chimo area) to investigate the feasibility of establishing a station there (Kohlmeister and Kmoch, 1814). Given the small and relatively inaccessible Inuit population in this area, this idea was abandoned. However, in 1830, a fourth station was established at Hebron.

By the early 19th century, the Mission was well-established in northern Labrador. Several developments emerged during this period and most of them centred on the issue of trade. As said, soon after establishing the Mission at Nain, the Moravians realized that Inuit must continue to exploit local natural resources so as not to become a burden to the Mission. A conflict emerged: on the one hand, the missionaries saw their basic purpose as religious; yet, at the same time they realized that local resources must be made to yield an income sufficient to support the Mission. The compromise that emerged saw the mission trade subsumed under the Society for the Furtherance of the Gospel (SFG),[2] while the missionaries ostensibly concerned themselves with conversion. Between 1771 and 1926, the organization of trade changed several times but the basic role of trade remained firm. Essentially, this involved a basic change in the Inuit economic cycle so as to harvest certain resources (codfish, seal skins, furs, and others) that had a European market value. Each summer, the mission supply ship imported basic staples (such as tea, metal goods, pork, gun powder, and others) to use as trade items and to supply the Mission itself. No cash changed hands during these transactions and the missionaries discouraged (by not stocking or overpricing) Inuit from obtaining what were considered luxury goods (for example, tobacco). For over a century, SFG trade flourished, enabling the Labrador Mission to help sponsor Moravian missionary work in other parts of the world. After about 1875, however, a drop in the market demand for seal oil, as well as other Labrador products, led to a decrease in profits until, in 1926, trading rights were leased to the Hudson's Bay Company.

A persistent difficulty in Moravian efforts to transform the Inuit economy was imposing values of saving, budgeting, and making profits onto a socio-economic system based on sharing. The Moravians came to Labrador with a rather ingrained 'Protestant ethic.' Consistent with this ideology was their subscription to so-called "rational" economic behaviour which, among other things, implied individual accumulation of goods, sometimes at the expense of one's neighbours. The emphasis in Inuit society on sharing has, therefore, consistently been viewed by the Moravians as wasteful and non-rational (Kleivan, 1966:65). Although many missionaries understood the underlying logic of sharing in Inuit culture, few were willing to condone sharing, and indeed, could not, if local trade were to support the Mission.

A final problem about mission trade revolved around competition, particularly during the early years of the Mission at Hopedale. Being the southernmost mission station (until the establishment of Makkovik in 1896), Hopedale was the community most exposed to external trade and change. Much to the regret of the missionaries, Hopedale Inuit became middlemen between southern traders and more northerly Inuit (Cranz, 1820:307). Typically, Hopedale Inuit ventured south to exchange whalebone (baleen) for wooden boats and iron wares, subsequently trading these items with their northern brothers. Although the Moravians attempted to curb such exchange, it persisted even after they established regular trade at the mission stations. Hopedale's southern location also placed the community in proximity, first to Euro-American fishermen, and later to permanent settlers. This explains why technological and social changes often occurred first at Hopedale and later at the more northerly communities. Lieutenant Curtis of the Royal Navy, in his survey work along the coast in 1773 describes Arvertok (later Hopedale) as the first settlement north of the Straits of Belle Isle and as having "the most [wooden] boats, by reason of [its] being nearest to the Europeans ..." (1774:387). Another problem faced by the early Hopedale missionaries was Makko, a Catholic French-Canadian who operated an independent trading post in the Kaipokok Bay area between 1780 and 1800 (Cranz, 1820:307). Details regarding Makko remain sketchy, but he apparently attempted to preach to and trade with both the Indians and Inuit – behaviour obviously distasteful to the Moravians. According to Davey (1905:248), the presence of Makko prompted the Moravians, in 1787, to consider establishing a mission station in the Kaipokok area, a plan subsequently abandoned.

A number of important changes took place in 19th century Inuit culture. Briefly, I discuss some of the more obvious, following the most recent and comprehensive source of the topic (Kleivan, 1966). First of all, in order to reduce the economic dependence of the Inuit on the Mission, the Moravians sought to transform Inuit hunters into cod fishermen. Efforts to do so were initially hindered by two factors: the cod-fishing season (August and September) coincided with the traditional caribou hunting season, the period when caribou hides were at their best for making into winter clothing; and cod fishing had been of minor importance in the pre-contact economy, usually involving only the women and children. Nevertheless, an increasing dependence on trade goods led to an "explosive expansion of the Eskimos' cod fishery" throughout the 1860s and 1870s (Kleivan, 1966:56).

Another technological change during the 19th century was the introduction of seal nets and/or the harvesting of harp seals in autumn (at Hopedale and further south, in spring). Excepting Schledermann (1971:56–7), who presents tentative evidence for the use of seal nets in the pre-contact period, students of northern Labrador believe seal nets were introduced by missionaries at the beginning of the 19th century. In any case, by the 1820s, the missionaries had mobilized Inuit workers for organized harp sealing, using nets owned by the Mission (Kleivan, 1966:62). This fishery, which lasted until the late 1920s, was lucrative for the Mission and beneficial to the Inuit who received shares of seal meat as remuneration. I believe it important to emphasize that few Inuit were able to afford the purchase of seal nets. Consequently, net sealing had little effect on the overall economic status of 19th-century Moravian Inuit.

Throughout this century, the demand for and consumption of European trade goods increased. Concomitant with increased demands were increased debts which Inuit accumulated at the mission stores. In 1866, the Mission tightened its credit policy, an act which produced considerable unrest among Inuit, likened by Kleivan to a revivalistic movement (1966:83–6).

Still another change occurring during the 19th century involved the transition from a semi-subterranean house-type heated by seal oil to European-styled wooden houses heated by wood stoves. This change of dwelling, beginning at Hopedale about 1840 (and moving further north later), was probably caused by two factors: moral pressure by missionaries and the desire to imitate houses occupied by nearby settlers. The adoption of wooden houses probably meant fewer people per household and, quite possibly, changes in sharing patterns (Kleivan, 1966).

By the mid-19th century, the mission goal of sedentary Moravian communities was realized. Such communities contained two to three hundred people during the winter season, and required methods of social control different from those of small hunting and fishing camps. Missionaries encouraged public men's meetings at which disputes were openly settled; they also chose respected men (and later, women) as chapel servants (*kivgat*) and, after 1901, introduced a new and elected role, that of church elder (*angajokaukatigik*) in the community. Elders coordinated spiritual and secular life in each community: they settled hunting and fishing disputes, decided punishments for violations of church policy, and occasionally administered food to poor and disadvantaged Inuit. In time, the status of elder became the important political office, a pattern which survives to some extent today, particularly in Nain (cf. T. Brantenberg, Ch. 19, this vol.).

Finally, the reaction of Inuit to change during the 19th century generated a number of interpretations by the missionaries about Inuit culture. The missionaries viewed the Inuit as simple children, inherently incapable of 'rational' economic behaviour. They remained perplexed by Inuit propensity towards sharing, an Inuit avenue to prestige, yet one antithetical to that of the Mission. The Moravians also describe what they believed to be a clear-cut association between periods of economic deprivation *and* increased spiritual interest on the one hand, and between periods of economic prosperity *and* decreased spiritual interest on the other hand (see, for example, Periodical Accounts, 1915 [Hebron]; Periodical Accounts, 1915 [Makkovik]). There can be little doubt that this was objectively the case (cf. Davey, 1905:198–199), suggesting that although the Inuit (and later, the Settlers) became Moravians during the 19th century, their relationship to Christianity was not that expected by the Mission.

Besides inducing many changes in the 19th century Inuit was of life, the Mission remained dedicated to preserving *what it saw* as essential to Inuit culture. This is particularly obvious in its efforts to maintain Inuit language, diet, and to protect converts from external agents of change. Ultimately, however, Moravian efforts to insulate the Inuit from external contacts while selectively transforming elements of culture and economy were to be challenged from two sources of change: permanent European settlers and Newfoundland fishermen. It is the first of these agents, the so-called Settlers, to which I now turn.

PART TWO: THE SETTLERS

Unlike other regions of northern Canada which saw Euro-Canadians arrive only recently to work as transient traders, administrators, or missionaries, the northeast coast of Labrador had experienced permanent European settlement as early as the 19th century. In what follows, special attention is given to the historical phases of the settlement, the processes by which Europeans became Labradorians, and the adaptations made by Inuit, Indians and the Moravian Mission to these Settlers.

During the 18th century, before the arrival of the Moravians, two Frenchmen, Courtemanche and Fornel, established independent trading posts at Bradore Bay and Northwest River, respectively (Zimmerly, 1975). After 1763, the French were barred from the coast. This prohibition created opportunities for independent English traders and larger trading companies, such as Captain George Cartwright who established two small fishing and furring posts, one at Cape Charles (1770–75) and another at Sandwich Bay (1775–86).

During the late 18th century, British trading companies, primarily from west England, such as the Hunt and Henley Company, John Slade and Company, and the King and Larmour Company, opened posts along the south and central Labrador coast, south of the area controlled by the Moravian Mission (cf. Gosling, 1910:382–89). Most early European settlers came to central and northern Labrador as employees of one of these trading companies or of the Hudson's Bay Company (HBC). During the 1830s, the HBC opened trading posts at Northwest River, Rigolet, Kaipokok and Aillik. Later in the century, posts were established at

Chimo, Saglek Bay, Nackvak, and Davis Inlet. Unlike the Mission, which obtained formal land grants before establishing each station, the HBC either purchased trading rights from independent traders or occupied posts by "squatters' rights" (Gosling, 1910). In the period following 1860, HBC trade was opposed by the Moravians, not simply because it threatened their own trade monopoly, but because they feared that Inuit would amass multiple debts with various trading companies. Competition between the HBC and the Mission reached its peak after the HBC opened the Nackvak and Saglek outposts, prompting the Mission to open a station further north at Ramah in 1871.

HBC personnel were recruited in England, Scotland, Norway, and Wales and were required to serve a minimum of five years with the company. They were mostly single men, and our interest is in those who decided to marry native women and remain in Labrador. Still other early northern Labrador Settlers were the sons of men who had come to work for one of the independent British companies operating in southern and central Labrador. Born and raised in southern Labrador, these second-generation Settlers moved into uninhabited areas of the north coast in the mid-1800s. Some married Inuit women, others chose wives from among the few Settler women on the north coast; their progeny, frequently bilingual and bi-cultural, became the foundation of Settler culture. These early Settlers engaged in some trade but also exploited local natural resources. Many attempted to retain the basic elements of European economy such as gardening and raising livestock. They chose to live along the "inner coast" (Kleivan, 1966:97) in well-wooded bays and inlets. In short then, the economic adaptation of early Settlers was generalized since it tended to blend trade, agriculture, trapping, fishing and hunting rather than, as occurred later, to specialize in one or two of these.

By 1873, most Settlers inhabited districts south of Hopedale. Citing the Moravian missionary Reichel's material, Kleivan (1966:93) reports that in 1873, between Davis Inlet and Hopedale, there were three Settler families, while between Hopedale and Cape Harrison there were sixteen Settler and three Inuit families (these data exclude the Inuit community of Hopedale). Further north, the Nain congregation of 1873 comprised 271 persons of which only 10 were Settlers. The fact that Settlers were more numerous south of Hopedale had profound implications for the development of Settler culture, as seen today in Makkovik and Nain (cf. Kennedy, and T. Brantenberg, this vol.).

Kleivan (1966) argues that the development of Settler culture throughout the 19th century occurred in two phases. In the first, which began about 1830 and lasted until about 1870, extensive cultural borrowing and inter-marriage took place between the first-generation Settlers and Inuit. As single males, Settlers were usually dependent upon the skills of their Inuit wives in order to lead a relatively independent life in Labrador. Items borrowed, including techniques for seal hunting, manufacture of skin boots, Inuit terminology and so on soon lost whatever symbolic association they had had with Inuit culture and became part of the emerging Settler culture. The same process also took place in the opposite direction. About 1870, the children of ethnically-mixed marriages had reached marriageable age. It is about this time that we see the beginnings of ethnic solidarity and social endogamy in northern Labrador (Kleivan, 1966:100). Although some second-generation Settler males, particularly in the Nain district, married Inuit women, most married those with whom they had greatest contact, namely other Settlers.

The role which the Moravian Mission played in creating and maintaining the Settler-Inuit distinction was substantial. Initially, the Moravians categorized first-generation Settlers with Newfoundland floater fishermen and transient white traders. However, when the aging Inuit wives of first-generation Settlers requested renewed spiritual contact with the con- gregations with which they had been affiliated, the missionaries had little choice but to accept them and, ultimately, their Settler husbands.

The critical factor regarding Moravian acceptance of Settlers hinged on their recognizing that the Settlers viewed themselves as distinct from Inuit. Once this occurred, Settlers no longer posed a threat to Moravian efforts to insulate Inuit from outside contacts. That Settlers perceived themselves as distinct from Inuit by the late 19th century is evident in the following quotation, recorded at the official opening (in 1873) of Zoar, the first Moravian station with a considerable Settler membership:

The English Settlers residing here were not a little gratified that, in the providence of God, the first infant baptized in the new church was the child of people of their own class ... They recognized in this fact, and did not hesitate to state it, that this station had been commenced specially on their behalf, in order that it might be a means of gathering them together, who before that time had been as sheep having no Shepherd (from Kleivan, 1966:103).

Notwithstanding that the Mission had, by this time, recognized the Settlers and even incorporated them into the fold, the views of individual mis- sionaries continued to differ regarding the Settlers: "Several of the mis- sionaries incline to prefer the native, pure blooded Inuit to the 'settler,' holding that the former is more open, more simple-minded, more genuine, more manageable, and of a milder disposition than the 'settler.' Others declare that the 'settler' is equally sober, more industrious, superior as a fisherman and hunter, more enterprising, and hardier'' (MacGregor, 1909:102). Whatever views individual missionaries entertained regarding the Settlers, the fact remains that by about 1870, they recognized two groups in northern Labrador, Settlers and Inuit. As will be shown below, the implication of this during the past one hundred years was that there *should be* two groups. Let us now examine more general changes in northern Labrador during the past one hundred years.

Several changes in the Settler economy precipitated the Mission's incorporation of the Settlers. Between the 1830s and 1870s, the HBC gained
control over its Labrador trade, and along with independent Settler traders, threatened Moravian trade. However, it is also during this period that
many independent Settler traders (or their sons) ceased trading, turning
instead to an economy based on hunting and fishing (Kleivan, 1966:102);
there are several factors to be taken into account here. First, few early
Settler traders realized much profit; indeed, some accrued debts. Secondly, many of the children of Settler traders were now communicant members
of a church that had always discouraged Settlers from trading. Finally, the
economic niche occupied by independent Settlers had been to supply trade
goods unavailable through the Mission. By the 1860s, however, such goods
became increasingly accessible through Newfoundland floater fishermen,
who, by now, appeared along the coast each summer.

Still another reason why the Mission accepted the Settlers was the
notable increase in their population during the latter half of the 19th
century. In 1892, for example, 177 of Hopedale's congregation of 352 were
Settlers. Thus, expansion of the Mission southward to incorporate the
Settlers and to intercept the annual intrusion of Newfoundland floater
fishermen was considered imperative. In 1857, a Hopedale missionary,
Brother Elsner, visited Northwest River and Rigolet to investigate establishing a station in Hamilton Inlet (cf. Zimmerly, 1975:97–102). Later,
another missionary, Brother Reichel, recommended the establishment of a
station to serve Settlers south of Hopedale (cf. Davey, 1905:243–45). Then
in 1892, responding to Inuit demands for a mission at Rigolet, Brothers Fry
and Hansen visited that community and explored Ailik Cape (near Makkovik) as well. Ailik and Rigolet were both considered, but Makkovik was
finally decided upon in 1895. The following summer, a prefabricated
church (constructed in Prussia), arrived at Makkovik and was officially
opened in early December, 1897.

From the Inuit perspective, first-generation Settlers were probably seen
as *kablunak* (white men), whereas the offspring of European-Inuit unions
were later called *kablunangojok*, literally half-white or almost like white
men. The implication of this appellation is that Inuit viewed Settlers as
beings, biologically and culturally, between real Inuit and real whites, and
(it is noteworthy) consequently as inferior to both.

Settler contact with indigenous Indians was somewhat different. Three
main areas of contact were Northwest River (Lake Melville) (see Zimmerly, 1975; McGee, 1961), Davis Inlet (see Henriksen, 1973), and to a lesser
extent, the Makkovik-Kaipokok Bay area. Settler-Indian marriages occurred during the early 19th century at Northwest River and Kaipokok Bay but
never assumed the proportions of unions between Inuit and Settlers. However, Settlers borrowed extensively from Indian culture and technology,
according to documents recorded during the fur-trading years in Lake

Melville (1836–1942). Settler trappers from Northwest River, Mud Lake, Sebaskachu, and Mulligan travelled into interior Labrador each winter. They used canoes, snowshoes, and light, Indian-styled moccasins; they also acquired a taste for relatively unsalted foods and boiled Indian delicacies such as porcupine, and they adopted elements of Indian nomenclature (Zimmerly, 1975; Tanner, 1944). But more remarkable, according to Goudie (1973:103), the Settlers of Hamilton Inlet developed a version of the Indian feast, *mokoshan* (see Henriksen, 1973 for a detailed description of *mokoshan*).

Although the impact of Indian culture on the Settlers of the north coast never equalled that of Settlers in Lake Melville, some contact did occur, particularly at Davis Inlet and the Makkovik-Kaipokok area, as mentioned previously. At Kaipokok Bay, for example, Montagnais trappers ventured to the coast each summer to trade with the HBC or with a Settler trader (himself married to an Indian) who, during the mid-19th century, operated a trading post just up the river from the HBC post. During the 1920s and '30s, Montagnais families, who trapped and hunted in the interior in winter, occasionally ventured to the HBC post at Makkovik in summer to trade furs for tea, flour, molasses and tobacco. They remained in the community for several days, often staying with Settler families to whom they gave meat and pemican (dried caribou meat) in exchange (Andersen, 1975:1–2).

PART THREE: 20TH CENTURY POPULATION DYNAMICS

At the beginning of the 20th century then, the settlement pattern was such that most Settlers lived in scattered family homesteads, only occasionally travelling to mission stations to trade; in contrast, Inuit resided at mission settlements during the winter season, and during other parts of the year, lived in small family groups at outlying fishing and hunting camps. However, this pattern was not to last. For just as the Moravians encouraged Inuit to remain (at least part of the year) at the mission stations, so they pressured converted Settlers to move to Hopedale, Makkovik, Zoar and Nain. Thus, prior to their selection of Makkovik as a mission station, the Moravians apparently used the issue of population concentration as a condition for their choice. In 1900, a Makkovik missionary commented that, "The people are not so ready to build houses for themselves at Makkovik as they were to promise to do so when first a station was spoken of" (Periodical Accounts, 1900:243). During the ensuing decades, however, the Moravian position prevailed, and gradually families abandoned their homesteads in bays and inlets along the coast and moved to the mission settlements.

The increase in the population during the first half of the 20th century of most northern Labrador communities can be explained by Settlers responding to the Mission's appeal to live permanently at mission stations; thus Nain's Settler population doubled (from 54 to 110) between 1905 and 1955, and in Makkovik it increased from 17 in 1905 to about 100 in 1951. By 1955 then, most of Labrador's population was concentrated into the four Moravian settlements listed below. (Beginning in 1956, however, a government-sponsored resettlement programme was to alter these figures.)

Moravian Stations	Population	Other Settlements	Population
Makkovik	100	Kaipokok Bay area	160
Hopedale	200	Davis Inlet	130
Nain	310	Nutak	202
Hebron	208		
Total	818	Total	492

Since the establishment of the first Moravian settlements in the late 18th century, Inuit have on occasion voluntarily moved from one mission station to another to marry, respond to reports of better hunting, or visit kinsmen. In addition, the missionaries and/or church elders sometimes banished deviant Inuit, or encouraged entire families to relocate to another, perhaps less-populated station. Then during and following World War II, military base construction offered the first opportunity for wage labour, attracting both Settlers and Inuit to the construction sites.

In the early 1950s, the provincial government acknowledged its responsibility for the provision of social and economic services to the small population distributed along the 260-mile coastline between Makkovik and Hebron. Shipping supplies in summer, and air-freighting them in winter posed difficulties and great expense. Until about 1959, for example, much of the air transport, which occasionally carried administrators and (less frequently) supplies to northern Labrador, flew from Gander, Newfoundland, a distance of approximately five hundred miles (Gander-Hopedale). These long and expensive flights were further complicated by unpredictable weather conditions.

In addition to the problems of servicing northern Labrador's small and dispersed population, administrators were concerned about the quality of life (as they saw it) among the coast's northernmost Inuit. For example, International Grenfell Association health officials believed that the houses in Hebron and Nain were overcrowded, unclean, and cold; fear was expressed of a major epidemic (cf. Jenness, 1965:79–81). Excepting Hebron, most Labrador Inuit had replaced the traditional sod houses, heated by seal blubber, with European-style houses, heated by firewood, in the mid- to late 19th century. In the Hebron area, itself, conversion to wooden houses did not occur widely until the late 1940s (cf. Kleivan, 1966: 40); however, that some families used wood as fuel by the early part of this century is evident in MacGregor's (1909:88) suggestion that Inuit be moved south *because* of the absence of firewood in the Hebron area. The difficulties of obtaining firewood at Hebron became increasingly evident in the mission accounts of the 1940s and '50s and was undoubtedly one reason for resettlement.

During this time, the potential for lumber and/or uranium exploitation in the Makkovik/Postville area became imminent, and would require a larger labour force than the 150 or so people living in the area. Although such an economic development did not occur at that time, it was believed that the Makkovik-Postville area would become the major population and industrial centre along the northern coast.

In summary, the problems of servicing the northern Inuit communities, concern for health and living conditions of the Inuit, and the potential for economic development further south led to the decision to close Nutak and Hebron, Labrador's two most northerly communities. Three agencies were involved in the decision: the Moravian Mission, Northern Labrador Affairs (DNLA – a division of the Provincial Department of Public Welfare), and the International Grenfell Association (IGA).

First, it was decided to close the DNLA store at Nutak, an outpost of the Hebron mission station since the influenza epidemic of 1918–19. The decision was made at a meeting between the former Superintendent of the Labrador Mission and members of the Northern Labrador Affairs Committee (P.A., 1956:25). The closing of the store affected some two hundred people who lived both at Nutak and throughout the Okak Bay area. Of these, some 182 were Inuit and 14, Settlers. Most were relocated to Nain, some to Makkovik and Hopedale, while a handful moved to Northwest River and Happy Valley.

Once the inhabitants of the Nutak-Okak Bay area were moved south in 1956, the decision to close Hebron, with its population of approximately two hundred Inuit, was inevitable. Initially, most of Hebron's population was moved to Makkovik though, as described elsewhere (Ch. 18, this vol.), in the period between 1961 and the present, many of these people later voluntarily moved north again – to Nain. In any event, with the closing of Hebron in 1959, Nain became the northernmost permanent community in northern Labrador.

Several implications of relocation must be mentioned briefly here. First, it has meant that some of northern Labrador's prime hunting and fishing resources remain unharvested during much of the year. On the other hand, the increase in population in recipient communities has put a strain on local resources, decreasing the possibilities of individuals obtaining a living through traditional economic pursuits. In some cases, this has made the realization of traditional values (see Ch. 16, this vol.) difficult and may be partially responsible for the increase in alcohol-related violent incidents. Thirdly, the process of relocation broke up many Inuit family units and this, along with the fact that Hebron and Nutak peoples did not want to relocate (RRCL, Vol. VI: 1215–17) have made many Labrador Inuit both resentful and suspicious of government programmes. It appears that those relocated had little understanding of the location to which they were being moved; many even believed they were being moved to an urban setting. One Makkovik informant, formerly of Okak Bay, told me, ''When we were moving here, we thought we were moving to an awfully big place, like we thought we'd be seeing cars and all sorts of things. [When we got here], it wasn't much different than being up 'home.' ''

It also appears that Nutak's and Hebron's former residents, most of whom spoke little or no English, were greeted with a mixture of curiosity and apprehension by the members of their new communities. At Makkovik, for example, virtually all of the Settler population spoke only English and the difficulties created by a sudden influx of non-English-speaking people were undoubtedly considerable. Makkovik Settler children were sometimes openly hostile toward their new 'neighbours'; and we find ''They (Settler children) treated us pretty bad sometimes. We used to get drove down to the ground sometimes with rocks. A whole bunch of Makkovik kids used to get at us with rocks and drive us under houses and keep us there; there were only four or five of us [from Okak] you know.''

The incidence of such open conflicts between Settlers and Inuit following relocation should not be exaggerated. More typical inter-ethnic relations are described by Ben-Dor (1966), T. Brantenberg, and Kennedy (this vol.); instead of open conflict, it has been more a matter of little interaction between Settlers, native to Nain and Makkovik, and the relocated Inuit.

PART FOUR: ADMINISTRATION, IDEOLOGY, AND ECONOMIC DEVELOPMENT

Any review of administrative policy in northern Labrador is complicated by the fact that few (if any) policies (past and present) affecting the region have been made there, and that 'Labrador policy' is thus a small part of British, Newfoundland, and Canadian policy. Labrador's political and economic status has been that of a colony, or at least one of dependency, and her peoples enjoy minimal participation in decisions affecting their region. A brief review of Labrador administration supports this interpretation and a subsequent section presents certain implications which are believed to follow from it.

In retrospect, 18th century British interest in Newfoundland and Governor Palliser's support for the Moravian Mission in Labrador established a precedent wherein Labrador was considered a part of Newfoundland.

Excepting the period between 1774 and 1809, when Labrador was administered by the province of Quebec, the region was formally considered part of
Newfoundland between 1763 and the present. Newfoundland's jurisdiction
over Labrador was further confirmed by the Privy Council's decision on
the boundary dispute in 1927. But whereas Newfoundlanders enjoyed
some elected representation between 1833 and 1934, Labrador was not
democratically represented until 1946.

In the summer of 1946, a vessel visited coastal communities to elect
Labrador's representative to the British-sponsored National Convention
convened to determine whether Newfoundland and Labrador would unite
with the United States, restore Responsible Government, or confederate
with Canada (Noel, 1973:245–48). In supporting confederation with
Canada, Labrador's delegate to the convention furthered the position
apparently favoured by many north Labradorians (P.A., 1947:56). Officially, Confederation meant Labradorians would, henceforth, elect members to the Provincial House of Assembly, and that the region would cease
to be a dependency of Newfoundland. In my view, however, the years
since Confederation (1949) have not significantly increased the control of
Labrador (or its people) over its destiny. To the contrary, although Confederation has improved the region's standard of living, the cost of that
increase has both reduced the socio-economic autonomy of Labradorians
and made them exceedingly vulnerable to fluctuations in provincial and
federal policy. In a sense, much of this was inevitable. Let us examine how
it came to be.

Administration and Ideology

The roots of contemporary administration in northern Labrador can be
traced to 1926 when the Moravian Mission, its trading operations on the
verge of bankruptcy, agreed to lease its trading rights and properties to the
Hudson's Bay Company for a period of twenty-one years. (The Mission's
trade failed mainly because of its humanitarian intentions and over-
extension of credit.) The company's aim, of course, was to generate profit
through the fur trade. By means of its rigorous control of credit, its total
monopoly, and incentives for the more productive trappers, the HBC was
able to increase fur production dramatically during the 1930s. In time, the
company's thirst for furs led to a disregard for the economic welfare of
Settlers and Inuit. This situation became still more marked when, in the
late 1930s, the Newfoundland government legislated an agreement with the
company in which the company was permitted to import all wares duty-free
in exchange for administering some public relief (Kleivan, 1966:129). The
details of this arrangement remain sketchy but it essentially involved the
government's reminding the company of its moral responsibilities as a
trading company. Coincidently, in 1937, the first law enforcement personnel, the Newfoundland Rangers, were dispatched to the northern coast.

Throughtout the 1930s, the Mission remained suspicious of the HBC's uncompromising strategy of profit-making. Although neither Labradorians nor the Mission welcomed the arrival of the Rangers, it soon became apparent that they had been sent to "care for the poor and invalid" of Labrador; that is, to administer relief (P.A., 1934/35:86) rather than simply enforce externally-derived laws. The Rangers did so until 1951, when many of them were absorbed into the RCMP.

In July 1942, insufficient profit forced the HBC to close the stores it had leased from the Mission sixteen years earlier. Again, neither the Mission nor the people complained of the company's decision, but both requested that the Newfoundland Government provide an alternative to the HBC stores. During the summer of 1942, the Northern Labrador Trading Operation (NLTO), a division of Newfoundland's Department of Natural Resources, took over the company's facilities and shipped essential goods to the coast. At the outset, NLTO was viewed optimistically; its experienced personnel promised a planned programme of economic rehabilitation in north Labrador, which was to include a housing project as well as sweeping changes in the fishery.

NLTO's plan to help Labradorians obtain self-sufficiency, in the view of Jenness (1965:67), involved discouraging "any further increase in trapping, advocating instead an expansion of sealing and cod-fishing, since fresh meat and fresh fish would provide the people with a cheaper and healthier diet than the store foods consumed by trappers." Whilst NLTO did discourage the specialized trapping economy fostered by the HBC, its success in promoting self-sufficiency among north Labradorians is more debatable. Furthermore, although NLTO advocated hiring Labrador people in its operations (P.A., 1943:151), most of its staff were actually former HBC employees (Division, 1952:6) or former Rangers.

Confederation brought about several major changes in the socio-economic lives of Labradorians. For the first time, money became available to Settlers, Inuit and Indians. By 1953, for example, Canadian citizenship qualified everyone for Old Age and Disability Pensions; yet, ironically, the rising cost of living reduced the impact of such benefits (P.A., 1953:14). For the Moravians, Confederation entailed a further erosion of their power and of their authority to control behaviour at the community level.

In 1951, the responsibility for trade and social welfare in northern Labrador was transferred to the Provincial Department of Welfare and a new agency, the Division of Northern Labrador Affairs (DNLA – henceforth referred to as the Division), was created to succeed NLTO. This change was precipitated partially because insufficient funding retarded NLTO's resource development programme. When Newfoundland joined Canada in 1949, the question of which government (federal or provincial) would assume responsibility for Labrador's Indians and Inuit arose. In 1951,

Ottawa acknowledged a moral, if not legal, responsibility for these native peoples with the provision of funds for health and welfare (Jenness, 1965:75). These funds were to be administered by the province by its newly formed Division. Federal involvement increased in 1954 with the signing of a ten-year agreement in which it assumed most of the responsibility for Indian and Inuit health services. In 1965, this agreement was expanded to include funding for the construction, maintenance, and development of Inuit and Indian communities.

Although federal funding had, since 1954, favoured communities with Indians and Inuit, the vagaries present in the northern Labrador ethnic structure meant that Settlers also benefited from the agreement (Jenness, 1965:74). Thus, until 1969, all communities north of Cape Harrison (see Map of Labrador) and the Indian community of Northwest River were included in the area of administration. Rigolet and Black Tickle, two Settler communities with some Inuit descendants, were added later. In 1970 and again in 1975, the federal-provincial agreement was renewed and extended, and worthy of note is that at the 1975 meeting, representatives of Labrador's native organizations were present for the first time.

The total impact of these agreements on the communities of northern Labrador is readily grasped when they are compared with the relatively segmented and impoverished (non-native) communities along the coast south of Black Tickle. Again though, ethnicity was the variable sponsoring government involvement. Tacit in each successive agreement was that the province, through the Division, would administer federal and provincial funding to communities inhabited by Inuit and Indians. The effect of this was to make the Division the most pervasive institutional force Labrador has ever seen, an agency which after 1951, increasingly came to affect most facets of life. Let us briefly examine the structure and ideology of the Division.

To begin with, like its predecessors, the NLTO, the HBC and the Mission, the Division was concerned with retail trade and the purchase of fish and furs. Each community had a depot (store) and other properties supervised by a depot manager who was responsible to the agency's director in St. John's. The responsibilities of the manager included requisitioning and shipping supplies, operating radio communication, supervising local economic development, and in some cases, acting as local postmaster or nurse. Depot managers were nearly always Newfoundlanders recruited through an intricate patronage network not uncommon in the civil service. Although Labradorians have occasionally worked as assistant managers, clerks, or interpreters, most are reluctant to risk possible allegations of conflict of interest on the part of a local person in the role of manager.

During the years between 1951 and the present, the Division's jurisdiction gradually expanded from socio-economic welfare to an umbrella-like organization that managed funds from other provincial departments (such as education, municipal affairs and health). During these years, three dominant themes in Division policy emerged from its Labrador experience and to some extent, helped shape it; they revolved around the issues of welfare, ethnic integration, and conversion to wage labour. Evidence for these policies reoccur in the Division's annual reports and provide some rationale for the particular manner in which the Division spent money in Labrador.

In many respects, the government commitment to the welfare of northern Labrador can be regarded as a predictable outgrowth of events described above: notably the Missions' declining role, the Rangers' presence during the late 1930s and '40s, and the new province's creation of the Division of Northern Labrador Affairs in 1951. While not denying that socio-economic problems existed in northern Labrador. I do not believe that the province's commitment to welfare in that area was based on real needs, but rather, in part at least, on the conviction (of policy makers) that native Labradorians were, in comparison to Island Newfoundlanders, culturally inferior and thus naturally dependent on their 'big brothers.'

This view that Labradorians are inferior has had a long history; although often softened by the altruistic rhetoric of liberalism, it basically assumes that native Labradorians are naturally incapable of managing their own affairs; that only by external guidance can their better interests, as drafted in St. John's, be realized. In its essential characteristics then, the ideology is the same as that which Paine (Ch. 2, this vol.) describes for the Northwest Territories as 'welfare colonialism.' A former Moravian missionary, for example, discussing Inuit language, concludes that: "The Eskimos are children of Nature, primitive and with a logic different from ours ... that they are not capable of analytical or abstract thinking" (Peacock, 1947:101) Similarly, we find the same ideology expressed by the first Director of the Division:

I was impressed with the desire of the Eskimo to take on more and more of our civilization. Perhaps this may be aptly expressed by comparing him to a younger brother holding out his hand to us and saying "May I come with you?" If we try to drive him back he will go on his own way, and perhaps be lost in the storm, and perish. On the other hand we may take him by the hand as an older brother ought to do, if he stumbles, as he is likely to do, we must patiently help him to his feet so that we may go forward into the future together (Division, 1951:12).

Again recalling Paine's discussion of welfare colonialism, we can only assume that the Division had little to gain by Labrador Inuit becoming "lost in the storm," and even less in seeing them "go on (their) own way."

There was also a geopolitical dimension to the provision of welfare services in northern Labrador. Though the present boundaries of Labrador and the territory's relationship to insular Newfoundland had been settled in the British Privy Council decision of 1927, I believe government policy-makers still felt the need, also on this account, for a provincial presence in Labrador; this could be most conveniently realized by providing basic services, in conjunction with the Federal Government, to native people. Whereas in 1955, the Division's actual presence in Labrador was restricted to five depots, distributed along the coast between Cape Harrison and Hebron, the area implicitly administered by the agency was described as being "... the strip of territory lying north of a line drawn from Cape Harrison *due west to the height of the land*; the northern panhandle of Labrador ... approximately equal in area to that of the whole of the Island of Newfoundland" (Division, 1955:76; emphasis added). A physical presence in northern Labrador ostensibly administrating welfare and basic services was, I believe, related to the more general (if, except for the fishery, unrealized) conviction that Labrador's natural resources might someday benefit the province – and Newfoundland, in particular. Whereas Newfoundland had, as recently as 1933, considered selling Labrador to relieve the 'national' debt, by the early 1950s its Labrador policy had evolved.

A second, more visible theme of Division policy concerns integration. The Division's Annual Report of 1956 states that "the Eskimos and the Indians cannot continue to exist as isolated minorities but must ultimately be integrated into the general body of our Society" (Division, 1956:73). Yet, only three years earlier, underlying the Division's commitment to integration was the belief that: "Eskimos and Indians have not as yet developed to the stage where they can be expected to compete on an equal footing with Whites in earning a livelihood, and, who, at least for some time to come, will need patient understanding and guidance in their adjustment to economic and cultural conditions into which they are increasingly being enmeshed and absorbed" (Division, 1953:82). To integrate the Labrador native population, the Division moved in two directions: relocation and education (see below).

Related to both welfare and integration was the Division's conviction that the Labrador subsistence economy be replaced by one centred on wage labour. As the Division saw it, hunting and fishing, along with the social and cultural practices these pursuits entailed, were inconsistent with efforts to modernize Labrador – something the Division believed desirable. In any event, the Division believed that hunting and fishing would barely allow north Labradorians to survive until the development of an industrial economy.

Economic Development

Until World War II, the main economic change occurred during the years of HBC tenure at the mission settlements between 1924 and 1941. As noted above, this period was characterized by a more specialized trapping economy, and yet certain continuities persisted; namely an absence of cash transactions and the relative independence of external administrators.

Initially, the development of northern Labrador following Confederation stemmed from two sources: American military base construction and mineral exploration. Base construction began during the summer of 1941 when the American, Canadian, and Newfoundland governments reached an agreement in which the Canadian government was granted a 99-year lease for a 120-square-mile military reserve at Goose Bay, near the head of Lake Melville. The effects of the base (and of related services) were far-reaching. Besides the influx of American and Canadian military personnel, many civilian Newfoundlanders, as well as Lake Melville Settlers and Inuit from the north coast were attracted to Goose Bay, where for the first time wage labour became available. In July 1944, eighty-five Labradorians were employed (Zimmerly, 1975:234), but by August, 1945, the hiring of civilian employees had ceased. Nonetheless, the new neighbouring village of Happy Valley, where most civilians employed in Goose Bay resided, continued to grow, ultimately becoming the main mercantile and distribution centre for coastal Labrador. In 1976, the amalgamated town of Happy Valley-Goose Bay had a population of 7,024 (Canada, 1976).

Some Settlers (and a few Inuit) from northern Labrador relocated (either temporarily or permanently) in Happy Valley, but U.S. bases built along the north coast during the 1950s lured many more from their hunting and fishing economy. During World War II, two American weather stations were constructed, one at Cape Harrison and another near Hebron (vacated in 1946). During the following decade, a number of American radar installations were built between Cut Throat in the south and Saglek in the north.

In the late 1940s, unusually low market prices for cod fish adversely affected the north-coast economy, which since 1942 had increasingly relied on the summer cod fishery. This situation magnified the effect that the Hopedale base had on the north coast; Settlers and Inuit from as far north as Nutak and from the Makkovik-Kaipokok area to the south went to Hopedale to work (temporarily or permanently). As was the case at other bases, most of them were employed as unskilled labourers.

Radar base construction naturally affected provincial government policy. Having accepted responsibility for the native peoples of northern Labrador, the government viewed the coast's economic future with some trepidation. The construction of radar bases meant two things: it provided Labrador men with several seasons of employment on one hand, and the Division with an economic model for northern Labrador on the other. This model rested on the hypothesis that Labrador men would rather 'work' than hunt or fish. In 1957, the Division's director wrote, "It is a fact that the Hopedale men have during the past four or five seasons, worked side by side with men from Newfoundland and other Provinces, doing the kind of work required on such projects, and which range from common labour to driving trucks and operating pneumatic drills'' (Division, 1957:77).

The logic of the Division's economic policy was now taken further. To its view that (a) the exploitation of natural resources could only be, even in the best of years, little more than 'holding operations,' The Division added that (b) Labrador people *could* work at construction work, and that (c) Labrador people would *rather* work than hunt and fish. Thus, in the Division's annual report for 1956, we read that,

The decision of the majority of the fishermen to seek other employment (e.g. base construction) rather than to continue at the codfishery reveals more clearly than words, their dissatisfaction with the present state of affairs, and a determination to strive for better conditions. This ambition can only be realized as remunerative employment becomes available and the people concerned are fully prepared for the duties and responsibilities the new conditions will demand (p. 74).

With base construction coming to an end (about 1960), and given the Division's stated commitment to provide wage employment, the problem then became a matter of where the employment would come from. I deal with this below, but first present some criticism of the Division's interpretation that Labrador people would rather 'work' than fish. First of all, had international market prices offered a reasonable return to north Labrador fishermen during the early 1950s, I believe the Hopedale 'experiment' would have yielded considerably different results. Here, one must keep in mind the traditional credit economy in which Settlers and Inuit transacted. Base construction provided one of the first real opportunities for converting labour into cash. Thus, the value of cash itself was elevated above its actual worth – it served as a hitherto unavailable vehicle to purchase commodities. What the Hopedale experiment showed was that the cash benefits (baby bonuses, old age pensions, and so on) available to Labrador people since Confederation were not considered sufficient. Further evidence for refuting provincial government logic appeared in May 1957 when for the first time, the Federal Government extended Unemployment Insurance Commission (UIC) benefits to fishermen. This meant that if a person fished during summer, he could qualify for a cash subsidy during winter. In effect, UIC benefits subsidized low fish prices (cf. Brox, 1972), and in Labrador, made fishing a preferable alternative to wage labour.

The Division's interpretation of the Hopedale experiment was tested anew at Cape Makkovik, where another American radar base was begun in the mid-'50s. Until 1957, the Americans had little trouble recruiting local labour. However, in the Division's Annual Report for 1958, we read that, ''The summer of 1957 saw a return to the cod fishery by a large number of fishermen who had been otherwise employed (i.e., base construction) for the past two or three seasons. Perhaps the principal reason for this was that fewer jobs were available, but undoubtedly the introduction of Unemployment Insurance to fishermen was a factor in this development'' (p. 121). Thus, the division realized that if fishing (and other subsistence activities) offered sufficient returns, Settlers and Inuit would fish rather than 'work.' Nevertheless, the Division appears to have resolved to encourage the development of wage labour opportunities. After the first federal-provincial cost-sharing arrangement; this began to be a possibility and appeared even more so after the second agreement.

From another perspective, the Division's decision to create local wage employment was a logical outgrowth of responsibility for the native people of Labrador. In order that Inuit and Settlers be able to enjoy services comparable to those of other Canadians, (education, health care, transportation, and others) the coast's dispersed population had to be centralized. Relocation also meant that economic opportunities would occur in fewer communities. In my view, relocation and the creation of wage labour must also be seen as emanating out of the Division's conviction that its policies were benefiting the people of northern Labrador. In many respects, this conviction disregarded traditional native culture and values, and stemmed from the view (which prevailed in Newfoundland politics) that industrialization was the key to the province's future. Other plans for economic development in northern Labrador, such as modernizing and expanding the production of local resources, were either not considered or ruled inapplicable. I now turn to some of the ways in which the Division developed local employment.

The first scheme introduced by the Division was a massive housing programme. Now it cannot be argued that such a programme was not needed. The 1955 visit to Nain of Dr. C. S. Curtis, the IGA Superintendent, provoked this comment: ''After entering every Eskimo dwelling in the settlement he [Curtis] had discovered only one, owned by a man who was working at Hopedale, which health authorities would not have condemned as unfit for human habitation. At Nutak and Hebron, he was told, conditions were more appalling still'' (Jenness, 1965:79). Also, relocating the approximately 500 people, primarily Inuit from the Nutak-Okak area and from Hebron, would necessitate the building of houses in their new communities. In short, although the Division's housing programme cannot be questioned on the basis of need, the fact that it became the basis of the Division's economic policy for northern Labrador occurred at the expense of developing local resources.

Between 1956 and 1963, 71 houses (66 in ''Eskimo communities,'' 5 in ''Indian communities'') were constructed in the northern coastal communities to which the Hebron and Nutak-Okak peoples were moved. These were small two-bedroom wooden structures, measuring 18 by 20 feet and costing between $1500 to $2000 to build. Inuit had been promised free housing upon relocation, and the only requirement was that they sign an agreement promising not to sell or renovate their homes for ten years, after which they would own the house.

Realizing that additional housing was required in north Labrador, the Division requested federal funds for this purpose. This second building period between 1963 and 1973 produced 313 more houses (206 in "Eskimo communities," 107 in "Indian communities") that were slightly larger (24 by 35 feet) and more costly. Occupants paid a small rent ($15 to $20 per month) and, as with the earlier arrangement, they would own their homes after ten years' occupancy.

In addition to new housing, other construction plans included several school buildings and teacher's residences, two fish plants (at Nain and Makkovik), retail store facilities, and other buildings. All these projects made use of local labour, and hence, the Division's dream of a wage-labour economy achieved fruition. They helped cushion the effects of the declining cod fishery, which began in 1968, and in offering workers several months employment each summer and fall, they further qualified them for UIC benefits during winter. Thus, within a period of about ten years, the economy of the north coast moved from one in which wage labour was all but non-existent (excluding base construction), to one which, in some communities, offered wage employment to everyone. This was especially true in Nain and Makkovik during the late '60s and early '70s, where in addition, the construction, maintenance, and operation of modern fish plants created new kinds of employment opportunities, most significantly, for women.

The implications of the coast's new wage economy are manifold; I shall mention but a few of the more obvious. As might be expected, incomes of construction workers were far greater than incomes from fishing or trapping. Concomitantly with increased earnings came increased purchasing and expectations. Some wage labourers have become dependent upon (and acquired a preference for) store-bought foods and, increasingly, upon stove oil instead of wood as fuel. This increase in the use of purchased commodities has led repeatedly to a depletion of stocks in Division stores, especially of frozen meats, fresh produce, oil and gas, a problem that is exacerbated by the awkward and inefficient requisition policies of the Division.

Secondly, wage labour offers an economic alternative to fishing (and hunting). Some men who annually work as labourers argue that earnings from fishing and hunting are insufficient to cover the risks involved. For other fishermen, who sold, or allowed to fall into disrepair, or did not replace fishing gear after the late 1960s, the option of obtaining wage labour is more a necessity than a choice; often fishermen take labourer jobs reluctantly, lamenting the loss of freedom associated with fishing, but viewing wage labour as a comparatively easy way to obtain money. It is also common to find men who fish during summer and take on construction work in the fall. Still others fish for salmon or char during summer and then jig for cod during the fall, though this strategy is less common than those described above. It is difficult to analyse the socio-economic benefits of fishing versus wage labour by concepts such as class, if by class one implies differential access to, or control over scarce resources. Some salmon-char fishermen realize incomes far in excess of those who 'work,' and vice versa. It is also difficult to identify fishermen and wage labourers by ethnicity: there are Inuit and Settlers in both categories. However, one thing can be said with some certainty: other factors being equal, the local status of successful fishermen-hunters is higher than that of labourers, especially because these traditional occupations remain identified locally with the image of the Labrador man.

At the time of Confederation in 1949, the average personal income in Newfoundland was $472 per year, and unemployment was five times the national average (Mathias, 1971:44). To counteract this situation, the provincial government sought to diversity the economy by attracting foreign industry and obtaining capital. One development scheme, which was to profoundly affect Labrador, was the creation of the British Newfoundland Corporation (Brinco) in 1953. A syndicate of international corporations and capital, it was granted major mineral, timber, and water power concessions in Newfoundland and Labrador. The best-documented and most controversial of Brinco's developments is the harnessing of hydro-electrical power on the Upper Churchill (Hamilton) River (cf. Mathias, 1971; Smith, 1975) and subsequent sale of its electrical energy to Quebec at low rates (cf. Gwyn, 1974). Although a small number of coastal Labradorians were involved in the construction phase of the Upper Churchill development, it is mineral exploration in Labrador, operated through a subsidiary of Brinco, British-Newfoundland Exploration Limited (Brinex), that has had, and most likely will have, the greatest socio-economic impact.

By the time Brinco was formed, most of Labrador's known mineral rights, primarily iron-ore deposits in western Labrador, were already controlled by American interests, restricting Brinex explorations to areas not yet conceded to other companies. During the '50s and '60s, large sections of the Labrador interior were explored and deposits of copper and uranium discovered. Using Northwest River as its base of operations, Brinex hired Labrador men to work as labourers, 'bushmen,' cooks and, less frequently, as prospectors. In 1956, uranium deposits were discovered at Kitts Pond, near Marks Bight, Kaipokok Bay.

I would emphasize that the actual number of men employed by Brinex was small (see Table 1).[3] More important than the actual numbers, however, was a growing conviction, especially after 1958, that the opening of a

TABLE 1

Brinco Employment 1953–1963

Year	N.W.R.	Postville	Makkovik	Hopedale	Nain	Total
1953	0	0	0	0	0	0
1954	3	0	0	0	0	3
1955	2	1	0	0	0	3
1956	17	3	3	2	1	26
1957	24	1	2	0	1	28
1958	18	6	0	0	0	24
1959	18	0	0	0	0	18
1960	20	0	0	0	6	26
1961	11	0	0	0	1	12
1962	6	0	0	0	0	6
1963	16	3	4	0	2	25
	135	14	9	2	11	171

major mining industry was imminent. Thus, each fall, after the summer season of mineral exploration, rumours would circulate in the communities that mining would begin "next summer." The government apparently also subscribed to such an expectation. The Nutak-Okak Bay people, as well as those from Hebron, were told that the Makkovik-Postville area would become a mining centre and that its population would, in a few years, outnumber those of Nain and Hopedale. However, this did not occur. During the late 1960s, Brinco continued exploration and conducted diamond drilling, occasionally on a year-round basis, at Kitts Pond and Seal Lake. By about 1970, falling demand on uranium led to a cessation of Brinex operations but, by 1973 and, increasingly by 1974, demands increased once again.

However, during the early 1970s the Federal Government responded to the energy crises with accelerated plans to manufacture nuclear reactors both for domestic use and export. Consequently, the Federal Government stepped up uranium exploration throughout Canada and encouraged exploitation of known deposits. By 1975 and early 1976, plans were being considered to open mines at Michelin Lake and Kitts Pond and to provide extensive ancillary facilities. Clearly, the almost certain development of uranium mining in the Makkovik-Postville area will profoundly alter both communities.

PART FIVE: HEALTH, EDUCATION, TRANSPORTATION, AND
COMMUNICATION

During the Moravian period of supremacy in northern Labrador, all services were controlled by the Mission. The following description shows how matters of health, education, transportation, and communication have become subsumed under one or another external agency.

Health

In the early years, the missionaries competed with the *angakoks* (shamen) in their medical role (cf. Davey, 1905). Gradually the missionaries gained ascendancy so that throughout the 19th and early 20th centuries, ailing Inuit and Settlers were taken to mission stations for routine as well as more serious ailments. In 1903, a hospital was founded in Okak (Hutton, 1912; Davey, 1905; MacGregor, 1909) which served the coast between Ramah and Hopedale. Persons from Hopedale south travelled to Indian Harbour, where the Deep Sea Mission (later the International Grenfell Association) operated a hospital (MacGregor, 1909).

Despite Moravian efforts to insulate Inuit from external influences, disease, frequently occurring as an epidemic, has been an unfortunate, yet inevitable, consequence of European invasion.[4] The world-wide Spanish influenza epidemic was brought to central Labrador by men returning from war (Zimmerly, 1975:221), and to the northern area by ailing crewmen on the Moravian supply ship, the *Harmony*. Between November 1918 and January 1919, the epidemic claimed the lives of over one third of the Inuit living within the mission area (Kleivan, 1966:181), reducing the population of 1,270 to 875 (Tanner, 1944:458). Hardest hit was Okak, where 207 out of 263 Inuit died, and Hebron, where 150 out of 220 died. Every man was killed in Okak, and it was decided to close the mission station there. Fortunately, other primarily Inuit communities such as Nain, Killinek and Hopedale were less severely affected.

Although much has been written on the 1918–19 epidemic, in my view, several points have not received adequate attention. Before the epidemic, MacGregor (1909:100–01) and others had noted that Settler deaths occurred far less commonly than did Inuit deaths, buttressing the generally accepted theory that Inuit lacked immunity, while Settlers, in contrast, illustrated the principle of "hybrid vigour." One cannot question the theory in the light of the influenza epidemic, but how does one explain the fact that the same disease claimed seventy people (presumably, many of them Settlers) in the Cartwright area and thousands more in Newfoundland and Canada – people of European descent?

Secondly, the severity of the influenza outbreak, when compared with earlier epidemics, dealt a profound blow to the "place group" settlement pattern characteristic of Labrador Inuit (cf. Williamson, 1964; Taylor, 1974). Kin groups formerly inhabiting the Hebron and Okak areas and affiliated with one of these two congregations, were either extinguished, seriously depleted, or resettled at Nain or Hopedale. Essentially, the congregation of the 'new Hebron' (after 1919) was composed of families from Saglek, Nain, and Okak who were encouraged to resettle in depopulated Hebron. In addition, with the closing of the Killinek station (because of the Labrador boundary dispute) in 1924, forty Killinek people moved to Hebron.

By 1924, then, Hebron was "more of a composite congregation than the others of the coast, and there [was] a lack of a good nucleus" (P.A., 1924:334), meaning that the Hebron missionaries encountered difficulties in obtaining chapel servants and elders, so essential to the organization of community life. In decimating much of the northern Inuit population, the 1918–19 epidemic caused a reshuffling of personnel and the creation of a composite congregation, rather than an integrated one common to other Moravian stations. It should also be noted that during the 1920s, some Inuit left the Hebron area to exploit the rich Okak area, a move further encouraged in 1926, when a HBC post was established at Nutak across the island from abandoned Okak. Officially, these people remained members of the Hebron congregation; yet, in reality, the seventy miles separating these districts limited contact. In addition, several Killinek (P.A., 1928:245) and Nain (P.A., 1929:419) families, who had been members of the Hebron congregation following the epidemic, returned to their former homes during the late 1920s.

In short, the 1918–19 epidemic ushered in a new era in northern Labrador, a period when population shifts became increasingly common. The difficulties which this new era presented to Inuit were further exacerbated by the HBC takeover of Moravian trade (in 1926), and its singular quest for furs.

A final point illustrated by the epidemic was the degree to which early 20th century Inuit subscribed to the medical practices of the Mission. More to the point, the epidemic points out the ambiguities inherent in early 20th century Inuit culture: on the one hand, in the fall of 1918, it appeared that the Inuit of Okak and Hebron ignored the warnings of missionaries, choosing instead to mix freely with the crew of the *Harmony*. Even after the epidemic had begun, many Inuit left as usual for their fall sealing stations. On the other hand, once sick, many returned to the missionaries, whose medical strategies had obtained some legitimacy among Inuit. Even though the heavens had foretold of danger,[5] by 1918 such a harbinger no longer served as an indication for action (or inaction).

At the beginning of the 20th century, except for Dr. Hutton's Hospital at Okak and Dr. Grenfell's work in northern Newfoundland and southern Labrador, medical services along the north coast remained limited. Several factors after this time led to the development of the present health care system. About 1900, two diseases that were new to Labrador, specifically tuberculosis and venereal disease, as well as increased consumption of Euro-Canadian foods, led to a deterioration in the health of Settlers and Inuit.[6] From 1920 (until 1950), medical services were provided by physicians, affiliated either with Grenfell's medical mission or the government officials who visited the coast in summer. These visits, however, probably served more as a comfort to missionaries than as a benefit to natives, who, during summer, were scattered at various outlying fishing stations. In 1929, a hospital was opened at Nain, a joint project of the HBC and the Moravian Mission. There were now two hospitals in Labrador.

World War II brought increased use of air transportation to Labrador. 'Mercy flights' parachuted medical supplies to missionaries or took ailing natives to hospital. By this time, improved communications, specifically the use of wireless telegraph, allowed missionaries to obtain medical information from the IGA hospital at Cartwright. Finally, after the 1954 Federal-Provincial Agreement health costs were largely funded by the Federal Government and administered through the IGA. During the '50s and '60s, government funding subsidized the construction and maintenance of IGA nursing stations, actually 'mini-hospitals' (RRCL, Vol. 1, 287), at Makkovik, Hopedale and Nain. These stations are staffed by full-time IGA nurses and provide routine health care. More serious patients are flown to the Northwest River IGA hospital which presently serves the north coast.

Education

From the earliest days of the Moravian Mission in Labrador, education has always been an integral part of religious conversion. Gosling (1910:281) attributes the religious 'awakening' of 1804–05 to a generation of teaching Inuit children. Benefiting from earlier missionary work in Greenland, especially the translation of New Testament scriptures into the West Greenland dialect, the early Labrador missionaries taught reading and writing, using fundamental Christian doctrine and liturgy (Jenness, 1965:38). This restricted curriculum was soon expanded to include sewing, arithmetic, geography and spelling (Davey, 1905:234). Until the arrival of permanent European Settlers in the Makkovik and Hopedale districts, instruction in all mission schools was given in Inuttitut, a conscious effort by the Moravians to preserve Inuit culture.

Another aspect of the early Moravian education system, striking when one compares present attitudes toward education, was the positive attitude Inuit children had toward school. "'The strongest punishment which can be imposed upon a child is to keep it away from the school,' says a missionary in 1824 about the work with the school in Nain and Hopedale" (Kleivan, 1966:80).

Providing education to Settler children presented problems to the Moravians. Their relatively dispersed settlement pattern and their infrequent contact with the mission stations left many first- and second-generation Settlers illiterate. To help remedy this, night classes for adult Settlers were opened at Makkovik in 1898 for instruction in reading, writing and arithmetic. Then, the Makkovik and Nain stations began providing accommodation for Settler and Inuit children during the fall and winter months. In 1899, a school building was constructed in Makkovik, and in 1919, a boarding school was opened, accepting students (primarily Settlers) from as far north as Nain. By 1931, there were thirty-five boarders and ten day students (P.A., 1931:174). Instruction was given in English. The Nain school offered instruction in both English and Inuttitut as early as 1905 (Schloss, 1964:11).

With certain minor changes, this system continued until Confederation, at which time education for all children between the ages of seven and fourteen became compulsory. Following Confederation, the basically religious character of the Moravian curriculum was replaced by a broad secular programme, built around the concept of integration – the notion that Labrador natives must obtain skills which would allow them access to Canadian socio-economic opportunities. One implication of this approach has been the lack of sensitivity to the unique character of Labrador life. For this reason, most north Labrador parents today argue that their children are receiving an education of little real value (RRCL, Vol. 1, 167). This kind of criticism has grown in the past several years and has been taken up by new native organizations, Indian and Inuit associations, which have urged the teaching of native language and cultural skills in the schools.

Transportation

Between 1770 and 1926, the Moravian Mission and the S.F.G. maintained an annual shipping service linking London with the Labrador coast. These annual voyages both collected locally-produced products (seal skins, cod liver oil, furs, and others) and supplied essential goods for trade and use by Settlers, Inuit, and missionaries, who all came to depend upon them. Until 1901, mission ships were sailing vessels and could make but one annual voyage; however, after that time, the use of auxiliary steam permitted two and occasionally three voyages. The voyage of the *Harmony*, under sail in 1888, gives some idea of the time involved (Wilson, n.d.:4–5). The return voyage London-Labrador took a total of 125 days, 53 of which were spent visiting the Labrador communities of Hopedale, Zoar, Nain, Okak, Ramah, and Hebron.

Even before the termination of Moravian trade and its replacement by the HBC in 1926, the Newfoundland government subsidized the operation of a coastal mail steamer which ran between St. John's and Nain once every two weeks (MacGregor, 1909:117). In addition to carrying mail, the government steamer transported floater fishermen (seasonal fishermen from Newfoundland), government wildlife, law-enforcing and medical personnel, revenue officers, and less frequently, government administrators.

By the beginning of the present century, the Canadian Marconi Company constructed five wireless telegraph stations for the Newfoundland government along the south Labrador coast, between Indian Harbour and Battle Harbour (MacGregor, 1909:76). Subsequently, a similar station was opened at Dunn's Island (outside Makkovik) but in 1930 this facility was moved to Hopedale (P.A., 1931:176). In addition, during the summer of 1915, the Newfoundland government erected and maintained six lighthouses along the coast, one at Ford's Harbour (east of Nain) and three in the Hopedale area (P.A., 1915:303).

The extension of transportation and communication northwards along the coast coincided with the expansion of Newfoundland's Labrador cod fishery. Although Settlers and Inuit may have indirectly benefited from a lighthouse at Ford's Harbour or a wireless station at Dunn's Island, such facilities primarily served to coordinate the Newfoundland fishery, which by the 1930s, brought 2000 to 2,500 schooners to Labrador each summer.

In addition to annual visits by the HBC supply ship, Newfoundland fishing schooners and the government mail boat, airplane transportation made its appearance during the 1930s. Over the decades to follow, it profoundly altered life in Labrador. After Confederation, the government, IGA, and Moravian Mission made extensive use of air transportation. In 1971, Labrador Airways began a regular bi-weekly passenger service to coastal communities, which was heavily subsidized by the provincial government. Formerly, most inter-community travel occurred during summer via Canadian National coastal boats. Within the past five years, air travel has become a regular feature of Labrador life, and excepting the snowmobile, more inter-community travel is done by air than by any other means (especially since air and boat fares are comparable).

Communication

Radio and other media have enjoyed a short and rather irregular duration in northern Labrador. In the period 1950–57, the Moravian Mission operated a radio station at Nain, broadcasting religious programmes reportedly received as far as 500 miles to the south (P.A., 1951:31). In 1975, a local FM station was opened at Makkovik, broadcasting music and local information in both English and Inuttitut. Hopedale has, for several years, received regular CBC network broadcasting via telephone circuit from Goose Bay, and in autumn of 1975, a Canadian communications satellite brought CBC television coverage to Nain.

Following Confederation, 16 mm motion pictures were introduced in Nain (1950) and Hopedale (1951). About the same time, electricity, radio telephone, and monthly air service (as far north as Hopedale in 1950) began to affect life on the coast. Telephone service, for example, linked the dispersed households in communities such as Nain and Makkovik, whereas monthly air mail service accompanied and, indeed, fostered greater dependence on external sources of welfare (for example, old age pensions, family allowances) and commodities such as those acquired through mail order companies.

Newspapers from St. John's have not been regularly available in northern Labrador, but several papers have from time to time been printed on the coast. In the early 1900s the Mission in Nain printed the annual *Aglait Illunainortut* ("the paper for everybody"), which "tells the people something of the doings in other lands, and it helps to stir their loyalty as British subjects" (Hutton, 1912:339). Sixty years later, a weekly, bilingual newspaper, *kinatuinamot illegajuk* ("concerning everybody") was printed in Nain. The newspaper, originally funded as a federal LIP (Local Initiatives) project, sought to improve communication between north Labrador communities and preserve aspects of Labrador's traditional culture (*kinatuinamot illegajuk*, 1972, No. 1:10). More significantly, this paper began to be used as a political tool, allowing individuals or groups a public forum in which to espouse their views. Perusal of several issues indicates that contributors to the paper wrote *as if* their views would be read beyond the local level, that bureaucrats in St. John's would take note of north Labrador's needs as expressed in the paper.

In 1972, a bilingual quarterly, the *Labrador Moravian*, was started by the missionary in Makkovik. The magazine carries reports from the various congregations and stories from the Mission's two hundred years in Labrador. Another quarterly, *Them Days*, published by the Labrador Heritage Society, began in 1975 and concentrates on the social history of south and central Labrador Settlers, with occasional contributions by residents of the northern coast. In recent years, several 'newspapers' have originated from Happy Valley, enjoying a few months or years of publication and some circulation along the north coast; the present publication is a weekly, *The Labradorian*.

Other Agents of Change

Certain new agents of change that have affected coastal communities since Confederation are the increased numbers of 'outsiders,' such as representatives of various government programmes and special interest groups, teachers, community development officers, and researchers who are presently a more or less regular part of each community's social landscape. The social and political impact of outsiders is great and often inversely correlated with their numbers, a fact probably explained by the traditional aura surrounding outsiders in Labrador.

Traditionally, the few outsiders who came to Labrador were usually representatives of one of four categories: the Mission, Newfoundland fishermen, government officials (including the Newfoundland Rangers during the 1930s) and the IGA. The more recent influx of outsiders discussed here is linked to two main results of Confederation: (1) the increased role of both Federal and Provincial governments, which has fostered a great variety of new programmes, and (2) radically improved transportation and communication. My intention here is not to evaluate the goals or motives of recent outsiders but rather to examine the impact of their presence.

Recent years have brought an increased number of trained teachers from Newfoundland and other parts of Canada, the U.S., and England, because of centralization, increase in population, and a programme aimed at improving pupil-teacher ratios. Outside the classroom, many teachers keep to themselves, a strategy facilitated by the recent construction of modern teachers' residences at Nain, Hopedale, and Makkovik. Other teachers who have, for instance, married local residents, exert considerable influence within particular communities over a longer period of time. Individuals who correspond to this last pattern have frequently recognized and occupied economic or political niches that local Inuit or Settlers have either failed to recognize or felt unqualified for.

Northern Labrador is perhaps one of the most thoroughly researched regions within the province of Newfoundland-Labrador. Most research has been conducted by individuals in the social and physical sciences, and has probably gone largely unnoticed by local residents. Recently, more publicized research, such as that conducted for the Royal Commission on Labrador and for two native organizations (the Labrador Inuit Association and the Naskapi-Montagnais Innu Association) has elevated expectations of more local control of Labrador policy. One can only speculate as to the local effects of this work. I believe it has made Inuit and Settlers more aware of their traditional culture. In other cases, such as the Royal Commission, the apparent failure of government to implement the Report's recommendations has caused some resentment and suspicion towards researchers.

In still other cases, researchers who have studied particular aspects of the natural environment, such as the fishery, and who publicly present their findings, may be roundly criticized by local fishermen who believe that only they should be privy to such information. If public meetings are held to inform residents of the scientific facts and their implications, heated debates may develop. The credentials of the researcher may be questioned on the grounds that he or she is "not from here," or "not a fisherman," and therefore cannot possibly know what the "real facts" are. Other debates might find one group within a community (the fishermen, for example) aligning itself with a researcher (who seeks neutrality) against another group (the wage labourers, for example), whose qualifications for attending a meeting on the fishery might be questioned.

Another type of outsider is one involved with community development organizations. Of those government-sponsored community development programmes which have mushroomed in recent years, I single out two: Memorial University Extension Service (the applied branch of the province's university) and the federally-subsidized (now defunct) Company of Young Canadians (CYC). Since 1972, both organizations have filled a rather extensive niche not occupied by other government agencies in northern Labrador. Advocating "local control," both earned credibility among the people. The Extension Service has been represented by an individual who is stationed at Nain and who is responsible for initiating economic and political development along the coast between Makkovik and Nain. Work focuses primarily on advising community councils and local fishery committees. The CYC, on the other hand, was stationed in Happy Valley, and it funded small groups in coastal communities to conduct research on local development. In Makkovik, for example, the feasibility of a locally-controlled fish camp and craft centre was studied, while at Hopedale, the implications of off-shore oil were studied and a craft council organized.

The effects of such organizations on the communities are manifold. First, residents who have worked closely with either organization are today more knowledgeable about existing government programmes; indeed, some individuals have acquired the skills of 'grantsmanship.' Secondly, the popularity of both organizations has elevated the political position of those who coordinate them. This is evidenced by the fact that the former Extension Service worker at Nain was recently elected to the Provincial House of Assembly. Third, concomitant with the increased political power of those outsiders who manage these organizations, is a decline in the authority of former patrons such as the Moravian minister and the LSD depot manager. This has occasionally created open political confrontations as in Nain (Ch. 19 this vol.). Finally, such development organizations may produce factions within local communities, since the coordinators or the approval of grants are seen to favour particular individuals or groups.

Some Concluding Thoughts

Rather than trying to summarize the materials presented above, I conclude with some thoughts, albeit speculative, about the future of northern Labrador.

During the past few years, Labrador's importance within the province of Newfoundland and Canada has suddenly been elevated. Labrador's resource potential – off-shore oil and gas, minerals, and hydro-electrical power – prompt authorities to include the region in any discussion of the province's economic future. Discoveries of natural gas by Eastcan Exploration Ltd. (a French-controlled consortium) have accelerated the jurisdictional dispute over whether Ottawa or St. John's should control off-shore petroleum revenues (Scarlett, 1977).

However, the matter of whether economic benefits would fall to native Labradorians is questionable. One scheme, which has been discussed, involves piping oil ashore, requiring service centres to store and transport the oil elsewhere. The employment of north Labradorians to construct and maintain such centres appears more likely than does training them to man technologically-sophisticated off-shore production facilities. Past experience with large-scale development, particularly military-base construction, offers native Labradorians some indication of the limited role they would play in the oil industry. Residents of Labrador's coast are particularly cynical of any possible benefits from an off-shore oil industry, while fearing, much like the Banks Island Inuit described by Usher (1971), that the costs, especially environmental damage, may despoil their livelihood as fishermen and hunters.

Any possible benefits to local communities that may result from other major industrial developments during the final quarter of the 20th century are equally debatable. Environmental damage attributed to the exploitation of uranium at Elliott Lake (Ontario) casts a foreboding shadow over the Makkovik-Postville area, where uranium-mining is likely to begin in 1978. Although hydro-electrical development on the lower Churchill River may not directly affect the north coast, mineral and/or off-shore petroleum exploitation could provide the essential infrastructure (roads, airstrips, docks, and so on) to facilitate hydro-electrical development on several northern coastal rivers. Plans to study the feasibility of further hydro-electrical development in Labrador have recently been revealed (*Evening Telegram*, April 4, 1977). These studies will determine the potential of several southern and central Labrador rivers, as well as the Naskapi, Canairiktok, Ujutok, Notakwanon and Koraluk Rivers in northern Labrador.

The consequences of large-scale economic development for northern Labrador's natural and social environment are difficult to predict. Three different views are currently held by different parties. Big industry, represented by spokesmen of the proposed Brinex Uranium development state and seek to prove that industrial development is compatible with the traditional Labrador economy – in this case, that salmon fishing and uranium mining can co-exist and that technological safeguards would reduce the possibility of environmental damage. As might be expected, this position finds a ready audience among members of the business community, especially those who, though not directly involved with a particular industrial venture, stand to profit from it through secondary or service industries. The recent announcement that the Labrador North Chamber of Commerce, composed of businessmen in Happy Valley-Goose Bay, support in principle the proposed Brinex uranium mine illustrates this point (*The Labradorian*, February 24, 1977).

A second view proclaims objective 'realism' and/or neutrality. Advocates of this view (privately) acknowledge that environmental damage will result from large-scale development, but that however unfortunate such damage may be, development ("progress") is necessary if the province is to realize its economic potential. Proponents of this view, be they government civil servants or members of the scientific community, argue that the traditional lifestyle of coastal Labradorians is no longer viable and that every effort should be made to train Labradorians so that they can be absorbed into the new economy.

Most coastal Labradorians and those in sympathy with them, predict that the consequences of large-scale development will be disastrous to the natural and social environments. Though not against all development, they resent the kinds of economic development proposed for Labrador; they remain cynical of industry and government assurances that Labrador will emerge unscathed from large-scale development. They argue that with proper management and technological refinements, the harvesting of renewable resources, such as fishing, would prove a viable and efficient economic base.

Whichever of these predictions one accepts, several points are clear. Northern Labrador is destined to become an area of "internal national expansion" (cf. Sanders, 1973), a region where major resource development will certainly occur in the very near future. It is also clear that the consequences of such development *could* produce changes on a scale far greater than ever before. In opposing major industrial developments of the sort currently being proposed, coastal Labradorians – Inuit, Settlers, and Indians – face formidable adversaries, special and influential interest groups whose strategy will likely be to try to convince government that its plans are in the best interests of the province, in general, and Labrador, in particular. In their struggle to maintain and improve a unique life style, northern Labrador's population, small and culturally diverse, isolated and relatively uneducated, faces its greatest challenge since early European contact.

Without question, north Labradorians are exceedingly vulnerable in what, I've suggested, will be an era of confrontation, a struggle over the region's future. Several organizations, most of them only recently founded, will doubtless be at the forefront in future disputes over Labrador's future. Although native organizations, such as the Labrador Inuit Association and the Naskapi-Montagnais Innu Association, foster the interests of separate cultural groups, they share the belief that native people must control the land in order that its renewable resources be properly managed and that native people benefit from future development. Regional organizations, such as the Combined Community Councils of Northern Labrador and a new organization, the Labrador Resources Advisory Council, will also contribute to the dialogue on the way Labrador will be developed. The work of this latter organization is particularly encouraging, since it has effectively drawn together Labradorians from all parts of the region and presented fundamental alternatives to several proposed large-scale industrial developments (cf. LRAC: Annual Report, 1976–77).

If the next several decades are marked by confrontation, then the problem of how decisions are made about development-related issues becomes paramount. Here the responsibility of government to honour the interests of both the broader society and north Labradorians is awesome. Should government prove insensitive to the concerns of north Labradorians, then the very existence of Labrador's native peoples as distinct and relatively independent cultural groups, as well as of the region itself, will be jeopardized. On the other hand, recognition of the region's ethnohistory and its unique problems, as well as a genuine effort to work *with*, rather than *against* coastal Labradorians will be in the better interests of northern Labrador and the province as a whole.

NOTES

1   Privy Council documents, vol. 9, pp. 206–7.
2   Society for the Furtherance of the Gospel, the British Mission agency, founded in 1741, to manage the Mission's trade.
3   Between 1953 and 1963, Brinex employed 171 Labradorians in mineral exploration. Of these, 135 were from Northwest River, 14 from Postville, 11 from Nain, 9 from Makkovik, and 2 from Hopedale. (Beaven, personal communication.)
4   See Jenness, 1965:43–4; and Kleivan, 1966:146 ff. for a list of the major diseases and their demographic effects on the peoples of the coast.
5   One element of traditional Inuit cosmology emphasized that *aksarnek*, the aurora borealis, was alive and its movement was considered to be the action of spirits playing in the sky (MacGregor, 1909:220; Hawkes, 1970:153); and if *aksarnek* was red, evil or danger was imminent (MacGregor, 1909:220). An aged Nain woman, who was 22 when the epidemic occurred, today recalls that the doctor in Okak warned the people of the flu at a time when the Northern Lights were bright red (*Them Days*, 1975:56).
6   Jenness (1965:64–6) discusses these in some detail and Weil's (1971) research in Nain updates earlier studies by Stewart (1939) and Suk (1927).

References

Author's Note: To ensure bibliographic consistency despite historical changes in title, I have referred to the Annual Reports of the Labrador Services Division as the 'Division' and the Moravian Mission Periodical Accounts as 'P.A.' in the text. Complete administrative details regarding both sources are listed below.

DIVISION (Labrador Services Division)
Annual Reports, Government of Newfoundland and Labrador, St. John's, Newfoundland.
    1952–67 Division of Northern Labrador Affairs (DNLA), Department of Public Welfare.

1968–72 Northern Labrador Services Division, Department of Public Welfare.

1972–73 Northern Labrador Services Division, Department of Social Services and Rehabilitation.

1973–76 Labrador Services Division, Department of Recreation and Rehabilitation.

June 1, 1976 – present is comparable to 1973–76 Labrador Services Division, Department of Rural Development.

PERIODICAL ACCOUNTS (Moravian) 1790–1961

Periodical Accounts relating to the Mission of the Church of the United Brethren established among the Heathen 1790 (vol. 1) – 1887 (vol. 34).

Periodical Accounts relating to the Foreign Missions of the Church of the United Brethren 1887 (vol. 34) – 1889 (vol. 34).

Periodical Accounts of the Work of the Moravian Missions 1890 (vol. 1) – 1961 (vol. 169).

Viewpoint from Distant Lands, 1962 (vol. 170) – present. London.

ANDERSEN, W. A.

1975 "The Nascapi Indians of Davis Inlet." Newfoundland Wildlife Service (mimeo).

BEN-DOR, SHMUEL

1966 *Makkovik: Eskimos and Settlers in a Labrador Community*. St. John's, Institute of Social and Economic Research, Memorial University of Newfoundland.

BROX, OTTAR

1972 *Newfoundland Fishermen in the Age of Industry*. St. John's, Institute of Social and Economic Research, Memorial University of Newfoundland.

CANADA

1976 *Census of Canada. Population: Preliminary Counts*. Ottawa, Statistics Canada.

CRANZ, D.

1820 *The History of Greenland: Including the Account of the Mission Carried on by the United Brethren in that Country*. Vol. 1. London, Longman, Hurst, Rees, Orme and Brown.

CURTIS, ROGER

1774 "Particulars of the Country of Labrador," extracted from the Papers of Lieutenant Roger Curtis of His Majesty's Ship 'Otter,' with a Plane Chart of the Coast. London, *Philosophical Transactions*, 64(2):372–87.

DAVEY, J W.

1905 *The Fall of Torngak*. London, S. W. Partridge and Co.

Evening Telegram

1977 "Energy study given 1 million price tag." St. John's, Newfoundland, April 4, p. 4.

GOSLING, W. G.
1910 *Labrador: its Discovery, Exploration, and Development.* London, Alston Rivers, Ltd.

GOUDIE, ELIZABETH
1973 *Women of Labrador.* Toronto, Peter Martin Associates Ltd.

GWYN, R.
1974 *Smallwood: The Unlikely Revolutionary.* Toronto, McClelland and Stewart Ltd.

HAWKES, E. W.
1970 *The Labrador Eskimo.* New York, Johnson Reprint Corp. (orig. 1916).

HENRIKSEN, GEORG
1973 *Hunters in the Barrens: The Naskapi on the Edge of the White Man's World.* St. John's, Institute of Social and Economic Research, Memorial University of Newfoundland.

HILLER, J. K.
1966 "The Moravian Expedition to Labrador, 1752." *Newfoundland Quarterly*, 15(2):19–22.

HILLER, J. K.
1967 "The Establishment and Early Years of the Moravian Missions in Labrador, 1752–1805." Unpublished M.A. Thesis, Memorial University of Newfoundland.

HILLER, J. K.
1971a "The Moravians in Labrador, 1771–1805." *Polar Record*, 15(99): 839–54.

HILLER, J. K.
1971b "Early Patrons of the Labrador Eskimos: The Moravian Mission in Labrador, 1764–1805." In R. Paine (ed.), *Patrons and Brokers in the East Arctic.* St. John's, Institute of Social and Economic Research, Memorial University of Newfoundland

HUTTON, S. K.
1912 *Among the Eskimos of Labrador.* Toronto, Musson Book Company Ltd.

JENNESS, DIAMOND
1965 *Eskimo Administration: III. Labrador.* Montreal, Arctic Institute of North America, Technical Paper No. 16.

Kinatuinamot Illegajuk
1972 Nain, Labrador, 1(10).

KLEIVAN, H.
1966 *Eskimos of Northeast Labrador.* Oslo, Norsk Polarinstitutt.

KOHLMEISTER, B. and G. KMOCH
1814 *Journal of a Voyage from Okak on the Coast of Labrador to Ungava Bay, Westward to Cape Chudleigh.* London, W. M. McDowall.

LABRADOR RESOURCES ADVISORY COUNCIL
1976–77 "Annual Report." Labrador, Happy Valley-Goose Bay (Mimeo).
(The) Labradorian
1977 "Chamber supports Brinex." Labrador, Happy Valley-Goose Bay, 4(8).
MATHIAS, P.
1971 Forced Growth. Toronto, James Lewis and Samuel.
MACGREGOR, W.
1909 Reports of Official Visits to Labrador, 1905 and 1908. Journal of House of Assembly, St. John's, Newfoundland.
McGEE, J. T.
1961 Cultural Stability and Change among the Montagnais Indians of the Lake Melville Region of Labrador. Washington, D.C., The Catholic University of America Press.
McGHEE, R. and J. A. TUCK
1975 An Archaic Sequence from the Strait of Belle Isle, Labrador. Ottawa, National Museum of Man, Archaeological Survey of Canada, Paper No. 34.
NOEL, S. J. R.
1973 Politics in Newfoundland. Toronto, University of Toronto Press.
PEACOCK, REV. F. W.
1947 "Some Psychological Aspects of the Impact of the White Man Upon the Labrador Eskimo." Nain, Labrador (mimeo).
PRIVY COUNCIL (Great Britain) Judicial Committee
1927 London, W. Clowes and Sons, 12 volumes.
PRIVY COUNCIL No. 457
1821 "Proclamation by Governor Hamilton as to Grant to Moravians." (Boundary Documents, Vol. 3:1347; Vol. 9:206–207.)
REPORT OF THE ROYAL COMMISSION ON LABRADOR (RRCL)
1974 St. John's, Newfoundland. 6 Volumes.
SANDERS, D. E.
1973 Native People in Areas of Internal National Expansion: Indians and Inuit in Canada. Copenhagen, International Work Group for Indigenous Affairs.
SCARLETT, M.
1977 "Some Aspects of the Newfoundland Setting for Developments of Offshore Oil/Gas Resources." In M. Scarlett (ed.), Consequences of Offshore Oil and Gas – Norway, Scotland, and Newfoundland. St. John's, Institute of Social and Economic Research, Memorial University of Newfoundland.
SCHLEDERMANN, P.
1971 "The Thule Tradition in Northern Labrador." Unpublished M.A. Thesis, Memorial University of Newfoundland.

SCHLOSS, B.
1964 "The Development of Nain School: 1771–1963." Unpublished Paper, St. John's, Memorial University of Newfoundland.
SMITH, P.
1975 Brinco: The Story of Churchill Falls. Toronto, McClelland and Stewart.
STEWART, T. D.
1939 "Anthropometric Observations on the Eskimos and Indians of Labrador." Anthropological Series, 31(1). Chicago, Field Museum of Natural History.
SUK, V.
1927 "On the Occurrence of Syphillis and Tuberculosis amongst Eskimos and Mixed Breeds of the North Coast of Labrador." Brno, Publications de la Faculté Des Sciences de L'Université Masaryk, 84.
TANNER, V.
1944 "Outlines of the Geography, Life and Customs of Newfoundland-Labrador." Helsinki, ActaGeographica Fenniae, 8.
TAYLOR, J. G.
1974 Labrador Eskimo Settlements of the Early Contact Period. Ottawa, National Museum of Canada, Publications in Ethnology, No. 9.
Them Days
1975 Goose Bay, Labrador, 1(2).
USHER, P. J.
1971 The Banklanders: Economy and Ecology of a Frontier Trapping Community. Vol. 3 – the Community. Ottawa, Department of Indian Affairs and Northern Development.
WEIL, G. J.
1971 "Biological Consequences of Acculturation: A Study of the Eskimos of Northern Labrador." Unpublished B.A. Thesis, Harvard College, Cambridge, Mass.
WHITELEY, W. H.
1964 "The Establishment of the Moravian Mission in Labrador and British Policy." Canadian Historical Review, 45(1):29–50.
WILLIAMSON, H. A.
1964 "Population Movement and the Food Gathering Economy of Northern Labrador." Unpublished M.A. Thesis, McGill University, Montreal.
WILSON, E.
n.d. With the Harmony to Labrador. St. John's, Creative Printers.
ZIMMERLY, D. W.
1975 Cain's Land Revisited: Culture Change in Central Labrador, 1775–1972. St. John's, Institute of Social and Economic Research, Memorial University of Newfoundland.

Shmuel Ben-Dor

The time when race and culture could be equated in northern Labrador ended as the first whites arrived in the area. The arrival of this group is responsible for the dual nature of the present social network. Theories which favour a 'proto' state of affairs may take the liberty of reconstructing an early stage in which there were two 'pure' races in Labrador and two 'pure' cultures. It might look neat but it would amount to fiction. From the very first days of contact, there was a large amount of give-and-take in both the cultural and racial spheres.

A big part of this exchange was to be expected. The Inuit possessed a wide variety of devices, some essential and others advantageous, for survival in an arctic environment, and their worth was quickly appreciated by the Settlers; and the Settlers brought with them many elements of western society which held a universal appeal and the Inuit in turn adopted them. The sexual mores of both groups and occasional inter-marriages promoted this process and resulted in the current racial picture. The present profile of northern Labrador is by and large the result of these forms of interaction.

I shall first clarify the terms Inuit and Settler, then proceed to examine the general pattern of interaction in northern Labrador, and finally the present circumstances in Makkovik.

Inuit versus Settler Identity

The terms Inuit and Settler may lead one to assume that we are dealing with two racial groups. This is not the case. True, there are racial distinctions among the people, and one can easily point out many 'Inuit-looking' or 'white-looking' individuals. What is more, there is a high degree of proba- bility that the 'looks' will agree with the category: the 'Inuit-looking' person is very likely an Inuit and the 'white-looking' is more likely a Settler than an Inuit.[1] Still, one cannot divide the groups along racial lines because of the continual racial mixture, the ever-present exceptions, and the result- ing intermediate group (which is not acknowledged socially).

Ruling out 'looks' as a means of distinguishing between the two groups has not ended the search, however meagre the results, for noticeable visual differences. One significant difference is found in the wearing of the white silapak. The present parka in northern Labrador consists of the inner *atigik* of blanket material and the outer *silapak* of cotton. People of both groups

* Excerpted from *Makkovik: Eskimos and Settlers in a Labrador Community* (Ben-Dor, 1966); not edited. All references to *Eskimo* have been changed to *Inuit* in keeping with all the essays in this volume (ed.).

wear it, but the wearing of the festive white *silapak* is an Inuit custom not found among the Settlers. The absence of this *silapak* among the Settlers agrees with the general pattern. The Settlers use the very effective Inuit parka but they do not share the Inuit notions of 'fashion.' A white *silapak*, therefore, may indicate that a particular individual is an Inuit but not necessarily so. There are a few exceptions.

A similar story can be told about footwear. The all-important skin boot is worn by people of both groups, but the ornamented creations which are highly esteemed by an Inuk are rarely worn by a Settler.

The above criteria are impaired by the recurring exceptions. The limitations are self-explanatory. One can improve the identifying tools somewhat by combining several visual aspects. It can be safely claimed that every Inuit-looking individual, wearing white silapak and ornamented boots is an Inuk, providing you do not refer to the one exception. Here we reach the border of the absurd. It must be concluded that although there are clear correlations between racial characteristics and items of clothing on the one hand, and social grouping on the other hand, neither race nor holiday garb provide a sufficient indication of social alignment.

An examination of linguistic differences yields more fruitful results. All unilingual persons, without exception, are easily and correctly identified. Those who speak Inuit only are clearly Inuit, and those who speak only English may be accurately placed with the Settlers. The very few who are fluent in both languages can usually be categorized according to the language in which they were brought up.

If a certain degree of ambiguity and confusion is evident, it is the problem of outsiders only. Local people do not share it. They know that all Inuit-speaking people who arrived recently from the north are Inuit, but Hans A. and his family are Settlers who lived "many years" in the north. They know that Anton N. who looks white, speaks both languages fluently, and wears European-type clothes was brought up by his Inuit grandparents and is 'obviously' an Inuk. They also know that Andrew A. may appear Inuit on account of his physical features, his command of the Inuit language, and his Inuit wife, but he is not. A son of Hans and Jane is unquestionably a settler. Every individual in the village knows unambiguously where he and his neighbors stand.

Generational Mobility

A major aspect of the dual interaction demands our attention first: mobility from one group to the other. One should not assume that it is a form of 'club membership' which can be discarded or adopted at will. We refer to mobility which is possible along certain lines only – generational lines. The nature of this generational mobility, its workable rules, and its extent can be best illustrated by the following case histories.

1. An American GI, stationed near Hebron 18 years ago, was responsible for the birth of at least one individual – Elias T. Elias can in all probability credit his fair skin, his tall, slim appearance, and his curly hair to that foreign progenitor. The Inuit mother was not married at that time and her son was adopted by her parents. Elias' biological background was known to the members of the community. He frequently visited our household and Magdalena never bothered to conceal her marvel, "Just like [his] daddy ... Just like [his] daddy." Her husband, Andreas T., enjoyed teasing the fellow about his "xabluna"-like features. Both Magdalena and Andreas, like the rest of the community, had no doubt though that Elias was Inuk. When his group identity was questioned, it was the sociological parents, Elias' biological grandparents, who determined the issue.

2. Julia L. was among the last Inuit 'exceptions' in the Settler-dominated area south of Makkovik. She and a few of her relatives shared the dubious distinction of being exhibited in the World's Columbian Exposition of 1893, "They went as Inuit ... skin clothes and skin boots ... A man promised to give them a lot of money but nothing came out of it." According to some, Julia "picked up"[2] her son in Chicago, but others claim it was a conventional case involving a Newfoundland schoonerman. At any rate, Julia gave birth to an illegitimate son who, in accord with the local custom, was adopted by her parents. The Inuit identity of this child was never a problem. Some years later the grown son married a Settler girl who came from the few Settler 'exceptions' in the Inuit north. One offspring of this match, Sam L., resides presently in Makkovik and the clear division between the groups places Sam and his family with the Settlers. Sam's children do not suspect that their grandfather, were he alive, would be classed with the Inuit.

3. John P. was among the very few Settlers who lived north of the Settler domain. He lived in Hebron until the village was abandoned. During his long stay there he married a daughter of the headman and became the proud parent of nine offspring. Each person in Hebron knew that John was a Settler and his wife Inuit, and each person knew also that all nine children were Inuit. John's eldest son, who lived in Makkovik during the fall of 1962, confirmed the above classification. There was no doubt that this young man regarded himself to be an integral part of the Inuit section. His Inuit neighbors and the Settlers in the village, including a couple of his first cousins, supported this sentiment.

4. Continuity on the one hand and change of identity on the other hand are subject to certain rules. Muriel A. seems to refute our evolving formula. She is supposed to be an Inuk, but it is common knowledge that Muriel is a Settler. Special circumstances explain this. Muriel was also an offspring of a temporary union between a Newfoundland fisherman and an Inuit girl. She was adopted by her mother's parents, and since they were Inuit, Muriel started her life as an Inuk. ... [However, certain developments

changed her identity.] Muriel attended the Moravian boarding school in Makkovik which was aimed at the Settler children; that is everything was taught in English. But it had a few Inuit youngsters of whom Muriel was one. Around that time her parents-grandparents died and the young girl was 'inherited' by her biological mother. This woman was married then to a Settler and Muriel could claim a different sociological background: no longer "My Inuit parents" but "My Inuit mother and Settler father." The road to a complete identification with the Makkovik Settlers was open. Muriel eventually grew up in Makkovik as an 'authentic' Settler.

These four cases exemplify the nature of social mobility.

1. Under 'normal' conditions a child assumes the social identity of his parents.

2. Variation of the 'normal' theme is represented by case 1. This case demonstrated that cultural, rather than biological, orientation prevails. Culturally-defined parenthood, regardless of biological 'contributions,' is the only determining factor.

3. Mobility is possible. In a significant number of cases, a set of grandparents who belong to one group find their grandchildren on the other side of the line. This process involves usually a mixed marriage constituting a transition of one generation. The grandparents witness first a marriage of their offspring with a spouse of the other group. The co-partners of such union do not lose their social identity. They remain "X the Settler and Y the Inuk." Their children, however, are associated from the start with one group only. Case 2 illustrated one route of this process in which the children of a mixed marriage obtained a Settler identity. Case 3 illustrated the opposite.

4. It should not be assumed that the acquired identity is an arbitrary matter. The case histories above and the conclusions so far may induce one to believe that children of mixed marriages have the prerogative of a choice. Neither children nor parents settle this question. It is determined by the social environment.

When one reads cases 2 and 3, one notices a careful mention of geographical locations. This is a decisive factor. Mixed marriages in Settler-dominated areas gave birth to baby Settlers, while similar unions north of Nain produced 'pure' Inuit. It is not surprising if one recalls the role of the parents and the importance of social environment.

5. The parents who form the transition stage pave the way for a complete integration of their offspring into one of the groups. Two processes, similar in nature but opposite in direction, accounted for it. In the southern regions of northern Labrador the Inuit were subject to the strong Settler influence, and in the north the relatively few Settlers were influenced by the locally dominant Inuit. The Inuit-Settler couple of case 2, for instance, spoke English whereas the mixed couple of case 3 spoke Inuttitut only.

6. The social environment constitutes a major factor in this process. It

starts the process by leading the partners in an Inuit-Settler marriage in one way or the other, and it shapes the social growth of their offspring. A child of a mixed marriage knows his social identity from a very early age, and at the same time he is aware of the attitudes of 'his' people towards the other group. He quickly acquires 'facts' and learns what the expectations are. A child in a Settler area, for example, hears regularly that "Eskimos never save caplin for dog feed." He cannot but notice the element of scorn; and he, in all probability, will conform later to "save the caplin" demand. A Settler girl, on the other hand, who lives in an Inuit area is very likely to produce one or more illegitimate children before she gets married. Nature and local values combine to defeat her mother's teaching.

7. Case 4 points out that variations are possible. These variations merit acknowledgement but should not be overplayed. This case, like several others, does not represent a major deviation from the general pattern and it does not call for new conclusions. The variations are simply an adjustment to cases of death, remarriage, and other facts of life.

It is apparent that mobility procedures could have resulted in a variety of classifications corresponding to the numerous racial shades. In a society where the consciousness of group identity is strong, where each group is associated with race, and where one group looks down upon the other one, it is at times surprising that racial categories have not emerged. The vague and often inaccurate "half," "half-breed" or "half-white," which are heard occasionally, is the extent of racial distinction. The minimal interest in racial differentiation concurs with the lack of concern for detailed genealogical background.

The social structure of northern Labrador admits two groups only – the Inuit and the Settlers. One may legitimately wonder whether latent sub-groups do not occur too. It is very unlikely that a Settler with an Inuit mother, for instance, will not acquire some Inuit cultural traits. The evidence does point to an intermediate group. It is even suspected that psychologically-oriented research will reveal more than one intermediate group. Four such groups are likely to emerge along a continuum: Inuit ... Inuit-Settler ... Settler-Inuit ... Settler. This hypothesis may serve as a basis of an interesting study. It is, however, beyond the limits of our present pursuit.

The "Mixed" Category

The argument that the social structure of northern Labrador admits two groups only seems to disagree with an earlier discussion of population in Makkovik. In that chapter* we referred to Inuit, Settlers, and people of "mixed background"; and a few chapters later we acknowledge the first

---

* Ben-Dor (1966: Chapter II) (ed.).

two groups only. What looks like a discrepancy becomes clear when we turn our attention from the general pattern of interaction in Labrador to the special circumstances in Makkovik.

The mixed category is a direct outcome of the sudden shift of populations. It consists of the children of an Inuit-Settler union who came originally from the Nutak area. The children started their life in an Inuit area and no one, not even the children themselves, questioned their Inuit identity. A drastic change in the social environment took place when the people of Nutak were moved south, and several families were sent to Makkovik. The youngsters found themselves in an overwhelmingly Settler setting and the road towards Inuit identity was reversed. To complicate matters, the Hebron Inuit were resettled in Makkovik three years later, and, at least numerically, matched the Settler position in the village.

No similar experience in the past is available to throw light on future development. There are, however, reasons to assume that the new circumstances are not likely to initiate a new trend. The few individuals involved would more likely represent another variation within the limits of the already established pattern (case 4 illustrated the possibility of variations accommodating 'facts of life'). The youngsters who started life as Inuit will very likely assume a Settler identity and maintain the old system.[3] A few incidents support this hypothesis. My field notes, for example, relate one such incident which occurred during the tug-of-war between Settlers and Inuit on Easter Monday. The visiting mountie had suggested the contest and the challenge was eagerly accepted. Excitement was great and spirits heated; many people sneaked quietly into the line after the count in both sides had been completed. Willie A., one of the individuals in question, rushed and joined the settlers.

Relations Prior to Hebron Resettlement

The clear knowledge of individual status among the residents of Labrador and the strong emphasis on group identity gained momentum in Makkovik as a result of the relocation project. The two groups with the least amount of contact in northern Labrador came suddenly into direct and immediate association. The impact of this encounter can be best understood against the background of limited contact in the past.

The presence of Inuit in Labrador was, of course, a known fact to all the Settlers of Makkovik, and the various 'truths' about these Inuit played a role in local lore. Not many Settlers, however, had experienced first-hand contact with the members of the other group prior to the resettlement of Inuit in Makkovik. A few Settlers heard from their parents about one Inuit family residing in the village around the turn of the century. "They stayed only a couple of years; then they moved to Hopedale because they were the only Eskimos in the area." Other persons in the village recalled that some

Inuit lived farther south. This last pocket of Inuit families south of Makkovik is remembered mostly by their direct descendants (see cases 2 and 4 above), a relationship which is not always acknowledged. Others remembered two Inuit who lived in the village during the 1920s: "Both lived on charity. One was old Joshua. He was crippled and he got many things from the Andersens. The other was an old widow. The people called her 'Granny Harris' and the children used to get her firewood. She died around 1928."

The younger Settlers in Makkovik could not even claim the meagre experience of their parents. The origin of many Inuit elements in their culture, as well as many Inuit ancestors, sank into oblivion. The 'truths' about the Inuit were no longer supported by crippled Joshua or old Granny Harris. They were carried on through accounts by parents, anecdotes by neighbours, rumours from the north, and chance visits with relatives in mixed communities.

The information furnished by the Hebron Inuit sounds similar. The Inuit were aware of the Settlers and distinguished between Settlers and other white people. Those Inuit who travelled south came across Settlers. Direct and immediate contact, however, was minimal. Hebron survived the fall of other communities in the north and it attracted many of their residents. Inuit from Ramah, Killinek and Okkak moved gradually towards Hebron. All these communities were north of the Settler area. As a result Hebron carried for half a century the title "most northern" and its people were known as "the northerns." Their greater isolation and lesser degree of contact with Settlers and whites marked them apart from other Labrador Inuit.

Only two Settlers lived in Hebron. Both lived in the village until it closed down in 1959. This scant population was no more a representative sample of the Settlers than old Joshua and Granny Harris were of the Inuit. Both Bill M. and John P. were on their way towards becoming Inuit. According to Inuit testimony, both spoke the language fluently. "They did not talk like foreigners. They did not talk like *avanimiut*.[4] They talked like Hebron people." Both married Inuit women who did not speak any English and the children of both unions completed the mobility cycle; they were raised as Inuit (see case 3 above).

Inuit Suspicion vs. Settler Resentment

The attitudes of the Inuit to the Settler and vice versa are an integral part of the world-views and practices of each group; they are completely different. The Inuit maintain a social organization which is based on kinship ties. All individuals, both Inuit and non-Inuit, who are situated outside one's own kin group are regarded with suspicion. The Inuit, in their association with non-kin have developed certain social devices, the *atitsiak* custom for example, which make limited contacts across the lines of kin-affiliation possible. These devices, however, are limited in their application: they do not operate beyond the limited range of the Inuit section. Suspicion, without means to counteract it, characterizes the attitude of the Inuit to their Settler neighbors.

The Inuit concept of Settlers reflects this distrust. Their world-view knows three types of individuals and their corresponding groups in the immediate social environment: Inuit, white, or *xabluna*, and Settler or *xabluangayuk* which means "half-white." The "half-white" image is supported by a rich lore describing the genealogical background of individual Settlers. This information is mostly imaginary, and the factual pieces are probably due to accident rather than to actual knowledge. Their stay in Makkovik has been too short to acquaint the Inuit with Settler genealogies. The Inuit further claim that Settlers conceal their Inuit ancestry and their knowledge of the Inuit language. The second argument is incorrect but the first has a truthful basis.

The rudiments of this lore were brought with the Inuit when they moved from the north and the particulars were added locally. Their resettlement to Makkovik created a situation which all Inuit have always tried to avoid; namely, living in an unfamiliar location in the midst of strangers. The unfamiliar habitat could be explored, but because of their particular type of social organization, they reacted with suspicion to the new and unfamiliar human environment.

The Inuit came upon a mode of life which had many elements of similarity to their known life, but at the same time, it displayed many manifest and latent differences. Settlers, for example, travel every spring to the head of Makkovik Bay where they place their seal nets. They believe that the location of the nets should be free from noise: motorboats are not allowed and one must refrain from shooting. These regulations are foreign to the Inuit who prefer to use guns instead of nets and discarded the kayak in favor of powered boats. The Inuit comply with the regulations by staying away from the area but their suspicions are aroused by these restrictions of movement.

All dealings on a community level which call for combined Inuit-Settler action are also stamped with a feeling of suspicion. The introduction of electricity, for example, created a need for a village body to collect fees. The Inuit wanted electrical lights but were slow to join the project. A special meeting of Inuit men was called to discuss the matter and many speculations were raised. Several individuals thought that the new engine was owned by a Settler who tried to get the community to pay his expenses; others suspected that the Settlers who contributed labor were paid, whereas Inuit were requested to volunteer their services.

This suspicion towards outsiders is strongly ingrained in an Inuk. It has roots in early childhood when individuals are threatened with *haloraluk*, meaning in children's talk "big-hello" [which represents an English-speaking person], and it continues throughout their lifetime. It is unlikely that they will develop means to overcome these feelings well enough to deal effectively with Settlers. Their means of dealing with Inuit outsiders are not applicable to Settlers, and evolving new means requires appropriate responses by the Settlers who are not interested.

The Settler attitude toward the Inuit derives from his confidence that the Settler way of life is superior to any other form. This ethnocentric view assumes a defensive note in discussions about city life, but it finds an aggressive expression in the attitude of Inuit. The Settlers link themselves with the rest of the 'civilized world' which does not include the Inuit. Their recent encounter with the Hebron Inuit reinforced these views and every Settler can recite rapidly Inuit characteristics which support the argument:

1. Eskimos do not prepare a supply of food for the winter. Not even one Eskimo salts and saves fish for the winter.

2. Eskimos gather firewood daily. They see the woodpiles of the Settlers but they do not learn.

3. Eskimos lack the ability to deal with nets properly and they catch less seal and fish.

4. Eskimos do not take good care of their dogs. They do not stock dog feed when it is available, and in time of need, they let their dogs stray to the Settler area.

5. Eskimos beg. Whenever a Settler brings home game they come and ask for meat.

6. Eskimos do not get along with one another. They lose control of themselves when they drink and the most violent fights erupt.

Their notions of superiority are complemented by a general feeling of resentment:

1. The Eskimos brought with them their problems of law and order. Makkovik was known before as a peaceful place but now there is a need for a permanent station of the Mounted Police. The Eskimos destroyed the good reputation of Makkovik.

2. The Eskimos ruined the weekly dance. Before the Eskimos arrived, the village hall was kept clean and dances were very successful. The Eskimos came drunk to the hall, they turned the hall into a dirty place, and the Settlers no longer participate in the dances

3. The Eskimo children get more attention in school than do Settler children.

4. The Eskimos do not take part in village projects. They are asked to volunteer their services but very few turn out.

In short, the Settlers feel very strongly that Makkovik was a better place before the resettlement of the northern Eskimos.

Bilingualism

The two groups were brought together with the customary tribute to an eventual merging of the two villages "into one prosperous community." Advocates of the plan stressed the similarities of the two groups while opposing parties pointed out differences. The various bodies raised the important questions of housing, transportation, economic possibilities, and the like. The everyday tools necessary for integration played a surprisingly small role in the arguments. The lack of a common language was not seriously considered.

From the early days of contact each group acquired many words from the other. Two processes were involved. The first one was a direct linguistic give-and-take in which an idea, an activity, or an item, and the term identifying it, were borrowed from the other group. The second process was the formulation of new words describing newly-introduced traits and concepts. Both processes were one aspect of the wider cultural exchange.

Both Settlers and Inuit borrowed words from one another, but only the Inuit utilized the second process and coined new words. The Settlers, for example, borrowed the Inuit word for a dog sled, *xamotik*, but their difficulties with the voiceless dorso-velar fricative "x" resulted in the Labrador *kamotik*. The Settlers talk about *mauya* in reference to deep snow, and the construction "deep *mauya*" is heard frequently. English and Inuit words are used interchangeably to describe various types of seals, but a seal on ice is always an *utuk*. The borrowed words were incorporated into the adopting language. The consistent replacement of the sound "x" with the sound "k" is an example of a phonological change. These phonological changes are accompanied by morphological accommodations. Settlers speak of many *kamotiks* and many *utuks* and when describing visits to friends in the village, they speak about *polaking*.

The Inuit of Labrador borrowed words, not from one, but two languages – German and English. The former played an important role in the past because of German missionaries, while the latter has increased in importance and lately has come to dominate the entire area. An Inuk may speak of *kartoflak* in reference to a potato, without knowing the word's German origin. His wife may borrow a *tipatik* from a neighbor and return the teapot the next day. Both may travel to church on a *pantik*, or punt to hear the missionary's sermon discussing *gotti* and *satanik*. Outsiders who try to departmentalize the two sources may find it confusing at times. The number system is the best example:

1. Numbers one through five, *atausik, maxok, pingasut, sitamat*, and *talimat*, are usually stated in Inuttitut.

2. The clock is always read in numbers which derive directly from the German: *aynts, suay, taray, fiyera, finfi*, etc.

3. German numbers account for references to numbers six through twelve: *saksi, siba, atta, nayna, sina, aylfa* and *suvaylfa*.

4. Larger numbers, from thirteen on, are stated in English. Only older people in the village can count in German-derived numerals beyond twelve.

The Inuit, very much like the Settlers, 'corrected' the original words to suit their linguistic requirements. The examples above illustrate that both phonological and morphological changes occur; *spoylilungilanga*, for instance, is a legitimate way to declare that one is not spoiled.

The other category of new words among the Inuit may be overlooked by descriptive linguists, but historically-oriented research may find it interesting. These words, like the previous ones, refer to cultural traits which were acquired through contact, but unlike the other words, they do not make use of foreign terms. New terms, based on Inuit words, were formed. There are numerous examples. The word for fire, *ikumak*, was employed to describe the concept "hell" as a place of fire, *ikumatsuak*. Later, it was the key to a new word, *ikumatik*, denoting an electric light. Referring to plane as *tingiyuk*, mail as *axlalitsiyuk*, asking for time with *sunaliak*, and discussing a meeting in the *katimavik* (church) are only a few examples. A choice example is the word *puvichuk* which describes both the squeak of mice and the act of kissing. ...

The discussion above deals with categories of words which were acquired through contact and were 'digested' in the speech of either the English- or Inuttitut-speaking populations. In addition, the people of Labrador learned words and expressions from their neighbours which remained foreign. These words are used only in dealings with the other group. Whereas an Inuit youngster, for example, does not realize that he is using German words to reckon time, he is aware that the greeting "halo" belongs to the other group. It is used only in association with Settlers and whites. The Settler, similarly, knows that the suffix "-ay," when added to a person's name is the Inuttitut form of greeting. He also knows that "ah" is the proper response. Almost all people can exchange niceties with members of the other group, and since the arrival of the Inuit in Makkovik several individuals have advanced beyond the occasional greeting. Of the 159 Settlers in Makkovik, only 8 speak Inuttitut fluently.* The question of bilingualism among the Inuit is more complicated. It is not a question of either ... or ..., but rather of a degree of knowledge. The position of the Inuit in the midst of an overwhelming English-speaking society is responsible for a consistent pressure towards bilingualism. The final results cannot be doubted but at present, very few individuals can use English freely.

All children are taught in English in school and any bilingualism found among school children is among the Inuit youngsters. The Settler children

* Detailed discussion of bilingual persons has been excerpted here from original chapter in Ben-Dor, 1966 (ed.).

do not know more than their parents do. There is no doubt, however, that the Inuit youngsters know English better than their parents ever did.

Among the 82 Inuit who are 16 and older one finds 14 who may be described as bilingual; 13 of them are in the 16- to 25-year range. Recent events account for this number, such as the change in school language from Inuttitut to English, and the move to Makkovik where English became a 'living' language rather than a school language. Many teenagers and several persons in their early twenties know a fair amount of English.

The effects of compulsory education and the continued incentive to learn English do not encounter opposition from the older Inuit. On the contrary, a certain prestige is attached to a knowledge of both languages. The first results of all these factors can be seen among the young Inuit in the village, but bilingualism on a large scale is at least a generation away.[5] The highest degree of bilingualism is found among members of the two social minorities in the community: the children of mixed marriages and the members of the group which we named 'others.' The use of both languages among these persons is expected and does not, in fact, alter the general linguistic picture.

Eskimo-Settler Relations: 1. Children

Inuit and Settler children of pre-school age never associate with one another. The absence of a common language may not seem a serious obstacle to children of this group, but this factor is not irrelevant if one considers the role of the parents in promoting associations of this kind. The geographical separation between most of the Inuit and Settlers prevents spontaneous relationships between these young children. The only way a child can break through the geographical barrier is by accompanying a parent on his visits "across the hill." This point is well-illustrated by the Inuit children from the Hebron and Nutak ends, on the north and south sides of the Settler area respectively, who join their parents for occasional visits to the other end of the linearly-structured community. The children have no opportunity to know Settler children.

One might expect to find closer contacts among school children. Both Inuit and Settler youngsters attend the same school and, unlike the old mission school in Nain, there is no division into English- and Inuit-speaking sections. The lack of formal division does not, however, erase the clearly marked lines. In addition to the universal knowledge of one's own group, there are linguistic barriers which contribute to significant age differences between Inuit and Settler children in each of the grades. Children start school at the same age but the English-speaking group has an advantage over their Inuit peers. In the fourth grade, for example, the average age of a Settler child is eleven whereas the Inuit average is thirteen years of age. Most Inuit children do not reach the higher grades.

All school children were asked to write down the names of their friends.

Among the 78 children, only 4 Settlers and 3 Inuit had each a name of a child from the other group.[6] This tendency to befriend children of one's own group results occasionally in two antagonistic camps and may find expression in sports activities.

Eskimo-Settler Relations: II. Adults

Visits between Settlers and Inuit are rare. If we were to draw a sociometric chart illustrating informal asssociations in Makkovik as a whole, we would come upon a complex network of intertwining lines for each of the two groups and almost no lines linking one group with the other. If we were to indicate frequent and recurring contacts only, we would have on our hands two separate charts disclosing the absence of informal associations between the Inuit and the Settlers. All school children were asked to name those persons who visited their houses, and although several children wrote down more than ten names each, no Inuit child mentioned a Settler name in his list, and among the many names submitted by the Settler children, only one Inuit name appeared, the name of a woman who is married to a Settler.

A general sociometric chart would reveal a third group in the village consisting of the missionary and his family, the nurse, teachers, and administrative personnel with a similar pattern of interaction. Several members of this group may claim various degrees of association, in addition to professional contacts, with members of the Inuit and Settler sections, but the major interpersonal orientation is within the group itself.

We found a more formal expression of the everyday informal association between adult members of the community in the custom of celebrating one's birthday. Participating in a birthday gathering, unlike a visit, requires a specific invitation; and this formality, which helped us understand interpersonal relationships in each group, points out also the absence of any close contact between the two groups. The Inuit who play up their birthdays invite Inuit only, and the Settlers, whenever they celebrate a person's birthday, invite only Settlers. The few exceptions support this argument rather than refute it. The Inuit attach great importance to a person's 50th birthday. Many individuals who are not invited by the celebrating family to participate in any other birthday may be asked to take part in one of the many meals which are served on one's 50th birthday. Invitations will be extended in this manner to unrelated Inuit, one or more Settlers, the missionary and other members of the administration.

Birthdays not only demonstrate the absence of contact between Inuit and Settlers, they also clarify the different principles of association which operate in each group and which are partially responsible for the lack of social interaction. The common denominator behind the assembled people at a birthday celebration indicates that the Inuit employ kinship whereas

Settlers combine kin, age and friendship factors in forming units of association. The Inuit group is therefore closed to other persons by the nature of
the group whereas the Settler unit is more loosely organized and allows, at
least in theory, numerous extensions. The lack of a common language is a
frequent claim in the Settler's overt reluctance to admit Inuit into their
associations. The attitudes and views shared by members of each group in
regard to the other group play an undeniable role.

The patterns of fraternization, informal or formal, throw light on other
forms of association: economic cooperation and political organization. The
economic quest offers, in theory at least, the best meeting grounds for the
two groups; the economic base is identical, the resources are shared
equally, and the amount of give-and-take in this area is notably larger than
in any other realm of human behaviour. As a result, tools, equipment, and
some methods and techniques are the same, and similar values concerning
the economic sphere are found among the members of both groups. These
favourable circumstances, however, do not produce economic cooperation across ethnic lines. Each unit is made up of members of either one
group or the other. A fishing crew or a sealing team is always composed of
Inuit or Settler persons and is never a mixed group.

These observations which are founded on the structure of various
economic units are further supported by many incidents. Two such incidents will suffice to illustrate the point.

1. A few Inuit men were engaged in a seal hunt during the late fall. These
men had been away from the village for five days when they noticed
another boat at a distance. The course of the first boat was changed
immediately and a certain degree of excitement was noticeable. About
halfway, the boat was turned and assumed its original direction. When I
asked for the reason, I received a one-word reply: "xablunangayuk"
("Settlers"). The next day we encountered another boat. This time it was a
group of Inuit who had left Makkovik that day. The two teams continued to
the nearest island where the ever-present kettle was put to use, news from
the village was exchanged for information about hunting conditions, am-
munition was supplied by the new arrivals in return for promises to pay it
back, and the two groups continued the search for game together until the
next day when the first boat returned home.

2. When the weather station at Cape Harrison was abandoned by the
government, several Settler and Inuit teams left the village by boat in order
to carry home some of the available goods. The people paid little attention
to electronic apparatus, burdensome instruments, and heavy equipment;
but the lumber of buildings, barrels of kerosene, tools, and the like provided a definite attraction. When I arrived there with an Inuit team, we met
two other Inuit groups and two Settler groups on location. The formation of
two larger groups, Inuit versus Settler, took place as soon as the teams

arrived in the area. Each group formed a social and working unit. Members of each group joined together for meals, for socializing purposes in the evening and for sleeping arrangements at night. The collection of goods was an individual matter, but the individual piles were transferred to the seashore and loaded on the boats by all members of the group. This joint operation was restricted to each group and no collaboration between members of the two groups took place.

Communication barriers, different principles of association, and views shared by members of each group were cited to explain the lack of fraternization between Inuit and Settlers. The absence of economic cooperation can be attributed to the same causes with an additional stress on differences in practices in economic activities. These differences, which ought not to be overlooked because of the many similarities in this sphere, stand in the way of shared experiences. We may recall, for example, that Settlers prefer to operate from the village most of the year, and only during the summer do they move out with their families to their fishing stages. The Inuit, on the other hand, are more mobile and several times during the year, leave the community with their families and establish temporary sealing or fishing camps. Under such circumstances economic cooperation is not likely to take place.

The political structure of the community advances our understanding of the inter-relationships between Inuit and Settlers. It was pointed out that governing bodies in the village are composed of members of both groups. The elected elders, appointed chapel servants and committees for specialized purposes represent a seemingly united front, but a close examination reveals that the two groups maintain their separate identities. It was possible to compare and contrast the relatively autonomous organization of each group. The two political systems operate similarly but separately.

The same barriers which blocked fraternization explain also the division of the village into two political units. The superimposed bodies of general representation pinpoint a complementary element which, in turn, acts upon all other forms of association. This element is apparent in all dealings on the community level.

The introduction of electricity required the creation of a committee whose major function was to ensure the proper collection of monthly rates. A general meeting was called in the village hall and the assistant store manager was asked to serve as an interpreter. After a few words of explanation in English and Inuit, the people were asked first to nominate Inuit; two Inuit were elected. The meeting proceeded with the nomination and election of two Settlers. The committee was deliberately planned to include an equal representation of each group.

The election of village elders which took place in church carried a more ceremonial note, but it demonstrated similar features. The missionary conducted the proceedings and acted as an interpreter. Four elders were elected – two representing the Settlers and two representing Inuit.

These examples and similar ones exhibit an exchange between two distinct groups. The general tone of the exchange is set off by the use of an interpreter, since the alternate uses of English and Inuit bring forth the presence of two groups. The composition of the elected bodies stresses the division between the groups and reinforces the dual image. It adds a formal stamp of regularity which helps to maintain the present socio-political structure of the community.

Eskimo-Settler Relations: III. Adolescents

Adolescents are grouped structurally by the two divisions of the Moravian congregation: the "Single Brethren's Choir" and "Single Sisters' Choir." By definition, a single brother or sister is a person over thirteen years of age and not yet married. A local tradition among the Settlers of Makkovik lumps the two groups together into a "young people's" division whose younger members overlap with the oldest student body in school. The somewhat ceremonial transfer from the Children's Choir to that of the Young People, the clear and cognizant point of termination of one's membership, the assigned seats in church in front of the married people but behind the children, as well as the separate "Young People's Day" serve to mark off the adolescents in much the same way that the other groups are stamped with their distinct identities.

The similarities between the adolescent and other choirs are external only. If we attempt to find here the already familiar lack of interaction between the Inuit and Settler individuals who make up the groups, we will reach negative results. This group of no-longer-children but-not-yet-adults accounts for most of the inter-group contact which occurs in Makkovik. This contact occurs between Inuit and Settler youths of the same sex and in the associations which develop occasionally between Inuit and Settlers of the opposite sex.

However, the general picture of strict contact with members of one's own group prevails. Inuit youths usually associate with other Inuit and Settler youths tend to meet and befriend other Settlers. Detailed sociometric charts for various individuals indicate, however, that the Inuit youths form associations which do not adhere strictly to the kin principle found among their parents. Adult Inuit maintain contacts, social and economic, within the limits of their own kindreds, but their teenage children may be found with age-mates of other kindreds. These may be temporary and they may change their composition frequently compared with the long and permanent associations of their parents.

In other words, Inuit, at this stage of their lives, admit principles of association which are foreign to their parents but are common among the

Settlers. Age and friendship outweigh, in many cases, kin connections. This development is not completely identical to the Settler pattern. The association of Inuit youth across kindred lines is restricted to social contacts and is not supported by economic cooperation. An unmarried Inuk may have friends from other kindreds, but he joins his elders in the economic ventures of his kin. His Settler peer, on the other hand, can establish a social and economic unit with non-relatives which may last a lifetime.

Our data indicate that young children associate freely with their peers, but many years before they reach the stage of adolescence, they fall into the kin-oriented pattern. How can this change be explained? Inuit and Settler membership in one church group is not necessarily a means to achieve inter-group cohesion. For that matter, the whole community belongs to one church and all children and adults are members of unified choirs, but this does not promote associations between Inuit and Settler individuals. The organization of the church and its activities contribute toward segregation (by holding separate services, for example) as much as it assists and encourages intergroup solidarity.

It seems that the temporary adoption of non-kin principles among Inuit youth may be attributed to the nature of the adolescent stage which spans the gap between physical maturity and the full assumption of adult responsibilities. Adolescence is new among the Labrador Inuit and the adaptation to this stage in the life-cycle includes the admittance of new forms of association. The reasons for the development of the particular forms are, in all likelihood, multiple; but sexual exploration and the search for a permanent mate may be assumed to play an important role by opening the gate for non-kin associations.

The causal explanations are not as interesting for our purposes as the consequences. Once an Inuit youth breaks away from the barriers of kin, he may well extend his associations to include Settler friends. This is facilitated by his knowledge of English. However, it is not suggested that the lines dividing the two groups will disappear completely, as the division which characterizes the social structure of Makkovik is bound to have its affects. The actual results can be best seen in the following examples.

1. Elias T., an Inuk, and Albert F., a Settler, became very friendly during the year. They could be seen together at the movies, dances and evening walks. In the spring, however, Albert joined a Settler friend for a combined venture of seal-hunting, and in the summer he joined a fishing team headed by his older brother. Elias, on the other hand, joined his kin on their spring migration to their sealing camp and in the summer he fished with the same group.

2. Anna A., a Settler, invited both Settler and Inuit youths to her 17th birthday party. Several Inuit youths who attended the party celebrated their birthdays later during the year, but they did not reciprocate. In the

Inuit way, close relatives were invited for a midday feast, others were invited during the afternoon and evening meals, but no Settler was asked to participate.

Occasionally, an Inuk, given the permissibility of non-kin associations, will meet a Settler who waives the notions shared by the members of his group about the Inuit. A friendship may develop; Albert and Elias were such a pair. They interacted socially but they did not share experiences of an economic nature.

Anna's birthday party illustrates another weak point in Settler-Inuit associations. Anna invited several Inuit friends to participate in her birthday party. Her parents explained, "You have to be neighbourly. We do not have Inuit friends but Anna has Settler and Inuit friends and she invited all of them." The Inuit guests did not have the social means to reciprocate.

It is evident that Settlers possess the social and economic means to cement their friendships into permanent associations. The Inuit lack them. The irony of the situation is that the Settlers are reluctant to do so. The barriers mentioned in the discussion about inter-relationships between adult members of the community, and above all, their overt resentment of the Inuit, stand in the way of contacts across ethnic lines. The Inuit, on the other hand, are willing to eliminate the general feelings of suspicion through closer ties with their neighbours. But their devices of dealing with non-relatives, the "atitsiak" custom, for example, are meaningless to non-Inuit and cannot be extended to the Settlers. The results are inevitable.

The only Settler-Inuit association which may escape its usual fate is courtship, providing it terminates in marriage. Young men and women in the village share a freedom of movement and similar experiences. They promenade frequently "on the road," they attend the weekly dance, go to the movies, and meet in private homes. The home allows more opportunities to meet persons of one's own group, Inuit or Settler, but there is at least one Settler house where the two groups can mingle freely. Associations between persons of the opposite sex are common. They vary from the temporary to the permanent union, which is formalized by marriage.

The similar courtship patterns lead to Settler-Inuit associations, but the separate identity of each group does not fade. This is evident in cases of rivalry over a woman. Rivalry between two Inuit is not uncommon and it may lead to a bitter fight between the two individuals; but rivalry between an Inuk and a Settler invariably results in two antagonistic camps of males who are ready to prove their group loyalty with their fists. The real or assumed nature of each group may influence some of the contacts. I was told by one Inuk that he did not like Settler girls because they refused to have sexual intercourse, and a Settler boy informed me that it was very easy to have intercourse with an Inuit girl but objected to the common consequence of venereal disease. These objections are not apparent in practice, and ties between Inuit and Settlers of the opposite sex do occur. Marriage is the only means of establishing contact with outsiders which is meaningful to both groups. Yet, Settler-Inuit associations between people of the opposite sex have the temporary stamp which characterizes similar associations between youth of the same sex. In the majority of cases, individuals marry members of their own group, and the few attempts to do otherwise are usually blocked by the Settler side of the prospective union. The different attitudes to intermarriage magnify the stand of each group on the question of general associations across ethnic lines. Inuit not only raise no objections, but they overtly welcome the occasion. Settlers, on the other hand, manifest strong objections which prove effective. In a few cases, the pressure of the family and public opinion did not stop a Settler from marrying an Inuk. Among the residents of Makkovik, there have been seven marriages since the arrival of the first Inuk in 1956, and one of these was an Inuit-Settler union.

In conclusion, various mechanisms combine to preserve the sharp distinctions between the two segments of Makkovik: clear-cut social boundaries, the absence of a mixed social group in spite of a small number of mixed marriages, the lack of a common language, crystalized concepts held by one group about the other, and conflicting principles of social organization. The contacts between Settler and Inuit adolescents are affected by these mechanisms. Whatever their extent, such contacts cease upon marriage and the assumption of adult responsibilities.

NOTES

1   The degree of correlation between the racial group and social category is higher in Makkovik than in other communities of northern Labrador. The recent arrival of the Inuit from the 'pure' Inuit area in the north is the reason for this.
2   A local term.
3   The younger ones who were born after the move to Makkovik will, in all probability, follow their brothers and sisters on their way to Settler identity.
4   *Avanimiut* actually refers to Inuit from the north and east of Labrador (Inuit who are not *karalimiut*; i.e., Greenlanders and who are not *animiut*; i.e., Inuit of the southern regions), but it is used to describe anything which is Inuit but different; e.g., the CBC radio broadcasts in Inuit bring comments such as: ''They talk like *avanimiut*.''
5   The Alaskan example may indicate a longer period. Birket-Smith wrote in 1936 that, ''The Eskimo language will probably disappear in Alaska'' (p. 213). A quarter of a century later, however, we learn that ''... only a handful of Alaskan Eskimos continue their education beyond high school graduation, and most of these drop out after the first year. The main stumbling-block, apparently is English, for neither in the elementary schools nor even in the high schools do they acquire proficiency in the language: its analytical character, indeed, and the virtual absence of any inflections, make it unlike their own highly inflected, polysyllabic tongue that it demands from them totally different thought-sequence'' (Jenness, 1962:62–3).
6   It is interesting that two school-children of a mixed marriage wrote down Settler names only. It supports the argument that the 'mixed' category of the present is moving gradually towards a Settler identity.

References

BEN-DOR, SHMUEL
1966 *Makkovik: Eskimos and Settlers in a Labrador Community.* St. John's, Institute of Social and Economic Research, Studies No. 4, Memorial University of Newfoundland.
BIRKET-SMITH, KAJ
1936 *The Eskimos.* London, Methuen.
JENNESS, DIAMOND
1962 *Eskimo Administration: I, Alaska.* Arctic Institute of North America, Technical Paper 10.

Ethnic Values and Ethnic Recruitment in Nain*

16

Terje Brantenberg

INTRODUCTION

The focus of my two contributions to this volume is on the ethnic relations between the Inuit and white Settlers of Nain in northern Labrador. These introductory remarks should serve both essays.[1]

Generally speaking, studies of ethnic relations deal with well-defined social groupings whose boundaries are maintained by differential control over productive resources, and whose members are consequently severely restricted in their interactions with persons outside the group (Barth, 1969). Nain, however, provides quite different circumstances for the study of ethnic processes inasmuch as both Inuit and Settlers exploit the same natural resources within the same region, the adaptation being a three-fold one of fishing, hunting, and trapping. Ethnic membership does not afford differential rights to the natural resources.

Inuit and Settlers meet in public and informal settings common to all the villagers; they can often be seen chatting together on the wharf, in the stores, and on the main road in the centre of the village; Settlers often speak Inuttitut and Inuit occasionally use English. It was often pointed out to me by members of both groups how individual relations between Inuit and Settlers are generally unproblematic – indeed, that relations can be of a positive and intimate kind. At first glance, this is confirmed by the number of intermarriages (Table 1). Even the fact that a number of Inuit who are descendants of these marriages today carry 'Settler' patronyms is, in itself, of no social consequence in the village.

Historically, both groups have adopted items from the other's culture. Changes in traditional Inuit diet, for example, are an outcome of Settler influence (cf. Kleivan, 1966: 115–16); and the same is true of the transition from the indigenous plural-family sod house to the one-family house made of wood. The Settlers, in turn, have adopted Inuit items of dress such as sealskin boots and parkas, and the dog team. Today, public services, cash incomes and modern technology (gasoline- or diesel-fuelled fishing boats, snowmobiles, factory-made nets, rifles, and so forth) are common to Inuit and Settlers alike.

Yet, ethnic identity is a matter of supreme importance in Nain, and an

---

* Excerpted from an unpublished manuscript, and revised (ed.).

TABLE 1

Ethnic Composition of Marriages (ethnic status
based on self-identification).

		MEN	
		Inuit	Settler
WOMEN	Inuit	99	12
	Settler	4	10

ethnic boundary *is* maintained between Inuit and Settlers. The first questions that spring to mind then are how are ethnic differences perceived by
the people themselves? How are they maintained? When (in what contexts)
are they insisted upon?

Most obvious of all is the segregation of neighbourhoods along ethnic
lines (see Map of Nain). Contact between neighbourhoods tends to be
minimal: apart from occasional strolls and visits during the evenings and
Sundays, Settlers are not seen in the Inuit neighbourhoods.[2] Certainly the
value placed on residential segregation[3] and the attitudinal behaviour
associated with it are in sharp contrast with the informal and unprejudicial
interaction in the public places in the centre of the village. Within the
confines of his (her) home and his (her) part of the village, a Settler or Inuk
may express stereotypic ethnic prejudices when interpreting an individual's behaviour. When challenged, the speaker is likely to agree that ''some
are different; not all are like that, you know!'' Yet, it is not supposed that
his original characterization is wrong.

I begin my analysis by looking at the respective economic adaptations of
the Inuit and Settlers, turning next to the process of ethnic recruitment, and
concluding with a brief note on ethnicity and stereotyping.

CONTRASTIVE ECONOMIC ADAPTATIONS

What does it mean to be a member of an Inuit household, or of a Settler
household in Nain?

Inuit Sharing

A central value among Inuit is the sharing of goods and services – the
sharing of meat being but one expression. The importance of sharing can be
seen in the Inuit notion of ownership: the fact that property is 'private' does
not exclude others from a moral claim to sharing it; were an Inuk to insist on
the exclusive use of his snowmobile, it would initiate controversy because
the individual would, in fact, be ignoring the needs of other persons or
households. In this way, the relationship between Inuit households is

characterized by an infinite number of exchanges involving a wide variety of goods and services. These exchanges normally begin by one person asking another for something or other. The person who is approached cannot expect definite counter-prestations; however, in most cases, the stress is not upon the recipient to reciprocate in kind, but rather to respond when the giver, in his turn, asks for some kind of assistance. Thus, sharing creates a form of social capital between individuals and households.

The value of sharing serves the Inuit as a criterion for judging the social morals of others. A person is positively rewarded for displaying willingness to share his resources with members of other households. Refusal to share is interpreted as negating the crucial content of social relationships, and may have stigmatic consequences. The ethos of sharing also underlines the interdependence of the household units in a community, especially with regard to the economy or management of resources. The crucial aspect of Inuit household economics is its limited self-sufficiency and hence, limited storing. Let us examine the implications of this.

A major problem throughout the seasonal cycle is maintaining the economic viability of the household. Seasonality implies variations in the supplies of subsistence items and cash. This problem can be exacerbated by the sharing practices that decrease supplies, especially subsistence items, of an individual household more rapidly. For instance, during the season of caribou-hunting, the meat from a particular hunt may last an average family only a few weeks, since there may be a continuous demand from neighbours and relatives for pieces of it. More than half the meat may be distributed to others, whereas the same amount would last several months were it stored and kept for private use. However, a successful hunter is motivated to share his meat as security against the future and the possibility of failure on the next hunt: "We give away our meat because we too may be starving some day." (I shall discuss other functions of meat sharing, below.) Thus, to be in a position of need does not necessarily inflict stigma on an individual or household, as sharing is seen as easing need between the periods of abundance in the seasonal cycle; indeed, ability to share is rewarded with prestige. Consumption habits within individual households do not lessen the problem of continuous availability of foodstuffs. Spending tends to be ostentatious and generous, with emphasis not on budgeting, but rather on enjoying momentary affluence. Thus, spending is as erratic as the ups and down of the seasonal cycle.

One begins to see how the organization of an Inuit household's economic activities is a compromise between satisfying the needs of one's family and the rules imposed by the community. The household must engage in a continuous effort in order to keep itself in basic subsistence items. Attempts at storing goods for future use are eventually discovered and pressure will be exerted upon the household in question to share the goods. Those who appear to be ignorant of this pressure, or resist it, are sanctioned, and become peripheral members of the neighbourhood – for as long as they appear unwilling to share.

The sharing of meat is especially highly valued, and hunting therefore becomes an important means of reinforcing social relationships. Except for sporadic sales of whole carcasses of seals (with or without skins), meat is, generally speaking, not conceived as being convertible to cash. Due to the demand for meat and limited opportunities for storing, hunting is sometimes pursued in conflict with, and at the cost of, other activities such as fishing or wooding.

Sharing firewood, although it can help to enhance a person's prestige, does not have the same social value as the sharing of meat. Although both serve the material needs of households, the willingness to share wood is less; indeed, constant demands for firewood tend to be regarded as a nuisance and often the owner will ask for counter-payments in cash. However, continuous insistence on payments is frowned upon as being contradictory to the values of sharing and neighbourliness.

The households adapt to this situation by deliberately keeping their supplies of firewood low. During the winter when firewood is constantly needed, this means travelling by dog team or snowmobile from ten to thirty miles several times a week. Because of weather and other travelling conditions, the small supplies are easily exhausted, thus rendering the household dependent on assistance from other households. This is an adaptation that, in its turn, tends to reinforce sharing as a mutual necessity among households. However, it can also promote dilemmas regarding the allocation of time and labour between hunting, fishing and wooding. When the N.L.S.D. depot – in response to the great demand for firewood – started to purchase wood locally on a large scale and to sell it at the same price, several households sold so much to the depot that their own supplies ran out; they then bought some back a few days later! By this somewhat roundabout way, households were able to obtain a stable supply of wood without exposing themselves to dilemmas in sharing.

In spite of sharing practices, there are marked differences between Inuit households. Both past and present accounts of Labrador Inuit society (cf. Kleivan, 1966; Taylor, 1968) show consistent differences in material wealth and productivity between households. The two periods are dissimilar, however, in an important respect. Whereas economic success in the traditional setting was predicated on the control of the labour of an extended household, as well as on the possession of individual skills, success today is allied to the use of modern technology, such as snowmobiles, and is thus predicated on the control of one's sources of cash income and expenditure. In this way the modern setting accentuates the dilemmas entailed in Inuit household practices, as well as actual socio-economic discrepancies between households.

This is most pronounced with regard to ownership of snowmobiles. In spite of the high value placed on owning a snowmobile and the great dependence on it as a means of winter transportation, only approximately 60 percent of the Inuit households owned snowmobiles in 1969/70 (there has been a concomitant decline in the use of dog teams). There seem to be several reasons for this relatively slow adaptation to the new technology; first, the kind of economic system described above restricts access to the level of income needed to purchase and maintain a snowmobile; second, the economic interdependence of households allows for partnerships and mutual assistance through the shared use of snowmobiles. In sum, the Inuit economic system helps households to overcome economic handicaps at the same time as it maintains economic and social differences between households.

Having purchased a snowmobile, the owner is immediately pressured to share it, and hence partnerships are formed. However, from the owner's point of view, such sharing seldom extends beyond helping the owner with gasoline expenses and minor parts: the monthly payments and major repairs are usually (exceptions are within households) left to the owner alone. Partnerships also increase the wear and tear of the machine as it tends to be in constant use all winter, pulling heavy loads in all kinds of weather and snow conditions. Naturally, this results in decreasing longevity of the machine and rapidly increasing costs of maintenance. In addition, the owner usually shares the produce (meat/firewood) equally with his partner. There is little willingness to enter into co-operative ownership of snowmobiles because the prestige of owning a machine is then reduced as well as the control over the use of the machine.

In other words, while unable to face the social costs of refusing to share his machine, the owner attempts to define the partnership as much as possible. This tactic may involve, for example, refraining from telling his 'partner' whether he plans to go off on a trip or not, or leaving as early as possible in the morning. At the same time, the 'partner' may exert pressure for the use of the machine, but be reluctant to enter into a contractual partnership covering joint sharing of total expenses. As such, he is unable to control the owner's decisions and actions, but attempts to keep himself informed by paying constant calls to the home of the owner.

The form of sharing I have attempted to describe represents a focal value: it generates esteem and respect; it expresses relations of solidarity in the moral community; it also provides for a variety of economic exchanges between individuals and households. On the other hand, sharing carries potential for friction and conflict within the Inuit community (as well as between Inuit and Settlers), and I think this is reflected in the somewhat ambiguous boundaries between private and public property. Sharing may, in fact, restrict the establishment of enduring cooperative relations among units within the extended (or multi-family) households, as well as within the nuclear family (cf. Ben-Dor, 1966:64–5). The whole matter becomes particularly problematic in the present-day Inuit economy where, on the one hand, there is the moral obligation to share and, on the other, the demands of the individualized cash economy confront each individual household. At present, the opportunity to share depends upon success in the cash economy, and the notion that sharing should occur both in times of material abundance and of scarcity (Paine, 1971) is being modified. Indeed, the incentive to achieve and maintain success in the cash sphere is being increasingly contrasted with the ideal of – and social pressure towards – heeding the needs of less successful individuals and households. While the 'have-nots' tend to insist on the primacy of sharing as ideal codes of behaviour, the more well-off would tend to stress the necessity for maintaining their own individual strategies. The present situation in Nain provides opportunities not only for increasing economic differences between Eskimo households, but also opportunities for redefining values related to economic activities and allocations.

As already suggested, these contradictions in the Inuit economy tend to be expressed particularly in relations between the constituent parts of extended (multi-family) households, their continued cooperation is hampered not only by an apparent ambiguity in the household members' statuses, but also through unequal distributions of pay-offs and commitments. Parents generally appear to have limited authority and control over the economic activities and incomes of their offspring as soon as they start to earn a regular income – even before marriage. Because of the lack of clear-cut rules as to the border between private and common household resources, conflicts easily evolve between the younger and older generations and between other members in a household. Because of the opportunity to form partnerships outside the household, there is a preference for neo-local residence among newlyweds. Extended-family households thus tend to be rather brittle and of short duration.

Settler Self-sufficiency[4]

The Settlers, in direct contrast with Inuit ideal behaviour, valued self-sufficiency as a way of life, particularly when they lived in widely scattered groups in areas with limited means of communication most of the year: in order to subsist, a family had to function on its own. But even today, when the majority of Settlers have left their homesteads and moved into Nain, household autonomy is still an important value. Dependence on others is to be avoided, and sharing restricted to close relations (friends or kin). Economic assistance tends to be defined as "borrowing" and "lending." If a person borrows some basic necessities in times of need, he will expect and be expected to return the same amount of goods. Being a recipient of government social welfare is regarded as socially degrading (which it is generally not so among the Inuit) because it implies the inability of the household in question to conform to Settler mores. However, welfare is acceptable in times of economic crises, such as failure in the fisheries.

Settler notions of private property do not allow for its public use, outside of close kinsmen and friends. All households appear to own the basic capital equipment such as motor boats, snowmobiles, and/or dog teams; and for one family to own more than one boat or snowmobile is not exceptional. Saving is the underlying factor making this form of adaptation possible; and saving, of course, implies the accumulation of capital and the ability to allocate resources for future consumption. With regard to subsistence items such as meat, fish and firewood, storing (per household) is of strategic importance in the light of the seasonal availability of natural resources. Meat and fish are preserved by means of smoking, salting, or deep-freezing.

Another aspect of saving is the organization of economic activities throughout the seasonal cycle. Settlers recognize the potential conflict in the allocation of time between gathering firewood and other subsistence activities such as hunting. Thus, a household reserves wooding to otherwise slack periods of the year only, and diverts all its efforts to cash-earning activities in peak seasons. In this way, the stock of fish, meat, berries and so forth is increased, and the money saved on food purchases can be allocated to something else.

In terms of economic organization, the Settler household acts as a corporate group, with each member co-operating in carrying out the activities under paternal rule. A father exerts great pressure on his sons to become contributing members of his team, particularly in fishing where they are expected to take on the role of sharemen. In some cases, a Settler father would equip his sons – when they became old enough to work with him – with their own dog teams, kamotik and boat. But all shares remain in one household. Normally, sons are never given their full share before they marry, and until that time the father has full control of the expenses and income. This state of affairs is becoming modified as Settler sons acquire various paid jobs, sometimes outside the community; but if they continue to live with their parents, the father still exerts control over their wages.

The corporate character of the Settler household is also reflected in the management of the family estate. Continuity in the household cycle was maintained in most cases by the practice of allowing the last son to marry to inherit the parental homestead (house, fishing berths, trap lines, and other equipment). In return, this son took care of the parents in their old age. Thus, there was statistical tendency towards *ultimogeniture*. However, when there were several unmarried adult brothers at the time of the father's death, the oldest would assume the parental management of joint incomes and expenses. In this way adult offspring were given an opportunity to be part of a household economy outside of marriage. In Nain there were no cases of bachelors or spinsters establishing separate residences (although there were a few in Makkovik).

The household, then, is the only unit in which allocation of goods occurs. By this means, Settlers can achieve economic success, and in times of high prices, even wealth. Those households which acquire costly capital equipment, such as cod traps and seal nets, are able to augment their income in good seasons. Settlers generally have been able to operate without either credit from the store or relief from the government.

Summary

The preceding observations indicate that different values produced contrastive economic adaptations within the same ecologic niche. These differences are reflected in the household organization and in strategies of production and consumption. In addition, the effect that cultural values have on each group's adaptation clearly shows up in their respective responses to such technological innovations as the snowmobile.

The differences in the socio-economic systems are also reflected in the respective relationships with trading agencies. Inuit often have a low credit rating because of the 'down' periods in their productive cycle; the problem of debt and credit regulations thus results in conflicts with these agencies. The Settlers, on the other hand, do not have the same problem and they have not actively supported the Inuit in their confrontations with the trading agencies.

The contrastive values of sharing versus self-sufficiency have become identification marks of Inuit and Settler ways of life, respectively, and so provide members of each ethnic group with a basis for comparison and judgement of others. For Inuit, sharing generates social esteem and credit, whereas Settler insistence on the private use of one's assets is regarded as stinginess. For the Settler, however, self-sufficiency is both a moral value and an economic and social necessity; they regard dependence on others for material support as laziness. As they are unwilling to ask for anything (or to ask for the return of something), when they do give away some meat or firewood, they complain that "Eskimos never give anything back!"[5]

LANGUAGE AND MARRIAGE

The differences in ethnicity are, however, not as clear-cut in matters of language and marriage. Language is the obvious identification mark of ethnic status insofar as Inutittut-speakers are Inuit and the Settlers speak English. But what of bilingualism and the sixteen families of Inuit-Settler marriage? Do these persons constitute a third category of 'mixed' ethnicity? And how do the people of Nain identify individuals whose descent indicates membership in one ethnic group but who use the language of the other group?

It is necessary to know, first of all, something about the changing historical circumstances of marriage and language patterns in Nain. The two crucial facts concerning the traditional circumstances of the Inuit population were these: (i) it always outnumbered the Settler population, and (ii) from 1791 to 1949, instruction was given exclusively in the Inuit language at the Moravian mission school. Among the implications of these circumstances for the Settlers have been (i) marriage to Inuit women, (ii) a need to be bilingual, and (iii) a need to distinguish their group identity from that of the Inuit (cf. Kleivan, 1966:100–103). The maintenance of Settler culture under such circumstances has depended upon striking a balance between these factors. For example, to counter the inevitability of marriage with Inuit, Settlers have resorted to ethnic endogamy, and this has meant first- and second-cousin marriages, and marriages with Settlers from other areas of Labrador.

But 1949, the year that Newfoundland became a province of Canada, was a watershed in the affairs of the people of Nain. First of all, Labrador came under the administration of the Newfoundland government, and this brought an influx of white officials, teachers, and medical staff. Ethnic segregation was discontinued in the schools and English became the language of instruction for all children. In sum, Nain was opened up to the outside world and especially to Euro-Canadian influences.

Today, besides the Settlers, there is a small resident population of white professional people and their families. Of no less significance, however, is the drain of Settler women from Nain during the past two or three decades: they have left Nain (an easier feat now) to marry Settlers or other whites in and outside Labrador, resulting in a severe shortage of eligible women. At the time of fieldwork there were only two bachelors under thirty years of age from the larger Inuit population in comparison to eight Settlers under thirty (and Settlers value marriage as much as the Inuit).

From this perspective, then, one sees how the notable frequency of Inuit-Settler marriages presented in Table 1, far from being an index of unproblematic Inuit-Settler relations, is an index of a problem from the Settler's point of view. In diachronic perspective, however, the increasing inclusion of Nain in the Euro-Canadian world now presents the Inuit population and culture of Labrador with some of the problems that the Settlers grappled with historically (and still do). In what follows, particular attention is paid to bilingualism and 'mixed' marriages in the process of ethnic recruitment in contemporary Nain.

Distribution of Language Skills

Our concern with the cultural context of language in Nain, forces attention upon the nature of the differences between language *skill* and actual *per-*

TABLE 2

Distribution of Language Skills among Households of Inuit-Inuit, Inuit-Settler and Settler-Settler Marriages. (Nain, 1971)

	Household Members of							
	Inuit-Inuit Marriages		Inuit-Settler Marriages		Settler-Settler Marriages		Total	
Language Skills								
Inuttitut only	214	45%	3	3%	—	—	217	34%
English only	—	—	42	45%	40	53%	82	13%
Bilingual	260	55%	49	52%	35	47%	344	53%
Total	474	100%	94	100%	75	100%	643	100%

TABLE 3

Language Skill According to Age among Inuit and Settlers, Excluding Inuit-Settler Households. (Nain, 1970)

	Settlers (of Settler-Settler Households)					
Age Category	English Only		Bilingual		Total	
3–30	30	99%	3	1%	33	(44%)
≦31	10	24%	32	76%	42	(56%)
Total	40	(53%)	35	(47%)	75	(100%)

	Inuit (of Inuit-Inuit Households)					
Age Category	Inuttitut Only		Bilingual		Total	
3–30	96	32%	206	68%	302	(64%)
≦31	118	69%	54	31%	172	(36%)
Total	214	(45%)	260	(55%)	474	(100%)

formance. The occurrence of bilingualism, for instance, appears to be highly contextual, depending on the status of the persons, their audience and the topic under discussion; even the *learning* of the second language – which might be assumed to be within the provenance of skill – is seriously affected by situational contexts.

Tables 2, 3, and 4 show the distribution of language skills, and are compared with language performance in Tables 5 and 6. An initial problem one faces here is the definition of "bilingual"; in the cultural situation of Nain, at least, it seems appropriate to make an operational definition based on minimal requirements (of both skill and performance). Accordingly, the category "bilingual" refers to persons possessing an elementary skill in the second language (English or Eskimo), sufficient for conversing on common local themes.

TABLE 4

Language Skill of Spouses in Inuit-Settler Marriages. (Nain, 1970)

	Language Skills			
	Inuttitut	Bilingual	English	Total
Inuit women married to Settlers	3	9		12
Inuit men married to Settlers		4		4
Settler women married to Inuit		9	3	12
Settler men married to Inuit		4		4
Total	3	26	3	32
	9%	81%	9%	99%

Table 2 shows that approximately half the population of Nain[6] is bilingual (as just defined), and there is little variation in bilingualism between the three categories of households that are otherwise distinguishable according to the ethnicity of the spouses at birth. Table 3 provides a breakdown in the ages of the population and thus reflects the post-1949 changes in the linguistic circumstances of Nain. Omitting the Inuit-Settler households, one finds a dramatic difference in the distribution of language skills between the younger and older generations among both the Settlers and the Inuit: whereas the Settlers are rapidly losing their bilingualism, the Inuit, almost as rapidly, are becoming increasingly bilingual.

'Mixed' marriages

Turning now to Inuit-Settler marriages, it is necessary to separate the data generationally here also, and the distinction between linguistic skill and performance proves to be particularly important.

Among the 32 spouses in this category of marriage (Table 4), bilingual skills are appreciably higher than those in the aggregate figures of Table 2: no less than 26, or about 80 percent, are able to communicate with his/her partner in his/her 'first' language. Of the 6 persons found to lack this skill, 4 were between 41–50 years old and all of them were women (3 Eskimo and 1 Settler).

TABLE 5

Language Skill and Performance among Inuit-Settler Couples. (Nain, 1970)

	Inuttitut Only	Bilingual	English Only	Totals
Skill	3	10	3	16
		(2) 1 (2)		
Performance	5	(6)	5	16
		1		
		6		

But what of actual bilingual performance? Here I turn to data collected within the fairly intimate settings of individual households: these show performance trailing behind skill. There are two different processes at work here. The first is a simple one of adjustment that takes account of the relative language skill of each partner, but the second is that of cultural selection whereby one of the languages is down-played. As shown in Table 5, although ten couples share the skill of bilingualism, only six perform bilingually in a domestic context. The language situation of these six couples suggests a plural type of relationship of this kind:

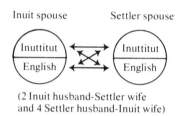

(2 Inuit husband-Settler wife
and 4 Settler husband-Inuit wife)

The remaining four couples with bilingual skill appear to choose only one language among themselves, although they may use their bilingual capacity in other social and cultural contexts. Inuttitut and English are separately chosen in two cases each:

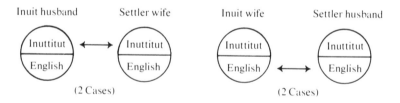

Also, in those marriages where one of the spouses appears to lack requisite skills for bilingualism, there is an equal distribution with respect to Inuit versus English cases and sex.

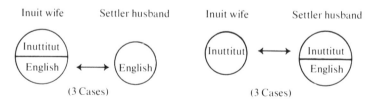

It should be noted that there is no evidence to suggest that these relation-

TABLE 6
Language Performance of Inuit-Settler Parents and their Offspring

Language	Language Performance of Parents	Language Performance of Offspring (per sibling group)
Inuttitut only	5	(4) 0
		(1)
Bilingual	5	(2) 6
		(3)
English only	4	(4) 8
	14 couples	14 sibling groups

ships are in the first stage of a process towards mutual bilingualism: three of the marriages are over twenty-years-old.

Offspring of 'Mixed' Marriages

A priori, the offspring of Inuit-Settler marriages, particularly in the six bilingual homes, exercise a choice over language, and in this way also indicate an ethnic commitment of their choosing. The next table sets forth the empirical relation between the language performance of these parents and that of their children. Of the 16 'mixed' marriages, 2 (1 bilingual couple and 1 'English only' couple) are without children of over 3 years of age; thus the table considers 14 couples and their offspring (a total of 62 over the age of 3 years).

One is struck by the fact that none of the groups of offspring speak only Inuttitut outside the school. Instead, usage is increasing in (a) 'English only' and (b) bilingual performances. It is safe to say that the English-language school exercises a strong influence, and in some instances even preempts any choice for the children: not only might the school influence which language they will use in the home, but it is also likely, in such cases, to influence their 'choice' of ethnic status as adults. Notice should also be taken of the roles parents play here: a Settler parent who speaks Inuttitut to his/her spouse might speak English to the children; other parents, however, may be helpless in this matter and their children left deeply affected by the cultural contrast between home and school (and the outside world).

However, there are six households in which parents and offspring all use Inuttitut and English interchangeably. It is true that the parents' culturally pluralistic outlook can make it difficult for the children to know how they should present themselves, or how they will be received by others according to ethnic criteria. Yet there is little ambiguity among them. Their behaviour sometimes shows a lack of specific commitments to an ethnic identity, but more noticeable is the tendency for *individual* expressions of ethnicity. Thus, one finds offspring from the *same* 'pluralistic' household stressing different aspects of their ethnic background: attitude towards traditional Inuit diet is a good example, as well as bilingual performance (perceptual as well as practical).

To answer the question posed previously, there is no indication of the existence or emergence of a socially-relevant third ('mixed') ethnic category in Nain.[7] Nor does this state of affairs appear to blur or neutralize the already-existing ethnic categories of Inuit and Settler. The marriages of the offspring of mixed marriages (historical data) support this point: marriage to an Inuk strengthens Inuit roles and commitment, and the status of *their* offspring will be unequivocally Inuit. (The complementary process occurs in marriages to a Settler or another white spouse.) Thus, the offspring of mixed parentage are usually quickly (within one or, at the most, two generations) re-distributed on either side of the traditional ethnic border.

In the past, the tendency to identify with the Inuit group predominated as a consequence of the numerical and cultural dominance of the Inuit. Persons of mixed parentage were likely to consolidate their Inuit identity by marrying an Inuk. But this process has slowed down and our tables indicate how its reversal is a possibility in the near future.

Little attention is paid to a person's ethnicity in terms of his 'descent'; particularly noteworthy is that common Inuit-Settler descent from generations back receives little social recognition. At the same time, each person's ethnic identity is public knowledge within the community, and should he(she) marry across ethnic lines, his behaviour continues to be interpreted, and judged, according to the canons of that identity.

Similarly, an Inuit-Settler marriage is unlikely to imply the dropping of the social network of one or other of the spouses, although there is much variance in the handling of this matter. In some instances, the spouses maintain ethno-specific social networks and there is little visiting between a spouse and his(her) in-laws; but there are also cases where the social networks of Inuit and Settler spouses overlap, where there is inter-ethnic visiting, and sometimes even partnerships in fishing and hunting.

In sum, language performance is both a criterion of ethnic status in Nain, and the means by which offspring of mixed marriages are able to make ethnic 'commitments' and affirm an identity. Language performance cannot be safely predicted either on the basis of the individual's language skills or on the basis of the parents' language performance, and siblings may make different commitments.

ETHNICITY AND STEREOTYPING

Both Inuit and Settlers fish, hunt, take odd jobs, have permanent jobs; both groups value a person who can catch a good supply of fish or who is a good shot with a rifle or who is clever at fixing engines, and so on. Yet as shown, there are important differences in values that result in contrastive house-hold management. Such differences become identified with ethnic stereotypes, thereby gaining additional significance.

Indeed, there seems to be no limit to the interpretation of behaviour in terms of ethnic categorizations – both of what 'we' are and 'they' are not. Inuit, for example, brag about their skill in walking on new ice, whereas the Settlers are proud of the care they take in preparing their fishing gear for use in the open water (they may forego the spring seal hunt in order to get their gear ready on time). Inuit skill in seal hunting, from which they draw prestige among themselves, as well as material rewards, on the first thin ice immediately after freeze-up is used by Settlers to confirm their view that Inuit are reckless and irresponsible. Similarly, the Settlers' refusal to participate in this early seal hunt confirms the Inuit views of their superior hunting skills and the Settlers' lack of daring. In this way, assertions about performance are transformed into other assertions about ethnic identity; and the local adaptations – despite the similarities betweem them – are found to provide a rich reservoir for the expression of contrastive iden-tities.

The situation with respect to food is worth special mention. In many ways the two groups share the same tastes and subsist on a similar diet; yet such differences as there are, are held as symbolic of ethnicity. Both Inuit and Settlers value fresh meat and fish as well as store food, and both groups generally boil or fry their food; however, the Inuit also value traditional foods such as raw, frozen, and old meat and fish. They associate these foods with their identity, and one reason for defining Settlers negatively is precisely because they do not eat, and do not value these foods. For the Inuit, these foods are good for one's health; for the Settlers, they endanger health – besides not tasting good.

Such stereotyping, as a group phenomenon, helps maintain ethnic boundaries. However, at the individual level of behaviour, the efficacy of stereotyping is much less; some Settlers adopt Inuit seal-hunting practices, and some Inuit have adopted activities that are part of Settler self-identity. Indeed, the notion of ethnic boundary itself pertains to the group dimension of ethnicity: that individuals may cross such a boundary is evidenced by the data on marriages in Nain; that individuals may be exempted from the pejorative labels that are attached to their group is evidenced by the unprejudicial interaction in certain parts of the village of Nain, and by the frequent comment ''... not all (of them) are like that, you know.''

This state of affairs helps explain the absence of an intermediate group between the Inuit and Settlers: persons are allowed to 'move' through the ethnic boundaries, only to end up at one or the other of these symbolically entrenched positions. This is so with respect to 'job' performance, but complications set in when it comes to language. Whereas it is 'separateness' that is stressed in stereotyping work performance, language performance provides opportunities for positive or integrative interaction between persons associated with each ethnic group. Although bilingualism has no necessary implication for job performance, it is the common means by which persons following different economic adaptations can have social relations. Thus, bilingualism is an important resource in the community: contrastive identities can be played down or considered contextually irrelevant.

However, language in Nain, and more precisely, bilingual skill has its own potential for generating confrontations along ethnic lines. The Settler who replies in Inuttitut when addressed in that language will be favourably judged, but the Settler who does not do so will be criticized and held in some suspicion by the Inuit. Settlers have reasons for not exercising their bilingual skills: some are reluctant to use Inuttitut in formal and public contexts because they are afraid that their lack of fluency may trigger ridicule from the Inuit public. But the Inuit interpret this reluctance negatively and criticize Settlers for their lack of participation in such meetings. Then the Settlers themselves are quite likely to re-construct the situation and say that as Settlers, the matters under discussion are of no interest to them.

Note should be taken here of the implications of the increasing use of English in community life. Although the ability to speak English is valued by them as a means of monitoring relations between Nain and the outside world, the older Inuit leaders are not only frustrated at not being able to speak English proficiently, but they also feel that their children's competence is a threat to what they define as the essence of being Inuit.

But can intermarriage and bilingualism be expected to annul or reduce the relevancy of ethnic categorizations? According to my data, no such conclusion would be warranted. Instead, the data suggest that there is increasing diversity of linguistic performances in accord with increasing diversity of linguistic contexts, and this, in itself, is one implication of the new inroads of English into community life in Nain. Particularly noteworthy is that intermarriage and bilingualism – in a situation of ethnic dichotomization such as prevails in Nain – seem to allow people who score 'low' on the cultural criteria of their natal group to become associated with the other contrastive group. Thus, a Settler who is judged negatively by other Settlers may find his failings (as perceived by the Settler group) assessed more positively or sympathetically by the Inuit community; a typical example would be a Settler who is characterized as "lazy" by other Settlers and who has an Inuk wife who appears not to be willing to share Settler values. This man is likely to experience a slow but unmistakable decline in his relations with other Settlers who, for their part, increasingly assess his performance as "Eskimo"; indeed, this judgement is likely (partly through a self-fulfilling process) to be increasingly validated as the man moves nearer to the Inuit community and its ways. This process can also be reversed. But we should be careful not to infer too much about ethnic mobility on this basis: to change one's ethnic identity (that is, to have such a change accepted by the community) is difficult, not easy; and unusual, not common.

However, the process just described – more a matter of shift in ethnic performance – is likely to be fulfilled in the next generation; in other words, it is one of the processes whereby each generation of offspring are afforded a relatively unambiguous ethnic identity, even if their parents' identity had been ambiguous.

Nevertheless, there is also evidence that a sense of ambiguity has long been present in Nain, and precisely in connection with the position in which young people of 'mixed' descent find themselves. The absence of any overarching system based on ethnic *stratification* is probably a factor of considerable significance here. Such stratification would have provided mechanisms and incentives for *unidirectional* recruitment and assimilation; as it is, the incentives are 'bilateral' and young people in Nain are quite likely to experience pulls and pushes from both directions. Accordingly, some individuals try to find a solution to their predicament by means of a strategy of 'implications' or ethnic 'tact,' in which demonstrable commitment to one group or another is kept to a minimum. What is surprising about Nain, then, is that the extent of ambiguity in individuals is not greater than it is. After all, the majority of Settlers are, in varying degrees, of mixed descent, as are many of the Inuit.

It is noteworthy that there is little evidence (except by transient whites) of the use of labels such as "half-breed" or "Metis." The nearest that this is approached in Nain is in the Inuit term for Settler: *kablunangajok*, "imitation white man." At one level, the implication is that Settler behaviour falls short according to both white and Inuit criteria. But at another level, the term has a *double-entendre* that encapsulates a way of life as well as the fact of mixed descent: "Settlers are *like* white people but they *do* have an Inuit background."

NOTES

1 At the time of fieldwork (1969–71) there were approximately 90 Inuit households, 12 Settler households, and 13 others with persons of mixed Inuit-Settler origin; there is also a small group of mostly transient Euro-Canadians whose role in Inuit-Settler relations is the topic in my other essay in this volume.
2 The Settler neighbourhood includes the school, hospital, R.C.M.P. headquarters, and the homes of the transient Euro-Canadian group; the Moravian church is in the centre of the village (along with the stores, fish plant, etc.).
3 There is evidence that this is a value, at least among the Settlers: because of land shortage and government housing projects, the segregated pattern has been disturbed a little and Inuit

households are now found in the traditional Settler/white part of the village; however, Settlers still appear to wish to remain segregated from the Inuit and there are cases of Settlers refusing government housing as this would mean moving into an Inuit neighbourhood.
4   The Settlers are a more heterogeneous group, economically and socially, than are the Inuit in Nain, and my remarks about them here, as a group, are necessarily generalized.
5   In fact, exchange practices among Inuit of Labrador, noted by Ben-Dor in Makkovik (1966:52–3), distinguish between *pitusak*, a prestation to be returned as soon as possible, and *tautilitsak*, to be returned when the recipient is able.
6   Children of three years and under are excluded from the tables, as is the white, non-Settler population.
7   Nor has there been in the past; Ben-Dor makes the same point for Makkovik.

References

BARTH, FREDRIK
1969 *Ethnic Groups and Boundaries*. Boston, Little, Brown and Company.
BEN-DOR, SHMUEL
1966 *Makkovik: Eskimos and Settlers in a Labrador Community*. St. John's, Institute of Social and Economic Research, Memorial University of Newfoundland.
KLEIVAN, HELGE
1966 *The Eskimos of Northeast Labrador. A History of Eskimo-White Relations 1771–1955*. Oslo, Norsk Polarinstitutt.
PAINE, ROBERT
1971 "A Theory of Patronage and Brokerage." In R. Paine (ed.), *Patrons and Brokers in the East Arctic*. St. John's, Institute of Social and Economic Research, Memorial University of Newfoundland.
TAYLOR, J. G.
1968 "An Analysis of the Size of Eskimo Settlements on the Coast of Labrador During the Early Contact Period." Unpublished Ph.D. thesis, University of Toronto.

The Marginal School and the Children of Nain

Anne Brantenberg

17

Introduction

This essay is concerned with educational policy and the problems arising from the divergent roles expected of the child in the home and at school, as observed in Nain, Labrador, in the period 1969–71. In underdeveloped countries and remote areas, the home and school represent two "worlds" with "separate ways of entrance" to adulthood (Wax, *et al.*, 1964; Hobart and Brant, 1966; Hoem, 1965, 1968; Nyerere, 1968). I shall attempt to show how this is the case in Nain.

In Nain, socialization in the home is informal and aims at producing an adult who can utilize the local natural resources; this process is common to both Inuit and Settler cultures (see Ch. 16, this vol.). Parental views on education and the resulting decisions are determined by the family's economic adaptation – whether it be in the traditional hunting/fishing economy or in the wage-earning market economy. These factors, together with its ethnic status, influence the child's interpretation of the pupil role, and his success or failure in playing it.

Socialization in the school, on the other hand, is comparatively formal, and the present teachers attempt to instill values and goals that belong to an urban, middle-class, southern Canada. A child growing up in a familial environment learns from its parents, helps them, and co-operates with them; a pupil in school learns from the teacher and accepts the values and premises the teacher puts forward, particularly those that refer to the pupil's future prospects as a member of society. Compulsory schooling demands that a child combine the role of family member with that of pupil; yet each role is defined differently by the two ethnic groups and even by individuals of the same ethnic group whose family circumstances vary.

In this essay, I shall discuss role definitions formed and acted upon by both parents and teachers, together with current and future consequences for the child. The question of the compatibility of the two roles is considered: is it possible for a child to fulfil parental expectations and play a satisfactory part in the family's daily life, and at the same time, be a successful member of the very different school environment? If the roles are compatible during childhood, will the child be able to mature satisfactorily and take its place in society for which the dual role has prepared him or her, if indeed such a place exists?

Education in Nain underwent a change in 1950 when the Government of

Newfoundland took over the responsibility from the Moravian Mission. Although the school was never an integral part of the community, school records and teachers' attitudes imply that the government school is more alien than its predecessor. Let us compare the Moravian school with the Canadian school.

Education in the Mission Period

Until 1950, Inuit and Settler children were taught by Moravian missionaries. Each group was taught in its own language, but in other respects the school curriculum was identical for both groups. School terms were short, discipline strict, and the curriculum consisted of little more than the 'three R's' and religious instruction. The primary aim of the school was to enable the children to participate in the social and religious activities of their own community and to provide them with a measure of competence for their limited economic dealings with the 'white world.' The Moravians felt, however, that their main duty was to educate the Inuit, and Settlers have implied that the teachers were more interested in the Inuit children and geared their teaching accordingly. The emphasis was on preparing children to take their place in the community, continuing in the traditional occupations of hunting and fishing, with a few religious offices providing the sole alternative. School terms were short so that pupils were able to participate in the hunting/fishing activities of their families throughout the yearly cycle. The Moravians, in fact, endeavoured to keep other whites out of the area, discouraged the Inuit from going south for more education, and punished Inuit caught speaking English.

The missionaries followed a policy of preserving Inuit (albeit Moravian-tinged) culture, and positively reinforced those Inuit practices that were compatible with Moravian Christianity. This was particularly true in the boarding schools where the children were fed local food, wore their hair in what the Moravians considered Inuit style, and were frequently dressed in skin clothing. Although the Settler children were taught in English, the Inuit were in the majority, and theirs was the language most frequently used out of class. Some Settlers claim to have learned Inuttitut from social interaction at school. Moravian institutions had a greater impact upon the Inuit than upon the Settlers, partly because the Inuit lived close together (in Nain) and the mission was centered in their community, and partly because the missionaries were dedicated to working among Inuit. The Mission monopolized education, religious instruction, and for a period, trade and health services, and thus earned the gratitude of the Inuit who began to feel somewhat dependent upon the mission. Positions of status created by the Mission, such as elders, or church wardens, were awarded exclusively to Inuit. For these reasons Inuit parents began to co-operate with the Moravian elders in matters of discipline, sanctioning, for example, unmarried people who did not return home before the 9 p.m. church bell; Inuit parents began to use corporal punishment in the home also.[1]

The independent and more scattered Settlers were, however, more reluctant to send their children to a school favouring Inuit. Whereas the Inuit in Nain have been literate since the 1840s (Kleivan, 1964:80), Settler children did not begin to attend school until 1919, and thereafter, the difficulty of getting young Settlers to attend school in Nain has been a recurring theme in the school records (Kleivan, *op. cit.*:104). The Settlers, most of whom originated in Norway or England, lived on homesteads outside Nain, and maintained much of their original way of life, placing great emphasis on the Protestant ethic of self-sufficiency and thrift (see T. Brantenberg, ch. 16). This independence, together with the isolation of most Settler households, meant that the parents were the main socializing influence on the children. Even today, children in a Settler home are more strictly brought up than their Inuit contemporaries, and they are reared in a hierarchical atmosphere where the authority of father and elder brothers is unquestioned.

By virtue of its monopoly, the Mission in Nain became a patron to its wards. (Hiller, 1971). The boarding school became, in many respects, an arena for the execution of this patronage, and for Inuit dominance in the community. The values taught by the missionaries were accepted for the most part, at least by the Inuit parents, so that the time spent socializing the children in school was not incompatible with their role in the family. Inuit children encountered no problems fitting into their own communities after they left school. Settler children, who had felt discriminated against at school, on the other hand, were sometimes able to move out of the area to look for work; in all likelihood they had relatives along the Labrador coast who helped them become established.

Education in the Contemporary Situation

The new government school is based on the melting-pot concept: all pupils' efforts and achievements are meant to bring them nearer the goal of becoming good Canadian citizens, and each grade from kindergarten up is a stepping-stone towards further education and the ultimate goal of a career in the national society. The school can be said to be based on the *vacuum* and *tabula rasa* assumptions (Wax, *et al.*, *op. cit.*), according to which children come to school as empty vessels to be filled with knowledge. No consideration is given to the cultural background or language of children from minority groups, the curriculum being designed for the norm: an idealized Canada where English, and sometimes French, are the only languages spoken, and the Protestant work ethic reigns supreme.

The school is under the provincial jurisdiction of the Department of Education in St. John's, Newfoundland and the Labrador East Integrated

TABLE 1a

Nain Pupils During the School-year 1970/71, according to Grade and Age

Age \ Grade	KG[1]	1	2	3	4	5	6	7	8	OC[2]	Total
5	11										11
6	14	7									21
7	2	9	10								21
8	1	9	12	2							24
9		1	3	7	1	1				1	15
10			4	9	8	3					24
11			1	3	4	5	2			3	18
12					6	5	6			2	19
13					3	2	4	3	1	3	16
14						4	3	6	2	1	16
15						1	1	3	1	3	9
Total	29	26	30	21	23	21	15	12	4	13	194[3]
No. of teachers	1		1	1	1	1	1	1		1	8

TABLE 1b

Average Age of Nain Pupils, according to Ethnic Status and Grade

Ethnic Status \ Grade	KG[1]	1	2	3	4	5	6	7	8
Settler/"mixed"	5	6	8	9	10	11	12	14	13
Inuit	6	8	8	10	11	12	13	14	15

Notes: 1 KG = Kindergarten
2 OC = Opportunity Class
3 104 boys, 90 girls

School Board in Happy Valley, Labrador. The local school committee has no say in matters concerning the curriculum, and there is no Parent-Teacher Association (PTA) in Nain. The Moravian mission retains some control over educational policies by virtue of its ownership and management of the boarding school and its position on the school board, a situation which is not common in Canada, but which is possible in Newfoundland because of the denominational school system in this province.

TABLE 2

Days Absent among Nain Pupils during School Year 1970–71, according to Grade and Reasons Given.

Causes / Grades	illness	unexcused	home-help	distance	weather	others	Total
1	244.5	3.0	3.0	310.0	11.5	4.0	576.0
2 + 3	293.0	12.0	28.0	257.0	1.0	211.0	802.0
4 + 5	387.5	13.5	62.5	120.0	3.0	32.0	518.5
6 + 7 + 8	56.5	6.5	22.5	27.5	—	28.0	141.0
Total	981.5	35.0	116.0	714.5	15.5	275.0	2137.5

The present school was built in 1956, and has been enlarged since. There are seven classrooms; nine grades (kindergarten to grade eight) and an 'opportunity class' (added in 1969) are taught. Schooling in Newfoundland is compulsory for children under fifteen years of age, and Nain children who have completed grade 8 and who seek further education can choose between the high school at North West River or the trade schools on the island of Newfoundland. In 1970–71, there were eight teachers (six of whom were new that year) and 194 pupils, most of them concentrated in the lower grades (see Table 1). Of the sixteen children over the age of fourteen, only four were in grade 8; this shows a considerable lag with regard to the age-grade norm set by the administrators.

Absenteeism, as shown in Table 2, was high during this period. Among the lower grades, the most common reason for an absence of more than a day, other than illness, was distance from school. Among the higher grades, absence was frequently unexplained, or the excuse given was that the children were needed at home. To understand this attitude, it is necessary to examine the hunting/fishing household economy in more detail, as the government school does not gear its schedule of instruction to the semi-nomadic life-style of these families as did the Moravians.

Home and School in an Economic-Ecologic Perspective
The basic unit in Nain is the nuclear family, although members of the extended family or adopted children may complete a household.[2] Domestic tasks and skills were, and are, strictly divided between the sexes, as are the social and religious activities; most personal relationships take place between members of the same sex. Female tasks are centred around the house or tent, and include the more repetitive chores such as cooking, washing, fetching water, making and mending clothes. Where the head of

the household is a fisherman or hunter, the woman is also responsible for preparing the catch, drying the meat or fish, and making articles from skins for family use and for sale. Male tasks include fetching firewood (and helping the women with the water), hunting, or earning wages. In the hunting or fishing households, the man also has to look after his equipment (skidoo or dogs, boat and nets).

In order for the children to learn their roles in such an environment, it is important that they participate from an early age. In hunting and fishing households, in particular, the boys must accompany their fathers or they would not learn where to find and how to trap the game. The girls must also be on hand if they are to learn how to prepare the meat and skins.

The household should be regarded as a unit whose members must make daily decisions about time and resource allocation. In this respect, then, education and being a pupil can constitute a dilemma. This dilemma fluctuates seasonally in fishing and hunting households where the family spends regular periods of time away from the local community. In contrast, parents who are sedentary, because the head of household earns a steady wage, do not require that their children stay home from school.

However, even in a hunting or fishing household, the pupil- and family-member roles can be combined successfully until a child reaches the age of about ten, since his responsibilities in the household do not become indispensible until this time. Nevertheless, children frequently start to help in the home before this, and parents do not like to leave even young children behind in boarding school when they go away on long expeditions. Today the conflict is less than it was in the past, since the age at which children are required to help in the family has increased slightly over the years, and there has been a slight decrease in seasonal mobility – the father being more inclined to leave his family in the village when he goes hunting. This fact has particularly relieved the pressure on female children, who now frequently do not learn skills related to hunting until marriage.

The high rate of absenteeism among young children in the school, however, suggests that conflict is engendered by the dual role, and that where conflict exists, the family tends to take precedence. As the children grow older, they become increasingly important in the household, particularly when the parents themselves are ageing. Then as the older children marry and set up their own households, the younger siblings have to undertake more responsibility. Even when the composition of a household is favourable for one or more of the children to attend school, it is usually financially impossible for them to move away and pursue further education; meanwhile the parents can only provide training in their own way of life. Once again, the pupil role becomes secondary. Hence, many pupils leave school as soon as they reach the age of fifteen, regardless of the grade

TABLE 3a

Nain Youth 17–19 Years of Age in 1970, according to
Residence and Economic Adaptation.

Alternatives / Yr. of Birth	Living in Nain			Living in the South		Total
	School	Apprenticeship	Job	School	Job	
1951	0	4	4	2	1	11
1952	0	3	1	1	0	5
1953	2	9	1	3	0	15
Total	2	16	6	6	1	31

TABLE 3b
Nain Youth with experience in Southern Schools, Classified according to
Type of School, Completion, and Return to Nain.

Type of Education	Drop-out/ Graduate	Returned to Nain	Remained in South	Total	
High School	do	5	2	7	15
	g	6	2	8	
Nursing School	do	2	0	2	10
	g	1	7	8	
Trade, Art School	do	3	0	3	7
	g	3	1	4	
University	do	0	1	1	4
	g	0	3	3	
College of Fisheries	do	3	0	3	3
	g	0	0	0	
Total	do	13	3	16	39
	g	10	13	23	

reached. Of those who leave the community (as shown in Table 3), some
pursue further education, some return home before graduation, while
others take jobs outside the community that do not correspond to their
level of education.

In some cases, pupils obtain jobs locally, thus remaining, to a certain
extent, part of the family's work team. The semi-nomadic life-style of the
hunting/fishing households creates problems for them too, since they are

inevitably caught in an employee/family member role conflict: the family still requires the child to help on the fishing and hunting expeditions, while the employer depends on the continuous service of his employee. Girls have fewer problems than boys in this respect, since their tasks in the family do not necessitate travelling, and their skills (domestic) are more easily applicable to such posts as a maid in a hospital or in a private household.

Parents with sedentary occupations usually require less of their children, partly because there are not as many manual tasks in a non-hunting household, and partly because a more predictable income makes the ownership of some labour-saving devices possible. Such parents are more likely to foresee a future for their children outside the family unit, and are more able to pay the expenses necessary for further education.

Generally speaking, paid local employment is regarded as a better alternative than further education for the following reasons: 1) in order to pursue further education, a child must leave Nain, and this entails financial cost; 2) in going away, an individual loses contact with potential local employers; 3) most of the local positions do not require an education but only on-the-job training; 4) the child who obtains work locally and lives at home can still be of use to his or her family; 5) a local employer is likely to have a similar and familiar life-style to the employee.

The Teachers

School records reveal many of the problems facing the teacher: classrooms are crowded and varied, often containing twenty pupils of different ages, ethnic backgrounds, and even grade levels. Absenteeism, as noted, is high and the possibility of success low. In order to further our understanding of the inefficacy of the present system of education, it is important to examine how the teachers manage their role in the school and in the community. This discussion is based on talks with both teachers and other members of the community, and it should be stressed that it describes the general pattern for Nain teachers, and not particular idiosyncracies and difficulties.

Teachers in Nain today are usually of middle-class Canadian, American, or English origin.[3] Some come straight from high school or teachers' training college, and most arrive with preconceived ideas about remote and ethnically mixed communities, and relatively fixed notions of a school's aims and methods. Most teachers regard their appointments in Nain as stepping-stones to better jobs elsewhere, or look upon the job as a highly paid stop-gap between school and college. There is, therefore, a high turnover among the teaching staff, and it is unusual for a real interest in the school and community to develop. Many teachers, indeed, do not remain long enough in Nain to rid themselves of their erroneous preconceptions, or to gain a sense of commitment to the area. On the other hand, some teachers arrive with a wish to reform the educational system, or improve the community's relationship with the rest of Canada. There are also those who realize and complain about the irrelevance of the curriculum and their own inability to speak 'Eskimo'; but these people have difficulty finding a remedy.

One reason for the lack of sensitivity to local needs stems from the fact that the school is administered from St. John's and Happy Valley; the teachers, books, and curricula are selected from outside the community. Any suggestions for improvements must be sent to St. John's and subjected to various administrative procedures before they can be put into practice. As mentioned before, there is no PTA and the local school committee has little or no power.

In a homogeneous society, the teacher can act as a go-between, presenting material and concepts in the manner intended by the authors and administrators of the school curriculum. But in a culturally marginal community such as Nain, the teacher's role has to be that of broker: he (she) might have to adjust the emphasis or even the content of the material he (she) presents in order to bring the message across (Paine, 1971). This work of redefinition and adjustment needs to be undertaken almost daily in Nain. Yet many of the teachers seem reluctant or unable to fulfil this middleman role, or are hesitant to take on the extra responsibility. Most bolster their teaching role by such means as emphasizing classroom discipline, or by appearing too busy to undertake anything out of the ordinary. Many lean on the administration and other members of white society rather than discuss problems with those they are supposed to serve – the local community. This segregates the teachers still further, and seems to diminish their effectiveness.

The majority of teachers do not understand the cultural history of the Settlers and Inuit, nor their economic and value systems. They base their judgement of a child's performance according to their own standards and draw conclusions about the children and their backgrounds only from what they see in school, using white, middle-class Canadian standards as their criteria. These attitudes persist because the teachers segregate themselves from the social life of the community, and by reason of their wages, life-style, and attitudes, form a class apart from the local people.

The teachers' problems are both caused and compounded by their lack of sensitivity and knowledge of the different ethnic backgrounds of the children.

Home and School in an Ethnic Perspective
Inuit and Settlers do not differ with respect to child participation in household tasks, but in other aspects of upbringing, there are important differences.

Bearing in mind the historical differences between Inuit and Settlers mentioned earlier, let us look at the expectations and rules of the present-day school in relation to the home. In the school, the child is expected to co-operate and interact with the teacher on his (her) terms. As already suggested, the teacher does not usually consider the cultural and social upbringing of the pupils, but rather stresses universalistic values such as quiet concentration and individual achievement. Errors and infringements of school regulations (however trivial they may seem to be to the child) are punished as they would be in a southern Canadian school.

The Inuit child enters this environment from a home composed of people of all ages, where few orders are given and where behaviour is not often criticized. The emphasis in the home is on responsibility, independence, and activity, and learning takes place through co-operation and participation. Punishment is reserved for significant wrong-doings, but is usually followed by immediate comforting of the child by another member of the family.

When the school was run by the Moravian missionaries, its rules and those of the home were similar because of the high integration of the mission with the society. The mission had a policy of preserving the Inuit culture and language and of being influential in the community, all of which the government school has been unable or unwilling to continue. This has made it harder for the present-day teachers to enforce their rules and regulations or to justify their demands regarding such matters as, for example, how the children must dress for school.

The Settler child has many cultural and social advantages over the Inuit in the present-day school system. The child speaks the same language at home and at school (albeit in a different dialect from the teacher's), and the Protestant ethic prevails both at home and school. In other words, Settler children and their parents are able to identify with the teacher and school curriculum more readily than Inuit because of the Settlers' relatively strict upbringing, their lack of dependence on the Moravian mission, and cultural similarities with the teachers. Settler parents seem to take more of an interest in the children's education and school work than do Inuit, prob-ably because the Settlers have more relatives and friends with higher education and steady jobs. Many teachers in the government school regard the Settler children as 'whites' (that is, not culturally deprived), and are surprised to find that those from hunting and fishing households – far from always succeeding in school – actually have high rates of failure and absenteeism, and frequently do not complete their education.

The Settlers are also more familiar with the teachers outside the school context than are the Inuit; besides the absence of a language barrier, the village layout (see map of Nain) makes teachers and Settlers neighbours. There have even been two marriages between teachers and Settlers.

Statistics relating to the inhabitants of Nain over two generations show an increase in bilingualism among the Inuit, and a corresponding decrease among the Settlers (see T. Brantenberg, ch. 16). This is attributable to the language policy of the government school, whose abrupt introduction of an all-Canadian curriculum (to the exclusion of the Inuit language) created difficulties for the Inuit pupils. Inuit parents today are content to have some knowledge of the English language, but because of the monolingual school, are concerned that their chlildren should speak English fluently, even in the home. The school is no longer a public place for bilingual interaction as it had been in the days of the missionaries, but rather a place where the differences between the two cultures are accentuated, to the detriment of the language and cultural traits of the Inuit. This situation has been commented on by Ben-Dor in Makkovik (1966:170). "Children start school at the same age but the English-speaking group has an advantage over their Eskimo peers. In the fourth grade, for example, the average age of a Settler child is eleven while the Eskimo average [is] thirteen years of age. In the fifth grade the average ages for Settler and Eskimo pupils are twelve and fifteen years respectively."[4]

In the past, the two ethnic groups had different attitudes towards education: the Inuit valued it mainly in relation to the mission as a source of prestige and a few positions; the Settlers, as bilinguals, used education as a means to secure a wider range of jobs, including those offered by the government and other white agencies. But neither group considered education very important; this attitude may not be changing with the current trend towards sedentary occupations and mechanization. Greater job diversification in a tight labour market will probably increase competition for existing jobs, thus making education more relevant. If existing conditions prevail, we may see differences in achievement and in the value put upon education by Inuit and Settlers. Educational achievement may also become a local idiom of ethnic diversity.

The government school also disrupts the gradual transition from child status to adult status in the maturation process. To some extent, the emergence of a youth culture is a result of this. The content and methods of the school and the rejection of further education all have a part to play in the local version of youth culture, which, in turn, stops the flow of out-migration (a phenomenon that is otherwise fairly widespread in other remote areas).

Youth and Youth Culture
Since white officialdom increased its activities in Nain, parents are no longer the primary models for teenagers; they now have a large network of relations upon which to model their behaviour. New educational possibilities, changing production processes, and an enlarged labour market are all part of the modernization process affecting Nain.

Change is also taking place in the hunting and fishing economies. The trends towards sedentary work and mechanization are having their effects; mobility is decreasing as more people settle in Nain so that the men, unable to take their sons who are in school, go hunting and fishing together, leaving the women and children at home. The transition from dog-team to skidoo has increased the household's need for cash and decreased the need for meat (for dog food). Father and son no longer have to co-operate over the handling and care of the dogs, and as their relationship changes, so also does that between the mother and daughters.

In the past, there were few outlets for local labour. In the 1960s, a federally-funded housing project provided construction jobs. But the job-market is still mostly seasonal, with poor wages and more potential employees than there are jobs. Seasonal odd-jobs are available only to males, who often take them to supplement their fluctuating income from hunting and fishing. Since the opening of a fish plant in the summer of 1971, however, females have achieved a little more flexibility. The alternative to the local labour market lies in fishing or hunting: both occupations give fluctuating incomes that often have to be supplemented by welfare or relief funds.

As the preceding pages have indicated, the government school is in-adequate as a training centre and as a stepping-stone to a career – both in and outside Nain. Few incentives are given at school and the majority of the pupils feel failure. Students see few, if any, opportunities or careers for themselves outside Nain. In Nain itself, there are few positions to attract those with higher education: nurse, technician, teacher, postmaster and clerk; so that reinvestment into the community of school-acquired skills is minimal. Those who do succeed at school usually take a job in the south and settle there. Some return to Nain without completing their education, or take jobs where they do not use it. The higher-paid administrative positions continue to be occupied by white outsiders. For all of these reasons, most Nain youth still find their employers or partners from among householders who make their living hunting or fishing. This means that they serve an apprenticeship before establishing their own households.

On the other hand, education being compulsory until the age of fifteen, and the curriculum being strictly south Canadian, young people do not get the necessary practice in the traditional skills. At an age when children, in the past, would have been serving as apprentices or partners, they are now at school, or in temporary odd jobs, or merely "hanging around." Such children are in a vacuum: economically dependent, socially neither child nor adult, and culturally influenced by both local and national values.

But as the traditional pattern of maturation was being disrupted, a youth culture emerged in Nain. It combines both modern idioms of expression and the traditional way of life. At present, the combination is not without conflict, as it is not yet clear which aspects are compatible with the adolescents' life at home and in the community.

Today, more money is available and there are more consumer goods circulating in Nain on which to spend it. Greater financial independence among adolescents facilitates the purchase of records, soft-drinks, fashionable clothes and other luxuries unconnected with the daily routine of the household. Local youth favour goods and attributes originating outside the community: pop music, movies, comics, and cosmetics, guitar playing, modern dancing, being fashionably dressed, and having a pretty or strong physical appearance. As this list shows, the school is not necessarily the donor of youth-culture idioms; many of the goods and ideas have been brought to Nain by adolescents who left to seek further education (often uncompleted) or jobs elsewhere, but who returned.

The new youth culture does not discriminate between Settler and Inuit, and relationships between the two ethnic groups develop. A youth club, patterned after the Canadian model and introduced by young teachers and emigré youth who returned, came into being; the club and the snack bar are the usual meeting places for young people. This does not necessarily imply opposition to the home milieu, even though such activities as dancing and singing in the hall are no longer enjoyably shared by different generations.

Besides the innovative qualities described above, the youth culture retains characteristics of a local traditional nature; for example, hunting trips are considered part of the 'good life' as much as dancing to pop music. This attitude is shared alike by Settlers, Inuit, boys, girls, hunters, fishermen and clerks. In other words, the local version of the youth culture is emerging in response to the local situation; emigration is negligible and most young people who leave Nain, return. The youth seem to adapt to the local scene and look south only to find idioms for expressing themselves in the new setting.

In summary then, the uncertainty evident among the young is related, to a great extent, to the fact that the school socializes them for careers and life-styles either not available to the local people, or not considered desirable by them. Because the youth milieu provides arenas for interaction where ethnic and economic differences can be ignored, there is an element of implied denigration of tradition, and this can lead to parent/child conflict and alienation. More significant, however, is the fact that the youth culture is an adaptation *to* the local scene, and not away from it. There are some tendencies towards proletarization and socio-economic distress, as well as conflicting values; and yet, participation in the youth culture, combined with other ties to the local community, give the youngsters a feeling of belonging. The young people seem to be able to give meaning and value to life in Nain. Most youth not only remain in Nain but eventually adopt life-styles (ethnically specific), and enter into marriages similar to those of their parents.

Conclusion: the Marginal School

Considerable government grants and an active interest are directed towards the schools in northern Labrador – at least in comparison to southern Labrador with its isolated Settler groups mainly engaged in fishing. In this sense, Nain cannot be considered marginal; and yet the educational system has not met with overwhelming success: perhaps it is the school which is marginal. The main reason for the seeming failure of the educational policy must be the ethnic and socio-economic gap between home and school. We have looked at this gap in this essay in terms of role compatibility and the situation of the youth.

The school has, indeed, been proven marginal in terms of the minimal reinvestment of school-acquired skills and their use in providing idioms for identity management – whether in relation to ethnic background or the youth culture. The influence of the school has, however, inevitable consequences with regard to the continuity, viability, and vigour of the local cultures, particularly that of the Inuit, whose language is disregarded in the school context, along with other cultural traits. Such disregard of a language that is predominantly oral is especially serious. The increase in bilingualism among Inuit and the decrease among Settlers have been mentioned, and there is growing concern about the communicative barrier between Inuit children and their parents as a result of changing language skills and usages. There is a tendency toward anglicization of the Inuit language.

Teachers in the government school are not unqualified in the national context, but their situation in Nain is difficult and frustrating. The teachers are aware of the problems and some make serious attempts to eliminate them. However, their ideas and projects seldom accumulate over time, partly because of the high turnover rate. Whereas one effect of the school is alienation from local values and life-styles, the school seldom provides the knowledge necessary for successful membership in the larger society. This gives both pupils and teachers a sense of inadequacy and failure. In its failure to provide alternatives which the locals could consider better than the traditional careers, the school has not become a proper "steel-axe" (cf. Sharp, 1952).

NOTES

1   There is a legend concerning this: A couple had two daughters. The oldest always had to work hard in the house and was often scolded and beaten. The youngest was very spoiled and was never asked to do anything and never beaten. However, she died as a girl. Some time after she was buried, her hand was seen coming up from the grave. Then they understood that she couldn't get rest and peace because she had never been punished. So the father opened the grave and hit the corpse with a stick. After that the hand never came up.
2   Cf. Kleivan's discussion (1964) of the transition from extended families to individual smaller units.
3   The standard of living enjoyed by the teachers in Nain would not be exceptional in a

national context, but it is dramatically different from that of the local population; the teachers enjoy such luxuries as running water, bathrooms, freezers and washers.

4 Compared to the data for Nain (see Table 1a), the average ages in Makkovik are higher for both groups of pupils, and there are greater differences between the averages of the two groups. The data for Makkovik, however, are for 1963. Another reason for the discrepancy may be that Makkovik was originally a Settler community, to which Inuit moved during the period 1956–59 (see Kennedy, ch. 18, this vol.).

References

BEN-DOR, SHMUEL
1966 *Makkovik: Eskimos and Settlers in a Labrador Community.* St. John's, Institute of Social and Economic Research, Memorial University of Newfoundland.

HILLER, J.
1971 "Early Patrons of the Labrador Eskimos: The Moravian Mission in Labrador, 1764–1805." In R. Paine (ed.), *Patrons and Brokers in the East Arctic.* St. John's, Institute of Social and Economic Research, Memorial University of Newfoundland.

HOBART, C. W. AND C. S. HOBART
1966 "Eskimo Education, Danish and Canadian: A Comparison." *Canadian Review of Sociology and Anthropology*, 3(2).

HOEM, A.
1965 *Samenes Skole an.* Oslo, Universitetsforlaget.

HOEM, A.
1968 "Samer, Skol og Samfunn." *Tidsskrift for Samfunnsforskning*, Bd. 9.

KLEIVAN, HELGE
1964 "Acculturation, Ecology and Human Choice: Case Studies from Labrador and South Greenland." *Folk*, 6.

NYERERE, J.
1968 "Utbildning Til Sjalvhtalp." In J. Nyerere (ed.), *Socialism in Tanzania.* Uppsala, Nordiska Afrikainstituttet.

PAINE, ROBERT
1971 "A Theory of Patronage and Brokerage." In R. Paine (ed.), *Patrons and Brokers in the East Arctic.* St. John's, Institute of Social and Economic Research, Memorial University of Newfoundland.

SHARP, L.
1952 "Steel Axes for Stone Age Australians." In E. H. Spicer (ed.), *Human Problems in Technological Change.* New York, Russell Sage Foundation.

WAX, M., R. WAX AND R. J. DUMONT, JR.
1964 "Formal Education in an American Indian Community." Supplement to *Social Problems*, 11(4).

Local Government and Ethnic Boundaries in Makkovik, 1972

18

J. C. Kennedy

Anthropoligical studies of small communities containing two or more ethnic groups[1] most frequently describe the nature of inter-ethnic relations in terms of conflict, or they conclude that in time, one group will absorb the other. Although it is obvious that no cultural or ethnic group persists in perpetuity, I suggest that another interpretation, based neither on conflict nor assimilation, should also be considered in describing relations across ethnic boundaries. This approach, hopefully clarified in what follows, assumes that two or more ethnic groups can co-exist independently of one another, at least for short periods of time. The character of individual transactions across ethnic lines can be quite variable even though the structural configuration describing the relations between the groups is more one of segregation than integration, of equilibrium rather than gradual blending of ethnic traits.

This essay is concerned with the way two contiguous ethnic groups maintain contrasting identities, and resist pressures to increase inter-ethnic interaction.[2] The analysis focuses on ethnic boundaries; that is, on those culturally-specific criteria determining group membership from two different angles that more or less correspond to the emic versus etic distinction of the new ethnography. The one views ethnic distinctions through the eyes of participants in the social system, or according to the local 'folk model'; the other examines both groups from a distance and concentrates on those factors explaining boundary maintenance.

Background Factors

Makkovik is situated on the north Labrador coast, approximately 135 air miles northeast of Goose Bay. First settled in the 1850s by a Norwegian pioneer, Makkovik remained primarily a Settler (that is, English-speaking and white) village for over a century. During most of that time, the village was immune to government influences, though not from the Moravian Mission, Hudson's Bay Company, and International Grenfell Association (IGA). Between the 1930s and 1950s, Settlers formerly living in scattered family homesteads along the bays near Makkovik were encouraged by Moravian missionaries to move into the community. Then in the late '50s, Hebron and Nutak, Labrador's two most northerly Inuit settlements were closed down by external authorities and their inhabitants resettled in Nain, Hopedale and Makkovik. Approximately one half of these people (about 150), the majority of them Hebron Inuit, were moved to Makkovik. By 1963 then, these convergent population movements had created a bi-ethnic community with its population of 324 roughly divided between Settlers and Inuit.

It should be emphasized that almost two hundred years of miscegenation between Inuit, Europeans, and to a lesser extent, Indians on the Labrador coast make physical characteristics misleading indicators of an individual's ethnic status: many Settlers have an Inuit appearance and vice versa (cf. Kleivan, 1966:90–94). Instead, what is important are certain behavioural criteria that define and signal ethnic identity. One should mention that there are also *intra*-ethnic cleavages, again the result of social, historical, and ecological forces. For example, Inuit from Hebron acknowledge differences (both linguistic and social) between themselves and those Inuit formerly living at Nutak.

Similarly, Settlers native to Makkovik distinguish themselves from the "bay" Settlers who moved to the community within the last 30 years. The former group represents the culmination of life in a mission settlement, with a mercantile tradition resulting from socio-economic contacts with Hudson's Bay Company personnel during winter and Newfoundland fishermen and traders during the summer. In contrast, the rugged existence of the Settlers whose early life was spent in the bays meant many months of isolation and only periodic visits to Makkovik. Two examples of the effects these differences have are: first, Settlers native to Makkovik differ from bay Settlers in their commitment to policies which benefit the community; for example, my attempts to initiate conversations with bay Settlers (and Inuit) regarding the prospects for a local airstrip and dock extension were met with considerably less interest than they did with Settlers native to Makkovik. Secondly, the exploitative strategies of both types of Settlers continue to differ: those native to Makkovik prefer to use techniques long successful in the immediate Makkovik area; for example, for several generations, they have used nets to catch migrating harp seals each spring and fall. Preparations for, and the actual process of netting seals are characterized by an almost ritual emphasis on quiet because harp seals are sensitive and believed to be easily frightened. After moving to Makkovik, bay Settlers (and Inuit) used rifles (as they always had) to shoot harp seals, and they either ignored or refused to adopt the traditional Makkovik Settler technique. Their behaviour was, and continues to be, criticized by the native Settler group and is frequently cited by them as responsible for the depletion of harp seals.

Although such differences within Makkovik's two ethnic groups can produce varying responses to any issue, I maintain that they do little to affect the primary Inuit-Settler distinction. Furthermore, each Settler and Inuk selects elements from the total constellation of *either* Settler *or* Inuit role behaviour without being disenfranchised of his overall ethnic status.

Makkovik's traditional economy was restricted to fishing, hunting and some trapping, but recent years have witnessed a decline in these subsistence activities. Whereas virtually all men (and boys) formerly fished for cod during summer and early fall, since 1968, declining cod stocks have signalled the diminution of this fishery and its partial replacement by salmon "catching,"[3] a labour-intensive fishery requiring less co-operative, more individualized productive units, and thus prosecuted by fewer full-time fishermen. At the same time, alternative means of livelihood were being introduced by government-sponsored wage-labour projects, which cushioned the effects of the decline of the cod fishery. At the same time many former cod fishermen were reluctant to invest their capital in entirely new equipment necessary to prosecute the salmon fishery. Thus, more men were turning to wage labour – an option not available in 1963.

These changes in Makkovik's economy are evident when the summer economic pursuits of adult men (over 20 years of age) in 1963 are compared with those of 1972: whereas 30 (22 Settlers, 8 Inuit) fished for cod during 1963, only about 14 (12 Settlers, 2 Inuit) prosecuted the salmon fishery in 1972. In 1963, whereas only a handful (cf. Ben-Dor, 1966:43) of adult men worked for wages in 1963, during the summer and fall of 1972, 12 men (11 Settlers, 1 Inuk) worked full-time on local construction projects, with another 18 (8 Settlers, 10 Inuit) working either at short-term labour or part-time fishing. In short, the period since 1963 has witnessed a re-orientation of the economy, prompted by declining cod resources and facilitated by increasing government capital expenditures on the north Labrador coast. The Labrador Services Division (LSD), a branch of the Provincial Government, has increasingly taken over the administration of both retail trade and economic development, both historically controlled by the once-pervasive Moravian Mission.

During the past ten years, Makkovik's population, specifically the ratio of Settlers to Inuit, has altered as a result of both a higher birth rate among Settlers and of Inuit out-migration (see Table 1). Many Inuit have moved to the more northerly community of Nain in order to rejoin kin living there and to exploit the richer resource base characteristic of the Nain area. Population movements are not new to coastal Labrador, but they have usually been determined either by external administrators (such as the relocation of Inuit to Makkovik between 1956–1959), or by the sporadic availability of wage employment (such as the movement of Settlers and Inuit to Goose Bay, Hopedale, and other military construction sites during the 1940s and 1950s). It is significant that this recent migration out of Makkovik of about half the Inuit who originally moved there was not caused by the usual circumstances.

The White Arctic

TABLE 1

Makkovik Population

Ethnic category	August 1963	July 1972
Settlers	159	204
Inuit	140	76
Mixed background	7	10
Others	18	16
Total	324	306

Note: Ben-Dor's category "mixed background" included the children of two mixed marriages, in which the husband was a Settler, his wife an Inuit. He speculated that although most of these children had considered themselves Inuit in their native Nutak, they would in time assume Settler identity in Makkovik (Ben-Dor, 1966:156–57). However, my data indicate that not all these children (plus an adult male we have classified as "mixed") have indicated choice of identity, despite temporary alignments with Settlers or Inuit. I have thus seen fit to include a mixed ethnic category though we suggest future situational factors (e.g., marriage to Settler or Inuit, place of adult residence, etc.) will facilitate an individual's management of a consistent identity. The category "others" includes "outsiders" (plus their dependents) temporarily working and living in Makkovik.

The Settler-Inuit Cleavage

In examining the nature of contemporary boundary maintenance and ethnic interaction in Makkovik, we shall refer to an earlier ethnographic study of the community conducted between 1962 and 1963 by Ben-Dor (1966). Ben-Dor's thesis questions the utility of anthropological definitions of the concept "community" (such as Linton's, 1936; and Murdock's, 1949) in describing Makkovik. He maintains that they characterize a community as an "integrated social village sharing a common culture" (*op. cit.*:3), and suggests that Makkovik might better be termed a multicellular-type community in which two ethnic groups, expressing separate cultures, are linked to a common territory by a "superimposed administration" (*op. cit.*:200).

Ben-Dor supports his contention by demonstrating the independence of each ethnic group from the other. He argues that whether one examines interaction networks, economic co-operation, or political organization, little interaction between the groups is evident. He cites one instance in which a number of Inuit and Settlers dismantled an abandoned government weather station to obtain building materials for local use; despite their common goal and the fact that they visited the site at the same time, each group worked separately during the dismantling process. Finally, Ben-Dor notes that although there is some social interaction between Settler and Inuit adolescents, such behaviour is not found among adults nor among the young children.

My data confirm, and go beyond, Ben-Dor's multicellular conceptualization of Makkovik in that it is the very cultural features (such as language, gestures, values and 'appropriate' role behaviour) enclosed by, and diacritical to, ethnic boundaries that inhibit interaction across ethnic lines. Contrary to Ben-Dor's conclusion that the Inuit way of life will become assimilated with that of the Settlers, I see little indication that this is occurring. Rather, there are definite signs, such as the recent establishment of the Labrador Inuit Association (see below), that the distinction between Settlers and Inuit remains vital. It is not my contention that no inter-ethnic interaction occurs, but that the little that does is overshadowed by cultural constraints restricting continuous interaction.[4] These constraints generate antitheses in the priorities which Settlers and Inuit accord institutions, people and events: Inuit accord primacy to kinship and fictive kinship ties in their socio-economic dealings, and relationships outside these categories are rare, or in any case, have little value; Settlers, on the other hand, value kinship ties, but strive to establish friendships[5] with unrelated Settlers and even "outsiders" (though not commonly with Makkovik Inuit).

The different emphasis each group places on kinship and friendship relationships is seen in Ben-Dor's (op.cit.:129–33) description of Inuit birthday celebrations and Settler parties. Birthday celebrations, introduced to Labrador Inuit by missionaries many years ago, include both religious and secular elements, notably the singing of hymns, saying of grace, dancing and feasting. Except for the more ritually important (for example, 50th) birthday celebrations, the invited guests are limited to members of the celebrant's *ilarit* or kindred. In contrast, Settler parties include no religious elements and are open to any Settler wishing to attend, particularly close friends. A party includes considerable drinking, either of locally produced "home brew" or commerically produced beer and spirits. After talking and dancing, it is concluded with a "lunch" or light meal.

Similar culturally-specific behaviour is manifested when the coastal boat calls at Makkovik to deliver and collect freight, passengers and mail. This event provokes some excitement, and it is common to see most of Makkovik's population (in segregated groups) waiting on the dock as the boat approaches. Once the vessel docks, Settlers rush aboard to renew friendships or to engage in any of a number of transactions with the crew (purchasing liquor, exchanging information, or obtaining freight). Meanwhile, Inuit remain on the dock, watching the activity and talking in small groups. Only after the initial excitement has died down do Inuit venture aboard, usually to gather in the ship's lounge, but seldom to engage in 'Settler' kinds of exchanges.

A similar situation in which Settlers and Inuit are found together but separate, and which also occurs on a 'neutral' stage, is in the self-service LSD store. Here members of one group rarely acknowledge the presence of members of the other; Inuit and Settlers shop 'together' but communication seldom crosses ethnic lines. Should communication occur, it is usually of a joking nature, consistent with the impression that some tension surrounds such contacts.

Ethnic behavioural differences show up in two other important domains of life in Makkovik: the mission and the community. Settlers express a greater sense of community than do Inuit, considering Makkovik *the* place to live; few Settlers, even those who have lived outside the community, express much interest in living elsewhere. Out-migration data reveal that few Settlers, even the young and educated, have permanently left Makkovik in recent years. Further, the predominance of Settler involvement in the community attests to the significance of community-related activities in the Settler value system. Since 1964, a 24 hour-a-day electricity service has made possible an extensive programme of events occurring at least five nights a week at the Community Hall. These events, particularly the bi-weekly movies, necessitated some organization, and so a Hall Committee composed of several young Settlers was set up. In addition, a small rock n' roll combo, also composed of Settlers, entertained at dances twice a week. Inuit of all ages attended these and other events at the Hall – bingo, benefit suppers, movies, and so forth – but seldom became involved in the leadership or organization of such activities. The extent to which Makkovik Inuit are denied such involvement is debatable; however it is my view that their behaviour is based on choice – they choose not to penetrate a traditionally Settler domain. In other words, Inuit avoidance of leadership/organizational roles in secular activities expresses not only the subordinate importance of such behaviour in their value system, but also the fact that this behaviour is seen by them as "Settler" and thus, not "Inuit." In my view, their choice is regarded as a boundary-maintaining mechanism. The Inuit are asserting their identity by enacting behaviour consistent with, and specific to, their value system which, in this case, implies rejecting involvement in secular or community events.

However, unlike most Settlers, Inuit do value active involvement in all mission-related activities, ranging from greater (than Settlers) attendance at church services to voluntary maintenance of the church and mission properties. Whereas the missionaries reward Inuit participation with counter-prestations (of praise, attempts to learn the Inuit language, gifts of clothing), they excuse, and reluctantly accept the relative absence of such involvement by Settlers. In this way, the mission reinforces ethnic differences.

Note should be taken here of the fact that Makkovik Inuit aspire to leadership positions in the church. Many years ago, the Moravians established a practice of having an elected body of church elders at each mission station to help maintain order, and to act as middlemen between the missionary and his congregation by disseminating (and obtaining) informa-tion. Elders mediated civil disputes, helped organize church events, and in the temporary absence of a missionary, even performed religious services. The number of elders in a community varied according to community size, with a theoretical ratio of one elder to every hundred members of the congregation.When I arrived in Makkovik, there were three elders, of which two were Settlers and one an Inuk.

Elders serve a three-year term, and in the autumn of 1971, a meeting was called to elect new elders. After several Settlers had been nominated and all had declined, the missionary requested one prominent Settler to explain his refusal. The man explained that many Settlers (in his view) no longer wanted to continue the custom of elders, emphasizing that the pressures incumbent on elders in mediating the increasing number of violent inci-dents were considerable, and that in the absence of formal law enforcement personnel (that is, RCMP), the newly established community council could, if necessary, maintain civil order. Other Settlers agreed, and they decided not to elect new elders. Next, the missionary, who privately supported this position, requested Inuit opinion on the matter. The vast majority of Inuit present voted to maintain the custom and, after some time, it was agreed that one Inuk elder should be elected; he was Paulus, a respected Inuk hunter.

The status of elder has long represented an avenue to leadership within the community. Interestingly, Settlers and Inuit have agreed on requisite personal characteristics of elders: they should be sober and enlightened men who earn respect by exemplary behaviour. Although Paulus' drinking habits deviated from this ideal, Settlers supported his candidacy because they thought his success as a hunter and his strong personality merited formal recognition, and they also sought a spokesman for the Inuit com-munity. Many Inuit, however, feared Paulus' violent temper. Neverthe-less, they agreed to his election over other candidates. What Settlers did not expect was that Paulus, as the only elder, would attempt to adjudicate Settler disputes. After drinking considerably one day, Paulus attempted to escort a drunk Settler home, but was prevented from doing so by several angry Settlers who reminded Paulus that (in their view) his jurisdiction was confined to the Inuit neighbourhood.

Before concluding my description of Makkovik's ethnic cleavage, men-tion should be made of the fact that ethnic boundaries are buttressed by collective assessments of *the other* group's life style and by convictions of group superiority; that is, by positive appraisals of whatever benefits are believed to accrue from affiliation with one's ethnic group. Ethnic assets generate boundary maintenance and act as a kind of *raison d'être* for Settler or Inuit identity, much as T. Brantenberg describes in his discussion of ethnic stereotyping in Nain (ch. 16). But the importance of each group's perceived assets alters through time, despite the persistence of the categories *Settler* and *Inuit*. An example lies in the changed caribou hunting practices of Makkovik residents. Until the mid-1960s, Makkovik people hunted the meagre-sized caribou herds of the wooded country southeast of Makkovik. The introduction of snowmobiles in the mid-1960s enabled hunters to pursue larger herds in the treeless interior west of Nain. However, Settlers, who cannot (or will not) construct snowhouses nor traverse barren country must hire an Inuk guide. The point here is that before Settlers hunted west of Nain, snowhouse construction and the ability to venture into the barren interior were both economically unnecessary and without social relevance. Although such skills would now be beneficial, Settlers show little inclination to learn them, acknowledging instead that "only Eskimos build snowhouses."

In my view, snowhouse construction has become symbolic of Inuit identity only since the change in caribou-hunting territory occurred. Prior to this, Inuit viewed snowhouses in a matter-of-fact manner. Presently, however, snowhouse construction not only bolsters Inuit conviction of their own cultural superiority, but also assumes social relevance among Settlers by demarcating the parameters of appropriate Settler and Inuit behaviour. I turn now to an examination of the ways Settlers and Inuit react to the increasing contact of Makkovik with the outside world.

The Introduction of a Community Council

In 1969, the LSD, in co-operation with the Provincial Department of Municipal Affairs, held meetings in most coastal communities to familiarize residents with the advantages of community incorporation with the province. In April 1970, Makkovik elected its first community council, thereby making Makkovik eligible for government support to an extent far greater than former "superimposed administrations" (Ben-Dor, 1966:200) could provide. Not since Newfoundland-Labrador's confederation with Canada in 1949 had residents witnessed such an influx of financial resources: the community council form of local government meant that Makkovik would automatically receive several annual provincial grants; and councillors soon learned that federal monies could be obtained also.

Although no single reason prompted Settler leaders to incorporate the community, there does seem to have been a general awareness that government funding was available only to incorporated municipalities. Davis Inlet (a Naskapi Indian community 100 miles north of Makkovik) and Hopedale (a Settler/Inuit community 50 miles north of Makkovik) established community councils before Makkovik did, and by 1970, all northern coastal communities (except the nearby Settler village of Postville) had done so. In these other communities, councillors have frequently been young Settlers or Inuit not previously part of the established political hierarchy. But in Makkovik, the first councillors were established Settler leaders. This meant that formalized local government did little to alter local leadership and decision-making patterns.

Early reaction to the council (before my arrival in the community) is difficult to determine, but a review of council records indicates that many residents, both Inuit and Settlers, responded favourably to the new services, notably the weekly garbage collection, even though it meant payment of a small per capita tax. It also seems that few residents knew much about community councils – who they represented, what their duties included, or what they could mean to a community. Nonetheless, during my time in Makkovik, I noted a growing awareness of formalized local government, in no small part encouraged by temporary wage-labour made available by the council to both Inuit and Settlers.

When I came to Makkovik in July 1971, the community's first council consisted of four elected Settlers; in addition, the assistant LSD store manager, an Inuk and a skilled accountant, was appointed by the council to administer its books. Three of the councillors were born and raised in Makkovik, each belonging to Settler families related to the community's founder. Amos, the chairman, was middle-aged, and a leader long-respected along the coast. Joseph, the vice-chairman, was a younger, more outspoken man with confidence in his "progressive" ideas and in his aspirations of higher political office. Both Amos and Joseph had been permanently employed by externally-based agencies previously, and thus felt at liberty to be outspoken on developments that were felt to jeopardize the positions of men employed locally (for example, by LSD). George, the third councillor, was an affluent businessman, operating a small general store and more recently, selling snowmobiles for a national firm. His relative affluence and longstanding outside orientation established him as Makkovik's innovator *par excellence*: he introduced the first speedboat, snowmobile, and truck to the community. Corresponding to one of Paine's (1963) two types of entrepreneurs, the "free enterpriser," George's breach of local values (particularly, with regard to consumption patterns) and his apparent disregard for the high social costs of his version of entrepreneurship made people wary of him, yet also made him a power to be reckoned with, both locally and otherwise. Samuel, the fourth councillor, was born and raised in one of the bays near Makkovik. A young man, his mild and unassuming manner contrasted with the more outspoken manner of his fellow councillors. However, Samuel was equally adept at various tasks both "in the country" and "in the community" and was more respected than any of his fellows who moved to Makkovik from the bays.

The council arrives at all its decisions in private meetings usually conducted in the living room of Amos or Joseph. Although opinions on council business might be requested from other Settlers, the meetings themselves were normally closed to non-councillors. Like Frankenberg (1957:71), I was thus unable to witness how, or with what difficulty decisions were reached, although it is believed that it was by consensus. This private and unilateral character of the council's decision-making was generally consistent with decision-making prior to the formalization of local government (Ben-Dor, 1966:86–87).

Settler Efforts to "Integrate" Makkovik

Since the formation of the community council, the Settler leaders have urged closer interaction between Settlers and Inuit. When the first relocated families from Hebron began leaving Makkovik in the early 1960s, their movement was considered seasonal, and thus went unnoticed by Settlers. However, Inuit out-migration increased in the mid-'60s and Settlers did begin to take note of it, particularly after the formation of the council, and the awareness among councillors that certain federal funds were granted only to communities having either Inuit or Indian residents. The council believed that unless something were done, Makkovik could return to its original status as an all-Settler community and thus become ineligible for these funds. Important here is that councillors expressed remorse over what they considered the "plight" of the Inuit, and attributed (mistakenly, I believe) Inuit out-migration to the failure of Settlers to help Inuit make Makkovik their home. In what follows, I want to consider in some detail how council sought to curb emigration by attempting to increase Settler-Inuit interaction.

Even prior to 1959, the rocky barren area south of the original Settler section of the village was considered by Settlers as an undesirable place to live. Here were housed the Hebron Inuit upon their arrival at Makkovik. It lay exposed to the icy north winds blowing in off Makkovik Harbour and lacked the spruce and willow trees that surrounded houses in the Settler section. Nonetheless, the decision to locate the Hebron arrivals there in 1959 was made by the administrators responsible for the evacuation of Hebron, together with the consent of Settler leaders. In effect, this isolated Inuit from important services: they had to walk nearly one mile to church and to the hospital while the children had about half a mile to go to school. As the years passed, what became increasingly significant was the impression of *de facto* segregation felt by outsiders visiting the village – particularly by government officials.

To remedy this situation, in 1970, the council began relocating Inuit families alongside Settler families in a newly-developed section of the community situated west of the original Settler section (see map of Makkovik). The funds for the construction of new houses were federal but administered provincially through the LSD which, in turn, delegated the matter of occupancy to the council. The power of the council was somewhat constrained by government stipulations that widows, widowers, the aged, and newly married couples receive new homes before all others. Applications were sent to the council which then made its decisions on the basis of the aforementioned stipulations and of relative need. Such decisions were not easily reached, and although they were occasionally criticized, the councillors appear to have been sensitive to local needs.

In 1970 and 1971, two Inuit families moved into this neighbourhood as did another family of five in 1972. Councillors were proud of their relocation programme but as yet there were no indications that it affected (and, I predict, will not affect) established Settler-Inuit interaction patterns. Over the several months I resided near that section of the community, there was little (if any) communication between Settlers and Inuit neighbours. Typically, Inuit living in this "integrated" neighbourhood walked back to the "Hebron end" for sociability (and the arrangement of economic partnerships), while the Settlers living there maintained interaction patterns established long before 1970.[7]

Quite as significant, yet either unknown or unacknowledged by councillors, is the fact that not all Inuit intended to accept new homes in this section of Makkovik. For example, one aging Inuk leader stated that he would not move *there*: if he moved anywhere it would be "back north." His view was by no means unique; rather, it reflected the growing desire among Makkovik's Inuit population to return to their homeland north of Nain.

In assessing this effort of council to "integrate" Makkovik, it is important to reiterate that councillors, as native Settlers, were concerned primarily with altering the community's public image and procuring government funding. In my view, council was acting on premises not necessarily shared by the community as a whole, nor even by all Settlers. That there was ambivalence among bay Settlers, as well as Inuit, concerning what council felt was important for Makkovik (in this instance, its "integration"), is not surprising. The situation was exacerbated by council's private mode of reaching decisions. For this tended to insulate its policies (particularly those that were potentially controversial) from possible contradictory views. By failing to communicate its rationale for policies, the council potentially undermined community support for what it hoped to achieve.

Inuit Rejection of a Broker Role

Late in 1971, a public meeting was held to elect a new council (in accordance with provincial local government regulations). In the days preceding this meeting, Joseph (the council's vice-chairman), had encouraged Marcus, a prominent young Inuk, to accept nomination as councillor. Marcus worked in and lived beside the LSD store between the Inuit and Settler sections of the village; he was exceptional in that he internalized many of the cultural features of both ethnic groups and could, at least theoretically, become "Settler." His Inuit status was potentially jeopardized because of his marriage to a Settler woman (one of two 'mixed' unions since 1963), his permanent government job, and his close relationship with his Settler in-laws. However, Marcus' potentially questionable identity was countered to an exaggerated (though still acceptable) extent by his constant co-operation (primarily hunting and sharing) with members of his kindred. In this way he asserted his Inuit identity. Marcus is neither straddling two identities nor engaging in *situational* ethnic identity (cf. T. Brantenberg, ch. 19, this vol.); he considers himself, and is considered, Inuit.

However, being bilingual, Marcus possessed an asset much in demand by councillors who were seeking a middleman between themselves and the Hebron Inuit. Also significant were qualities such as his industriousness, infrequent and non-violent drinking habits and personable manner, all of which corresponded to Settler norms of what constituted "acceptable" Inuit behaviour. Indeed, the other councillors strongly supported Joseph's efforts to recruit Marcus, expressing the need to "translate the idea of community councils" to Inuit. Finally, and not insignificantly, the council was embarrassed by the fact that of all the ethnically-mixed communities on the coast, only Makkovik lacked representation from both Settlers and Inuit on its council. To the councillors then, Marcus could, as cultural broker, solve a problem that disturbed the council since its inception.

Of the forty-seven voters in the community hall on the evening of the election, no less than half were Inuit; however, Marcus was not there and thus made himself ineligible for nomination. Nonetheless, the large number of Inuit voters present appeared to ensure the election of any Inuk nominated. After the chairman opened the meeting with a short address, two impartial moderators (the missionary and school principal) offered their services in conducting the vote for a new council. In addition, a bilingual Settler was asked to translate the voting procedures which called for eight nominations, of which the four receiving the greatest number of votes would constitute the new council. Given the absence of Marcus, another Inuk, James, was among those nominated and seconded by Settlers. Although not as fully bilingual as Marcus, James was respected by both Settlers and Inuit.

With 47 voters present, a total of 188 votes could be cast, each voter casting four votes. However, when the votes were tallied, only 169 votes had been cast and four Settlers had won the seats on the new council – three being former councillors. James was placed fifth, with only fifteen votes. In contrast, Amos, the re-elected chairman, had received 41 votes, Joseph, the re-elected vice-chairman, 33 and Samuel, 30. George, the fourth original councillor was replaced by Clyde, a popular young Settler. In my judgement, these elections returns raise several points about ethnic processes in Makkovik.

Admittedly, the nineteen-vote discrepancy between the potential and actual total vote is difficult to explain. Most likely, however, some voters, probably Inuit, voted for only one or two candidates, rather than for four. It is unlikely that the voting instructions were misunderstood by the Inuit, as the interpreter was both impartial and competent. Furthermore, most Makkovik Inuit, though reluctant to speak English, understood a great deal of it.

Assuming that most of the nineteen votes not cast were in the hands of Inuit voters, and given the large number of Inuit voters present, it is clear that a united Inuit vote could have assured James' election. Why then, did this not occur? I suggest that James was not elected because most Inuit decided against voting for him. Further, I believe most Inuit voted for one or more Settlers. Several factors support my contention. To begin with, I learned after the election that of the fifteen votes James received, at least five were cast by Settlers. Clearly then, less than one-half of the Inuit present voted for him. In contrast, Amos (the re-elected chairman) received forty-one of forty-seven possible votes, meaning that many Inuit voters supported his candidacy. A possible explanation for this may have been the recent events surrounding the introduction of the Labrador Inuit Association.

Briefly, since its foundation in 1973, the Labrador Inuit Association (LIA) conducted three presidential elections, each one won by a person of mixed ethnic status. Most recently (autumn, 1975), the Association re-elected a man of mixed ethnic status as president and another as vice-president. Of cardinal importance here is that persons of mixed ethnic background are bilingual, and therefore, I maintain, are believed by northern Labrador Inuit to be more successful in communicating with the English-speaking outside world. While supporting the LIA, Labrador Inuit attach primary significance to fluent bilingualism as a criteria for leadership and are thus willing to be represented by persons of ambiguous ethnic status.

Returning to the Makkovik council election, it appears that Makkovik Inuit supported Settler councillors both because they were reluctant to see Inuit on the "Settler council" and, in any event, because they believed such positions better filled by English-speaking Settlers. This leads me to conclude that James' failure to win a council seat and the voluntary absence of Marcus from the election meeting indicate that many Inuit view council leadership as "off limits" to them. I suggest that both men were restrained directly or indirectly, from enacting behaviour inconsistent with the value system of Makkovik Inuit (in this case leadership in secular institutions). In Marcus' case, acceptance of the council nomination would have upset the unique and delicately balanced configuration of social facts affecting his ethnic identity (his mixed marriage, permanent employment with LSD, his close relations with his own kindred), and thereby would have ruptured his relationships with fellow Inuit. Moreover, after the election, Marcus expressed his intention to ''remain his own man'' and clearly recognized what some of the implications would have been of adopting a broker role – especially with respect to the services expected and values returned. In other words, he believed that the 'ethnic costs' of a council position would have been greater than any value it might have conferred – such as a higher social status among Settlers. James, on the other hand, was not elected by his own ethnic group: one may say that an 'ethnic check' was placed on his political activity.

Conclusion
What conclusion can be drawn from the materials presented above? To begin with, the council's efforts to 'court' Inuit represent a dramatic departure from the previous absence of socio-economic contact between Settlers and Inuit and is, in part, an unforeseen consequence of the establishment of a community council. On the other hand, the council was perceived by some Settlers as a necessary instrument for opening new avenues for financial support; at the same time, this meant adherence to government priorities favouring integration. Thus, the council's rationale for attempting to check emigration was moved more by pragmatic (developing Makkovik) than normative concerns, despite the *noblesse oblige* declaration of the council to ''do something for the Eskimos.''

But I have also pointed out how the Settler councillors misconceived the causes of Inuit out-migration, and mistakenly believed that if the impression of integration were created, out-migration would cease. In fact, the Hebron Inuit have adapted, and integrated – as far as they are willing – to an unfamiliar and Settler-monopolized environment; and after fifteen years of involuntary relocation in Makkovik, they still find traditional values important. Their out-migration is directly related to the better realization of these values.

Although supporting Ben-Dor's multicellular conceptualization of Makkovik, the data presented above indicate that, *contra* Ben-Dor, Inuit remain hesitant to abandon behaviour they perceive to be symbolic of their identity. Clearly, members of each ethnic group are 'holding the line,' as if increased ethnic interaction and relaxation of ethnic boundaries would contaminate the salient principles of ethnicity. Thus, as with other bi-ethnic northern Labrador communities, ethnicity in Makkovik remains a vital theme of social organization.

One might question whether it is Inuit values or other variables that sustain Makkovik's ethnic schism? Although my interpretation is that the schism is perpetuated primarily by differing values, I do not deny that other factors also play some part. I would stress, for example, that unlike other Labrador communities, Makkovik was originally a Settler village. To Makkovik Settlers, Inuit relocation there was both unexpected and unwelcome. For their part, the Hebron Inuit have been encouraged to relocate several times during the present century (see ch. 14, this vol.) and were neither consulted nor given a choice as to their destination when moved in 1959. As stated, adaptation to Makkovik's heavily-wooded and Settler-dominated environment was by no means easy, a fact which prompted many Inuit to voluntarily move north to Nain. In 1972, the Inuit population was less than half that of the Settlers and their minority situation and inability to speak English made them even more hesitant to interact with Settlers. Finally, Inuit undoubtedly realized why Settlers sought to "integrate" Makkovik and elect an Inuk councillor; and they believed they could gain few advantages from the council's policy.

Finally, three reasons, not necessarily mutually exclusive, may now be offered to explain ethnic boundary maintenance in Makkovik. First, I adhere to the view that repeated and stable exchanges between two parties (in this instance, ethnic groups) will generate a "congruence of codes and values" (Barth, 1969:16) and eventually a reduction of boundary-maintaining mechanisms: in short, integration. However, in order for an exchange to occur, the interests of both groups (usually neither totally different nor identical) *must* be valued by both parties (Wilson and Wilson, 1968:101). The absence of exchange, or the strict maintenance of ethnic boundaries in Makkovik, is partially explained then by the fact that neither Settlers nor Inuit see significant values in the other group's assets. Indeed, in my view, this is why Makkovik's Inuit are reluctant to respond to Settler efforts ostensibly aimed at increasing ethnic contacts. Secondly, ethnic boundary maintenance assists each group's contention that it is superior to the other. Feelings of superiority, however well-founded, exaggerate and perpetuate ethnic boundaries and thus assure continuation of distinct ethnic statuses. Finally, boundaries persist because of the proliferation and transmission of cultural differentiae signalling group membership. Such differences, described above in terms of ethnically-specific priorities, place imperative role constraints on the actors of each group, and thereby canalize and circumscribe the nature and extent of inter-ethnic interaction.

NOTES

1   My use of the term *ethnic group* borrows much from Barth (1969), as well as from Shibutani and Kwan (1965). Ethnic groups (or categories) are considered "ascriptive and exclusive" (Barth, 1969:14). *Cultural features* (e.g., dress, physical posture, values, language, ideas, etc.), signalling identity and/or allowing an actor to manage a particular identity,

constitute both the content and criteria of *ethnic boundaries*. As a type of status, the management of a particular identity constrains an actor's choice of roles according to boundary-specific criteria. This approach to ethnic groups recognizes that situational factors (e.g., when identity implies stigma; cf. Eidheim, 1969) may compel the incumbent of an ethnic status to temporarily de-emphasize identity without necessarily abandoning it. In short, this approach acknowledges the dynamic character (both persistence and change, without necessarily the loss) of ethnic boundary criteria and ethnic identity, and thus implicitly rejects the inevitability of the assimilation model of a plural society.

2   Data for this paper were collected between July 1971 and May 1972 and between July 1972 and September 1972 in Makkovik, Labrador. All names are fictitious for purposes of anonymity. Field research was conducted for and sponsored by the ISER, Memorial University of Newfoundland. I would like to acknowledge the many helpful comments and criticisms on earlier versions of this paper given by Tord Larsen, Frank Manning, George Park, and especially Robert Paine.

3   On the Labrador coast, as in parts of Newfoundland (cf. Faris, 1972:26–8), the category 'fish' refers only to cod, and 'fishing' describes only the procurement of that species. Other terms apply to other species; thus, men go salmon 'catching' or 'trouting.'

4   Inter-ethnic exchange remains constrained by an absence of prescriptive rules governing such exchange. Thus, when possible, Inuit and Settlers avoid contact; when this is impossible, encounters are lighthearted and momentary.

5   In reviewing some of the comparative literature on friendship, DuBois (1975) concludes that whereas casual friendships can override ethnic boundaries, close friendships seldom do. My use of the term friendship describes dyadic personal relationships, generally distinct from kinship, and typically between fellow Settlers and/or a Settler and an "outsider."

6   During brief return visits to Makkovik in May–June 1973, and August 1974, I observed increased interaction between Inuit and Settler children living in this integrated neighbourhood. This was not so among adults.

References

BARTH, FREDRIK
   1969 *Ethnic Groups and Boundaries*. Boston, Little, Brown and Company.
BEN-DOR, SHMUEL
   1966 *Makkovik: Eskimos and Settlers in a Labrador Community*. St. John's, Institute of Social and Economic Research, Memorial University of Newfoundland.
DUBOIS, CORA
   1975 "The Gratuitous Act: an Introduction to the Comparative Sociology of Friendship Patterns." In E. Leyton (ed.), *The Compact: Selected Dimensions of Friendship*. St. John's, Institute of Social and Economic Research, Memorial University of Newfoundland.
EIDHEIM, HARALD
   1969 "When Ethnic Identity is a Social Stigma." In F. Barth (ed.), *Ethnic Groups and Boundaries*. Boston, Little, Brown & Company.
FARIS, JAMES C.
   1972 *Cat Harbour: A Newfoundland Fishing Settlement*. St. John's, Institute of Social and Economic Research, Memorial University of Newfoundland.

FRANKENBERG, RONALD
1957 *Village on the Border*. London, Cohen and West.
KLEIVAN, HELGE
1966 *The Eskimos of Northeast Labrador. A History of Eskimo-White Relations 1771–1955*. Oslo, Norsk Polarinstitutt.
LINTON, RALPH
1936 *The Study of Man*. New York, Appleton-Century.
MURDOCK, G. P.
1949 *Social Structure*. New York, Macmillan.
PAINE, ROBERT
1963 "Entrepreneurial Activity without its Profits." In F. Barth (ed.), *The Role of the Entrepreneur in Social Change in Northern Norway*. Bergen, University Press.
SHIBUTANI, R. and K. M. KWAN
1965 *Ethnic Stratification: A Comparative Approach*. New York, Macmillan.
WILSON, G. and M. WILSON
1968 *The Analysis of Social Change*. Cambridge, Cambridge University Press.

Ethnic Commitments and Local Government in Nain, 1969–76*

19

Terje Brantenberg

My earlier essay in this book described the contrastive value systems of the Inuit and Settlers in Nain and the consequent streaming of persons to one or the other ethnic group. An important question to ask is whether these values would have endured the passage of time had the local populations been left to themselves instead of being under the influence of an 'outside' agency since the late eighteenth century. We should first consider, then, how the Moravian Mission, and other agencies after 1949, contributed to the persistence of Inuit-Settler ethnic categorizations.

A second and closely related objective of the present essay is to assess recent (post-1949) socio-political changes in Nain for what they mean to Inuit and Settler interests. These changes have not only been in the direction of modernity, with strong implications of secularization in the management of public affairs, but of ethnopolitics as well (see ch. 13).

I

'Moravian Eskimos' and Settlers

Because of its historical and virtually exclusive presence along the coast of northern Labrador (since 1771), the Moravian Church has greatly influenced Inuit society and culture. This prolonged contact resulted in the gradual disappearance of many traditional Inuit notions and institutions, especially those concerned with religion,[1] and in the substitution of Moravian ones. In important respects, the Inuit themselves now regard items of their pre-contact culture as incompatible with their present status as 'Moravian Eskimos.'[2]

Nevertheless, the Mission also believed that the spiritual and material welfare of the Inuit involved maintaining a basic Inuit identity. Assimilation was regarded as detrimental. Thus, knowledge of the Inuit language has always been a prerequisite for the missionaries, and Inuit children were taught to read and write in their own language; adherence to their traditional diet and skills was also encouraged. The hold of the Mission over the Inuit, as patrons, enabled them to sanction and supervise any contact that the native population had with other white agencies (cf. Hiller, 1971).

This policy of ethnic preservation and cultural isolation was largely

---

*Excerpted from an unpublished manuscript, and revised (ed.).

reversed in the years following World War II. These were years of increasing outside contact, and of greater mobility due to the opening up of a labour market at the American Air Force base in Goose Bay, Labrador (Zimmerly, 1975). The resettlement of the northernmost communities and the shift of the Mission's headquarters from Nain to Happy Valley in 1957 were related to this change of policy. However, the population resisted pressures to move south into more urban-like centres, and the present practice of the Mission is to provide religious services to the Inuit and Settler populations in their existing settlements.

Activities associated with the Moravian congregational culture provide the Inuit of Nain with the principal formal and public expressions of their ethnicity. Rituals and practices of Moravian origin are now seen by them as inherent to religious life, and the Inuit elders, as spokesmen of the congregation, consider the maintenance of Moravian traditions to be one of their main tasks; for example, recent changes in ritual, instituted officially by the Moravian Church, were unanimously opposed by the elders and by most of the Inuit population. We return to this later.

Whereas the Moravian culture came to provide a context for the formation of a new Moravian 'Eskimo' identity, mission contact with the Settler population was of a different order. The Mission was highly critical of the first generation of Settler immigrants, particularly because their trading activities were considered as a threat to its Inuit clientele (Hiller, 1971). However, with the transition of the Settler economy to one of fishing and trapping (c. 1860–80), the suspicious and even hostile relations between Mission and Settlers gave way to a more positive attitude on the part of both. It was also in this period that the scattered and isolated Settlers began to express a need to strengthen their separate identity *vis-à-vis* the Inuit. Although the Mission did not provide the Settlers with a basis for formulating a new identity, from about 1910 its presence along the coast became for them also, the main forum for publicly maintaining their identity. (The Settlers would come into Nain for the major church celebrations [Kleivan, 1966:101–04].) At present, the importance of the Moravian Church seems less pronounced for the Settlers because of increasing contact with the outside and the presence of alternative representatives of white society in Nain.

The Settler approach to religion differs markedly from that of the Inuit. For the Settler, being a Moravian does not mean a public and traditionalistic expression of religious life; to some extent, he sees his religious status as separate from his church activities; it belongs more to the private sphere of life, and derives from personal conviction. Generally speaking, then, they do not stress Moravian congregational culture as the ultimate religious experience.

The Inuit, on the other hand, emphasize the public expression of religious conviction, and this is demonstrated in the relatively high attendance at Inuit services. Ritual participation is seen as fundamental to religious experience and esoteric qualities are attributed to various rituals, especially to *rites de passage*. The details of Holy Communion are thus kept secret until candidates start training for confirmation. Until recently, this secrecy was also practised with regard to the marriage ceremony, inasmuch as children and youngsters were not allowed to attend the service. Similarly, in the household of an Inuit elder, the book containing the regulations and doctrines of the Labrador Moravian Church is not to be read by anyone but the elder himself. This ritual secrecy is still maintained today, independent of the will of the missionary, as a means of increasing the value of religious activity.

A word is necessary here about the actual organization of the local congregation. It is based on separate church choirs, each representing the different status of the members according to age, sex, and marital status. Thus, the unmarried are divided into the children's choir (all under thirteen years of age), and the separate choirs of unmarried men and boys, and of unmarried women and girls. The rest of the congregation belongs to the "married choir" (including widowers) and the "widows' choir." Settlers and Inuit are members of the same choirs. Each choir celebrates its annual festival days with services (widows and widowers have theirs in combination with the married people's day).

Services are conducted in Inuttitut, English, or bilingually as follows: a bilingual service is held every Saturday night; separate Inuit and English services, as well as a bilingual service, are held on Sundays. Major services such as Holy Communion and the Love Feasts are conducted in both languages at the same time. The Inuit and Settlers (including other whites) have their own choirs for their separate services.

From what has already been said about the religious attitudes of each ethnic group, it is not surprising that certain church activities are dominated by Inuit. The brass and string bands are composed of Inuit only – not because of any formal rules of segregation, but because Settlers are not interested. This disinterest in participation is also indicated by the fact that only one out of the nine chapel servants is a Settler and *no Settlers have been elders* during the last few years.

These different canons of religious behaviour can become the cause of confrontations. A Settler was once approached by an Inuk and criticized for not going to church regularly; observing that his critic was somewhat drunk, the Settler retorted that as far as he was concerned, it was far worse to be drunk in public than not go to the church services. He added later that *he* did not need to attend every service to prove his moral integrity. Another Settler related how he had spent one Sunday fishing from the wharf located beside the church. During the Inuit service, he was spotted from the church by an Inuk elder who immediately ran out and ordered him to stop fishing; the Settler ignored the command. Later the same evening, all the elders visited him and furiously scolded him for refusing to listen to the orders of an elder and for breaking church rules.

Although Inuit and Settler Confirmation candidates receive instruction separately, both groups attend the one bilingual service of Confirmation and Holy Communion at which the Inuit (as at all major rituals) generally wear the white *silapak* (cotton parka) and sealskin boots. A Settler related to me how he went to church as a candidate for the Confirmation service in his new dark suit. On entering, he was stopped by an elder who told him to go back home and change into a white *silapak* which the other (Inuit) candidates were wearing. Refusing to accept this, he went over to the missionary who readily gave him permission to remain as he was. This action resulted in a heated discussion between the elder and the missionary. The same man had the same problem at a celebration of the "single brethren's choir" for which the choir wore colourful ribbons and decorated caps. When seen in his suit by an elder, he was told to go home and dress like the others; having nobody to appeal to, he just left and stayed home; he discontinued attending thereafter.

We see, then, how on some formal occasions – particularly those involving members of both groups – items of dress can assume a symbolic significance that they do not otherwise have.[3] From the Inuit point of view, the *silapak* at the Confirmation service is a religious symbol and, for this reason, should be worn by Settlers as well as Inuit. The Settlers, on their part, conceive the *silapak* to be an Inuit garment in precisely such a setting – and therefore an ethnic symbol. Politically, the confrontation described above demonstrates how (i) the Settlers' insistence on remaining distinct in outward appearance at some public functions is (ii) negatively sanctioned by the Inuit (through the elders who see it as their responsibility to sanction deviance from traditional behaviour). The result is (iii) increased segregation along ethnic lines and the abstention of Settler participation from several aspects of the Moravian Church and congregation in Nain.

The Council of Elders

It should be emphasized that the Moravian Mission provides an organization for its congregation through which leadership roles may be exercised. Prior to 1901, the official roles were chapel servants appointed by, and responsible mainly to, the minister; since 1901, elders have been added, and together, they constitute the Congregation Board.

The elders are elected on a three-year basis, one per every hundred parishioners; candidates are proposed and elected by the congregation in a public meeting. The council of elders was established in order to bring a degree of self-government to the congregation. The elders' functions are broad in scope, covering "... all the general affairs of the congregation, internal as well as external" (Church Book of the Moravian Church in Labrador Province). The different tasks focus on enforcing church discipline, and on maintaining social control within the village in general; the elders settle disputes, organize public meetings and administer village affairs such as the spring clean-up and care of the aged and sick; they also have a voice in the appropriation and use of congregational funds.

Even though the Moravian Mission controlled most of the community affairs, until the last few decades, the elders were an important political body within the village. Since the Inuit, at that time, constituted almost the entire village population (the Settlers lived in homesteads dispersed outside Nain), they dominated the council of elders from the beginning. Because 'church' and 'village' (or 'congregation' and 'local community') are perceived by the Nain Inuit as so closely interrelated as not to be properly separable, the responsibilities of the elders are of a broad nature. Also, because they are chosen by popular vote, they are able to exercise a high degree of independence from the missionaries; indeed, they have sided frequently with the villagers in confrontations with the missionaries.[4]

The traditional importance of elders in the maintenance of social control and administration of community affairs can be seen in the regulations which they have made and enforced. For instance, they instituted a detailed set of rules regarding the division of shares in seal and caribou hunting, and in cod fishing, as well as setting local prices for seal carcasses, firewood, and other items. They forbade travel by boat or dog-team, as well as noisy conduct, before and after freeze-up, in order to prevent the migrating schools of harp seals from being frightened out of the bays close to Nain. Although some of these regulations have slowly fallen out of use, Inuit still look to elders for settling grievances regarding the access to and sharing of major game.

Thus, in addition to the public functions laid down by the Mission (for example, rounding up children after 9 p.m.), the elders assumed an active part in local affairs on their own. It was they who were instrumental in initiating and organizing the construction of the town hall (named after a former chief elder). The elders also played an important part in settling interpersonal conflicts; although generally refraining from involving themselves in cases of private violation of personal ethics, they would intervene, and attempt to reconcile the opposing parties when hostility erupted in public fights.[5]

It was not until 1907 that a Settler was elected to the body of elders; but Settler representation has never been continuous and in recent years, there has been none. Accordingly, the council is really regarded as an Inuit organization and the position of chief elder, in particular, as a platform for influential and able Inuit. The lack of Settler assertiveness and surrender of influence cannot be accounted for exclusively by their numerical minority. As has been mentioned, Settlers have expressed an unwillingness to speak Inuttitut (which is what is expected of them by the Inuit) at such a formal and public gathering as the council of elders; they are afraid, they have said, of being ridiculed for mispronouncing words (Kleivan, 1969:114). This is in marked contrast to the relative ease and fluency with which Settlers speak Inuttitut at informal occasions. Also, Settlers have sometimes claimed that the elders and their meetings serve Inuit interests only, and that when Settlers have attempted to get problems discussed which are of an interest to them, little understanding or interest has been shown for their views by the elders.

Beginning of Change
The last decades have seen the steady transfer of responsibility and influence for the affairs of Nain from the Moravian Church to the Newfoundland Government. The rationale behind the presence and policies of the Newfoundland Government in northern Labrador is directly connected with the presence there of native people (Indians and Inuit), and with federal funds ear-marked for use in northern Labrador (for the benefit of the native peoples). This special status of the area is reflected in the setting up of the Northern Labrador Services Division (N.L.S.D.) to the general neglect of southern Labrador, officially an all-white region (see Ch. 14, this vol.).

But, paradoxically, the change of fortunes brought by this special status are as noticeable among the Settlers in Nain as among the Inuit.[6] The Settlers have much more to win from change; in the traditional setting, it was the Inuit – through the structure provided by the Moravian Mission – who were in control of the main political arenas; Settlers were exposed to Inuit sanctions and Inuit interests prevailed. But under the new circumstances, the Settlers fulfill an important role because of their status as 'whites' with bicultural capabilities: they have been recruited by the Provincial and Federal Governments as "middlemen" (Paine, 1971) in dealings with the local Inuit population. They serve as clerks, interpreters, and hold other similar positions.

One implication of the new situation is the marked trend towards Settler dominance in the economy of Nain. This is seen in their ownership of shops, a snack bar, a bakery, and the selling of snowmobiles and spare parts. Still more compelling evidence is that about 75 percent of the total number of persons employed by Euro-Canadian institutions in full-time wage-work are Settlers.

From the Settlers' own perspective, perhaps the most important change is in the arrival of personnel representing a number of Euro-Canadian agencies that provide Settlers with alternative means for expressing their identity as whites. Although the Moravian Church and its activities are still valued by the Settlers, it is no longer the context in which Settlers stress membership in white society and culture. The new personnel are of different ages, backgrounds, and occupations; they include government white collar workers, R.C.M.P. officers, nurses, teachers, bush pilots, seamen, and others; although they are classified as temporary residents, some of them have been in Nain for several years with their families. Socially remote from the Inuit population and residing within the general Settler area (see Map of Nain), these persons provide Settlers with opportunities for Euro-Canadian social life (from which, as a rule, Inuit are excluded) of a more diffuse and intimate kind than they had with the resident Moravian officials: visiting, parties, card-playing, hunting partnerships, and so forth. Several marriages have taken place, and although the Settler wives generally leave Nain when their husbands are posted elsewhere, there have been several recent instances of southern Canadian wives settling in Nain with their Settler husbands.[7]

There are two particulars to be noted about the Settlers' recent* management of identity: on the one hand, there is what amounts to an 'over-communication' of what the Settlers perceive as 'white' values, and on the other, they are able to pass onto the transient Euro-Canadian group their stereotypic ideas about the Inuit and Inuit culture. Also at this time, the influence of the elders, and indeed, the traditional basis of 'Eskimo Moravianism' were challenged from an unexpected quarter: the Mission. The Nain missionary announced changes in the Confirmation practices, changes aimed at reducing the formal importance of public rituals.

The instruction of candidates for Confirmation was based on a printed manual of questions and answers covering the main Moravian doctrines, which also form the foundation of the Confirmation service. In instructing Inuit candidates, the missionary was always assisted by an older Inuk, one of the chapel servants, whose main role was to ensure as fluent and complete memorization of the manual as possible (in contrast to Settler practice; cf. Ben-Dor, 1966:106–10). Opposed to this mere recitation of text, the missionary in Nain assumed all responsibility for the instruction of candidates, stressing comprehension and discussion, instead. In this, he was ardently opposed by the former assistant as well as by the Inuit congregation at large. Inuit ideas of proper religious observance seemed to them to be threatened. However, the will of the missionary prevailed (for the time being at least): he dismissed the objections of the congregation as "empty formalism." With regard to the Confirmation service itself, the missionary abridged the traditional formal hearing from the manual, causing much dissatisfaction among the Inuit: "This is not an Inuit Confirma-

---

* That is, during the 1960s. Still more recent changes in Settler identity management are discussed in Part II of this article (ed.).

tion – it's not the way we do it!'' Attempts to introduce more modern hymns were met with the same reaction among the Inuit, with their elders in the forefront.

Ethnic Separateness

After this review of the influence of the Moravian Mission in Nain, we can return to the question of the ways the Inuit and Settlers of Nain have maintained distinct ethnic identities through time. The thesis of the present essay is that the process has been considerably facilitated by the presence of 'external' agencies, in particular the Moravian Mission.

By separating the two groups for ritualistic and other activities, the Mission provided each with a context for the expression of their ethnicity; this is true even though the Mission has always been explictly supportive of the 'Eskimo' language, diet, hunting skills and so on. Through what amounted to Moravian patronage, the Inuit came to re-define their identity as 'Moravian Eskimos.' As for the Settlers, the Mission provided them with an additional and most significant context for confirming their separate ethnic identity as a hard-pressed local minority.

Each group judges the other according to its own standards of behaviour: Inuit are inferior to Settlers and vice versa. Nevertheless, there has been little direct confrontation between the two groups, a situation that can also be attributed to the degree of separation imposed upon them by the Mission. Where this separation has not been enforced, confrontations have occurred (at Confirmation services and, as will be shown below, at town council meetings, for example) and their usual outcome is, in fact, separation.

As long as each group was able to express mutual superiority and inferiority, there was little likelihood of uni-directional ethnic change in Nain, and there was an absence of any clear-cut stratification between them. Instead, in each generation there has been an allocation of individuals to each group – by processes I attempted to describe in my earlier essay. However, I do not mean to suggest a state of affairs in which there is an easily-held homeostasis. For generations, it was the Settlers who were in particular need of maintaining their numbers and distinguishing their culture from the Inuit. Now that Nain is becoming integrated with Euro-Canadian institutions, the Inuit face some of these problems. It is a paradox of Moravian patronage that the Inuit, in their present circumstances, are in the role of Moravian conservatives, accusing the Mission itself of not being sufficiently Moravian. In stressing their separate identity vis-à-vis the outside world, it has become crucial for the Inuit to control the cultural and institutional expressions of Moravianism as they knew it.

It is, however, group conduct that we have been describing, and much about inter-personal relations in Nain escapes the strictures of ethnicity – a point also made earlier. Indeed, it is possible for an individual, Settler or Inuit, to be censured and ridiculed by his fellows for his inappropriate attention to ethnicity. Especially interesting here is the notion of *context*; dress and language, for example, may be seen as ethnic symbols in church and at other public meetings, but not on informal occasions. Settlers refuse to wear the *silapak* in church, yet are pleased to use it when outside in cold weather and about their ordinary business; that there is no contradiction in this conduct indicates how there is, after all, a wide spectrum of social life in Nain in which Inuit and Settlers are not facing each other as competitors or adversaries.

II

So far, we have been concerned with Nain until 1970 – a relatively simple scenario; after 1970, however, events become considerably more complicated with the addition of two new institutional foci: a community council in July 1970, and in September 1972, the Labrador Inuit Association. First, let us consider the establishment of the council.

The First Council: 1970
The formation of community councils was recognized as a step in the provincial government's policy to modernize the communities along the Labrador coast. Other coastal settlements to the south already had councils when some years previously, government-inspired attempts to form a council in Nain had failed. This was attributed to the lack of local response stemming from a failure to appreciate, it was said, the need for an additional organization besides the council of elders. The initiative for the establishment of a council at that time had come from the local N.L.S.D. depot manager (as was the case in the other coastal communities). But when the public meeting was called at Nain (the depot manager used an Inuk elder as his interpreter), the elders and their congregation were not only at a loss to understand what the projected role of a council would be in Nain, they were also deeply apprehensive.

The second attempt in 1970 was initiated by a number of young Settlers, who clearly recognized that a community council would be a more important political arena than a council of elders, and one Inuk, along with the help of various government personnel. This small group of persons combined a variety of Euro-Canadian experiences and skills: high-school education, jobs with the N.L.S.D., and specialized training acquired in urban centres; most of them could also speak Inuttitut fluently. Also of importance was the fact that the previous N.L.S.D. depot manager had been transferred, and his replacement was experienced in starting up a community council.

At a public meeting, this group presented to the community, in both languages, the rationale and advantages of a council. They stressed that municipal status would bring Nain financial support for public projects; they pointed out that the council of elders could not be acknowledged by municipal regulations, and therefore, a town council was the sole means to further development and modernization in Nain. They received a great deal of support from both Settlers and Inuit who, at that time, accepted them as honest brokers or as "go-betweens" (cf. Paine, 1971:21). The entire group were voted into the council (almost unanimously), together with one Inuit elder. The group of initiators had taken the trouble to meet with the elders before calling their public meeting (and the posters they distributed around the village were written in both languages). As a result, the chief elder attended the public meeting and there urged everybody to support the idea of a council and to vote for the slate of councillors that had been prepared.

A great deal of enthusiasm was generated at this time and a number of promises made. There were promises of such services as garbage collection, street lighting, and fire fighting; there would even be a lobby pressing for an airstrip. The council also undertook to call frequent public meetings, to ensure consistent and proper translations into both languages of all communications, and to provide careful accounting of the council's revenue. After this successful start, however, conflicts developed.

Ideally, the two community organizations – the council of elders and the community council – represented separate fields of responsibility, the elders serving the needs of the congregation, and the town councillors the needs of the community *vis-à-vis* the outside world. Initially, the community members accepted this arrangement even though they recognized that the elders' traditional spheres of influence were being restricted by it.

It is important to note that none of the Settlers voted onto the council would have had much of a chance of being elected an elder; similarly, the few Inuit who had been suggested as candidates for council received little support (with the sole exception of the elder who was included on the successful slate). This seems to show quite clearly how, at the outset, the two different community organizations were associated not only with different tasks but also with different realms of expertise, each of which were, in turn, associated with specific ethnic membership.

In practice, however, the two bodies had difficulty restricting themselves to their respective spheres, and this tendency was aggravated by ethnically-conditioned views concerning the proper management of local public affairs. Thus, the issue was not the existence of a council as such, but the attempt of the first council to re-define the management of public affairs and interests – management that was identified with the elders. Whereas attention had been given to explaining the formal functions of the council, what had been left out of account, not unexpectedly, was how the

differences of interest within the local community were to be accommo-
dated. It had been hoped that these differences would be resolved through a
mutual division of influence; in fact, the presence of a council alongside the
body of elders served to accentuate differences of interest.

The councillors insisted on giving the village a new face: cleanliness,
street lights, no loose dogs, public notices written in correct English, and so
forth. They also demanded control of the community hall and proper
bureaucratic procedure concerning public funds derived from municipal
activities. The issue of the community hall was presented to the elders
within a few days of the election of the council. The majority view among
the councillors was that the hall was public property, as it had been built
largely through voluntary labour and cash donations from local persons.
The elders were divided among themselves over this issue; however,
control of the hall was given to the council. The actual use to which council
put the hall gave rise to a sharper confrontation in which the council had to
call in the R.C.M.P. to enforce their decisions.[8]

The elders had to surrender on other issues and there were other confrontations; the aggregate effect was to place the community in a mild
condition of shock. Although some people were glad to see the rule of the
elders rudely terminated (as it seemed at the time), there were many more
who were perturbed by the council's comparative liberalism and its opposition to the traditions upheld by the elders.

Inevitably, the council lost some of its earlier support among the Inuit
whose loyalty reverted to the elders. Confidence in the council was also
reduced by its failure to realize some of its promised projects: funds
received from government for street lighting remained unused and their
were even problems with the weekly garbage collection. The difficulties of
the council were exacerbated by disagreements between councillors (beginning with the handling of the town hall issue) and the periodic absences
from Nain of the chairman. (While he was away attending courses in
municipal management, he failed to delegate his office properly.) Within a
year, then, the council began to experience some of the criticism that used
to be raised against the elders. Particularly damaging was the talk about
possible misappropriation of public funds and also the ineffectiveness of
council: unfavourable comparisons were made (by the Inuit) with the
success elders had had in getting people to work together on community
projects.

Perhaps the opinions of resident and visiting whites in Nain were of some
importance also. Commenting on the difficulties of the first council, a
storekeeper stated that he had become less inclined to vote for Settler
candidates as, in his view, they did not command sufficient respect and
authority, especially among the Inuit. A visiting public official compared
the organizational skills of the first council unfavourably with those of the

elders. He had sat in on several committee meetings of both councillors and elders. However, in my judgement, the public meetings of the first council were handled in a manner not inferior to the meetings of the elders. (Knowing the importance local people would attach to this, the councillors provided complete bilingual coverage, something that did not ordinarily happen at the public meetings of the elders.)

But even if disenchantment with the council at this time meant a renewal of support for the elders, changes in the place of the elders' authority in the community must not be overlooked. We should begin by mentioning that ever since the arrival, in 1935, of a police detachment in Nain, the elders' role in maintaining order had been on the decline. Nevertheless, they still intervened in social problems that fell outside police jurisdiction, as in cases of serious and continuous marital conflict. The elders also insisted on attempting to use the ultimate sanction of traditional Moravian discipline; that is, expulsion of troublesome individuals from the village. This was one of the actions that the council objected to, for the first time, demands by the elders that certain individuals leave the community were successfully resisted.

But of still greater significance, the consensus traditionally given to elders' authority was disturbed with the resettlement to Nain of 32 families from the more northern, predominantly Inuit communities of Hebron and Nutak during 1956–59.[9] Neither the majority of the northerners nor the people of Nain had been in favour of the resettlement, as they knew it would mean increased competition for local resources – be it wild game or firewood, hunting and fishing places, or jobs and amenities within the village. Indeed, there were conflicts between members of the two groups when Nain Inuit showed reluctance, and sometimes refused, to allow northerners to use their hunting and fishing places; and northerners believed that the Nain elders' rules in this regard were deliberately prejudicial to them. Arguments, joking, and mock fights (about differences in dialect, or hunting and fishing skills) easily erupted into serious fights during the first years. Relations were also strained because of the government housing scheme: the Nain Inuit were left in their old homes, whereas the newcomers were placed in new houses in a separate neighbourhood.[10]

Although there have been several marriages between the two groups, as well as hunting and fishing partnerships, the northerners still described their situation as one of estrangement and dislocation ten years after resettling; and they have repeatedly (and unsuccessfully) petitioned the government to re-locate back north.[11] Nor were the northerners able to exert themselves politically within the community of Nain; although some of them served as chapel servants and elders, as a group they had little influence. One reason for this is that on the basis of numbers only, Nain Inuit controlled the majority of votes for the election of elders; another

TABLE 1

Nain Councillors, 1970–74

No.	Inuit (I) Mixed (M) Settler (S)	Place of Birth	Age on Election	Bilingual Rating	Occupation	Other Status
1	M	Hebron	32	high	NLSD, grocery store	
2	I	Nain	45	low	Fishing and sealing skipper	elder
3	S	Nutak	25	low	NLSD, postmaster	
4	S	Nutak	28	low	power-plant operator	Inuk wife
5	S	Nain	32	high	Bell Telephone, janitor	Inuk wife
6	M	Nain	22	low	store clerk, postmaster	
7	I	Nutak	32	low	fisherman-hunter	elder
8	I	Nain	24	high	fisherman-hunter	interpreter, reporter
9	I	Nain	30	high	power plant operator	
10	I	Nain	38	low	fisherman-hunter	elder
11	M	Nain	25	low	nurse	female editor
12	S	Nain	49	high	fisherman-hunter	

reason is that the chief elder of the Hebron community resettled in Mak-kovik (Ben-Dor, 1966: 86–9), leaving those in Nain without their most influential spokesman. The northerners have been reluctant to accept the Nain Inuit leaders as their spokesmen; indeed, their criticisms so upset the chief elder in Nain that he threatened to resign unless he received an unambiguous vote of support.

Yet, of the small group who successfully initiated the idea of a community council, three were northerners and all were elected to the first council (Table 1: nos. 1, 3 and 4).

Let us summarize the relations between elders and councillors, between Inuit and Settlers, and between Inuit during the early years of the council. The council came into being in response to two locally-perceived causes. The first had to do with the younger generation of Settlers' increasing identification with local public affairs. In general, the council was con-

TABLE 2

Changing Representation on Community Council, 1970–74

(a) according to the individuals identified in Table 1

Councillor	1st Council 1970	2nd Council 1971	3rd Council 1974
1	X		
2	X		X
3	X[1]		
4	X	X	
5	X	X	
6	X[2]	X[1]	
7		X	
8		X	
9		X[2]	X
10			X
11			X
12			X

Notes: [1] resigned
[2] replaced resigned councillor

(b) according to ethnic and other statuses

	Inuit	Mixed	Settlers	Nain	Northerners	Elders
1970	1	2	3	3	3	1
1971	3	1	2	4	2	1
1974	3	1	1	5	0	2

ceived as a means of modernizing the community according to Canadian standards; in particular, it was recognized (by the activist group) as an alternative and more up-to-date mode of management than the traditional ways of the elders. The second cause was the northerners' dissatisfaction; although there were a few prominent Settlers among them, the northerners were another Inuit group. These two causes were joined, in the beginning, to make the political platform for a council. But as soon as the council came into being, two closely-related issues came to the forefront: the division of responsibility between elders and councillors, and the continuance of the elders' authority as an inclusive symbol of Inuit hegemony in Nain.

Notwithstanding public statements about the division of authority between the elders and council, most Settlers of Nain saw the one being replaced by the other. One Settler declined an invitation to stand for election as an elder, something he would not have done (he later explained) before the establishment of a council; for this respected Settler and others like him, the council became the only relevant civic institution. The majority of Inuit felt that the council was to be simply an additional instrument of local government.

An early effect of a council in Nain was to provide the Inuit elders with the occasion to defend 'traditional' values; this implied a selection of priorities on the part of the elders and gave a new significance to questions of commitment to alternative codes of conduct. The confrontation in which the elders found themselves with the Moravian Mission over traditional religious practice should be recalled here, for there is no doubt that this strengthened the bonds between the elders and their Inuit followers at a time when it seemed possible that the relationship might become severely compromised.

It is also significant how the establishment of a council placed new distance between those Settlers who were now councillors and the Inuit public as a whole (even the younger generation and northerners). This was particularly the case whenever the councillors turned their attention to (what they saw as) problems within the village. As brokers working on behalf of the community with outside agencies, the Settler councillors were more acceptable; though even here, Inuit resented the Settlers' early monopoly of (broadly defined) entrepreneurial and brokerage roles. For it should not be forgotten that, aside from the administrative skills and the local authority of the Inuit elders, the younger generation of Inuit were improving their bilingual and bicultural skills.

Subsequent Events: 1971–75

An examination of the changing composition of the community council up to 1975 helps reveal some of the political developments that were – in some cases but faintly – presaged in the aftermath of setting up the council in 1970. The second and third councils were elected in the autumn of 1971 and in January 1974 (Table II).

Only two of the original five councillors continued in office for a second term: both were younger Settlers, one a northerner (no. 4) and the other from Nain (no. 5); they became chairman and vice-chairman, respectively, of the second council. Both of them were married to Inuit women. Indeed, the father-in-law of no. 5 was the chief elder of Nain; it was this councillor who, in 1970, found himself at odds with other Settlers on the council over the disagreement with the elders on the matter of the community hall. Because of this and similar incidents, he became characterized by other Settlers as "Eskimo," politically (see Ch. 16).

One man who was not re-elected was the only Inuk on the first council (no. 2) and a Nain elder. The other two not re-elected were northerners, one a Settler (no. 3) and the other of Inuit-Settler parentage (no. 1). The latter had been part of the small group who had urged the idea of a council on the community, later becoming the chairman of the first council; this councillor resigned several months before the second election in anticipation of the problems he sensed were under way.

Two of the new councillors were Inuit; one, a northerner, was an elder (no. 7), and the other, from Nain, was an interpreter who became a reporter for the newspaper started in March 1972[12] (no. 8). The third new councillor (no. 6) was a young man of Inuit-Settler parentage who recently returned to the community after going to school elsewhere and replaced no. 3 for the last few months on the first council; he himself resigned from the second council in the autumn of 1972 and was replaced by another young Inuk from Nain (no. 9).

The results of the third council election in January 1974 followed the trend set in the previous election, even though four out of five of the councillors were replaced (no. 9 remained). Of the four new councillors, one was the Nain elder (no. 2) on the first council; another was also a Nain elder (no. 10); the third was a young nurse from Nain (no. 11) of Inuit-Settler parentage, who also served as editor of the Nain newspaper; and the fourth was an older Nain Settler (no. 12).

In summary, by the time of the third council, none of the original Settler activists remained on council, the influence of the elders had grown stronger (two elders on the third council), and the earlier Settler and 'northerner' majorities were reversed in favour of Inuit and Nain representation (see Table IIb).

Since 1974, the council has increasingly become an arena for cooperation between Inuit and Settlers as both groups realize its importance in obtaining local control of local affairs. As far as the Settlers are concerned, they realize that such an electoral system makes them heavily dependent on the local Inuit majority, and a Settler who wishes political office in Nain has to win the trust of that majority. To achieve this trust, public criticism of local Inuit codes of conduct must be scrupulously avoided; *on this basis* the Inuit of Nain are increasingly prepared to recognize the importance, among those seeking local political office, of such abilities as public speaking.

III

At the very time that the community of Nain was trying to adjust to the place of a municipal-type council in their community alongside its traditional council of elders, a new form of political organization, with different ideals, made its appearance in northern Labrador. In February 1972, representatives of the Northern Quebec Inuit Association (N.Q.I.A.) visited Nain for the first time, travelling by snowmobiles from George River. A month later, the chief elder of Nain was invited by the National Inuit Association (I.T.C.) to participate in a conference held in Frobisher Bay, and during the following summer, representatives of I.T.C. visited the main Inuit coastal communities.

The Founding of the Labrador Inuit Association
The people of Nain followed these events with great interest. Apart from the Northerners from Nutak and Hebron who kept in touch with relatives and friends in the settlements of Northern Ungava, Nain Inuit and Settlers had had very little contact with, or knowledge of, Inuit outside Labrador. At a public meeting in Nain, a representative from N.Q.I.A. stressed that Inuit society had been long divided by provincial borders running north-south; now, he urged, it was time to cross these borders and revitalize the earlier unity found among the native peoples of the north.

This statement, though generally appreciated by those attending the meeting, was viewed with grave concern by several resident whites and by government personnel on the coast and in St. John's. They regarded it as tantamount to inciting the Labrador Inuit to oppose the authority of the Provincial Government, and even to aiming for the separation of northern Labrador from Newfoundland rule. A white community worker, believed to be sympathetic to these aims, was threatened with a charge of inciting public disorder. The proclamation of a state of emergency was even discussed, but eventually the situation, which had had little impact outside the closely-knit white neighbourhood, settled down.

A more far-reaching event was the meeting held in Nain in September 1972, to establish a Labrador Inuit Committee intended as the foundation of a Labrador branch of the *Inuit Tapirisat* of Canada. This meeting was attended by about 120 people and was opened by the chief elder of Nain (father-in-law of councillor no. 5), who informed them that a chairman had been selected for the proposed committee at a recent combined meeting of elders, chapel servants and councillors. Their choice was ex-councillor no. 5. The local newspaper *Kinatuinamot Illengajuk* noted that "people agreed with this choice and nobody expressed any discontent with it" (1972:24). Nominations were then invited for the three remaining places on the committee. Six Inuit (including two women) and two bilingual women Settlers were nominated and seconded by the Inuit. Those elected were councillor no. 7 (the Inuit elder) as vice-chairman, the wife of the chairman as secretary, and her brother as treasurer. The chief elder was elected as asvisor to the committee.

Most people probably failed to understand the full implications of this kind of political development. However, it was realized that native people elsewhere were starting to organize themselves on such issues as hunting regulations and language, and that Nain should have similar aims. Since the beginning of this century, the elders of the Moravian communities had continuously petitioned Newfoundland officials to take into consideration the special needs of the northern population with regard to various hunting regulations. As the elders were not always successful – indeed, they were often ignored – the new committee came to be regarded as a proper channel for furthering such interests.

However, this first committee had certain difficulties in organized activity, one reason being lack of funds; for example, the committee originally intended to arrange the election of five additional members to represent Hopedale, Makkovik and Happy Valley, but due to the lack of outside financial support, this plan could not be implemented. Thus, the establishment of the Labrador Inuit Association and its incorporation into the national organization (I.T.C.) was delayed.

In September 1973, Nain was once more visited by Inuit representatives from outside: the I.T.C. president and the editor of the *Inuit Monthly* (published by I.T.C.). At a meeting held on September 26, it was explained that the role of the I.T.C. was to unite the Canadian Inuit in order to achieve greater Inuit independence, and to further Inuit interests and needs with regard to hunting regulations, education, language and political representation. In addition, the establishment of the Labrador branch should help the people to "know who you are and where you are going." At the same meeting, the chairman of the committee asked those attending to elect a new chairman and three board members; he stressed that those elected would not only have to keep in touch with the Federal Government, but also attend meetings outside Labrador.

Thirteen candidates were proposed for chairman: 7 had an Inuit background (several of them were elders); 2 were from a mixed Inuit-Settler background (one with a clear Inuk status within the community); and the remaining 4 were Settlers (including the chairman of the first committee) who were either married to Inuit women and/or were bilingual (one of these Settlers had served as an elder in Nain). The chairman of the first committee (ex-councillor no. 5), a Settler, received an overwhelming majority with 60 votes, and the chief elder (advisor to the first committee) 20 votes; none of the other candidates received more than 10 votes.

Then followed the nomination of nine candidates for the three positions as board member: 5 of the nominees were Inuit (3 being elders), 3 were of mixed background, and 1 was a Settler married to an Inuk. The last four spoke Inuttitut. All nine candidates were nominated and seconded by Inuit. In the end, three Inuit were elected: two of them had been on the original committee (the vice-chairman and the secretary) and the third was an Inuk of mixed background (who was elected as elder the following year).

Subsequently, the other communities also elected representatives to the new committee: two were from Hopedale, two from Makkovik, and one from Happy Valley. All were Inuit, though two had a mixed background.

The following month (October 1), all members attended a board meeting in Nain at which the I.T.C. president, the chief elder and his predecessor were also present. The latter, then 84 years old, still exerted some influence in Nain, and was unanimously appointed as an honorary life president of the L.I.A. After a unanimous confirmation of the previous election of the chairman, the Labrador Inuit Association was formally established and made an affiliate member of *Inuit Tapirisat* of Canada. Nain was chosen as the location for the head office of the association.

The association adopted the following aims and objectives:

"(1) To promote the Inuit wants and rights, and all matters affecting the Inuit people of Labrador through the democratic system of Canada.

(2) To share all democratic, social, economical, recreational, legal and human rights with the citizens of Newfoundland and Canada.

(3) To promote and preserve Inuit culture and language, and develop dignity and pride in Inuit heritage amongst the Inuit people of Labrador.

(4) To promote and protect the traditional hunting, fishing and aboriginal rights of Inuit people of Labrador.

(5) To promote effective communication among Inuit people of Labrador through all available sources.

(6) To provide access to an interpretation of Government policies affecting Inuit people of Labrador.

(7) To promote public awareness of Inuit aspirations for Inuit people of Labrador." (From a public statement of the L.I.A. 2 October, 1973.)

Membership eligibility in the association was an important issue to settle, also. Naturally, the discussion turned on the eligibility of Settlers, especially those who were not fluent in Inuttitut. Some members suggested a liberal approach, reminding the meeting of the difficulties some Settlers were experiencing further south along the coast in speaking Inuttitut, and that even some of the younger Inuit there could speak only English. However, other members took a harder line, proposing that board members should be fluent in Inuttitut. This was consequently adopted as one of the by-laws. In the first public statement of the L.I.A., the following restrictions on membership were made.

This brief summary of the founding of the L.I.A. should illustrate how the association, from its very beginning, was embedded in ambiguity and potential contradiction: it mixed the desire for Inuit independence with the need for Inuit and Settler co-operation. As we shall show, the problem was aggravated by the involvement of the L.I.A. in intra-ethnic relations (with I.T.C. and another native association in Labrador) and inter-ethnic relations (with the Federal and Provincial governments).

Inuit Politics and Ethnic Commitment: The Local Scene
Initially, both the founding committee and the L.I.A. were explicitly urged by the I.T.C. to emphasize their identity as Inuit organizations, and to stress the importance of Inuttitut fluency as an essential qualification for full membership. Another factor that inspired the need for Inuit solidarity in Labrador was the exposure of L.I.A. representatives to the larger pan-Inuit community throughout the N.W.T. When comparing their own life style and traditions with those of the *Inummariit* ideal (Brody, 1975) in the N.W.T., they felt inferior; that is, less Inuit. They also noticed the strong cultural pride and apparent unity among Inuit of the N.W.T., in contrast to the divisions and conflicts in their own Labrador communities.[13]

It is not surprising, then, that L.I.A. representatives agreed to revitalize Inuit cultural traditions as one way of counteracting the consequences of Inuit exposure to white society and culture. This emphasis on 'Inuitness' was also related to the political and economic rationale of the concept of aboriginal status, so important for the (on-going) negotiations of Inuit land claims with the Canadian government.

Settler status in L.I.A. was, however, still ambiguous (even for those eligible for full membership), as it was not specified in the aims and objectives of the association, but only in the membership rules. As far as the L.I.A. was concerned, the basis for Settler involvement in Inuit politics was the fact that they shared Inuit cultural traditions, and was not due to their status as Settlers. But many of the Settlers were in a dilemma whether to join L.I.A. as a full or associate member, or to remain outside the association; in short, every Settler had to make a decision as to his/her commitment to Inuit and non-Inuit (white) interests, even at the risk of causing internal divisions between themselves.[14]

Since the founding of the L.I.A., Nain Settlers naturally have become increasingly concerned with the possible outcome of Inuit politics and how it could affect their own situation. Several Settlers joined the association early, but the majority of them feared that the existence of L.I.A. would strengthen the position of Inuit by making them a dominant group in Nain and elsewhere along the coast. Group interests of Settlers were not included in the association's aims and objectives. Moreover, Inuit legal claims to the land are based on their status as the aboriginal inhabitants of Labrador, and the complexities of native law in Canada provide only "squatters" rights to those Settlers who are unable to prove their aboriginal status in Labrador.[15] This fact makes some Settlers afraid of losing their hunting and fishing rights, even within their homestead areas – rights that had traditionally been recognized by both Inuit and Settlers. Some Settlers have become suspicious of L.I.A's attitude, and possible role, in this matter, and they have often reacted indignantly to Inuit statements that Settlers could claim land only if they were able to qualify for full membership in L.I.A. (that is, if they qualified as Inuit). Some Settlers in Nain, who formally qualified for full membership, regarded the association as a threat to the traditional Settlers' interests, and even expressed their readiness to actively oppose L.I.A. if they found their suspicions confirmed.

It is worth mentioning that after the founding of the L.I.A., some local Inuit representatives advocated an unconditional admission of Settlers to the native association. Their main argument in favour of this was the similarity of Inuit and Settler interests along the coast of Labrador. They recognized that a political coalition with the Settlers would likely strengthen their mutual interests.

The electoral procedure made it possible for Settlers to obtain leading positions in the association; the first president of the Labrador Inuit Council was a Settler. This suggests that when selecting individuals for political tasks, people in Nain attached importance to other local factors besides bilingual skills and ancestry. For example, it was particularly advantageous for a candidate to have a wide kinship network; the president's included the most influential people in Nain (both Inuit and Settlers). (It was, however, necessary for a candidate to show ability and willingness to use Inuttitut, as well as a general commitment to Inuit values.) Such an interpretation of Settler eligibility for membership certainly reflected the fact that the concept of aboriginal status was, in general, new for both Inuit and Settlers. (In addition, there was only limited information on the legal and political implications of native law in Canada.) Results of the first elections to the native association in Nain clearly show that the Inuit part of the population did not regard Settlers' participation in the work of the association as a factor that might hinder the attainment of its objectives.

On the other hand, it was the growing self-awareness of Inuit, as Inuit, that gave rise to difficulties in the relations between Inuit and Settlers. There were cases of open conflict when some Settlers heard individual Inuit say that "all whitemen are to be driven out of Labrador." To this, Settlers retorted that their families could prove a longer residence on the Labrador coast than some of the Inuit who moved there from Ungava. (However, this sort of argument between the two groups has never, as far as I know, been publicly expressed in Nain.)

In view of the considerable number of marriages between Inuit and Settlers, the question of Settlers' rights in any future land claims' settlement generated much anxiety, and was discussed in the context of the

I.T.C. requirement that Settlers be at least one fourth Inuit. Even persons who previously enjoyed an unquestionable Inuk status in the community became worried; some who feared that they would not qualify as Inuit started opposing the L.I.A. For those of mixed ancestry who had already experienced difficulties in finding their own identity, these developments only added to their personal frustrations and difficulties in their dealings with other Inuit and Settlers. On the other hand, some who had opposed L.I.A. became its supporters after realizing that they had misunderstood the criteria for gaining Inuk status. Then the fact of being formally classified as Inuk supported their self-identification as Inuk. Before L.I.A. came into existence, the majority of persons with a mixed ethnic background used to emphasize their white descent, whereas now they made every effort to confirm their Inuit background and identity. Such a change in identity management was positively received by the rest of the Inuit population.

Summing up the early period of ethno-political development in Nain, we find tension and ambiguity both in the relations between the Inuit and Settlers and within each of these groups, but especially among Settlers. If left unsolved, these problems might have led to a sharpening and deepening of the divisions between Inuit and Settlers. There was also the danger that the Settlers might be treated locally as a non-status group (as, for instance, the non-status Indians and Métis elsewhere in Canada) with all the unfavourable consequences of such a 'status.'

Rival Associations

A further complicating factor was the activity along the coast of the Native Association of Newfoundland and Labrador (N.A.N.L.). This organization was formed in Newfoundland in February 1973 by persons of Mic Mac ancestry, but Inuit and Settlers were subsequently admitted to membership. N.A.N.L. introduced itself on the coast by launching and funding a housing programme for the native populations. The project started in the southern communities with N.A.N.L. supplying building materials and financial means, and Settlers in the southern communities started supporting the N.A.N.L. and not the L.I.A. By the fall of 1973, the project had reached Nain.

Another matter that added to the conflict between the two associations was a N.A.N.L. by-law that gave members of the community council positions as board members in the native association. In this manner, the association attempted to secure the ethnic representation and support of Inuit and Settlers, as well as Indians. Consequently, the question as to which of these two organizations should be the legitimate spokesman for Inuit interests became an issue. When L.I.A. applied to D.I.A.N.D. for funds to finance its own land claims project in 1974, the application was

turned down on the grounds that there were Inuit board members in
N.A.N.L. and that this association had received a grant-in-aid, earlier that
year, for a land claims study project.

In the rivalry between the two associations, the allegiance of the Settlers
became a crucial matter, and N.A.N.L.'s liberal policy of admitting
Settlers as full members (and as members of the board of directors),
regardless of their language skills, clearly put L.I.A. into a difficult position. During the founding period of L.I.A., the majority of members came
from Nain,[16] but even there, the attitudes of the Settlers had been highly
ambivalent (as shown above). Now, however, for most Settlers it was not a
question of whether they should support the native associations, but a
question of which of the two they should support. L.I.A.'s response to this
situation is worth particular attention. At the annual meeting of the L.I.A.
board, held in Makkovik on October 3–5, 1974 (some days before the
meeting with N.A.N.L.), the board added four temporary members. All of
them came from Nain, and two were of Inuit background (one acting as a
member of the community council, the other being the chief elder of Nain
and the former adviser to L.I.A.). The remaining two were bilingual
Settlers, one of them a councillor who also qualified as "Inuit" on the basis
of one-fourth Inuit ancestry. All four were appointed to L.I.A.'s land
claims study group (L.I.A. Annual Board Meeting 1974, Resolution 2).

Still more significant was the revision made at the annual meeting of
L.I.A.'s official policy regarding Settlers and their rights in any land
claims:

"*Whereas* the Settlers of Northern Labrador cannot be included in any Aboriginal Claim to
land of the Inuit of Labrador North under Federal Law, and
Whereas the Settlers of Northern Labrador are entitled to only Squatters' Rights under
Federal and Provincial Law, and
Whereas the Settlers of Northern Labrador have coexisted with the Inuit of Northern
Labrador for over a century, and
Whereas the Settlers of Northern Labrador have hunted, fished, trapped and intermarried
with the Inuit of Northern Labrador,
it is hereby resolved that;
The Inuit of Northern Labrador recognize the Settlers of Northern Labrador as having *equal
rights in all Land Claims Settlements and accompanying Hunting and Fishing Rights*"
(author's emphasis).
(From L.I.A. Annual Board Meeting 1974, Resolution #1)

Although this message was directed both to the N.A.N.L. and the
Settlers in general, L.I.A. and its appointed advisers paid special attention
to Nain. Here they started campaigning for broad support of the association: a liason officer (a young bilingual Inuk) contacted all persons or
households who were known to doubt L.I.A., its membership and land
claims policies. Also helping the L.I.A.'s campaign was the fact that in
1974, the annual I.T.C. conference, with representatives from all over the

Canadian north and from Ottawa, was held in Nain. As a result of meetings held in 1974–75 between N.A.N.L. and L.I.A., the latter was officially recognized as the sole representative for Inuit and Settlers on the Labrador coast. At the same time, negotiations between L.I.A. and the federal and provincial authorities resulted in funds for financing L.I.A.'s own land claims project. (N.A.N.L. became split into two organizations – one representing a membership on the island of Newfoundland, and the other, Labrador Indians.)

Towards Ethnic Incorporation Within L.I.A.
All in all, these events helped to reduce tension and misunderstandings in the community; many persons who previously opposed L.I.A. now started supporting the association, although some still clung to a more passive wait-and-see attitude. These events were also accompanied by changes in the self-ascription of Settlers; in some cases, persons who used to identify themselves as English or Irish now emphasized their Inuit ancestry. Some Settlers even started questioning the very term "Settler," regarding it as an inadequate description of their background. As an older Nain Settler said: "I don't like to be called a Settler! It is not right to call me so; there are no Settlers in Nain any more! We have been born here – our parents were born here. The first ones who came to the coast were Settlers, but not us! If you are going to use the word about people in Nain today, it can only be with reference to persons like Mr. ... [a store-owner in Nain, born outside Labrador]. We are Labradorians!"

At the annual general meeting of L.I.A. held in Nain on November 3–7, 1975, the idea of a native-born Labradorian was repeatedly put forward by both Inuit and Settlers. This meeting brought together fourteen delegates from the communities of Hopedale, Makkovik, Postville, Rigolet, Mud Lake, Northwest River and Happy Valley, eight delegates from Nain, guests from the Labrador Indian Association, and government representatives. One of the more important topics of discussion was the question of changing the criteria for membership in L.I.A., particularly with regard to the position of Settlers in the association. The board proposed new rules allowing all Settlers to become full members; the language criterion was to be taken into consideration only in electing board members and the president of the association. The former chief elder of Nain summed up the discussion by saying: "Whether Inuit or Settlers, it doesn't make any difference! Settlers are all Labradorians as we ourselves are! Outsiders should not make by-laws for Labrador people! I feel that the by-laws should not have been there at all!" The proposal for full membership for Settlers was unanimously accepted.

At the same time, it was explained that bilingualism should remain one of the important criteria in appointing the board members and the president:

abolition of this requirement would open the way for a non-Inuit leadership, creating doubts about L.I.A.'s being an Inuit association. However, not all speakers agreed entirely with this; some, including the former chief elder of Nain, insisted that only the president ought to be fluent in Inuttitut. The question of the outsiders' status in L.I.A. was also mentioned in the course of the discussion, and one of the most debatable issues was the question of outsiders married to Inuit; some were in favour of granting them full membership while others were against it.

At the same meeting, the following proposal was put forward concerning membership rules: a member must

"1. a) be at least 18 years of age
     b) be of Inuit or Settler ancestry, or
     c) be the child of a marriage between a white and an Inuk or [between a white and] a Settler.
  2. The president must be able to speak Inuttitut fluently."

This proposal was to be treated as a temporary solution, open for alterations if it should prove inadequate. In the course of discussion, most speakers expressed concern at the prospect of outsiders (non-Labradorians) joining the association. An Inuit delegate expressed it in this way: "Outsiders come here and we don't know what they are doing! *We* should rule our own communities and be able to tell outsiders what to do!" The delegates were no longer worried by the prospect of Settlers' participation in the association. When it became clear that the proposed by-laws were open for later changes, the chief elder of Nain moved that the proposal be accepted and it was, without further discussion.

The candidates were proposed for the post of president, and all of them delivered their introductory speeches in both languages. The former president was re-elected by a clear majority of 33 votes. The candidate who received 17 votes was appointed the vice-president; he was of mixed Inuit-Settler descent and regarded himself as Inuk. The third candidate (13 votes) was an ex-councillor, an Inuk from Nain. Neither of these men were newcomers to L.I.A.; the former had previously been employed by the L.I.A. as a field worker, and the latter had acted as the Land Claims Director of the association.

In the election of board members, secretary and treasurer, only two members of the old board were re-elected, both of them Nain Inuit. Among the five new members, two were Inuit (one of them of mixed background), while the other three had a Settler background; none of them was fluent in Inuttitut. It is noteworthy that two of these five new members came from Makkovik. For the first time in L.I.A.'s short history, Settlers from communities other than Nain were elected to the board. In sum, the developments of the last few years reflected the change in the status of Settlers with

TABLE 3

Changing Representation on the L.I.C. and the L.I.A. Board

	Inuit	Inuk-Settler	Settler	Residence Nain	Residence Other	Nain elders
1972 L.I.C.	4		1	5		2
1973 L.I.A.	5	3	1	4	5	1
1974 L.I.A.	7	3	3	8	5	2
1975 L.I.A.	3	3	3	4	5	1

L.I.A. (see Table 3): from associate and temporary membership, they reached the status of full members, and the Settler representation on the board increased.

The wider significance of these events is that the focus of local politics shifted from separate Inuit and Settler interests to commitments involving both groups, thus providing new contexts for ethnic categories which can then take on new meanings (for example, "Inuit"). For the Inuit, obviously, the L.I.A. brought them in contact with pan-Inuit (and other native) politics in Canada. In addition, membership in the association provided Settlers and persons of mixed Inuit/Settler background with a public forum in which to present themselves (though not without problems of ambiguity) as Inuit. It should be stressed that this took place with surprisingly little conflict or disagreement. At the annual L.I.A. meeting in 1975, as we saw, the question of outsiders was considered more important than the position of Settlers, and no proposals were put forward to fix quotas of Inuit and Settler representatives. Then at the 1977 annual meeting in Hopedale (Feb. 28–Mar. 4) the following motion was passed: "To respect the rights of native settlers, to invite participation by native settlers in all the objectives of the Association and to share equally with them all benefits such as the Association might obtain for its members" (*Kinatuinamot Illengajuk*, 1977:2).

Ethnic Status: Local Versus Other Definitions
It should be noted that such progress among the Inuit and Settlers towards (political) ethnic incorporation is happening against a backcloth of national and provincial uncertainty and even contradictions. For example, at a meeting between L.I.A. representatives and the minister of D.I.A.N.D. in September 1974 in Ottawa, the minister was asked to state his views on eligibility to Inuit status. In the subsequent L.I.A. report, he is quoted as having "stressed the difficulty of this problem today. He said the decision of how to handle this should be worked out in accordance by the Inuit and it was not his business to resolve the matter." By contrast, the unconditional

Settler participation in L.I.A. leadership was described by I.T.C. advisers as being contrary to L.I.A.'s position *vis-à-vis* the federal authorities (as well as contrary to I.T.C. philosophy). Each of these statements need to be strongly qualified, however. In fact, any (Labrador) Inuit proposal regarding eligibility to ethnic status, as soon as it is linked to a substantive issue (such as land claims), would need approval by the Federal Government. On the other hand, there exists an official "re-definition" of "Eskimo,"[17] which, when applied to northern Labrador, includes even a large number of Settlers.

The question of Inuit status is no less complex at the provincial level. Prior to Confederation, neither the British nor the Newfoundland Governments had negotiated any treaties with the Inuit of Labrador; nor was there any reference to their special aboriginal rights in the laws of Newfoundland. After Confederation, the Newfoundland and Federal Governments (while debating their respective constitutional responsibilities on behalf of the Labrador Inuit and Indians), agreed to a joint programme to assist Labrador aborigines in health, education and welfare. It was to be administered by the Provincial Government and financed by the Federal. In 1965, a federal-provincial agreement established the constitutional responsibility of the Federal Government towards the Labrador Inuit and Indians in terms comparable to the rest of Canada.[18] However, two of the provincial agencies administering the programmes use different definitions of "Inuit" (Lewer, n.d.a:33–34). The Labrador Service Division of the Department of Rehabilitation and Recreation have the following criteria:

"(i)   patrilineal descent of person historically identified as an Eskimo
 (ii) marriage to a male Eskimo
(iii) issue of union(ii) above; and, illegitimate issue of female Eskimo
(iv)   self-identification and acceptance by the community as an Eskimo."
Loss of definition as an Eskimo is achieved by:
"(i)   female Eskimo marrying non-Eskimo
 (ii) issue of such union" (*ibid.*, p. 33).

The International Grenfell Association, on the other hand, is reported to use the following criteria:

"(i)   some quantum of Eskimo blood, as evidenced through racial physique and appearance;
 (ii) Eskimo cultural orientation – inclined to lead the traditional Eskimo way of life
        (economic) and use of Eskimo language
(iii) paternity, where it can be established" (*ibid.*, p. 34).

The I.G.A. reportedly registers new-born babies according to their criteria and, in addition, practises a continuous re-evaluation of adults. Lost of "Eskimo" status is defined as follows:

"(i)   self-identification as "white" or "settler," regardless of eligibility in (i)–(iii) above; and
 (ii) if relocated to wage-earning communities and independent means of employment"
        (*ibid.*, p. 34).

The striking thing about these definitions is that the relative importance of the various criteria is not mentioned: although self-identification as an Inuk is counted as positive, subsequent marriage to a non-Inuk (a Settler) or wage employment invalidates such an identification. Also, except for the purpose of census-taking, these definitions have so far had little practical significance in Nain: services are administered on a community rather than an individual basis.[19] Whereas the definitions are examples of the difficulties in which the Newfoundland administration finds itself when trying to cope with the question of ethnicity in northern Labrador, it should be noticed how the definitions bear little relation to the actual processes of ethnic recruitment in a community like Nain (see my earlier chapter). Not surprisingly, some L.I.A. representatives of mixed ethnic backgrounds have been challenged by government officials in St. John's regarding the legitimacy of their position in an Inuit association. Similarly, in the course of his presentation of L.I.A.'s eligibility policy, one of L.I.A.'s white advisers was asked by a government official to define "Inuk" and "Settler"; unable to do so (he considered that ethnicity in northern Labrador could not be categorically defined), the policy was rejected.

IV

Returning to the emergence of the process coined as ethnopolitics, let us examine in greater detail how the L.I.A. succeeded in establishing itself as a context for an incorporational relationship (Barth, 1966) embracing both Inuit and Settlers.

The Transformation of Ethnicity
Traditionally, the striking feature of group relations between Inuit and Settlers was their lack of complementarity (Kleivan, 1966; T. Brantenberg, 1973). The ethnic structure in Nain had been based on a dichotomy between Inuit and Settler categories (Part I of this essay), with an ensuing privatization of meaning (Paine, 1976) on the part of each group. These circumstances buttressed the exercise of tutelage by the Moravian Mission and, latterly, the Provincial Government. Now, the L.I.A. (and also the community council) had been the principal instrument in the gradual dismantling of such tutelage. The need for co-operation between Inuit and Settlers had been impressed upon the community, and its achievement has been facilitated by the multi-purpose character of the L.I.A. For example, as an intermediary between government agencies and the coastal communities, L.I.A., from the start, provided public funds for both Inuit and Settlers in connection with a diversity of projects: Summer Student Employment Programmes, Emergency Repair Programmes, and the Nain newspaper (among others).

Also from very early on, L.I.A. was used as a mouthpiece to voice local problems of a varied nature. These ranged from petitions to government departments about the 50-mile fishing limit and inadequacies in caribou-hunting regulations, to applications for grants to establish a Legal Aid Center on the coast, and requests to improve the L.S.D. services and the system for collecting fish from fishing camps. Most of these issues were raised by Inuit and Settler participants at L.I.A. meetings. As they generally concern assertions of deficiencies in the services provided by the Provincial Government, the association fosters political interests of a community-sized order that other political forums, for one reason or other, have failed to cope with successfully.

During L.I.A.'s annual meeting in Nain in 1975, discussion was centred not so much on topics of Inuit interest (except for proposals concerning Inuit language and a new writing system), but on a host of everyday problems relevant to both Inuit and Settlers. A salient feature was the way in which the dichotomy between "outsiders" (in most cases synonymous with the Provincial Government) and "us" (native-born Labradorians) was communicated. As an elderly Nain Inuk succinctly stated with regard to new game laws: "We should all work together on this. We should make our voice heard. We've lived in Labrador all our lives, we know the land. We shouldn't have to follow rules made by outsiders. We are Labradorians!" This particular case concerned new regulations on caribou hunting proposed by the provincial Wildlife Department, which are based on concepts of southern sports hunting and ignore the significance of hunting to the northern Labrador natives' life style. They were so actively resisted in all the northern communities that the administration was forced to amend sections of the proposal.

The above case clearly shows how (despite any eventual outcome) local and regional common interests, in confrontation with the actions of outside agencies, generate a feeling of shared identity between Inuit and Settlers. In addition, it shows how political mobilization *vis-à-vis* shared restrictions imposed from the outside leads to the re-interpretation of relationships, not only with "outsiders," but also between Inuit and Settlers themselves. It is particularly significant that the idiomatic context of the rhetoric of 'sharedness' is provided by contexts that otherwise (see Ch. 16) have served to express the dichotomy between the Inuit and Settler communities. For example, although the Nain Brass Band is still made up of Inuit players, their performance at various events, such as the closing ceremony of the L.I.A. annual meeting in 1975, now provides additional content to the sense of common regional identity for both Inuit and Settlers (from the northern communities), while also underlining the dichotomy between Labrador and Newfoundland.

Although the strategies for ecological adaptation and economic management have differed between Inuit and Settlers, they have all been expressed within the same habitat, and within an increasingly similar technology encompassing the same general activities of hunting, fishing and trapping. In fact, when Nain Inuit express concern for the younger generations' possible loss of ability to live in harmony with the land (as they themselves and the "inummariit" of the old generation did), they define the skills, insight and endurance of these veterans not in terms of pre-contact Inuit society, but more in the context of the plural cash/subsistence economy of the first decades of this century. Despite specific differences between Inuit and Settlers during this period (for example, snow houses versus canvas tents), older Settlers employ the same terms of reference (hunting, fishing and trapping) when evaluating toughness, endurance and skill. Inuit and Settlers share an identical concern for the eventual loss of expertise in these fields. Thus, some of the hunting and travelling stories told by older Inuit men (published in the Nain newspaper), describing the traditional Inuit way of life, are closely matched by tales told by Settlers. Such stories are recurrent themes in the day-to-day communication between Inuit and Settlers, as well.

Another contributing factor to the process under discussion may be the absence of any clear-cut class distinctions between Inuit and Settlers. Most of them are dependent on the same wage-earning activities: construction work and odd jobs during the summer months, combined with hunting, fishing, trapping and other subsistence-oriented activities. Settlers in Nain and other communities, however, take on entrepreneurial positions more often (between local and outside markets).

It does not necessarily follow that traditional expressions of ethnic differences between Inuit and Settlers, in a community like Nain, have been completely obliterated. However, this essay attempts to demonstrate how ethnic categories and commitments, if not altogether changed, have gained new meanings and relevance through the circumstances provided by the L.I.A. Although no radical change in more private spheres of interaction have taken place, it seems significant that the public forums provided by L.I.A. supply Inuit and Settlers with opportunities for positive sanctioning of each others' commitments to common political interests, while simultaneously retaining a sense of ethnic uniqueness.

Conclusion

The communities of northern Labrador during the last decade have become increasingly involved with the developments in Canadian society as a whole, and as a result, they have experienced changes. This chapter has focused on select aspects of this process of modernization, such as the development of local government in a context of ethnopolitics, with particular reference to the community of Nain.

Both the introduction of ethnopolitics, by the L.I.A., and of modern local government, by the community council, were stimulated and initiated by non-Labradorian outside agencies. The former was introduced by Inuit politicians, and the latter by representatives of the Provincial Government. In addition to originating within highly different political fields, both institutions initially represented contrastive local ethnic commitments; hence, the community council was to some extent used by Nain Settlers as an alternative and competitive arena to that held by Inuit elders. The L.I.A., in contrast, was presented as a means for maintaining and defending Inuit interests *vis-à-vis* white influence. Besides the concomitant ambiguity and contradiction generated by these issues among both Inuit and Settlers, this period of time presented both groups with opportunities for decision-making that could have been critical in deepening the traditional Inuit-Settler dichotomy on the coast. However, as witnessed in the subsequent events, Inuit and Settlers did not split into two factions, neither in Nain nor on the coast in general.

As documented in Nain, both political arenas were characterized by an increasing amount of Inuit-Settler cooperation. Most importantly, this came about by local insistence, despite the opposition expressed by outside sponsors (principally I.T.C.) and government. Note should also be taken of the restrictions placed on Settlers, when devising possible political strategies, by the existence of a local Inuit electoral majority. At the same time, however, Inuit came to depend upon Settler support within L.I.A., particularly because of another competing native association (N.A.N.L.).

A particularly significant effect of this development has been the dramatic decline of the role of the Moravian Mission as a third party controlling Inuit-Settler relations. Whereas the present situation might seem to provide the population of northern Labrador with a choice of potential third parties, the integration of the fields of local government and ethnopolitics in Nain effectively places serious restrictions on such a role.

The main problem of Inuit and Settlers today may be seen as one of maintaining and increasing the emerging inter-ethnic unity between them. On the other hand, the population of northern Labrador is facing the problem of how to get its decisions understood and acknowledged by outside parties. An underlying purpose of this chapter has been to demonstrate how politics and ethnicity in northern Labrador have to be understood in terms of the local culture of Inuit and Settlers themselves. (Labrador Inuit cannot be understood as "less" or "more" white or Inuit than Inuit elsewhere in Canada, nor Settlers as something "less" than Inuit or whites.) Similarly, the amount of inter-ethnic co-operation and incorporation between Inuit and Settlers in Nain today demonstrates that there is there no clear-cut division between local-level (and regional) politics and ethnopolitics. In fact, a key to understanding the current scene is that politics in northern Labrador is, at the same time, both local-level and ethnopolitical. Consequently, a proper interpretation of ethnic commitments has to take consideration of the ascriptions and definitions made by local people themselves; to do otherwise would only serve the dialectically opposite purpose: that is, the maintenance of tutelage.

NOTES

1   For the missionaries it was not just a matter of attacking what they termed "superstitions"; they were concerned with the construction of a barrier between their early Inuit converts and the pagans; they also wished to prevent a 'hybrid' religious system in which pagan and Christian elements were mixed (cf. Kleivan, 1966:70–71).

2   The following incident may illustrate how Inuit in Nain today (1971) regard their aboriginal past. Some years ago the missionary obtained a copy of recordings of traditional Inuit music from Alaska and the Canadian Arctic, some of which he played to an Inuit audience during a social event in the community hall. Soon afterwards the Inuit elders came to the missionary, criticizing him for what he had done. They felt it was wrong – and especially wrong of the missionary – to play recordings of (what they assumed to be) the songs of angakok, the aboriginal shaman. To my knowledge, the record was never again played in public.

3   In point of fact, both groups now avail themselves extensively of factory-made clothing; the silapak and seal-skin boots are the two principal traditional items still in everyday use as they are considered essential in rough and cold weather.

4   However, all decisions of the congregational board have to be confirmed by the missionary who may reject them.

5   In 1935 a detachment of the Newfoundland Rangers was stationed at Nain; prior to that time Nain would be visited each summer by a magistrate accompanied by a police officer.

6   This is not to say that Settlers do not complain about Inuit being favoured by government. The housing programme sponsored by the N.L.S.D. is one example: despite the fact that Settlers have been offered new housing facilities, several have expressed resentment against what they consider to be government preoccupation with Inuit. Indeed, the programme is often referred to as the "Eskimo housing project" by government officials both in Nain and in their annual reports. Settlers have also criticized government officials for being more lenient towards Inuit when issuing short-term social assistance (that is, relief); the Settlers say that they have a hard time qualifying for such assistance when, for example, the fishery fails.

7   Leaving aside marriages between persons born in Nain after they had left the community (no reliable data), there were seven marriages for the period 1965–71 with persons coming to Nain from outside Labrador: five Settlers, but only one Inuk, and one person of 'mixed' parentage.

8   The decision by the council to show films in the town hall over the week-ends provoked vehement protestations from the elders and the missionary (up to this time, cinema showings had been strictly kept to days when there were no church services): indeed, they went to the hall to try to stop the first of these week-end showings: the R.C.M.P. was called to order them out of the hall.

9   This represented an increase over the 1955 population of Nain (198 Inuit and 110 Settlers) of approximately 50 percent; later, other families and individuals who had been resettled south of Nain moved into Nain to join friends and relatives resettled there.

10   Cf. Ben-Dor (1966) and Kennedy (this volume) on residential neighbourhoods in Makkovik arising out of resettlement.

11   In fact, seasonal fishing and hunting trips out of Nain and up to the north are of economic importance to the majority of the northerners in Nain.

12   The first issue of the newspaper Kinatuinamot Illengajuk ("To Whom It May Concern") appeared in March 1972. A project initiated by Memorial University and funded by the Federal Government through its Local Improvement Programme, the newspaper was operated independently by a local staff of young Inuit and persons of Inuit-Settler background,

together with Settler reporters in Makkovik. It was the only newspaper ever to have been concerned with the Inuit and Settler communities of northern Labrador (the Moravian Mission had published an annual news sheet between 1902 and 1922 but it had dealt mainly with foreign events). It went out of publication for a period in 1974 through lack of funds but since then has appeared regularly.

13   Even at the time of the founding of the L.I.A., individuals were involved in I.T.C. work (as delegates from Labrador) concerning Pan-Inuit problems. Similarly, L.I.A. members became involved in the work of the Inuit Cultural Institute (I.C.I.) based at Rankin Inlet. The main task of I.C.I. is to preserve the culture, identity and lifestyle of the Inuit people (I.T.C., 1976:5). The Institute has been carrying out several projects aimed at collecting and preserving the remains of Inuit cultural tradition (e.g., tales and legends) in northern Labrador; several Labrador Inuit were trained in the N.W.T. to work on these projects.

14   Note should also be taken here of the difference between the L.I.A.'s and the national association's (I.T.C.) membership rules. For instance, Settlers in communities like Nain, who were eligible for membership by virtue of their bilingual skills, could attain only associate status in I.T.C. if unable to prove 1/4 Inuit ancestry. Some Nain Settlers were uncertain about the interpretation of these criteria.

15   Very few Settler homesteads had been directly bought or obtained by any formal transaction. Owners of homesteads situated within the Moravian territory do not have unquestionable rights to ownership of the land on which they stand; in fact, the legal aspects of the Moravian land grant in Labrador still remain an unsolved issue.

16   This can be demonstrated by quoting the number of full and associate members of L.I.A., as given in the president's report at the annual general meeting, 1975:

Community	Full	Associate	
Nain	70	9	
Hopedale			
Makkovik	7	2	
Rigolet	3	1	
Postville			
Happy Valley	22	2	
Totals	102	14	116

Until 1975, L.I.A.'s activities were centred in Nain and the association did little campaigning in other communities.

17   In 1975, at the request of I.T.C., the Department of Environment re-defined "Eskimo" for the Northwest Territories Fisheries Regulations (the Narwhal Protection Regulations and the Quebec Fishery Regulations): "Inuk means a person who is a direct descendant of a person who is, or was, of the race of aborigines commonly referred to as Eskimos and possesses at least one-quarter of Inuk blood." A person of "mixed blood" was defined as being of "mixed Indian (or Inuk) and non-Indian blood – at least one-quarter Indian or Inuk." (See Lewer, n.d.b.:7–19.)

18   The constitutional position of Inuit in Canada was settled by the British North America Act (B.N.A.A.) (1867, Section 91[24]) which gave Parliament exclusive jurisdiction over "Indians and Lands reserved for Indians." In 1939, this section was referred to by the Supreme Court of Canada when defining Inuit in the province of Quebec as "Indians." In 1966, the Supreme Court extended this definition to cover all Canadian Inuit, but Parliament did not include Inuit in the statutory definition of Indians in the Indian Act, as amended in 1951. Thus, Inuit have been spared the problems caused by the Act, which discriminates between "status" and "non-status" Indians. No definite set of criteria have so far been established by Canadian law to provide a uniform definition of a "native person" (see Cumming and Mickerberg, 1972: 6–9).

19   But Inuit re-settled in the communities of Goose Bay and Happy Valley have not qualified for the assistance provided under the federal-provincial agreements.

References

BARTH, FREDRIK
1966 *Models of Social Organization*. Royal Anthropological Institute of Great Britain and Ireland, Occasional Papers No. 23.

BEN-DOR, SHMUEL
1966 *Makkovik: Eskimos and Settlers in a Labrador Community*. St. John's, Institute of Social and Economic Research, Memorial University of Newfoundland.

BRANTENBERG, TERJE
1973 "Kultur og Identitet. Etnisk artikulasjon blandt Eskimoer og hvite i nord-Labrador." Unpublished M.A. thesis, Tromsø University.

BRODY, HUGH
1975 *The People's Land: Eskimos and Whites in the Eastern Arctic*. Aylesbury, Penguin Books.

CUMMING, P. A. and MICKENBERG, N.
1972 *Native Rights in Canada*. 2nd edition, Toronto, General Publishing Co. and the Indian Eskimo Association of Canada.

HILLER, J.
1971 "Early Patrons of the Labrador Eskimos: The Moravian Mission in Labrador, 1764–1805." In R. Paine (ed.), *Patrons and Brokers in the East Arctic*. St. John's, Institute of Social and Economic Research, Memorial University of Newfoundland.

INUIT TAPIRISAT OF CANADA
1976 *NUNAVUT: A Proposal for the Settlement of Inuit Lands in the Northwest Territories*. Ottawa.

KINATUINAMOT ILLENGAJOK
1972 No. 24, Nain, Labrador, Newfoundland.

KINATUINAMOT ILLENGAJOK
1977 No. 47, and 48, Nain, Labrador, Newfoundland.

KLEIVAN, HELGE
1966 *The Eskimos of North-East Labrador. A History of Eskimo-White Relations 1771–1955*. Oslo, Norsk Polar-Institutt.

KLEIVAN, HELGE
1969 "Culture and Ethnic Identity: On Modernization and Ethnicity in Greenland." *Folk*, 11–12.

LEWER, ELSE
n.d.a *Report on Labrador Eskimos' Eligibility for Federal Government Development Programs for Eskimos*. Mimeograph.

LEWER, ELSE
n.d. b *Systems of Definitions used in Canada by the Government, Courts of Law, and the Native Peoples in Identifying an Aborigine of Canada*. Unpublished manuscript.

PAINE, ROBERT
1971 "A Theory of Patronage and Brokerage." In R. Paine (ed.), *Patrons and Brokers in the East Arctic*. St. John's, Institute of Social and Economic Research, Memorial University of Newfoundland.
PAINE, ROBERT
1976 "Two Modes of Exchange and Mediation." In Bruce Kapferer (ed.), *Transaction and Meaning*. Philadelphia, Institute for the Study of Human Issues.
ZIMMERLY, DAVID W.
1975 *Cain's Land Revisited: Culture Change in Central Labrador, 1775–1972*. St. John's, Institute of Social and Economic Research, Memorial University of Newfoundland.

This bibliography is restricted to the *Identity and Modernity in the East Arctic* research project, financed by grants awarded by the Canada Council as part of its Izaak Walton Killam Awards Programme. (An inclusive bibliography of arctic research conducted out of the Institute of Social and Economic Research at Memorial University in recent years is to be found in the ISER Reports.)

Three categories of writings are distinguished:
pre-project: work incorporated into the design of the project;
project: principal topics of investigation during the project years (1968–72);
**post-project*: subsequent work arising out of the project or directly related to it.

BRANTENBERG, ANNE
published
  1977 "The Marginal School and the Children of Nain." In Robert Paine (ed.), *The White Arctic: Anthropological Essays on Tutelage and Ethnicity*. St. John's, Institute of Social and Economic Research, Memorial University of Newfoundland.
unpublished
  1975 Kvinner i Nain: Kjønnsforvaltning i et multi-etnisk lokalsamfunn i forandring. (Women in Nain.) Unpublished M.A. thesis, University of Tromsø.
BRANTENBERG, TERJE
published
  1977a "Ethnic Values and Ethnic Recruitment in Nain." In Robert Paine (ed.), *The White Arctic: Anthropological Essays on Tutelage and Ethnicity*. St. John's, Institute of Social and Economic Research, Memorial University of Newfoundland.
  1977b "Ethnic Commitments and Local Government in Nain, 1969–76." In Robert Paine (ed.), *The White Arctic: Anthropological Essays on Tutelage and Ethnicity*. St. John's Institute of Social and Economic Research, Memorial University of Newfoundland.
unpublished
  1973 Kultur og identitet: Etnisk Artikulasjon blant hvite og Eskimoer i

Nain, Labrador. (Ethnicity in Nain.) Unpublished M.A. thesis, University of Tromsø.

BRIGGS, JEAN

published

*1968 *Utkuhikhalingmiut Eskimo Emotional Expression*. Ottawa, Northern Science Research Group.

*1970a *Never in Anger. Portrait of an Eskimo Family*. Cambridge, Cambridge University Press.

*1970b "Kapluna Daughter." In P. Golde (ed.), *Women in the Field. Anthropological Experiences*. Chicago, Aldine. Reprinted in *Transaction*, June 1970 and I. L. Horowitz and M. S. Strong (eds.), *Sociological Realities*, 1970. Harper and Row.

*1971 "Strategies of Perception: the Management of Ethnic Identity." In Robert Paine (ed.), *Patrons and Brokers in the East Arctic*. St. John's, Institute of Social and Economic Research, Memorial University of Newfoundland.

1972a "The Issues of Autonomy and Aggression in the Three-Year-Old: The Utku Eskimo Case." *Seminars in Psychiatry*, 4.

**1972b Review of *Seasons of the Eskimo* by Fred Bruemmer. *Natural History*, LXXXI.

**1973a Review of *Pitseolak: Pictures Out of My Life. Natural History*, March.

**1973b "Comment on the Place of Fieldwork in Anthropology." *Western Canadian Journal of Anthropology*.

1974a "Eskimo Women: Makers of Men." In Carolyn Matthiasson (ed.), *Many Sisters*. New York, Free Press.

1974b "Eskimo Family Life." In R. Prince and D. Barrier (eds.), *Configurations*. Toronto, Lexington Books.

1974c "The Origins of Nonviolence: Eskimo Aggression Management." In Warner Muensterberger (ed.), *The Psychoanalytic Study of Society*. New York, International Universities.

unpublished

*1969 "An Anthropological Method for Studying Emotional Concepts and Expressions." Prepared for Killam Project Colloquium.

1976a "The Consistency in Ambivalence: Inuit Personality Structure." Read at the Universities of Bergen and Oslo, Norway.

1976b "Serious Play: Inuit Value Maintenance." Read at Universities of Bergen and Oslo, Norway.

1976c "Morality Play: Inuit Style." Presented to the American Anthropological Association.

FREEMAN, M. M. R.

published

*1969a "Development Strategies and Indigenous Peoples in the Canadian Arctic." In M. M. R. Freeman (ed.), *Intermediate Adaptation in Newfoundland and the Arctic: A Strategy of Social and Economic Development*. St. John's, Institute of Social and Economic Research, Memorial University of Newfoundland.

*1969b "Adaptive Innovation among Recent Eskimo Immigrants in the Eastern Canadian Arctic." *Polar Record*, 14.

*1970a "Studies in Maritime Hunting: 1. Ecologic and Technologic Restraints on Walrus Hunting, Southampton Island, N.W.T." *Folk*, 11–12.

1970b "Ethos, Economics and Prestige – a Re-examination of Netsilik Eskimo Infanticide." *Verhandlungen des XXXVIII Internationalen Amerikanisten Kongresses*, 2.

1970c "Productivity Studies on High Arctic Musk-oxen." *Arctic Circular*, 20.

1970d Review of *Hunters of the Northern Ice* by Richard Nelson. *Arctic*, 23.

*1971a "Tolerance and Rejection of Patron Roles in an Eskimo Settlement." In Robert Paine (ed.), *Patrons and Brokers in the East Arctic*. St. John's, Institute of Social and Economic Research, Memorial University of Newfoundland.

1971b "Population Characteristics of Musk-ox in the Jones Sound Region of the Northwest Territories." *Journal of Wildlife Management*, 35.

1971c "The Significance of Demographic Changes Occurring in the Canadian East Arctic." *Anthropologica*, 13.

1971d "A Social and Ecological Analysis of Systematic Female Infanticide among the Netsilik Eskimo." *American Anthropologist*, 73.

*1971e "Patronage, Leadership and Values in an Eskimo Community." *Verhandlungen des XXXVIII Internationalen Amerikanisten Kongresses*, 3.

1973a "Polar Bear Predation on Beluga in the Canadian Arctic." *Arctic*, 26.

1973b "Demographic Research in the Canadian North: Some Preliminary Observations." In K. R. Greenaway (ed.), *Science and the North*. Information Canada, Ottawa.

**1974a *People Pollution: Sociologic and Ecologic Viewpoints*. McGill-Queen's Universities Press.

**1974b Review of *Hunters in the Barrens: The Naskapi on the Edge of the White Man's World* by Georg Henriksen. *Man* (N.S.), 9(4).

and L. M. HACKMAN

**1975a "Bathurst Island N.W.T.: A Test Case of Canada's Northern Policy." *Canadian Public Policy*, 1(3):402–14.

1975b "Studies in Maritime Hunting II: An Analysis of Walrus Hunting and Utilisation Southampton Island, N.W.T., 1970. *Folk*, 16–17: 147–58.

**1975c "Assessing Movement in an Arctic Caribou Population." *Journal of Environmental Management*, 3(3):251–57.

EDITOR of:

**1976 *Report of the Inuit Land Use and Occupancy Project*. 3 volumes. Department of Supply and Services, Ottawa.

unpublished

1971 "The Utterly Dismal Theorem: A Contemporary Example from the Canadian Arctic." Presented to the Canadian Sociology and Anthropology Association.

**1977 "Anthropologists and Policy-Relevant Research: The Case for Accountability." Presented to the Canadian Ethnology Society.

HENRIKSEN, GEORG

published

*1971 "The Transactional Basis of Influence: Whitemen among Naskapi Indians." In Robert Paine (ed.), *Patrons and Brokers in the East Arctic*. St. John's, Institute of Social and Economic Research, Memorial University of Newfoundland.

1973 *Hunters in the Barrens: The Naskapi on the Edge of the White Man's World*. St. John's, Institute of Social and Economic Research, Memorial University of Newfoundland.

**In press "The Naskapi of Davis Inlet: Nomadic Hunters and Sedentaries in White Tutelage." In *Handbook of North American Indians*. Smithsonian Institute of North America.

**In press "Land Use and Occupancy among the Naskapis of Davis Inlet." Report to the Naskapi Montagnais Innu Association.

unpublished

1970 "Indian Reservations in the Maritimes, the Contemporary Situation. A pilot study." I.S.E.R. file.

KENNEDY, JOHN

published

**1974a Review of *Circumpolar Problems: Habitat, Economy, and Social Relations in the Arctic*, edited by Gösta Berg. *American Anthropologist*, 76.

**1974b Review of *Circumpolar Peoples: An Anthropological Perspective* by N. H. H. Graburn and B. S. Strong. *American Anthropologist*, 76.

1977a "Northern Labrador: An Ethnohistorical Account." In Robert Paine (ed.), *The White Arctic: Anthropological Essays on Tutelage and Ethnicity*. St. John's, Institute of Social and Economic Research, Memorial University of Newfoundland.

1977b "Local Government and Ethnic Boundaries in Makkovik, 1972." In Robert Paine (ed.), *The White Arctic: Anthropological Essays on Tutelage and Ethnicity*. St. John's, Institute of Social and Economic Research, Memorial University of Newfoundland.

unpublished

1973a "From Cod to Salmon: Changing Fishery of a Labrador Community." Presented to the Atlantic Association of Sociologists and Anthropologists.

**1973b Brief to the Royal Commission on Labrador. (Mimeo.)

1975 "New Ethnic Minority Organizations in Northern Labrador: Some Preliminary Observations." Presented to the Society for Applied Anthropology.

1976 "Ethnic Groups in Process." Presented to the Atlantic Association of Sociologists and Anthropologists.

**1977a "Community Reactions to the Proposed Uranium Development in Northern Labrador." Presented to the Canadian Ethnology Society.

**1977b "The Information Gap Syndrome: A Policy-Discussion Paper." Presented to the Newfoundland Liberal Policy Convention.

LANGE, PHILIP

published

1977 "Some Qualities of Inuit Social Interaction." In Robert Paine (ed.), *The White Arctic: Anthropological Essays on Tutelage and Ethnicity*. St. John's, Institute of Social and Economic Research, Memorial University of Newfoundland.

unpublished

1972 "Social Flexibility and Integration in a Canadian Inuit Settlement: Lake Harbour, N.W.T., 1970." Unpublished M.A. thesis, University of British Columbia.

PAINE, ROBERT

published

*1968 "Toward a Model of Programmed Research: With Particular Reference to Research Continuity and Multidisciplinary Relationships." In J. J. Bond (ed.), *Proceedings of the 2nd National Northern Research Conference*. Edmonton, Boreal Institute, University of Alberta.

*1971a "Introduction." In Robert Paine (ed.) *Patrons and Brokers in the East Arctic*. St. John's, Institute of Social and Economic Research, Memorial University of Newfoundland.

*1971b "A Theory of Patronage and Brokerage." In Robert Paine (ed.), *Patrons and Brokers in the East Arctic*. St. John's, Institute of Social and Economic Research, Memorial University of Newfoundland.

*1971c "Conclusions." In Robert Paine (ed.), *Patrons and Brokers in the East Arctic*. St. John's, Institute of Social and Economic Research, Memorial University of Newfoundland.

1977a "Introduction." In Robert Paine (ed.), *The White Arctic: Anthropological Essays on Tutelage and Ethnicity*. St. John's, Institute of Social and Economic Research, Memorial University of Newfoundland.

1977b "The Path to Welfare Colonialism." In Robert Paine (ed.), *The White Arctic: Anthropological Essays on Tutelage and Ethnicity*. St. John's, Institute of Social and Economic Research, Memorial University of Newfoundland.

1977c "An Appraisal of the Last Decade." In Robert Paine (ed.), *The White Arctic: Anthropological Essays on Tutelage and Ethnicity*. St. John's, Institute of Social and Economic Research, Memorial University of Newfoundland.

1977d "The Nursery Game: Colonizers and the Colonized." In Robert Paine (ed.), *The White Arctic: Anthropological Essays on Tutelage and Ethnicity*. St. John's, Institute of Social and Economic Research, Memorial University of Newfoundland.

1977e "Leaving the Nursery?" In Robert Paine (ed.), *The White Arctic: Anthropological Essays on Tutelage and Ethnicity*. St. John's, Institute of Social and Economic Research, Memorial University of Newfoundland.

1977f "Tutelage and Ethnicity, A Variable Relationship." In Robert Paine (ed.), *The White Arctic: Anthropological Essays on Tutelage and Ethnicity*. St. John's, Institute of Social and Economic Research, Memorial University of Newfoundland.

unpublished
*1968 "Identity and Modernity in the East Arctic: Research Statements." St. John's, Department of Sociology and Anthropology, Memorial University of Newfoundland.

RICHES, DAVID
published
**1974a "Baffin Island Eskimos." In *Peoples of the World* (encyclopaedia). London, Tom Stacey Limited.

**1974b "The Netsilik Eskimo: A Special Case of Selective Female Infanticide." *Ethnology*, 13:351–61.

1975 "Cash, Credit and Gambling in a Modern Eskimo Economy." *Man*, 10:12–24.

1976 "Alcohol Abuse and the Problem of Social Control in a Canadian Eskimo Settlement." In L. Holy (ed.), *Knowledge and Behaviour*. Belfast, Queen's University Papers in Social Anthropology No. 1.

1977a "Neighbours in the 'Bush': White Cliques." In Robert Paine (ed.), *The White Arctic: Anthropological Essays on Tutelage and Ethnicity.* St. John's, Institute of Social and Economic Research, Memorial University of Newfoundland.

1977b "An Inuit Co-operative: The Contradiction." In Robert Paine (ed.), *The White Arctic: Anthropological Essays on Tutelage and Ethnicity.* St. John's, Institute of Social and Economic Research, Memorial University of Newfoundland.

1977c "Discerning the Goal: Methodological Problems Exemplified in Analyses of Hunter-gatherer Aggregation and Migration." In M. Stuchlik (ed.), *Goals and Behaviour.* Queen's University Papers in Social Anthropology 2.

unpublished

1975 "A Study in Social Change among the Killinirngmiut Eskimo of Canada's East Arctic." Unpublished Ph.D. thesis, University of London.

ROBBINS, EDWARD

published

1974 "Class and Ethnicity in Wabush." In M. Sterns (ed.), *Perspectives on Newfoundland.* St. John's, Extension Service, Memorial University of Newfoundland.

1975 "Ethnicity or Class: Social Relations in a Canadian Mining Town." In J. Bennett (ed.), *The New Ethnicity.* Minneapolis, West Publishers.

unpublished

**1973a "Brief to the Royal Commission on Labrador."

1973b "The Class Analysis of an Industrial Town in Labrador." Unpublished Ph.D. thesis, University of Michigan.

SAMPATH, H. M.

published

1974 "Prevalence of Psychiatric Disorders in a Southern Baffin Island Eskimo Settlement." *Canadian Psychiatric Association Journal,* 19.

1976 "Modernity, Social Structure, and Mental Health of Eskimos in the Canadian Eastern Arctic." In R. J. Shephard and S. Itoh (eds.), *Circumpolar Health* (Proceedings of the Third International Symposium, Yellowknife, N.W.T.). Toronto, University Press.

unpublished

*1970 "The Characteristics of Hospitalized Psychiatric Eskimo Patients from the East Arctic." Prepared for Killam Project Colloquium.

1971a "Fieldwork and the Personality of the Fieldworker." Prepared for Killam Project seminar.

1971b "On Doing Psychiatric Field Research in the Eastern Arctic. Anxiety and Stress in Fieldwork." Presented to Faculty of Medicine, Memorial University.

1972a "The Psychiatrist as a Fieldworker." Presented to the American Psychiatric Association.

1972b "The Identification of Mental Illness by Baffin Island Eskimos." Presented to the Canadian Sociology and Anthropology Association.

1972c "Modernity and Mental Health of Eskimos in the East Arctic." Presented to the Canadian Psychiatric Association.

1972d "Migration and Mental Health of the Non-Eskimos in the East Arctic." Presented to the Third International Conference on Social Science and Medicine.

1972e "Cultural Relativism and Cross-cultural Psychiatric Research." Presented to the Atlantic Provinces Psychiatric Association.

1973 "Eskimo Perception of Psychopathological Behaviour." Presented to the American Psychiatric Association.

1974 "The Battered Wife Syndrome of the Eskimos of the Canadian Eastern Arctic." Presented to the Canadian Psychiatric Association.

1975a "Environment and Mental Health. A Comparative Study of Psychiatric Morbidity in Newfoundland and Labrador." Presented to the Royal College of Physicians and Surgeons of Canada.

1975b "The Bushed Syndrome: Environment and Mental Health in the Canadian Eastern Arctic." Presented to the Canadian Psychiatric Association.

ZIMMERLY, DAVID W.

published

1972 "Winter Seal Hunt in the Eastern Arctic." *North*, 20(3):32–6.

**1973a *Qiqirtarjuamiut Udlumi (Broughton Island Eskimo Today)*. 16 mm film, color, optical sound, 23 minutes. Ottawa, Ethnology Division, National Museum of Man, National Museums of Canada.

**1973b *Woman of Labrador*. By Elizabeth Goudie; edited and with an introduction and photographs by David W. Zimmerly. Toronto, Peter Martin Associates Ltd.

1975 *Cain's Land Revisited: Culture Change in Central Labrador, 1775–1972*. St. John's, Institute of Social and Economic Research, Memorial University of Newfoundland.

unpublished

1971 "Research Report from Broughton Island, N.W.T.." Institute of Social and Economic Research files.

List of Institute Publications